Democracy After Slavery

Florida A&M University, Tallahassee
Florida Atlantic University, Boca Raton
Florida Gulf Coast University, Ft. Myers
Florida International University, Miami
Florida State University, Tallahassee
University of Central Florida, Orlando
University of Florida, Gainesville
University of North Florida, Jacksonville
University of South Florida,Tampa
University of West Florida, Pensacola

Democracy After Slavery

Black Publics and Peasant Radicalism in Haiti and Jamaica

Mimi Sheller

University Press of Florida

Gainesville/Tallahasee/Tampa/Boca Raton
Pensacola/Orlando/Miami/Jacksonville/Ft. Myers

Published in the United Kingdom as part of the Warwick University
Caribbean Studies Series by Macmillan Education Ltd., London
and Oxford

Published simultaneously in the United States of America by the
University Press of Florida

05   04   03   02   01   00   6   5   4   3   2   1

Printed in China

Library of Congress Cataloging-in-Publication Data
Sheller, Mimi.
Democracy after slavery: black publics and peasant radicalism in Haiti and
Jamaica/Mimi Sheller.
p.   cm.
Includes bibliographical references (p.–) and index.
ISBN 0-8130-1883-8
1. Haiti—History—1804–1844. 2. Haiti—History—1844–1915. 3. Jamaica—
History—19th century. 4. Jamaica—History—Insurrection, 1865. 5. Haiti—
Foreign relations—Jamaica. 6. Jamaica—Foreign relations—Haiti.   I. Title.
F1924.S54 2000
972.92'04—dc21   00-057696

The University Press of Florida is the scholarly publishing agency
for the State University System of Florida, comprising Florida A&M
University, Florida Atlantic University, Florida Gulf Coast
University, Florida International University, Florida State
University, University of Central Florida, University of Florida,
University of North Florida, University of South Florida, and
University of West Florida.

University Press of Florida
15 Northwest 15th Street
Gainesville, FL 32611
http://www.upf.com

Acknowledgement
The author and publishers wish to acknowledge, with thanks,
the following photographic source:
Lithograph by Daumier, © Collection Viollet, p. 83

Preface

Democracy After Slavery is an important comparative study of Jamaica and Haiti at a critical period in their histories. Sheller focuses on two moments in post-emancipation Haiti and Jamaica: the Piquet Rebellion of 1844 and the 1865 Morant Bay Rebellion. Both rebellions highlight the popular movements for democratization which characterized the two societies after the abolition of slavery. For Sheller, ex-slaves in Haiti and in Jamaica 'did not simply retreat into a world of peasant subsistence and conservative values. They turned their collective energies toward changing structures of domination wherever they could'. However, in each case, former slaves met with resistance: elites were reluctant to move toward real democratization, resulting in the two major rebellions Sheller describes. Despite the efforts of freedmen and freedwomen, there was a significant retreat from democracy in Haiti and Jamaica during the nineteenth century.

Sheller places the Jamaican and Haitian situation in the context of other societies emerging from slavery. She sees similar patterns elsewhere, especially in the American South, but also in other parts of the Caribbean and Latin America, and this comparative perspective adds considerably to the importance of her book. She is also aware of the significance of Haiti in the Americas, not only because of the Haitian Revolution, but also because of the image of Haiti in the century which followed. Planters never forgot Haiti, but neither did slaves and freed people. The anti-slavery and anti-colonial stance of the Haitian Republic stood out in the nineteenth century.

Sheller's nuanced account of peasant radicalism adds significantly to our understanding of resistance after emancipation. She rightly devotes considerable attention to the role of women in resistance, and she concludes with a fascinating discussion of the personal and political ties between Haitians and Jamaicans in the mid-nineteenth century. Yet it was more than these personal contacts which makes her comparison so intriguing; there was also an overlap in the 'conceptual worlds' of former slaves in these two societies. In highlighting that shared ideology, Sheller has provided a new perspective on the world after slavery ended.

Gad Heuman

Contents

Acknowledgements

This project originates in many ways out of my recognition of the injustices of Europe and North America dominance in the production of academic 'knowledge' about the Caribbean. If, as Dorothy Smith (1987) suggests, 'relations of ruling' always shape academic practice, then it is better to acknowledge how we are embedded in those relations than to believe we can easily escape them. Therefore, I want to acknowledge up front that I am in a position of unequal power in relation to many people in the Caribbean. I come from a country (the U.S.) that has throughout its history had an invasive and detrimental effect on the Caribbean, and I write from an academic position in another country (the U.K.) partly responsible for slavery and colonialism in the region. I believe that the past history of slavery and colonialism has had a strong impact on global relations in the contemporary world. Thus, I feel an ethical obligation to critique North Atlantic hegemony (both political and academic) in the Caribbean region by rethinking some of the basic tenets about core 'Western' values such as freedom, democracy and equality from the perspective of those who have been enslaved by Western countries. In seeking to contribute to Caribbean historical sociology, I admit to my own limited vantage point, but hope that we can all learn from the Caribbean experience, which is our shared history.

Thanks in part to this privileged structural location, research for this book was generously supported by the MacArthur Program in Global Change and Liberalism, by an Elinor Goldmark Black dissertation fellowship from the New School for Social Research, and by the Janey Program in Latin America and the Caribbean. I am also thankful for the time for revisions provided by a Du Bois-Mandela-Rodney postdoctoral fellowship at the University of Michigan's Center for Afroamerican and African Studies.

Many people have supported this work over the eight years that it has taken to reach this particular point (more a starting point than an endpoint). First of all, I want to thank my Ph.D. dissertation supervisors, Charles Tilly, William Roseberry and Mustafa Emirbayer, for their exemplary teaching, research and guidance. I did my best to heed their advice, and the wise counsel of Harrision White, but the still flawed final product remains my own responsibility. Other teachers to whom I am very thankful include Janet Abu-Lughod, Seyla Benhabib, Jose Casanova, Diane Davis, Donald Scott, Louise Tilly and Aristide Zolberg. Special thanks are due to Gad Heuman who first assisted me during a Visiting Fellowship at the Centre for Caribbean Studies at Warwick University, and who has ever since made wonderful efforts to introduce me to colleagues in the Society for Caribbean Studies and the Association of Caribbean Historians. Thanks also to colleages at the Center for African and Afroamerican Studies, and to Rebecca Scott for academic support. At Lancaster University, I must thank all of my colleagues in the Sociology Department and at the Institute for Women's Studies for helping me to juggle teaching and research in my first year, and for inspiring me in new directions.

The archives and libraries in several countries are owed thanks not only for opening their doors to me, but also for offering archivists, librarians and staff who were always helpful and patient. In Jamaica, I thank the National Library, the Jamaica National Archives and the University of the West Indies for use of their valuable resources. In France, I extend thanks to the Archives Nationales, the Archive du Ministère des Affaires Étrangères and the Bibliothèque Nationale. All translations from the French are my own, including primary and secondary sources, unless otherwise noted in the bibliography. An effort has been made to maintain original spellings in direct quotations, including British and Jamaican spellings and those that represent various degrees of Creole language.

In England, I especially appreciated the use of the wonderful public resources of the British Public Record Office and the British Library. I am thankful for the use of the Wesleyan Methodist Missionary Society and London Missionary Society archives held at the School of Oriental and African Studies, London; and for the Bodleian Library and Rhodes House Library at Oxford University. I am also grateful to the Baptist Missionary Society for permission to quote from their collection at the Angus Library, Regents College, Oxford, where the archivist Mrs. Susan J. Mills was especially helpful. In New York, I have benefited from use of the Bobst Library of New York University and the New York Public Library's excellent collection at the Schomburg Center for Research in Black Culture.

I want to give special personal thanks to Mrs. Cybil Hall and her family for welcoming me into their home in Kingston, and to Randall Hepner for introducing me. I also want to thank Charles Arthur, Laurie Richardson and other members of the Haiti Support Group in London for giving me such an intense introduction to the people, places and politics of Haiti. The many dedicated activists whom we met were a living testament to the commitment of the Haitian people to the ongoing project of social change. Thanks also to fellow graduate students who supported my work and inspired me with their own, especially Anne Mische and Gina Ulysse.

Finally, I could not have carried out this research without the love and support of my family. Many, many thanks to my mother who has been an inspiration and a guide in so many ways; to my father who has made me strive for excellence in all things; to Jamie for always looking out for her little sister; to the rest of the family for keeping my heart in Philadelphia; and especially to Simon, who has cooked so many dinners, put up with so many long absences, and made so many moves back and forth across the Atlantic. Thank you all.

List of tables

List of figures

List of abbreviations

AMAE	Archives du Ministère des Affaires Étrangères (Paris, France)
AN	Archives Nationales de France (Paris, France)
BMS	Baptist Missionary Society Archives (Angus Library, Oxford)
CCC	Corréspondence Consulaire et Commerçial (AMAE, France)
CP	Corréspondence Politique (AMAE, France)
FO	Foreign Office Archives (PRO, England)
JRC	Report of the Jamaica Royal Commission
LMS	London Missionary Society Archives (SOAS, London)
NYPL	New York Public Library
PRO	Public Record Office (England)
WMMS	Wesleyan Methodist Missionary Society Archives (SOAS, London)

Part one

Democracy in the Post-Slavery Caribbean

'Rockstone a' riber bottom no know how sun hot'

From a letter to the editor of *The Sentinel*, Jamaica, March 24, 1865
Signed 'S.C.C. alias Niger'

Wòch nan dlo ap fin konnen doulè wòch nan soley
'The rocks in the water are going to know the suffering of the rocks in
the sun'

From President Aristide's Inaugural Address
(Farmer 1994: 163)

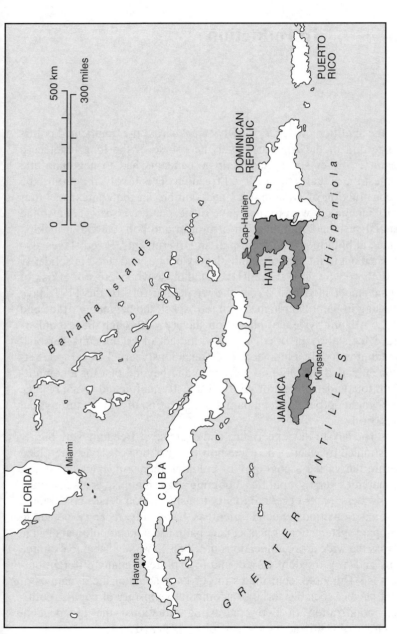

Figure 1 Map showing the proximity of Haiti to Jamaica

Introduction

As the abolition of slavery slowly swept across the fragmented political terrain of the Americas over the course of the long nineteenth century, former slaves and their descendants had to negotiate and contest the actual terms of lived freedom. This involved not only the reconstruction of communities and families in the context of bitter daily interaction with former slave-owners and overseers, but also the crucial sustained mobilization of protest and political claim-making aimed at both local and metropolitan governments. Freed slaves also reached out to international anti-slavery publics and stood in solidarity with those who were still enslaved and those who were still at risk of enslavement in Africa. From the wrenching fury of the 1791 slave uprising in Saint Domingue — in retrospect, the beginning of the end of the Atlantic system of plantation slavery — through the last unheralded legislation in Brazil in 1888, the act of establishing personal freedom was only a first step. Each tenaciously struck but fragile settlement called for ongoing vigilance, and beyond that for a commitment to a wider project of political transformation and social change that would uproot the dehumanizing institution of slavery throughout the world.

The day-to-day experience and exercise of freedom were highly constrained by when, where and how the abolition of slavery unfolded within the varied topography of colonial versus independent states, monarchies versus republics, booming sugar regions versus forgotten backwaters, paths of revolutionary transformation versus constrained gradual transitions. Social scientists have only recently begun to compare systematically post-emancipation social and political change across the wide array of locations in which slavery existed, to examine how and why freedom varied, and to explore its many different outcomes.[1] This book contributes to our knowledge of the dynamics of post-slavery societies through a comparative history of popular political mobilization in two contrasting situations, the independent Republic of Haiti and the British colony of Jamaica.

The French colony of Saint Domingue (which became Haiti) and the British colony of Jamaica had been the two most profitable sugar-producing (and slave-killing) colonies in the world in the late eighteenth century (Knight 1990: 114). However, Haiti became the first place ever to end slavery through revolution and established itself as only the second independent state in the Americas in 1804. Jamaica, in contrast, went through a gradual process of abolition in the 1830s and remained a colony until 1962. Although their contrasting paths to emancipation situated Haitians and Jamaicans in quite different political landscapes, there were nevertheless certain similarities in the development of peasant communities in both islands. With mountainous interiors and well-developed 'proto-peasantries' during the period of slavery, both islands became exemplary of the post-emancipation pattern of strong peasant development based on customary land tenures and expansion of internal markets (Mintz 1979, 1989; Knight 1990; Besson 1995).[2]

The central thesis of this book is that those who struggled out of slavery in Haiti and Jamaica also developed a shared radical vision of democracy based on the post-slavery ideology of freedom. In addition to the clear demand for full political participation and equal citizenship, it was an ideology that included an explicit critique of white racial domination and of the unbridled market capitalism that built a world system of slavery. It was at times accompanied by demands for (and moral justification of) some degree of economic redistribution and land reform as reparation for generations of enslavement. This alternative path to a future free from domination provided not only a counter-narrative to modernity and an ethical critique of capitalism, but also an alternative vision of true grassroots democracy. The popular legacy of this peasant democratic ideology, as I shall refer to it, had a deep impact on the development of Caribbean radicalism throughout the nineteenth century, and was later carried onto an international stage by generations of Caribbean migrants and activists (Rodney 1981, 1982; cf. James 1998).

To trace the genealogy of this subaltern political ideology, I offer a detailed analysis of two major crises of political contention and violent conflict over democracy and the rights of black citizens: Haiti's Liberal Revolution and Piquet Rebellion of 1843–44, and Jamaica's Underhill Movement and Morant Bay Rebellion of 1865. My narrative of these events features the creation, transformation and changing relations of various publics in the two islands, focusing on the degree to which former slaves and their descendants took part in public claim-making, political protest and rebellion. I also consider how their forms of collective identification, political communication and social mobilization changed over time. In addition to comparing and contrasting these two cases, I will also be highlighting the relationships between them, as well as placing them within a wider comparative framework of relevance to the entire Atlantic world.

The primary purpose of this comparative analysis of popular politics in post-revolutionary Haiti and post-emancipation Jamaica is to examine the general shift *away from* democratic political systems following the abolition of slavery. As many historians have noted, there was no cataclysmic social transformation after slavery's abolition; instead, almost everywhere, 'ruling social and economic institutions carried on with remarkable continuity…[while] former slaves and generations of descendants remained largely landless, impoverished, unschooled, and disfranchised' (Lowenthal 1995: 179–80). The struggle for freedom continued in the face of both the personal tyranny of former slave-owners and the political tyranny of the various governments that reluctantly admitted the once enslaved as tenuous citizens. In explaining this, I argue that processes of *de*-democratization were crucial to the transition out of slavery. Contrary to teleological assumptions about the triumph of enlightenment or the forward-march of modernity — with its supposedly ineluctable progress towards broader and more equal citizenship — abolition entailed a retreat from democracy.

At first, this may sound counter-intuitive, given prevailing notions of slave emancipation as a facet of humanitarian progress, a crowning achievement of one of the classic social movements of the 'age of democratic revolution'. Yet, despite the pressures towards democratization which were felt in all the states of the Americas in the nineteenth century, all failed to fairly incorporate as full citizens the people of African origin who had survived enslavement and become free. In faithfully exercising democratic rights, fulfilling obligations to the state, demanding political inclusion and generally seeking freedom, freed slaves flushed out and publicly exposed the severe limitations of liberal ideologies that were deeply complicit with white racial dominance and economic exploitation of the lands and people of the Caribbean archipelago. Even in Haiti, the overarching 'racial project' of European colonialism could not easily be escaped, and the outcomes of the revolution were curtailed (see Chapter 3). Why did the abolition of slavery have such bittersweet results? How and why was its transformational potential so pervasively thwarted and everywhere contained?

While massive research efforts have gone into explaining the rise and fall of the Atlantic system of slavery (see Chapter 1 for a synopsis), far less attention has been given to researching the conditions and outcomes of slavery's abolition. Recent attention to comparative post-emancipation histories 'has tended to highlight the transformation of the slave population into a free labor force and to narrowly focus on the social and economic ramifications this change had for the sugar plantations' (Olwig 1995: 3). Commonly utilized economic and state-centred structural variables too often downplay the political agency of freed slaves, while theorists of resistance often ignore structural variation and its differential effects on political processes. We now need better explanations not only of the unfolding of labour emancipation in comparative economic contexts, but also of slavery abolition's role in processes of political emancipation and state formation, on the one hand, and in transformations of colonial and post-colonial civil societies, on the other.

In so far as freed men (if not women) were in some places momentarily enfranchised and welcomed as soldiers, jurors, tax-payers, even elected officials, they and their children soon enough found themselves clapped back into the shackles of enforced impoverishment and political exclusion. Many 'freed people throughout the Caribbean shared common grievances in the wake of emancipation', argues Gad Heuman, because their 'ideas of freedom clashed with those of the ruling elite.... In the face of pressure from below, planters and administrators [in the British West Indies] generally sought to abolish the system of representative government and replace it with direct rule from London' (Heuman 1995: 132–3). This backward movement is not unique, but occurred in a whole series of post-emancipation settlements. Where it was resisted, the backlash was all the more stinging. Thus, a pattern can be discerned of brief democratic openings, popular protest and political mobilization met with harsh suppression, and finally retreat from representative government (and from 'democracy' in so far as it existed).

As W. E. B. Du Bois presciently recognized, the 'true significance of slavery in the United States to the whole social development of America lay in the ultimate relation of slaves to democracy. What were to be the limits of democratic control in the United States?' (Du Bois [1935] 1992: 184). The expansion of democratic rights for white men, he argued, proceeded hand in hand with the disenfranchisement of freed slaves, the reversal of the reparative policies of the Reconstruction Era, and the undermining of the Fourteenth Amendment by the U.S. Supreme Court (cf. Harding 1981; Foner 1988). The same could be said for other states adjusting to the aftermath of slavery. There is no simple story of progress, moral victory or ethical triumph; instead we find case after case of disappointment, defeat and anti-democratic reaction. In identifying this policy reversal as a common post-slavery trend throughout the Americas (even in revolutionary Haiti where there was no white landowning minority left to appease), this book raises fundamental questions about the development of democracy in the modern West.

The large-scale changes in the boundaries of citizenship that accompanied emancipation made political negotiation between former slaves and nominally democratic governments an overlooked cornerstone in the construction of modern Western states. A second purpose of this book is to challenge prevalent assumptions about the social 'disorganization' and political 'apathy' of post-slavery peasantries and the 'late' development of Afro-Caribbean working-class consciousness. Recentring our thinking about *where* the impetus for democratization arose and reconsidering *how* subaltern groups engage in politics, my account highlights the ideologies, collective actions and political agency of slaves and their descendants. Rather than metropolitan governments bringing democracy to the Caribbean, it was Caribbean freed slaves who pushed hardest for full democratization.

The significance of post-emancipation politics lies in its critique of the limitations of liberal democracy and its proposals for more radical ways forward. Democracy in the Americas, as elsewhere, owes a great deal to working-class contention (Tilly 1995a; Rueschemeyer, Stephens and Stephens 1992) — in this case, that of the slave's struggle for freedom, the freed person's struggle to implement that freedom and their children's defense of whatever small victories were won. My approach rejects both top-down models of elite-led 'tutelary democracy' (an oxymoron from this perspective) and Eurocentric models of modernity that extol the (male) industrial proletariat of the 'core' countries as the key agent of 'history from below'. Rather than assuming that post-slavery Caribbean states were not capable of democracy, or the people 'not ready', we must consider the actual contours of the struggle that took place. Of relevance to this argument are recent agrarian studies that have compellingly reformulated the wider realm of peasant political agency in Latin America and Africa.[3] As Florencia Mallon suggests of nineteenth-century Mexico and Peru, 'through the very processes of participation, political creation, and repression, rural people transformed both themselves and the polity they struggled to expand....[Thus] popular creativity and political action put identifiable marks on the state being constructed over the years' (Mallon 1995: 141).

Once seen as apolitical, conservative, distrustful, socially undifferentiated, lacking in associational life and accommodating to elites (cf. Booth and Seligson 1979), accumulating evidence shows that the 'reconstituted peasantries' of the Caribbean actually resisted coercive labour regimes, created long-lasting oppositional cultures and often joined in public political protest (Turner 1995). I argue that the peasants and 'semi-proletarians' of the Caribbean were not merely beneficiaries of European developments, but contributed as much to the citizen/state bargaining that drove nineteenth-century states toward extensions of democracy as did political mobilization in the metropolitan heart-lands. Extending C. L. R. James' classic argument in *The Black Jacobins* that the slave revolution of Saint Domingue was the most radical expression of the Jacobin thrust of the French Revolution, one could add that post-slavery political contention held the potential for revolutionary transformation of Western society by its most oppressed group. Moreover, the tool for achieving that transformation was democratization. Evidence for this specifically democratic peasant radicalism exists in the words and actions of the black publics and peasant radicals of Haiti and Jamaica, as I hope this book will demonstrate.

The title of this work, *Democracy After Slavery,* is a reminder that slavery was practised by nominally democratic governments (including those of the 'model' democracies of France, Great Britain and the United States), and that it also continues to haunt those states today. As Orlando Patterson has grasped, slavery is in some very troubling way fundamental to the emergence of democracy and to the valuation of freedom in Western culture (Patterson 1991). We forget slavery at our own peril. Secondly, the title reminds us of Du Bois' question: what is the relation of slaves to democracy? What exactly occurs in the transition from a system of slavery to a democratic system and is this transition really complete in contemporary post-slavery societies? It was only in recognizing that former slaves turned to democracy and wielded it against ruling elites that I began to question our taken-for-granted understandings of what democracy is and from what social and ideological origin it arises. Democracy's radical potential remains unfulfilled in part because of the failure to complete the transition out of slavery.

When I presented this research in various forums, I was often told that 'peasants are not democratic' and that there could not have been 'peasant democratic' movements in the Caribbean in the nineteenth century.[4] As Barrington Moore demonstrated, the social origins of democracy lay in bourgeois-led revolution, which was impossible wherever an agrarian elite depended on labour repressive agriculture (Moore 1966). I thank those respondents for making me think more carefully about the wider implications of my argument. Indeed, it was only after completing my research that I realized the significance of Jeffery Paige's analysis of the rise of democracy in Central America to this study of the Caribbean. In *Coffee and Power: Revolution and the Rise of Democracy in Central America*, he challenges Moore's widely accepted thesis that democracy is a product of bourgeois revolution. In so far as there was an alternative route to democratization 'through revolution from below' (Paige 1997: 324) in coffee republic like Nicaragua, El Salvador and Costa Rica, the ideological roots of such democratic 'peasant-proletarians' must lie deeper in the longstanding resistance to coercive labour systems and colonial regimes. I want to suggest that similar cycles of democratic struggle can be found earlier in the nineteenth century, especially within a wider American context that includes the Caribbean.[5]

The key pattern found throughout the Americas is one of elite retreat from democratization in the face of popular demands for civil and political inclusion. In Haiti, the radical demands of the Haitian Piquets in 1844 (and their black collective identification) led the liberal elite to retreat from democracy and resort to authoritarianism when faced with an alliance of small landholders and a rural peasantry demanding full democratic rights. In the case of Jamaica, it is even clearer that both colonial and metropolitan elites reneged on democracy. The view that West Indians were 'taught' democracy by colonial tutelage is grossly misleading not only because it misconstrues the ideological position of the local elite, the colonial government and the British Colonial Office, but also because it fundamentally misconstrues the ideological position of the colonial working classes and peasantry It purposely misreads and silences the political struggles of the Caribbean people.

We will fail to understand democracy in the Caribbean (and elsewhere) so long as we fail to recognize the radical democratic ideologies of the post-slavery peasantry in their struggle against *limited* liberal democracy.[6] It is simply tautological to attribute Caribbean democracy to the inheritance of British parliamentary institutions, and its failure to the absence of a pre-existing democratic political culture forged over centuries (Payne 1993). Comparative historical sociology can help us to rethink the social origins of democracy. Rueschemeyer, Huber Stephens and Stephens, among others, emphasize the importance of civil society in installing and consolidating democracy. In order to trace the formation of post-slavery civil societies and to track their engagement in struggles over democracy, I argue that a more complete analysis will be required of post-emancipation 'plebeian publics'. The actual lived reality of freedom depended to a great extent on the facility with which political communication was possible between freed slaves, local authorities, colonial governments, civil and military arms of distant imperial states and periodically concerned international publics.

I will examine relationships among multiple Caribbean public spheres and associational networks in order to better understand popular political cultures and processes of democratization in the post-slavery period of transition, when new forms of citizenship were being tried and tested. Moving beyond Jürgen Habermas's influential model of the transformation of the bourgeois public sphere, I draw on recent reconceptualizations based on a multiplicity of non-bourgeois publics.[7] These theorists extend the concept of publicity beyond the confines of European Enlightenment and explore the boundaries that implicitly exclude people from full citizenship on the basis of race, gender, class or other social distinctions.

In seeking to broaden theoretical conceptualizations of the public sphere in democratic societies, I systematically analyze the specific patterns of popular claim-making and political mobilization that emerged in Haiti and Jamaica in the decades after slavery was eradicated. People freed from slavery had to manipulate creatively every opportunity and means for making claims on the state and for gaining a voice in decision-making. The concept of 'plebeian publics' has generally been thought out in relation to modern democracies in Europe and the United States, but could be even more useful if extended to colonial and post-colonial networks of political communication. The advantage of considering publics from the point of view of the colonial periphery is that it highlights the complexity of multiple publics, right from the earliest moments of formation of the 'bourgeois public sphere' in Europe. Publics can be defined as open-ended flows of communication that enable socially distant interlocutors to link positions, identities and projects in pursuit of influence over issues of common concern (Emirbayer and Sheller 1999: 154–63). Multiple publics with different diasporas or 'imagined communities' are always in tension with each other. Drawing on the concept of a 'black public sphere' or 'black counterpublic', which has been developed particularly in the United States,[8] I characterize Haitian and Jamaican subaltern publics as 'black publics'. This is possible because of their explicit self-identification in terms of colour or African ethnic origin as well as their self-conscious critique of white domination.

Another aim of this book, then, is to inquire into the public articulation of racial and national identities, and to explore the relationship between collective identities and political practices. Paying close attention to the actual words and symbolic structures used in the context of public contention can tell us a great deal about political narratives and the ideologies informing them. Different understandings of 'race', ethnicity and class were elaborated in the process of post-emancipation adjustment. It was in the heat of contention that former masters and former slaves together framed, defined and mobilized around identities such as 'white' or 'black', citizen or subject, mechanic or merchant. What were the sources and conditions for the elaboration of 'Black' or

'African' identities in the post-slavery period? Where and when did people of various classes and colours draw boundaries between terms such as 'Black' or 'Brown', Creole or African, British or Jamaican, Haitian or Dominican? When were national identities trumped by racial identities? When were racial identities shattered by class and colour stratification? And what role did gender play in all of this?

The colour terminology used throughout this book will refer to socially constructed and politically contested categories that appeared in discourses of the period, which included class and status valuations within them.[9] In Jamaica, the major categories were *black* (or *negro*), *coloured* (or *brown*) and *white* (or *buckra*). In Haiti, the main categories were *nègre/sse* (used today by most Haitians to refer to themselves), *noir/e* (black), *mulâtre/sse* (mulatto), and *blanc/he* (white, but referring today to any foreigner). As a Creole saying that originated at the time of the Piquet Rebellion recognized, '*Nègue riche qui connait li et écri, cila mulâte; mulâte pauve qui pas connait li ni écri, cila nègue*' [The rich negro who can read and write is mulatto; the poor mulatto who cannot read or write is negro] (d'Alaux 1860: 112). In other words, Haitians have long recognized that wealth, literacy, status and power are bound up with racial/colour categories that only emerge through the cultural work of politically motivated 'racial projects' (Omi and Winant 1994; and see Chapter 3). This meant that the politics of inclusion and exclusion in a democratic polity was also a politics of race, class and social belonging.

Emancipation concerned not only who would be defined as a citizen on paper, but also which rights and obligations would be enforceable in particular times and places, and, most importantly, what actions would be considered legitimate means of making rights-based claims or calling for the enforcement of obligations. Citizenship can be defined as 'rights and mutual obligations binding state agents and a category of persons defined exclusively by their legal attachment to the same state' (Tilly 1995b: 369). However, I also heed Somers in emphasizing the *public practice* of citizenship over the legal definition, i.e. citizenship as 'a set of institutionally embedded practices' that vary locally according to regional 'contexts of activation' (Somers 1993). A key determinant of the quality of freedom experienced by former slaves and their descendants was the extent to which political communication became possible between new citizens and the state. By political communication, I refer to the ways in which freed people could make their demands and grievances heard and thereby gain influence over decision-making.

In so far as the formation of publics were one means for transmitting such influence, the capacity for publicity was dependent upon colonial histories, the timing and mode of emancipation, and ongoing local struggles to adopt, adapt or create what Tilly calls 'repertoires of contention'. The study of contentious events offers pertinent guidance on how to go about studying the dynamics of publicity. My methodological approach builds on the work of Tilly and others on repertoires of contention, but pays greater attention to language in terms of both narratives and claim-making genres. To understand historical publics, we must turn to the contexts of political communication and of its framing within particular linguistic registers, idioms and genres.[10] Evidence of competing publics exists in the claim-making documents produced in instances of communicative and contentious interaction. I define 'public texts' as the set of actively claim-making documents that are produced during episodes of political contention. They are public in so far as they have been published in a newspaper, posted in a public place, submitted and recorded through official channels or in some other way committed to the public record. They are 'active' in so far as they embody an interactional speech act between two or more identifiable interlocutors. My aim is to systematically document interactions between black publics, their targets and brokers, as well as between geographically segmented publics including interactions between colony and metropole, between local regions and national government and among international or even transnational publics.

The basis for this comparative historical study, then, is original archival research in Caribbean and European government archives, missionary archives and national libraries, gathering evidence of the 'geography of publicity' over roughly a thirty-year period in postrevolutionary Haiti (focusing on 1818–1844) and post-emancipation Jamaica (focusing on 1834–1865). Key moments leading up to peasant rebellions have been chosen because of the numerous types of public texts that were produced in the flurry of political activity surrounding Haiti's Liberal Revolution and Jamaica's Morant Bay Rebellion, along with crucial debates about publicity, freedom of the press and freedom of association. Drawing on consular correspondence, parliamentary papers, government records, missionary correspondence, local newspapers, contemporary memoirs, histories and political pamphlets, I have collected a range of Haitian and Jamaican public texts, supplemented by information on participants, places and modes of publication. Methodologically, therefore, this book contributes to ongoing efforts to conjoin two major strands in contemporary sociology. Historical and comparative sociology, which largely employs a macro-comparative structural approach, has been resistant to the 'narrative turn' brought about by the post-modern 'epistemological crisis' (but see Sewell 1980, 1992; Somers 1992, 1993). The sociology of culture, on the other hand, embraces investigation of narrative and symbolic meaning structures, but has to some extent been less successful in analyzing temporal processes and social change (but see Swidler 1986; Sewell 1996; Abbott 1996).

I combine large-scale relational analysis of social and institutional networks with text-based discourse analysis of 'claims-in-action' (based on primary sources such as petitions, resolutions, proclamations and other public texts). My analysis of popular political participation in the post-slavery Caribbean demonstrates that Haitian and Jamaican former slaves did not simply retreat into a world of peasant subsistence and conservative values. They turned their collective energies toward changing structures of domination wherever they could. By carefully examining the repertoires and situational contexts of public contention, the production and dissemination of specific types of public texts and the actual narratives of citizenship, rights and obligations recorded in those texts, I show how modes of political communication structured Haitian and Jamaican freedom in significantly different ways. These differences are evident even in the kinds and range of public texts that remain in the historical record, with far more non-elite voices recorded for Jamaica. While the majority of the population was illiterate in all post-slavery societies, in Jamaica there was an intermediate set of brokers and institutional arrangements that gave the labourer or peasant access to a greater range of channels for political communication. Patterns of Creole language are themselves traces of the extent of public political communication across class and racial divides (Holm 1988; White 1995).[11] The Native Baptist Church, for example, offered organizational resources and 'safe spaces' much in the way that Black Churches did in the United States Civil Rights Movement, while also shaping the language of Jamaican political claims.[12]

The suppression of publics and the dearth of public texts in Haiti should not preclude us from comparing the kinds of popular claim-making that did occur. Instead, it offers us the opportunity to explore why Haiti's potentially democratic public formations were constantly undermined by military solutions with lasting recursive consequences, still evident today. Evelyne Huber suggests that the success of democracy in the English-speaking Caribbean rests first on the strength of civil society (associations, unions, religious organizations, etc.), and second on civil control over the state's armed branches of military and police. In modern Haiti, in contrast, '[a] still relatively weak civil society and party system confront a military apparatus with sufficient coercive capacity to terrorize the society but with insufficient institutionalization and professionalization to constitute a reliable partner in negotiations about democratic consolidation' (Huber 1993: 88). As

Tilly suggests, 'armed men who exercise autonomous state power inhibit democracy' and 'military power and autonomy depend on the polity's transnational connections' (Tilly 1995b: 382–83). Where elite actors can resort to armed force, as in many parts of Latin America, there will be a tendency for 'democratic opening and popular mobilization [to be] followed by violent and authoritarian elite reaction' (Paige 1997: 335).

In sum, a crucial overlooked factor in the history of emancipation is the subtle transformation of local environments of civic participation and political interaction in which plantation workers, peasants and semi-proletarians first exercised specific freedoms and tested the practical meanings of citizenship. Freed people's efforts to wrest actual freedoms from resistant states had a far more definitive impact on the development of citizenship and democracy in the modern West than has previously been recognized. Modern states (and we as citizens within them) have been indelibly marked by the project of unmaking slavery. Democracy itself has been shaped by the powerful political projects of former slaves and their descendants, not necessarily in the direction sought by them. The following questions will inform my analysis of post-slavery politics. How does emancipation, understood as an ongoing political process, vary in different contexts? How did former slaves exercise freedom and shape citizenship in interaction with different states and in the context of different civil societies? What impact did peasant or proletarian ideologies of freedom and practices of citizenship have on state-civil society relations? What effect did differing governing institutions (especially armed forces) have on post-slavery civil societies and political cultures?

Democracy After Slavery is organized into three sections. Part One first offers an overview of the historiography of abolition and emancipation in order to develop a more robust comparative framework for post-emancipation studies; it then begins the empirical analysis of the comparative decline in planter economic, political and civil control in post-slavery Haiti and Jamaica. The remaining two parts of the book zero in on parallel accounts of black publics and peasant rebellions in Haiti (in Part Two) and Jamaica (in Part Three). The analysis in each case moves from a comprehensive overview of the development of post-emancipation black publics and peasant agency over a thirty-year period, to an event-centred analysis of the parallel periods of crisis during 1843–44 in Haiti and 1865 in Jamaica. Thus, the overall organization is case-based and chronological, yet several sections emphasize the relational and international contexts that link the two countries. The Conclusion develops these linkages and reflects on the comparative findings, on their significance in popular political memory, and on their far-reaching implications for explaining the unfinished creation of democracy after slavery.

Notes

1 For some recent important contributions, see Rebecca Scott, 'Exploring the Meaning of Freedom: Postemancipation Societies in Comparative Perspective' in *Hispanic American Historical Review* 68 (1988): 407–28; Frank McGlynn and Seymour Drescher, eds., *The Meaning of Freedom: Economics, Politics and Culture After Slavery* (Pittsburgh and London: University of Pittsburgh Press, 1992); Karen Fog Olwig, ed., *Small Islands, Large Questions: Society, Culture and Resistance in the Post-Emancipation Caribbean* (London: Frank Cass, 1995); Mary Turner, ed., *From Chattel Slaves to Wage Slaves: The Dynamics of Labour Bargaining in the Americas* (Urbana: University of Illinois Press, 1995).

2 The definition of 'peasantries' has been much debated in Caribbean historical anthropology. Freed agricultural producers working smallholdings in family units are 'reconstituted peasantries' (the term comes from Sidney Mintz, 'Slavery and the Rise of Peasantries', *Historical Reflections*, [1979], 6:1: 213–42) in so far as they formed *after* capitalist penetration of the region. Because they often participated in occasional wage labour, they were 'precipitates of capitalism' rather than 'traditional' solidary communities (William Roseberry, *Anthropologies and Histories: Essays in Culture, History and Political Economy* [New Brunswick: Rutgers University Press, 1989]). See also Mintz, 'The Rural Proletariat and the Problem of Rural Proletarian Class Consciousness' in *Journal of Peasant Studies*, 1:1 (1973): 291–325.

3 For related arguments concerning peasant agency, see Florencia Mallon, *The Defense of Community in Peru's Central Highlands: Peasant Struggle and Capitalist Transition, 1860–1940* (Princeton: Princeton University Press, 1983) and *Peasant and Nation: The Making of Postcolonial Mexico and Peru* (Berkeley and Los Angeles: University of California Press, 1995); James Scott, *Weapons of the Weak: Everyday Forms of Peasant Resistance* (New Haven: Yale University Press, 1985); Jean Comaroff and John Comaroff, *Of Revelation and Revolution: Christianity, Colonialism and Consciousness in South Africa* (Chicago and London: University of Chicago Press, 1991); Frederick Cooper et al., *Confronting Historical Paradigms: Peasants, Labor, and the Capitalist World System in Africa and Latin America* (Madison: University of Wisconsin Press, 1993); and Steve Stern, ed., *Resistance, Rebellion and Consciousness in the Andean Peasant World* (Madison: University of Wisconsin Press, 1987).

4 Thanks are owed especially to Aristide Zolberg, who helped me to clarify this point along with other members of the Proseminar on Global Change and Democratic Governance at the New School for Social Research in 1995–96.

5 Also missing from Paige's analysis, which a study of the Caribbean can contribute, is greater attention to racial formation and inequalities based on ethnicity and colour. Although Paige refers to the indigenous peoples of Central America, questions of race, ethnicity and colour are not theorized within his class-centred approach.

6 The neo-liberal democracy being advocated or imposed in the Caribbean region by the United States and the world financial institutions (through means such as military intervention, structural adjustment programmes and 'democracy enhancement'

programmes) is faulty not because it produces 'fragile' democracies, but because it is not truly democratic. Herein lies the contemporary relevance of this book.

7 See, for example, John Keane, *Public Life and Late Capitalism: Toward a Socialist Theory of Democracy* (Cambridge: Cambridge University Press, 1984); Joan B. Landes, *Women and the Public Sphere in the Age of the French Revolution* (Ithaca and London: Cornell University Press, 1988); essays by Craig Calhoun, Geoff Eley, Nancy Fraser and Mary Ryan in Craig Calhoun, ed., *Habermas and the Public Sphere* (Cambridge: MIT Press, 1992); and Mary P. Ryan, *Civic Wars: Democracy and Pubic Life in the American City during the Nineteenth Century* (Berkeley, Los Angeles and London: University of California Press, 1997).

8 Elsa Brown, 'Negotiating and Transforming the Public Sphere: African American Political Life in the Transition from Slavery to Freedom' in Collective, ed., *The Black Public Sphere* (Chicago and London: University of Chicago Press, 1995), pp. 111–51; Paul Gilroy, *There Ain't No Black in the Union Jack: The Cultural Politics of Race and Nation* (Chicago: University of Chicago Press, 1991) and *The Black Atlantic: Modernity and Double Consciousness* (Cambridge: Harvard University Press, 1995); Eleanor Higginbotham, *Righteous Discontent: The Women's Movement in the Black Baptist Church, 1880–1920* (Cambridge and London: Harvard University Press, 1993); Robyn Kelley, *Race Rebels: Culture, Politics, and the Black Working Class* (New York: Free Press, 1996).

9 On varieties of Caribbean racial formation, see H. Hoetink, '"Race" and Color in the Caribbean' in Sidney Mintz and Sally Price, eds., *Caribbean Contours* (Baltimore and London: Johns Hopkins University Press, 1985), pp. 55–84.

10 For historical applications of discourse analysis, and narrative analysis I am influenced by Margaret Somers, 'Narrativity, Narrative Identity, and Social Action: Rethinking English Working-Class Formation' in *Social Science History* 16: 4 (1992): 591–630; George Steinmetz, 'Reflections on the Role of Social Narratives in Working Class Formation: Narrative Theory in the Social Sciences' in *Social Science History* 16:3 (1992): 489–516; Marc Steinberg, 'The Dialogue of Struggle: The Contest Over Ideological Boundaries in the Case of the London Silk Weavers in the Nineteenth Century' in *Social Science History* 18: 4 (1994): 505–542; and Roberto Franzosi, 'From Words to Numbers: A Set Theory Framework for the Collection, Organization, and Analysis of Narrative Data' in P. Marsden, ed., *Sociological Methodology* 24 (1994): 105–137.

11 This social and political bridging would also explain why Jamaica has a 'creole continuum', while Haiti has a situation of 'diglossia' in which there is a clear break between a majority of Kréyol-speakers and an elite minority of French-speakers. See John Holm, *Pidgins and Creoles* (New York: Cambridge University Press, 1988); Mervyn Alleyne, 'A Linguistic Perspective on the Caribbean' in Mintz and Price, *Caribbean Contours*, pp. 155–80; Frederic Cassidy, *Jamaica Talk: Three-hundred Years of the English Language in Jamaica* (London: Macmillan, 1982).

12 On church-based 'safe spaces', see Albert Raboteau, *Slave Religion: The 'Invisible Institution' in the Antebellum South* (Oxford: Oxford University Press, 1980); Sara Evans and Harry Boyte, *Free Spaces* (New York: Harper and Row, 1986); Doug McAdam, *Political Process and the Development of Black Insurgency, 1930–1970* (Chicago: University of Chicago Press, 1982); Aldon Morris, *The Origins of the Civil Rights Movement* (New York: Free Press, 1984). And for critical discussion, see Emirbayer and Sheller, 'Publics in History'; and Francesca Polletta, '"Free Spaces" in Collective Action' in *Theory and Society* 28 (Feb. 1999): 1–38.

1 | Caribbean configurations of freedom

How can we make sense of the long, complex chronology of the century-long process of abolition of slavery in the Americas? Looking at the painfully slow unraveling of the Atlantic system of slavery over the course of the 'long' nineteenth century, we find a confusing pattern of scattered progress, stubborn stasis and occasional retreat. In some places,7 emancipation was propelled forward by violent rebellions or revolution, in others it happened by gradual reform. It occurs in both independent republics and colonial domains, in areas experiencing economic decline, and those experiencing economic growth. Slavery held on even when all around it was swayed toward emancipation, and was in some instances reinstated against all the odds in places where it had already been eradicated, with unthinkable human costs.

Social science has attempted a number of strategies to explain the strange temporalities of slavery abolition, and in this chapter, I want to highlight one major theme in the debate: structure versus agency as causal factors in history. Structural phenomena are the macro-level processes of economic development and state formation that drive large-scale historical change, such as capitalist growth, urbanization, state centralization or the expansion of European empires and the wars among them. These impersonal processes to some extent 'caused' first the spread and then the decline of slavery throughout the Americas. However, they do not entirely satisfy one's attempts to explain the patterning of the process. Other accounts focus on the 'agency' of specific actors or groups, from the slaves who ventured violent rebellion to secure freedom, to the planters who maintained slavery, and the abolitionists who fought for slavery to be outlawed. If social scientists have at times seen these as mutually exclusive modes of historical explanation, there has also been a trend towards unifying structure and agency. Some of the most convincing arguments in explaining the overall pattern and timing of slave emancipation are those which identify variations in the degree of agency exercised by different actors in situations constrained by certain types of structural limits.

In his essay 'Democracy is a Lake', Tilly (1995b) suggests that theories of democratization tend toward one of two extremes of temporality. One set of theorists focus on long-term, largescale processes that take centuries to achieve, moving so slowly and gradually that they are comparable to the geological formation of oilfields. Another set of theorists look at much smaller timeframes, in which political actors quickly cultivate democracy in a manner comparable to gardening (often emphasizing elite actors). In contrast to both of these, Tilly suggests that democratization actually is more like the formation of a lake. That is to say, it may form through a number of processes of differing timescales, but which produce a similar endresult, recognizable as a lake whether slowly formed over glacial centuries (as in Britain's parliamentary system) or quickly man-made like a reservoir (as in recent 'democratic transitions'). I want to suggest that a similar metaphor can be applied to grouping and interpreting the various historical explanations of the abolition of slavery in the Americas.

This chapter will present an overview, in the very broadest strokes, of some of the major historiographical debates over the abolition of slavery (in part because embedded within these debates one discovers the original impetus for the prominent emergence of the field of post-emancipation studies in recent years). I begin with a set of explanations that focus on gradual, slow developments similar to Tilly's idea of the formation of oilfields. These often involve macrostructural changes such as growth of the capitalist world economy, state centralization or proletarianization, but also may include largescale cultural changes such as new ideological structures brought about by the Enlightenment. The causal mechanisms here are largely external to the Caribbean region. Then, I turn to another set of explanations that focus on agency, on the sudden creation of conditions for emancipation through the concerted efforts of various collective actors, particularly the resistance and rebellion of slaves themselves. These approaches are far closer to the gardening metaphor and depend on causal mechanisms generated within the Caribbean region itself. In contrast to both, I propose a middle-level causal analysis that includes aspects of both structure and agency, external and internal processes, and which bridges the pre- and post-emancipation periods. Finally, I apply this multi-causal ('lake') approach to sketching a preliminary comparative model of different types of transition out of slavery.

Oilfield explanations of slavery's abolition

Massive efforts have gone into explaining the rise and fall of the Atlantic system of slavery from the perspective of European abolitionist movements. One of the most important lines of historiography on this question focuses on the slow structural changes that led to modernization of European capitalist economies and the accompanying ideological changes that have variously been linked to the Enlightenment, the Protestant Ethic, British Nonconformist Dissent or the Age of Democratic Revolution. Whether one views the process of change as rooted in economics or in ideologies, the general thrust of this outlook is that the ending of the Atlantic system of slavery took place because of large-scale changes that occurred over long periods of time in imperceptibly gradual steps. The causal mechanisms driving these processes occur outside of the Caribbean, at the level of European empires or the 'world-system' as a whole.

Consider examples drawn from British history, where a classic debate occurred between those who attributed emancipation to a humanitarian movement rooted in European culture, and those who attributed it to forces of capitalist development on a world scale. The 'humanitarian thesis' was the dominant paradigm for at least the first half of this century. Its focus was the changing religious and moral beliefs of a select group of Englishmen (many of them Quakers) known as 'the Saints'. Nonconformists such as William Wilberforce and Thomas Clarkson combined a moral imperative to act against slavery with an ability to mobilize political campaigns of petitioning and parliamentary lobbying (Anstey 1975). The spread of abolitionism in this scenario is attributed to the gradual spread of these progressive values throughout the Atlantic world, until slavery became morally repugnant for increasing numbers of people who simultaneously had increasing power over government policy. More recent versions of this argument expand the notion of culture to include not simply ideologies but cultural practices, 'recipes for action', and 'cognitive styles' brought about by the changing nature of the market economy (Haskell 1985). Others introduce the concepts of social movement theory to more powerfully delineate the precise impact of ideological change ('frame transformation') on social change (d'Anjou 1996).

In contrast to this approach, the 'economic thesis' proposes that the real causal force in human history is not cultural change and elite ideologies, but the powerful forces of capitalist expansion and class struggle that have shaped the modern world. The Trinidadian historian and politician Eric Williams prominently framed this thesis in his classic book *Capitalism and Slavery* (1944). He argued that slavery and the slave trade were major economic contributors to the British industrial revolution of the eighteenth century and that after the loss of the North American colonies in 1776, slave plantation colonies declined in importance to Britain's economy. Therefore, slavery could be abolished because British capitalism no longer required it. The economic details of the Williams thesis have been rightly challenged in many regards, yet the general thrust of his argument remains an important influence and still has many adherents. The most significant modification has been the inclusion of a cultural and ideological dimension to the capitalist rejection of slavery.

Building on the Williams thesis, David Brion Davis argues that not just structural change, but also a shift toward bourgeois 'hegemony' was the crucial factor in the abolition of slavery. Shifting hegemony brought about a new ideological conjuncture of laissez-faire economics, utilitarianism and precepts of rational behaviour for which various reform movements — including opposition to slavery — provided a kind of moral cloak. Here the ideological shift is seen as a kind of superstructural adjustment led by more fundamental structural changes. Another proponent of this view is Michael Craton who argues that there are overwhelming continuities in capitalist exploitation of Caribbean workers both before and after the abolition of slavery (Craton 1997). Thomas Holt's analysis of the problem of freedom in Jamaica also suggests that abolitionism and free labour ideology together validated British liberalism and the new bourgeois class who came to power in the mid-nineteenth century (Holt 1992). In each case, it is argued that slavery had become economically irrelevant to the dominant class in society, as well as morally repugnant to some.

One of the major critics of the economic thesis is Seymour Drescher, whose book *Econocide* (1977) aimed to demonstrate that slavery and the plantation system were in decline neither at the time of Britain's abolition of the slave trade in 1807 nor during the period when slavery itself was abolished. In fact, if anything, British colonial slavery as an economic system was still thriving and expanding up until the early 1830s, according to Drescher; thus to end it was a form of economic suicide. Moreover, in answer to the neo-Gramscian thesis of shifting hegemony, Drescher (1987) points out that capitalists were not the only (nor even the primary) promoters of abolition of slavery. In fact, it was the new working classes of the industrializing north of England who mobilized the massive petition campaigns that put so much pressure on Parliament. If capitalist expansion had any impact on abolitionism, it was in creating an industrial working class in England, which ultimately changed the balance of power there.

Drescher also argues, quite convincingly, that all of the economic and ideological factors attributed to 'causing' British abolition were present in the Netherlands, yet there was no significant anti-slavery movement there (Drescher 1994); in the absence of a mobilized working class, no amount of elite ideological pressure would end slavery. Conversely, France abolished slavery during the French Revolution in the absence of a powerful anti-slavery campaign like Britain's and with little apparent bourgeois support for abolition. With regard to the United States, the work of David Eltis, Robert Fogel and Stanley Engerman also supports the argument that slavery was not only economically viable right up until its abolition, but was of great significance to world markets. Their work undermines the basic tenets of the economic thesis, for they show capitalism and slavery growing hand in hand. Indeed, sugar booms in Cuba and Brazil in the second half of the nineteenth century intensified slavery even while introducing new technologies, industrial processes and links to an expanding world market (Moreno Fraginals 1976).

In arguing that economic growth, rather than decline, accompanied the abolition of slavery, several analysts turn to a more state-centred explanation. The traditional 'humanitarian' thesis was partially state-centred in so far as it emphasized public pressure on Parliament leading to changes in state policy. More recently, however, historians have examined precisely how structural changes in both the modern economy *and the state* enabled the anti-slavery mobilization to succeed in Britain, and not, for example, in France (except during a brief radical phase of the Revolution). Eltis, for example, attributes Britain's abolition of the slave trade in 1807 to its combination of certain advanced characteristics (compared to other European states) of both its national economy *and* its state (Eltis 1987). A similar awareness of the crucial role of the modern state (along with the economy) is also apparent in the work of Du Bois and others who have studied the Reconstruction Era. For example, Anthony Marx emphasizes the crucial impact of forces of centralization of state power in both the abolition of slavery and the development of segregation in the United States, much like apartheid in South Africa (Marx 1998). State-centred theories focus on the relatively autonomous effects of state centralization in bringing about abolitionist outcomes, rather than subsuming the state under the ideological superstructure of bourgeois hegemony.

A slightly different account of the importance of structural change to the abolition of slavery is offered in the world-system theory of Immanuel Wallerstein. This is perhaps the most 'oilfield' inspired point of view, for in contrast to historians who focus on questions of economic and cultural change within metropolitan centres, Wallerstein

(1980) shifts the focus to creeping change in the global economy as a whole. He describes the emergence of a world economy with a capitalist core in Europe and a shifting zone of 'semi-peripheries' and 'peripheries' as this core expands. In his view, the fifteenth- to sixteenth-century Spanish American periphery was replaced in the seventeenth to eighteenth century by the Caribbean, which was then superceded by plantation development in India, South East Asia, the Pacific and Africa. In this paradigm, the development of slavery is a tool for the expansion of the capitalist world system, which is just as easily dropped as new peripheries are incorporated with new forms of labour exploitation such as indenture, contract labour, debt peonage, share cropping, etc. (cf. Beckford 1972). Which social actors actually abolished slavery is less important than which phase the world-system has reached in each place. This approach sidesteps the question of agency altogether, whether by abolitionists or rebel slaves.

All of these approaches locate the causal factors and processes of change driving the abolition of slavery wholly outside of the Americas, whether the motors of change are within Europe or exist at some kind of global level. Changes in the global economy and in the class and state structure of European countries may be necessary components of any argument about the abolition of slavery, but are they sufficient? As Steve Stern has argued in a critique of Wallerstein, just as crucial in understanding the timing and patterns of slave emancipation are the actions taken by people on the supposed periphery (Stern 1988). We must take into account resistance, rebellion and revolution by working classes against the system that exploits them, as well as the horizontal linkages that develop among Creole elites who may act to protect regional interests against the imperatives of imperial powers or global economies. An important new question then emerges: what is the relationship between slaves' struggles for freedom and Creole elite struggles for autonomy from metropolitan interference? Beyond underlying structural and ideological changes, it is the interplay of these two driving forces that plays a major part in determining the actual *timing* of slavery's abolition. In this sense, we can say that there are both external and internal causal mechanism driving the abolition process forward.

This certainly seems to be a key factor in the case of Cuba's relatively late abolition of slavery in 1886. Rebecca Scott argues that neither changes in the plantation economy nor changes within the Spanish state, alone or in combination, explain why emancipation took so long or why it was resisted both by Spanish and Cuban elites. Instead, she argues, we must expand our analysis to include other actors: slaves, freedmen, peasants and insurgents. While pressure for reform in Spain certainly played a part (i.e. the liberal reforms of 1868) along with external pressures such as the abolition of slavery in the United States in 1865, it is also important to consider new perceptions and scope for activity on the part of slaves themselves. The Ten Years' War (1868–78) centred in the mountainous eastern province of Oriente and led by Afro-Cubans like Antonio Maceo brought about the 'ameliorative' policies of the Moret Law, while war and reform together offered new opportunities and latitude for individual strategies of self-emancipation through fighting, flight or self-purchase. As Spain moved toward formal abolition of slavery in the 1880s, bargaining between workers, landowners and special courts known as *Juntas Protectadoras de Libertados* made for a dynamic process of emancipation. Most importantly, emancipation was not so much experienced in the legal distinction between free and slave, but in the very struggle by slaves to assert their rights and actively test their freedom. That is why self-purchase remained an important form of self-emancipation even when slavery was about to end.

Garden explanations of slavery's abolition

Here we begin to see why slave agency became so important to reinterpreting the whole current of historiography described above. It was 'bottom-up' analyses like Scott's that fed into a new phase in the study of slavery and emancipation. Unlike the previous emphasis on great shifts in ideological or economic structures bringing about abolition, a new cohort of historians began to delve into individual cases and close study at the local and regional level, exploring emancipation from the 'grassroots' up, so to speak. The 'gardening' metaphor is particularly appropriate here, not only because emancipation began to be seen as something that slaves themselves helped to bring about in particular local time-frames, but also because gardening was, literally, an important site for the cultivation of freedom. The slave's kitchen garden and provision ground has come to be understood as one of the most important mechanisms through which slaves could build some degree of autonomous life, community and kinship (Mintz 1979; Besson 1979, 1995). The economic and social space of the garden was crucial to the making of a 'culture of resistance' even during slavery, and it became the seed-corn from which post-emancipation freedom could be cultivated.

Whereas previous debates over the abolition of slavery usually located the 'motors of change' outside of local political interactions (Stern 1993), neglected Caribbean civil societies and completely overlooked slave and peasant political cultures, the focus has more recently shifted to slave resistance. As Hilary Beckles observes, 'slave resistance had long been conceived of as a lower species of political behaviour, lacking in ideological cohesion, intellectual qualities and a philosophical direction'; he calls instead for 'closer investigation of slaves' political culture' (Beckles 1988: 1–3). This approach to the making of freedom began, as do many Caribbean gardens, with the process of '*dechoukaj*', or uprooting and cleaning of the land. Slashing and burning away the debris of Eurocentric history, it places the foundational moment of emancipation not in European enlightenment, but in slave rebellion, of which the Haitian Revolution is exemplary. The violence of self-liberation is seen as a necessary and cathartic process, much like Frantz Fanon's understanding of the violent catharsis necessary for decolonization (Fanon 1967).

Many historians from the Caribbean, along with some metropolitan anthropologists, challenged the Eurocentrism of the 'oilfield' approach by shifting the focus of attention to the New World, and to the agency of enslaved people themselves. James was one of the first writers to suggest that the Saint Domingue Revolution was 'a thoroughly prepared and organized mass movement' by slave gangs who were 'closer to a modern proletariat than any other group of workers in existence at the time' (James 1989 [1938]: 86). Building on the work of James and other Caribbean Marxist scholars such as Walter Rodney, Caribbean historiography in the 1970s and 1980s began increasingly to highlight slave rebellion and labour resistance. The initial emphasis was on armed uprising or marronage as the most important political instruments of the enslaved (Aptheker [1943] 1993; Price 1973; Genovese 1979). It is now clear that violent resistance to slavery was endemic, from the revolts on slave ships during the middle passage to the scores of attempted rebellions and discovered plots in the New World (Geggus 1997).

Slave agency now has to be taken into account more fully in any explanation of the abolition of slavery. In studying slave rebellion and how it changed over time, however, a number of new debates emerged. In *The Sinews of Empire* (1974), Craton identified a pattern of differentiation between early Maroon-led slave revolts that predated sugar monoculture and often aimed to exterminate whites; African-led rebellions that had liberationist orientations and attempted to recreate African society on the plantations; and late Creole-led rebellions with Christianized elite slaves as leaders and more limited aims of reform within the European colonial system. In later work, Craton recognized the shortcomings of his chronology, and has admitted his failure to examine the potential ideological positions of different slave rebels, and particularly the impact of the Haitian revolution. Nevertheless, he still sees slave ideology as based in the proto-peasant (non-revolutionary) aims of small landholding, which continued into the post-slavery period (Craton 1997).

In contrast, Eugene Genovese argued that slave rebellions prior to the French and Haitian revolutions were traditionalist and simply reacting against enslavement, but did not radically challenge the system as a whole, whereas those following the period of revolution adopted the radically revolutionary ideology of equality of all men. Thus, they challenged the entire existence of the slave system. Genovese, like James, tried to bring slave political consciousness to the fore by depicting slaves as 'proto-proletarian' revolutionaries. More recently, historians like David Geggus have questioned whether slave uprisings ever adopted this kind of revolutionary democratic ideology; many, in fact, appear to have appealed to conservative monarchism and rumours of royal emancipation proclamations well into the nineteenth century (Gaspar and Geggus 1997).

These debates have important implications for how we interpret slave uprisings and their revolutionary potential; most importantly, they shift the locus of attention away from Europe and into the world of the slaves themselves. Beckles (1988) attacks Craton, Davis, Anstey, Drescher, Blackburn and others for still focusing on white humanitarians, and seeing the slave's struggle for freedom as peripheral or secondary. In suggesting that we focus on the 'self-liberation ethos' of the slaves, and the multiple political ideologies and strategies they may have used to further this ethos, Beckles pits not only Marxist against non-Marxist views, but also Caribbean scholarship against that produced in the metropolitan core. Indeed, he raises fundamental questions about the production of knowledge and its impact on how we understand the meaning of freedom. Does the slave's ideology of freedom contain a more radical kernel than the discredited ideologies of Western modernity, the very ideologies that justified slavery?

One sociologist who has placed slavery at the centre of understanding the Western valuation of freedom is Patterson. In a bold inversion of common logic, he argues that '*without the institution of slavery America would in all likelihood have had no democratic tradition and would not have come to enshrine freedom at the very top of its pantheon of values*' (Patterson 1987: 545, [italics in original]). Tracing a passage from ancient Greek household slavery through the slave plantation system of imperial Rome, and into the Christian ideology of redemption, he contends that 'the very idea and valuation of freedom [in the West] was generated by the experience and growth of slavery' (Patterson 1991: *xiv*). If he is correct that freedom is a constitutive Western value not in *spite* of slavery but *because* of it, then it becomes imperative that we re-evaluate the relationship between the Atlantic system of slavery and the democratic revolutions and expansions of popular citizenship that occurred alongside it. Even if one rejects Patterson's strong hypothesis, he is at least correct in noting that the rights of free citizens were originally defined 'in contradistinction with the non-native, the most extreme case of which was the slave[;]...the alien population both enhanced and defined the values of citizenship' (Patterson 1991: 78, 91). By interrogating the constitutional freedoms enshrined in the modern democratic state with sensitivity to their roots in institutionalized slavery, we are perhaps in a better position to understand the limited implementation of freedom in post-slavery contexts.

Patterson returns us to the temporal scale of oilfields, but clings to the small causal mechanism of the human spirit and its powers of moral cultivation. Yet, it is clear that self-emancipation does not occur in a vacuum. We still need to ask how macro-structural changes occurring in the world system, and affecting different colonial powers at different rates, shaped the timing and impact of slave resistance and rebellion. And from the opposite perspective, what impact did their resistance and rebellion have on the system as a whole? Did slave resistance accelerate metropolitan anti-slavery action in any way? As Arthur Stinchcombe notes, we face a question not simply of how the valuation of and struggle for freedom arose, but also of how it got translated into political action at the level of the state. The crucial question is what 'channels' existed between colonial populations and metropolitan governments, both from the pro-slavery viewpoint of the planters and from the anti-slavery viewpoint of the slaves (Stinchcombe 1996: 224).

One of the shortcomings of the early debates over slave agency was the failure to examine the relationship between violent acts of rebellion and forms of non-violent resistance and day-to-day political consciousness. The initial (one might say Fanonian) emphasis on violent rebellion as the only truly political act available to slaves precluded the possibility of more subtle forms of resistance and of analysis of the long-term development of 'cultures of resistance'. It also tended to overlook the political agency of women. Some historians have redressed this imbalance by exploring not only the extent to which women participated in violent fighting and flight from plantations, but also the more Foucauldian question of the 'infrapolitics' of resistance. Recognizing multiple forms of resistance adds a richer texture to our reconstruction of the political culture of slaves, and may help resolve some of the debates over slave political consciousness. Recent work in this area brings into focus more subtle forms of 'everyday' slave resistance as integral parts of an overall culture of resistance (Besson 1995; Craton 1982; Heuman 1986; Okihiro 1986; Olwig 1985; J. Scott 1985, 1990). Acts of resistance such as foot-dragging, attacks on property, appropriation of goods from masters, or 'hidden' actions such as poisoning, abortion and witchcraft have all come into view (Bush 1990; Beckles 1989; J. Scott 1985).

It has become increasingly apparent that if we are to understand the full range of ways in which slaves and freed people challenged the limited project of liberal democracy and radicalized its ideal of freedom, then we will need an expanded notion of what constitutes politics. The fundamental impetus behind this line of reasoning is to challenge the idea that valued 'social goods' like abolition of slavery, democracy and freedom came first from developments in Europe and then percolated down into Caribbean societies. Both approaches, the Fanonian and the Foucauldian, emphasize how slaves contributed to building free societies; they show that slave agency is an important internal causal mechanism for explaining the ending of slavery. Yet, neither approach pays a great deal of attention to the question of transmission of influence. By focusing so closely on psychological catharsis and everyday action, they either lose sight of the larger timeframe and political contexts in which these actions were taking place, or simplify them into evolutionary schemas that do not hold up to close scrutiny.

The notion that there is some monolithic form of political resistance in different periods or at different stages of 'creolization', for example, has served to obscure varieties of political orientation and differences in political access in different places and for different groups of people at different times. Elsewhere, I have begun to research women's post-emancipation political participation in Jamaica in order to understand the interplay of civil modes of political protest with those frequent occasions when women did resort to violence (Sheller 1998). Here a new set of questions arises. What is the relationship between labour disputes, strikes, demonstrations, petitions, public meetings, voting, riots and rebellions? How, when and under what circumstances did Caribbean women and men of different classes, colours and ethnicities resort to particular repertoires of contention? And how did different state actors react to them? I have found that women were in fact central to popular political mobilization in Jamaica, and were recognized as such by plantation owners, missionaries and state personnel who had to deal with their resistance. In spite of disfranchisement and lack of rights, black women clearly had an acute sense of collective agency and were not totally excluded from the public realm. Their struggles for freedom, dignity and survival politicized their everyday lives. As a Haitian saying puts it, 'Nou lèd, nou la' — we're ugly but we're here.

While occasionally verging on romanticization of the rebel slave, the Maroon, or the slave woman as 'natural rebels' (Beckles 1989, but cf. 1998), the recovery of slave agency has certainly re-invigorated a whole branch of historiography. While Geggus may be correct that rebel slaves in many instances turned to isolationist, conservative, royalist or militaristic political solutions in the early nineteenth century, such findings have not been proven for conspiracies and rebellions after the 1820s. Moreover, if one investigates post-slavery political movements among people who had themselves been slaves, or whose parents had been slaves, one finds there were clearly radical democratic ideologies in circulation. One of the objectives of this book is to demonstrate that many Afro-Caribbean activists in the period from the 1840s to 1860s were certainly not conservative in their aims, ideologies and political outlooks. My research corroborates findings that there were significant currents of peasant and proletarian radicalism in the mid-nineteenth century Caribbean, including democratic, republican and socialist ideologies. A far cry from the old bugbear of 'resistance versus accommodation', our task now is to understand how these movements emerged under particular favourable conditions, and to what extent they were suppressed under unfavourable conditions.

Towards a multi-causal explanation

Social scientists have only recently begun to systematically compare post–emancipation social and political patterns. As Karen Fog Olwig observes in regard to the Caribbean, 'the social sciences have concentrated mainly on present-day societies, whereas historical research has largely been devoted to slavery' (Olwig, 1995: 3). Yet, rather than focusing on the crescendo of forces leading to formal decrees of the abolition of slavery and stopping there, we should instead be looking at variations in the degree of freedom exercised by workers in the American plantation zone both during and after slavery. In other words, by shifting our point of view to that of the plantation worker, we see that the formal abolition of slavery may itself be less important than the ongoing struggle for actual on-the-ground freedoms. The paradox of democratic values is that they flourished in the soil of slavery, and once slavery ended, they were often limited and curtailed (at least for several generations until new movements could push forward, like the Civil Rights Movement in the United States). Emancipation was a multi-sided, dispersed and constantly interrupted struggle for local expansion in the breadth and depth of democratic rights wherever and whenever progress could be made, accompanied by breathtaking assaults on those same rights in countervailing periods of retreat and retrenchment.

This suggests a far-reaching transformation in how we think about and study the processes of abolition and emancipation. Rather than seeing freedom as a status guaranteed by law that one either has or does not have, it should be seen as something that one has more of or less of in different situations, and at different times. Workers throughout the Americas continued to struggle for fundamental rights that were still denied them after emancipation, so the process of self-liberation did not end. Following Stinchcombe, I understand freedom as a continuous variable, a sliding continuum of pragmatic relationships rather than an existential state or legal status. Emancipation is not a single moment when one becomes free, but is attached to a long-term process of interaction between former slaves, former masters and state personnel, along with various brokers or mediators ranging from missionaries and judges to overseers and abolitionists. Emancipation, then, was not the triumphal march of humanitarian progress depicted in earlier celebratory accounts of the abolition of slavery, yet neither can it be grimly reduced to the grinding imperatives of one-way capitalist exploitation and hegemonic adjustment, as pessimistically depicted in recent neo-Gramscian accounts. Understanding the interaction of structural constraints with human agency requires an account that allows room for both the possibilities and impossibilities of social change, and for multiple causation.

Stinchcombe — who is neither a historian nor a 'Caribbeanist' *per se* — has brought to bear sociological tools of generalization in studying variation across the Caribbean. He argues that each of the European empires transmitted the ideology of freedom associated with the age of democratic revolution to its sugar colonies at different times and with different intensities. This transmission then met with more or less resistance depending on the degree to which a particular colony was a 'slave society'. The degree to which a Caribbean island was a slave society depended on two factors. First, there was the timing of the sugar frontier, that is, the boom in plantation-formation and associated large-scale importation of slaves. Before the sugar boom, there are usually adventurer-bachelor societies made up of rich and poor whites, free coloureds, and small slave populations. During the sugar boom, there is a transformation into a small white settler population controlling a large population of newly imported largely young, male, African slaves. After the boom, there is a period of 'creolization' during which the slave population stabilizes into families, with higher numbers of locally born and 'racially mixed' people; there also tends to be a diversification of crops (where practicable) and the growth of a native merchant class with distinct local interests. Slave society is most intense at the height of the sugar boom, and less intense before and after its coming.

The second factor in determining a slave society is the degree of autonomy of the local government. Where planters' legislatures are autonomous from metropolitan interference (and the upper class is socially and politically cohesive and organized), they will have more power over slaves; where there is more metropolitan interference, planter power may be somewhat mitigated by legal protections for slaves. In this model, we see how slowly evolving structural features such as changes in the plantation economy and state institutions *also* affect the more immediate degree of agency of elite actors. Stinchcombe also discusses the degree of agency of slaves themselves, insofar as it produces intra-island variations in freedom. Some slaves enjoy more freedom than do others if they are in positions requiring trust and some degree of independent decision-making, i.e. special occupations or close personal relationships with whites. In general, such positions of trust were more likely to be experienced by urban slaves, mulatto slaves and Creole (non-African) slaves, while rural, darker, new arrivals from Africa experienced the least independence, hence the least freedom. However, beyond this intra-island variation in personal freedom, Stinchcombe makes little effort to explore the political implications of slave agency. In fact, he only makes slight (though crucial) reference to the ways in which black and free coloured political grievances might be channeled into the imperial system through links with republican centres of power in the metropole (Stinchcombe 1996: 224–25).

Slaves in different positions would have not only experienced more or less day-to-day autonomy, but also would have developed differing political ideologies and different means of political action, ranging from violent rebellion, to everyday forms of resistance, to political organization and civil participation. These differences arose from and fed back into links with republican and/or abolitionist movements, and thus affected the outcomes of emancipation. The ideology of freedom was grasped, transformed and, to some extent, created by slaves and ex-slaves; in other words, as Patterson argues, there is an independent internal logic to the slave's valuation of freedom. Yet, the influence of Afro-Caribbean political ideologies and mobilizations were also channeled in different ways into varied metropolitan political situations, so multiple causal mechanisms produced abolition and democratization in different ways.

In contrast to studies of the emancipation process that begin either at the macro-level of large scale economic and state transformations or at the micro-level of violent catharsis and 'infrapolitics' of resistance, my approach focuses on a more contingent intermediary level. I am concerned with the interactional process by which future-oriented human agency is transmitted into indeterminate structural transformation via political struggle. That is, while accepting both the long-term causality of macro-structural change and the more immediate causality of personal agency, my main interest is in the dynamic and unpredictable interaction between structure and agency. The locus of action is neither the European metropoles, where colonial policy was hammered out and imperial rivalries settled by war or diplomacy, nor the day-to-day politics within plantation societies, where particular groups of slaves struggled against a seemingly permanent system of personal domination. Instead, I look for the politics of emancipation between the external and the internal, between the macro-dynamics of the world system and the micro-dynamics of psychological warfare: here lies the social terrain of collective interaction, political communication and contentious politics.

The relational networks of the Caribbean region itself are at the centre of this analysis, as are the Afro-Caribbean people who struggled to shape the actual outcomes of emancipation from slavery. As Vincent Harding has argued, in 'seeking out their own way, defining their own freedom, taking the initiative to build their own institutions and speak their own convictions, black people [in the United States] necessarily addressed the future of the larger society as well' (Harding 1981: 264). In challenging the system of slavery, the people of Haiti and Jamaica also addressed the future of their societies and of Western society as a whole. Rather than attributing democracy to an ideology that was simply transmitted from Europe to the New World, I argue that we should begin with the struggles for self-determination within the colonized and enslaved communities, and determine how they interacted with concurrent metropolitan transformations.

In the following chapters, I extend Stinchcombe's model into the post-emancipation period, but also critically evaluate some of its presuppositions and shortcomings, particularly in regard to peasant agency. I introduce a tripartite model of social structure wherein figure not only the state and the economy, but also civil society and the public spheres that mediate between these institutional realms. To what extent did a ruling planter class continue to exercise economic, political and civil power after the abolition of slavery? What degrees of freedom did former slaves exercise, in which situations, and with what results? What were the political ideologies of post-slavery peasants and other workers? Perhaps most importantly, what effect did the ongoing struggle for actual freedom (i.e. even after formal emancipation) have on processes of democratization?

Preliminary comparative model

In order to explore the political participation of freed workers and their descendants in Haiti and Jamaica (including impacts of this New World dynamic back on Europe), we need a preliminary comparative model for post-slavery transitions. In order to understand the making of different types of freedom in Haiti and Jamaica, I first want to compare them to several other contexts, in order to clarify some of the parameters of variation in their formation. Taking another hint from Sidney Mintz and Stinchcombe, I apply a 'systadic' rather than a 'synchronic' approach. This means that rather than looking at several cases in a single slice of time, I look for a single process that occurs in many places but at different times. The process that concerns me is a pattern of change that I have identified in a number of post-emancipation settings. It consists of a window of opportunity for democratic expansion occasioned by the extension of citizenship to a large class of people who were previously enslaved, followed by a period of restriction of those rights. In many cases, efforts to extend rights to former slaves (often through cross-class alliances) were thwarted, leading to peasant rebellions, state repression, reactionary elite consolidation and what I am calling *de*-democratization.

In Haiti, this occurred in the 1840s, in Jamaica in the 1860s. Despite contrasting paths to the abolition of slavery (the former revolutionary and anti-French, the latter gradual and British-controlled), these economically and symbolically important islands experienced surprisingly similar post-emancipation political processes, including government claims to represent the emancipated population, oppositional reform movements, peasant/proletarian protest and rebellion and finally *de*-democratization. If attempts to exercise freedom or extend its meaning were at the forefront of the overall movement for democratization in the nineteenth century, then it is clear that democratic movements could take place even in those historical settings most riddled with social injustice, economic inequality and violent repression. Indeed, it was these very conditions that made the ongoing project of liberation all the more urgent once slavery was abolished in some places and still to be abolished in others.

Table 1 depicts the distinctive pattern of anti-democratic transition out of slavery in four exemplary cases: Haiti, Jamaica, the United

Table 1   Comparative Emancipation and De-democratization Processes

Country	Context of Slave Emancipation	Attempt to Expand Black Rights	Peasant Rebellion	Retreat from Democracy
Haiti	Revolution and War of Independence: 1791–1804	Liberal Movement 1838–1843	Piquet Rebellion 1844	'Politique de Doublure', i.e. Mulatto Power
Jamaica	Gradual colonial 'apprenticeship' 1834–1838	Underhill Movement 1865	Morant Bay Rebellion 1865	Martial Law and Crown Colony Rule, 1865-
United States of America	Post-Colonial Civil War 1861–65	Radical Reconstruction 1865–1877	X	'Redemption' Jim Crow Laws 1877-
Cuba	Gradual reform: 1870 Moret Law, 1880–6 Patronato	Independence Wars: 1868–78, 1895–98	Guerra Chiquita 1879	Massacre of Partido Independiente de Color, 1912

States and Cuba. For each case, the columns present a series of chrono-logical events. First, there is the context for slave emancipation, which is associated with different historical periods and different types of abolitionist process in each country. Then, there is a post-emancipation attempt to expand the rights of those who were freed from slavery, usually related to the disappointment of freedom for a disillusioned younger generation (possibly in alliance with other oppositional groups). The failure of each of these movements prompts (under certain condi-tions) a 'rebellion' among populations identified as 'peasants' or small landholders. Finally, each country experiences a retreat from democ-racy, recognized in each of their historiographic traditions as a kind of swindle of the promise of freedom. The end result in every case is that the hopes and raised expectations of the former slave population were crushed under the weight of continuing oppression.

In Haiti, the emancipation process began with the slave uprising of 1791 and the abolition of slavery in the context of the French and Haitian Revolutions. Two decades of civil war and state consolidation followed, but eventually a liberal reform movement emerged that called for a more democratic constitution and for fuller popular partici-pation in political life. Though succeeding in the overthrow of President Boyer, the 'liberal revolution' failed to consolidate a new government and instability led to party fragmentation along colour lines ('mulatto' vs. 'black'), peasant rebellion in the Southern province, and the breakaway of the Dominican Republic. The final settlement of this fumbled attempt at democratization was the installation of a black president in what came to be known as the 'politique de doublure'. This refers to a populist-fronted system in which real power was held behind the scenes by a traditional (in this case mulatto) group of power-holders, backed by the army (Trouillot 1990; Nicholls 1996; and see Chapter 5).

In Jamaica, the gradual process of movement towards abolition included the first British abolition campaign in the late eighteenth century; abolition of the slave trade in 1807; the 'amelioration' pro-grammes of the early nineteenth century; the enfranchisement of the 'free coloured' population in 1830; and finally the apprenticeship system of 1834-38. Plantation-owners' control of the local House of Assembly, however, led to discriminatory laws that penalized the freed population. In response, an alliance of missionaries, non-white politi-cians and Native Baptist religious leaders led a campaign of public meetings and petitioning in pursuit of greater black political enfran-chisement. Governor Eyre's refusal to acknowledge the demands of this movement sparked the rebellion at Morant Bay and its harsh repression under martial law. The Jamaican House of Assembly was then abolished and replaced by Crown Colony Rule, thereby ending the brief post-emancipation period of openly flourishing popular political contention and electoral participation (Heuman 1981; Holt 1992; and see Chapters 7 and 8).

In the United States, abolition of slavery was gradually introduced in the industrializing North, but vehemently resisted in the agrarian South until the Civil War. The war at first caused *de facto* mass self-emancipation for some slaves (through desertion of plantations); later emancipation was codified and extended to the majority by the wartime Emancipation Proclamation of 1863. The final abolition of slavery and end of the war in 1865 led to a period of democratic opportunity for freed men (and to some extent women [cf. Brown 1995]), now able to own land, vote in elections, sit on juries and hold public office (Du Bois 1992; Harding 1981). However, the period of Radical Reconstruction with federal troops occupying the South came to an end in 1877 as federal policy turned toward reconciliation with white Southerners (Foner 1983, 1988; Marx 1998). Here, retreat from democracy was achieved without a peasant rebellion as catalyst and excuse, but with equally devastating outcomes.

In the economically burgeoning Spanish colony of Cuba, a gradual process of emancipation began with Spain's liberal reforms of 1868 and the Moret Law of 1870 (freeing children and the elderly, and outlawing whipping), which came into effect in the context of the Ten Years' War of 1868–78. The combination of war and reform led to the freeing of around one third of the enslaved population (R. Scott 1985). Although colonial control persevered until a second War of Independence in 1895–1898, the process of slavery abolition was nevertheless caught up in the ongoing anti-colonial debates and armed struggles — in contrast to the state-contained experiences of the United States, the British Colonies or Brazil. The Guerra Chiquita of 1879 was associated with Afro-Cuban anti-colonial leadership (Helg 1995), and Spain finally introduced the gradual *patronato* system in 1880, culminating in full abolition in 1886 (two years before Brazil). However, following Cuban independence from Spain, the United States occupations of 1898 and 1906 had a major impact on the post-slavery settlement. Proletarianization of small farmers combined with racial polarization led to Afro-Cuban protest and in some regions renewed armed conflict. The strength of the Partido Independiente de Color after the United States withdrawal demonstrated that racial inequality was still a central issue in Cuba. The army's massacre of 3000 blacks in the 'Race War' of 1912 presented the typical pattern of anti-democratic backlash that we have found elsewhere (Helg 1995). It also led to the persecution of a large population of migrant Haitian and Jamaican sugar plantation workers, who sought protection and solidarity in the burgeoning Universal Negro Improvement Association. By the mid-1920s, Cuba hosted one of the most important Garveyite networks outside the United States (Martin 1976: 49).

Note that there is also an overall chronological progression from the top of the table to the bottom, so each case may have been influenced by what had gone before. In other words, the pattern of citizenship and political culture in each case was partly dependent not only on the internal path by which slavery was locally abolished, but also on the external impact of previous paths taken in surrounding cases. Thus, all slave-holding empires lived in fear of the example of the Haitian Revolution (as discussed in Chapter 3 below), while a gradual programme such as Britain's apprenticeship became a model for Cuba's *patronato*. Furthermore, there was also a flow of influence from imperial centres of power to dispersed colonial sites, as news, people and governing agents flowed in this direction. Ideas, discourses, models and events in France, Britain or Spain provided warrants and stimuli, resources and constraints, for the formation of political movements in Haiti, Jamaica or elsewhere in the Caribbean. The French Revolution itself, the July Revolution of 1830, the British Reform Act of 1832 or the European events of 1848, for example, all influenced the direction and timing of cycles of protest which reverberated across the Atlantic and sent ripples throughout the Caribbean. At times, though, such waves of influence were also reflected from the Caribbean back to Europe, as when events in Haiti sparked terror in Europe or emulation among anti-slavery activists.

Table 2 categorizes these various configurations of the emancipation process into four possible types. On the one hand, the abolition of slavery could either be war-driven and relatively sudden, as it was in the Haitian Revolution and the United States Civil War; or policy-driven and gradually introduced, as it was in Jamaica's or Cuba's planned systems of apprenticeship. On the other hand, we see that the abolition process could either be intimately associated with the overthrow of colonial rule — as it was in Haiti (towards the end of the Revolution) and Cuba (drawn out over several wars of independence).

Table 2   Types of Abolition of Slavery

	State-overturning	State-contained
War-driven/immediate	Haiti	United States
Policy-driven/gradual	Cuba	Jamaica

Or it could be carefully contained by the existing state (as with federal government control of emancipation in the United States and British colonial control in Jamaica).

These broad differences in process and outcome of abolition patterned the type of post-slavery citizenship that emerged in each case and the kinds of public practices in which citizens could engage. Even more importantly, the timing and type of emancipation process also impacted on overarching formations of class, racial, colour, ethnic and national distinctions, for each country marked these social boundaries in significantly different ways. If Afro-Caribbean working classes shaped the meaning and practice of freedom through robust interaction with land-owning and mercantile elites, missionaries and state actors, then the very process of that interaction also marked out the political identities and fluid boundaries between groups. Military-led transformation, for example, had a significant impact on subsequent models of citizenship and public participation quite different from cases of gradual political alliance building; likewise, integration into an existing state shaped the potential for nationalist consciousness in quite different ways than did anti-colonial war.

The new economic, civil and political formations that emerged in Haiti and Jamaica in their respective post-emancipation periods both shaped popular political participation and were themselves shaped by the repeated incursions of freed men and women seeking to test and define their freedom. Jamaican freed slaves were not simply bequeathed the 'boon' of British freedom, nor were they just handed down previously used scripts and worn costumes from the British repertoire of contention. Contention depends on political skills of creative adaptation, timing, local action and tactics; to develop these, freed slaves had to forge their own relationship with a stubborn colonial wing of the state, albeit one that had certain pre-existing patterns of response and control. Likewise, Haitians created their own unique state from the remnants of the destroyed French colonial government, building on a fiercely independent republican military and borrowing constitutional models from the United States (though bringing in original features such as the constitutional abolition of slavery). Previous histories and new public forays together established a range of safe and dangerous channels that ordered the possibilities of collective action and also shaped what might be called state 'repertoires of coercion'.

Where collective action crossed into danger zones, the question of the state's ability to use armed force and coercion became crucial. Armed force was always crucial to the maintenance of slave societies, and there is no reason to think that it should simply have disappeared as a factor in the post-emancipation political calculus. Geggus argues, for example, that slave uprisings in the Greater Caribbean are patterned according to levels of military garrisons and linked to the timing of military campaigns in various regions (Geggus 1997). This is commensurate with a wider hypothesis that black political mobilization of all types in both slave societies and post-slavery societies varies indirectly to the degree of military autonomy and available armed force. Thus, Winston James observes that the absence of political protest and uprisings in Barbados (in contrast to Jamaica) is not a function of a quiescent political culture or Little England mentality. It was due, rather, to the military odds stacked against blacks in Barbados, as first made evident in the brutal suppression of Bussa's Rebellion in 1816 (James 1998).

Subordination of the military to civil control is a crucial factor in the key period of post-slavery reconstruction of polity, economy and civil society, just as it would be in later efforts at democratization in the region (Rueschemeyer, Stephens and Stephens 1992; Paige 1998). Equally important is the international context in which that military operates. The Haitian military's autonomy and national significance were an inescapable legacy of its revolutionary overthrow of slavery and the hostile international response, but it had an overwhelmingly negative impact on the ability of its citizens to build public channels of communication between the state and civil society. Jamaica's colonial position, in contrast, meant not only that the military was not under direct control of local landowners, but also that there were 'spaces' for civil association to develop. Afro-Jamaicans exploited channels of publicity to build alliances not only internally, but also with British abolitionists, the British labour movement, or even with international actors such as Haitian or African-American political activists and intellectuals. The impact of armed coercion on publicity only became apparent in Jamaica in the aftermath of rebellions when martial law was imposed; even then, it caused controversy back in Britain. Understanding why peasant mobilization in Haiti differed from that in Jamaica or Cuba (and how the states' reactions to such mobilizations differed in each case) will bring us a long way toward understanding the varying constructions of citizenship, freedom and democracy in the post-slavery Caribbean.

In this regard, the Haitian case is not an anomaly, as many previous historians have argued, but can in fact be explained by the same set of causal mechanisms that are found in other post-slavery settings. Rather than seeing some peculiar cultural exceptionalism in Haiti's historical trajectory (to which even Stinchcombe falls prey), we should recognize it as one type of outcome of a conjuncture of relational causal factors that were also at work in other cases. The apparent uniqueness of its outcome lies, of course, in its rare combination of a military-imposed emancipation married to an anti-colonial war of independence. The United States enjoyed the former, without the latter, which had already been achieved in 1776; thus, like Haiti, its abolition of slavery was militarily imposed, but, unlike Haiti, its government (and with it the military) was under civil control. Cuba tried to achieve independence militarily, while studiously avoiding the imposition of island-wide immediate emancipation, which would have undermined white support for independence. The British managed to head off both outcomes, as did Brazil, though in different fashions. The French colonies flipped back and forth unsteadily between all of the options, first abolishing slavery, then re-imposing it, suddenly losing colonies, then regaining them. In the next chapter, this multi-causal model of post-slavery transitions will be applied to charting the different routes of emancipation taken in Haiti and Jamaica, yet ultimately converging on the same direction: the decline of planter economic, political and civil control.

Given the multiple paths to, and outcomes of, emancipation, it should not be surprising that those who were going through it adhered to a number of conflicting political ideologies and programmes. Some historians have been at pains to point out *either* the radicalism *or* the conservatism of Caribbean peasants as a group, to emphasize either the racial-consciousness or the class-consciousness of Caribbean political actors (as if the two were mutually exclusive). These debates originate in the initial polarization of the field between oilfield versus garden models of emancipation, as discussed above. The key question is really: Under what conditions does one or the other tendency prevail? Evidence from popular political movements in Haiti (as will be discussed in Part Two) suggests that peasants there were not politically 'apathetic' as many historians have assumed. Not only did some Haitians agitate for an expansion of black political and civil rights, but they also did so in the name of the democratic ideals of the Haitian Revolution and in defense of the republican and anti-colonial foundations of the Haitian State. Evidence from Jamaica (as will be discussed in Part Three) suggests that the conjoined peasant/proletarian activist networks, political discourses and forms of political agency were far-reaching and sophisticated. Moreover, there is a crucial parallel in the struggles for black rights in both Haiti and Jamaica, and clear indications that black peasants and proletarians in both countries were aware of their positional similarities and used this knowledge to develop their own democratic ideology.

The decline of planter control in Haiti and Jamaica

Defining freedom as a continuous variable

Neither independent Haiti nor British Jamaica made a smooth transition to widespread black enfranchisement, and attempts to broaden political participation and ensure equality of citizenship failed. In Haiti, the reform movement and Liberal Revolution of 1843 ended in violent conflict between a mulatto-dominated state and black cultivators in the south, led by Jean-Jacques Acaau; in Jamaica, the 1865 Underhill Meetings ended in a rebellion by black small settlers in St. Thomas-in-the-East, led by Paul Bogle.[1] In both cases, self-consciously black-identified publics emerged in conjunction with democratic reform movements claiming to represent the interests of the black majority and calling for the extension of black civil and political rights. Yet, at these pivotal moments in their respective histories, both the Jamaican and Haitian liberal reform movements were overtaken by armed peasant rebellions expressing far more radical claims for racial equality, social justice and participation in governance. In both cases, fragmented elites regrouped, dissent was brutally suppressed and democratization attempts failed, leading in Haiti to the authoritarian military regime of Emperor Faustin Soulouque and in Jamaica to the replacement of the two-hundred-year-old House of Assembly with direct rule from London. These were opposite outcomes in terms of racial power, but both profoundly anti-democratic in political terms in so far as they excluded the bulk of the population from the small taste of political participation they had previously had.

Comparing these parallel cycles that ultimately undermined democratization in both contexts offers insights into the routes of potential development that were not taken in the nineteenth-century Americas — above all, the failure of democratization movements that might have led to greater inclusion of peasants and workers. Haiti and Jamaica are especially fruitful for comparison because they shared many initial economic similarities, but went through opposite political processes of emancipation (one revolutionary, the other gradual) with contrasting outcomes (one an independent republic, the other a colony). They were the two most profitable colonies in the world in the late eighteenth century, and were among the most important producers of sugar just prior to their respective abolition of slavery.[2] Occupying relatively large mountainous territories (compared to the Lesser Antilles or the low coastal zones of the Caribbean), both countries combined extensive sugar plantations on their plains with cattle grazing on upland savannas and coffee-growing on higher slopes. They also became exemplary of strong peasant development, with a post-slavery expansion of small landholding and crop diversification. However, they developed contrasting kinds of state-citizen relations, with major implications for popular politics.

With populations that were nearly 80 percent black at the time of emancipation, both islands were seen not only as tests and proving grounds of the claims of abolitionists, but also as measuring rods of the 'advance' of the black race worldwide. In French Saint Domingue, with an area of roughly 10,000 square miles, there were approximately 452,000 slaves just prior to the revolution, while in Jamaica, with an area of 4244 square miles, there were 311,000 slaves just prior to the apprenticeship period in 1834.[3] These slaves, however, experienced opposite modes of emancipation as the overthrow of slavery unfolded within wider national and international political transitions that were reshaping France, Great Britain and their colonies. The punctuated timing of the abolition of slavery coincided with wider cycles of social mobilization and transformation of political contention. France and its overseas colonies took the path of revolution, but Great Britain took a less violent route with an emerging national field of public opinion wielded through extra-parliamentary claim-making, petitions and the press (Bradley 1986; Tilly 1995a). Haiti's slave-led revolution and independence, and Jamaica's gradual emancipation and colonial integration set up contrasting political models that marked out the opposite poles of a symbolic field in which the meaning and practice of 'freedom' and black citizenship were tested and transformed.

In his ambitious comparative study of the political economy of the Caribbean, Stinchcombe has argued that the 'sociology of slavery and freedom has been crippled by not treating freedom as a variable. Part of the problem is that in the United States, freedom is thought of as a legal concept defined in the Bill of Rights, or in France, as in the Declaration of the Rights of Man, so that it is either guaranteed or not' (Stinchcombe 1996: 150–51). Instead, it should be conceptualized as a 'possibility set under different causal conditions'. Just as slaves could enjoy more or fewer practical liberties, so too could 'freed' men and women become more or less free in different kinds of states and in occupying different positions within society. If emancipation everywhere led to struggles over the liberties that planters would lose, and the liberties that ex-slaves would gain, one should be able to identify some regular patterns, and apply the same set of causal mechanisms to explain many different cases.

It is often assumed that colonial Jamaica inherited the 'Westminster system' from Britain and so therefore benefited from 'tutelary democracy' (cf. Payne 1993; Maingot 1996), while Haiti was bound to be autocratic because it lacked democratic traditions on which to build civil institutions (cf. Weinstein and Segal 1992). Stinchcombe, in contrast, suggests that Haiti had one of the most democratic governments in the Caribbean region in the nineteenth century because of its revolutionary independence from imperial ties, even if it did not qualify as a 'good' democracy. In Jamaica, on the other hand, the 'racist oligarchic parliamentarism of the British islands, backed by a more or less nongoverning colonial office, provided stability and some civility, but its tutelary democracy had provided more tuition than democracy, and not much of either' (Stinchcombe 1996: 13). Neither country was very democratic, then, but each had certain aspects of democratic rule after slavery ended, plus a strong potential for further democratization. My approach, then, is to compare the actual forms of political claim-making and state-citizen interaction that existed in the post-slavery period in each island. There is no reason to believe that Haitians could not have enjoyed broader and more equal citizenship than any country in the Americas under a democratic constitutional system, given the right conditions; nor is there any reason to believe that colonial Jamaica was particularly conducive to fostering democracy or inculcating democratic values and outlooks. To the contrary, the Haitian Revolution enshrined the values of equality and liberty, while the colonial state in Jamaica more often than not acted directly contrary to democratic values. In this regard, rather than being a retrospective historical account, looking back along one path from the past to the present, what is required is a 'prospective history', highlighting the 'opening and closing of possibilities...[in] a process of selection strongly constrained by previous history' (Tilly 1993: 17).

In synthesizing a great deal of previous research by historians of various Caribbean territories, Stinchcombe provides some of the sociological tools with which to attempt an overall mapping of the parameters of freedom. As mentioned above, he suggests that there are general causal mechanisms which determined whether a slave-holding island in the Caribbean was more or less of a 'slave society'. The two main variables in his model are the degree of planter dominance (which determines inter-island variation in freedom) and the degree of slave agency (which determines intra-island variation). Planter dominance depended on the importance of sugar in the economy, the degree of solidarity within the planter aristocracy and the extent to which the local planter-dominated governments were left to run island affairs independent of imperial interference. Slave agency refers to the exercise of choice and decision-making in everyday life, i.e. the degree to which slaves were treated like free people. This, in turn, depended on the type of tie in the master-slave relationship based on 'the slave owner's need for the slave's consent and enthusiasm as a trusted agent'.

These general mechanisms can be extended to the post-slavery period in order to see how freedom for former slaves varied both between and within islands. First, though, we must shift Stinchcombe's 'slave society' variables to a post-slavery context. The question of planter dominance continues in a very similar form after emancipation because big landowners remained a prominent political force throughout the Caribbean; however, the timing of the 'sugar frontier' recedes in causal prominence while the timing of expansion and diversification of peasant crops moves forward.[4] Peasant landholding as an alternative to sugar monoculture became the key terrain for wresting economic power from planters, and with it political and civil power as well (Mintz 1989; Rodney 1981; Fick 1990). In this sense, it seems appropriate to refer to this cluster of variables as the degree of 'planter control' of both economy and polity, for then it can be weighed against the degree of 'peasant agency', which only emerges as a political possibility after slave emancipation. I also disaggregate this variable into three areas of control, reflecting different institutional settings: economic, political and civil.

Second, the question of slave agency must be translated into a new question of peasant agency. Variations in post-slavery peasant autonomy in different Caribbean regions have been attributed to a combination of economic, geographic and political factors that together determined availability of land for peasant settlement (Mintz 1989; Higman 1995; Stinchcombe 1996). The main economic variable is the timing and rate of plantation development and decline: where the sugar frontier had already passed its peak, more land was available after emancipation for peasants. Geographically, peasants 'gained a more secure foothold in the larger and more mountainous territories... [and] were more attenuated or constrained in smaller or flatter islands' (Besson 1995: 73). At the regional level, this meant that peasants were prevented from gaining a foothold on plains and valleys dominated by sugarcane, but were able to concentrate landholding in hilly or moun-

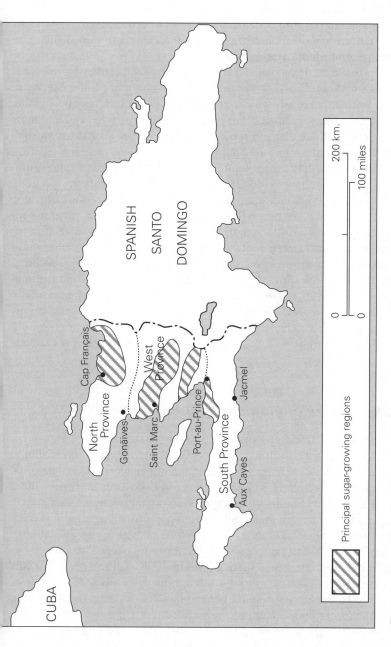

Figure 2   Map of Saint Domingue showing sugar-growing regions in 1790

tainous areas not suitable for cane (see Figure 2). Finally, differences in the process and context of emancipation affected the degree to which ex-slaves who became 'free' were afforded an equal status of full citizenship; the more that planter control was constrained, the more that peasant agency could expand

How were Jamaican and Haitian planters affected by slave emancipation? This chapter tracks the decline not only of planter economic and political control, which we would expect in old sugar colonies with growing peasantries, but also the decline of what I call planter 'civil control', an element somewhat neglected (at least theoretically) by Stinchcombe. Because many analyses of the post-emancipation period focus solely on economic changes at the level of the plantation, and political changes concerning the state (particularly relations between local and metropolitan government), they overlook changes in the constitution of civil society. I bring all three institutional spheres into focus by thematizing them in this chapter in relation to the decline in planter control in Haiti and Jamaica. In subsequent chapters, I show how changing configurations of economic, political and civil control allowed for the emergence of both elite oppositional publics and radical subaltern publics, whose successful democratic alliance would spell the end of plantation society. Yet it was a movement for democratization whose time had not come, as post-slavery societies throughout the Americas retreated from the radical implications of freedom.

The decline of planter economic control

Extending Stinchcombe's model into the post-slavery period, we can hypothesize that a decline in the economic importance of sugar should have had a negative impact on the degree of planter social and political dominance. In both Haiti and Jamaica after slave emancipation, there was a rapid decline in sugar exports accompanied by an increase in production of 'provisions' and small export crops. As sugar waned in economic importance for both islands, land was made available to freedmen, via distribution to soldiers in Haiti (Lacerte 1975) and the free village system in Jamaica (Mintz 1958; Turner 1982). In this sense, planter control over land was visibly decreasing. Nevertheless, all big landowners struggled to maintain control over the plantation labour forces and to continue sugar production against unfavourable odds: the sugar frontier was long gone, and many plantations were encumbered with deep debts, exhausted soil and uncooperative 'free' labour forces.

In Haiti, annual sugar exports plummeted from over 141 million pounds on the eve of the French Revolution in 1789, to 18.5 million pounds during the War of Independence in 1801 (only 13 percent of former levels), falling to a meagre 2.5 million pounds in 1820 (less than two percent of pre-revolution levels) and by 1841 to practically negligible amounts; almost all of the post-independence exports, moreover, were of less valuable unrefined muscovado.[5] At the same time, annual coffee production fell from a high of almost 77 million pounds in 1789 (when coffee exports matched white sugar exports in value) to a low of 24 million in 1822 (34 percent of former levels). It then stabilized around 35 to 40 million pounds over the next two decades, indicating viable production.[6] Some export growth occurred after 1820 in cotton and mahogany in the west, tobacco and dyewoods in the east; however, most of these exports leveled off or fell by the late 1820s.[7]

James Franklin, a British businessman who visited Haiti in the second and third decades of the 1800s, described how various methods of keeping the big estates cultivated had failed since the abolition of slavery.[8] First share cropping was tried on government-owned land, with the cultivators given one-third, and later one-fourth of the crop. This had to be abandoned, and the next experiment was 'to purchase canes from the cultivator, who was put in possession of the land, the Government, or Owner, retaining the Mill, Boiling house, etc. in his possession, and grinding the canes purchased from the cultivator'. This, too, failed, according to owners, because the central factories could not obtain enough canes, and because the cultivators continually disputed the prices being offered. Finally, the little sugar being produced had to be paid for by wages, with men offered $3 per week and women and boys $1.50. As the unsympathetic British Consul General Charles Mackenzie reported in 1828, the big sugar plantations had been broken up and labour could not be enforced:

> The whole of these estates [on the plain of Aux Cayes] are, more or less, in a dismembered condition, from the small grants made by the government to the military of from five to thirty carreaus, and from similar sales having been effected by many of the large proprietors.... The very little field labour effected is generally performed by elderly people, principally old Guinea negroes. No measure of the government can induce the young creoles to labour, or depart from their habitual licentiousness and vagrancy.... I am satisfied that, in general, a want of population, of industry in the existing population, and the subdivision of land,

counteract the wishes of the government to produce
systematic labour.[9]

Thus, the most significant change in agricultural production after independence was a shift to small-scale coffee production. 'Just as the less
prosperous among the whites and the freedmen of Saint Domingue had
found an economic alternative in coffee', observes Michel-Rolph
Trouillot, 'so a growing number of the post-revolutionary peasants and
small landowners had turned to that crop for similar reasons. It
required little start-up capital, its cultivation and processing required
much less labor than did sugar cane, and it sold well on the export
market' (Trouillot 1990: 60). By 1859, Haiti was the fourth largest
coffee producer in the world (after Brazil, Java and Ceylon), and
coffee constituted 70 percent of its exports (Dupuy 1989: 95). Other
small exports included cacao, indigo, molasses, hides, tortoise, horns
and wax.

Without a large-scale plantation economy, the state became
increasingly dependent on taxation of trade. A good picture of the
highly-wrought government control of trade is provided by the
Licensing Law of 1819–1821, which gives a detailed schedule of
license fees that were required for a wide variety of commercial activities, divided into fine gradations (see Table 3). It also clearly depicts
the pyramidical structure of regional trade networks, with several
regional hierarchies, all culminating in Port-au-Prince.[10] Article 31
required that all licenses be shown on demand to 'police officers, justices of the peace, administrative or treasury agents, and to members
of the Councils of Notables'. Three classes of occupations were
exempted from holding licences: (1) farmers or cultivators; (2) public
functionaries, army officers and salaried employees of the nation; and,
(3) day workers, domestics, and hired wage workers. Fishermen who
sold their fish or carried freight had to hold licenses, as did carters
whether they used wagons or animals; blacksmiths, builders, carpen-
ters, wheelwrights and other skilled craftsmen also were licensed to
work.

Foreigners paid particularly dearly for trading licenses, they could
not own property and they were allowed to operate only out of seven
designated open ports. Given the weakening of planters and the key
position of foreign merchants in the economy, the latter had increasing
influence over state policy, especially following the indemnification
treaty with France in 1825. President Boyer agreed to pay 150 million
francs, over five years, to former French colonists in compensation for
their loss of property (after which France promised to recognize
Haitian independence). Haitian ports were also opened to foreign trade,

Table 3 Haitian License Law (Loi sur les Patentes), 1819–1821
[license fees in gourdes]*

Class: Occupation:	1st Class	2nd Class	3rd Class	4th Class	5th Class	6th Class
Wholesalers	60	45	30	20	12	8
Speculators	60	45	30	20	12	8
Retailers	30	20	15	10	6	4
Fat Sellers	10	8	6	5	4	2
Provision Sellers	8	7	6	5	4	3
Produce Dealers	8	7	6	5	4	3
Bon-bon Sellers	6	5	4	3	2	1
Tripe Sellers	6	5	4	3	2	1
Peddlers (between communes)	8	–	–	–	–	–
Carters (between communes)	25	–	–	–	–	–
Cafe License	50	40	30	20	15	10
Innkeeping License	40	30	20	15	10	6
Haitian Consignee	400	300	200	150	–	–
Foreign Consignee	1200	–	–	–	–	–

1st Class = Port-au-Prince
2nd Class = Aux Cayes, Jacmel, Cap Haïtien
3rd Class = Acquin, Jérémie, St. Marc, Gonaïves, Port-de-Paix
4th Class = other major regional markets
5th Class = local market centres
6th Class = small village markets
* Adapted from Linstant, *Récueil Général des Lois*, 1860, Vol. 3, pp. 120–40.

with France receiving preferential low tariffs. A 30 million-franc loan to pay the first debt installment led to resistance to the plan among the Haitian elite. Eventually, after defaults on interest payments, the terms were renegotiated, and an agreement made in 1838 for Haiti to pay 60 million francs over thirty years (still a heavy drain on a depleted economy).[11] Marking the first major debt-repayment crisis of a 'Third World' nation, Haiti paid a heavy price in both symbolic and real terms for its revolution.

In Jamaica, sugar production during the apprenticeship period (1834–38) was only 77 percent of what it had been in the decade prior to abolition. It then continued to decline, especially rapidly during the first decade after slavery's abolition, until 'by the eve of the Morant Bay Rebellion in 1865, the annual product stood at just 38% of the pre-abolition level' (Holt 1992: 119). Though less precipitous a decline than Haiti's, Jamaica suffered a far worse decline than other British colonies, some of which were increasing sugar production after emancipation. Coffee exports had already been falling prior to emancipation, and fell by 76 percent between 1834 and 1850, with only a slight rise after that date (Holt 1992: 122; Green 1991: 223, 252). Barry Higman has summarized data collected by the Jamaican House of Assembly showing that '140 sugar estates were abandoned between 1832 and 1847, with a total area of 168,032 acres and employing 22,553 slaves in 1832[;]...some 465 [coffee] plantations were abandoned, with an area of 188,400 acres and a slave population of 26,830, more than half the total employed in coffee in 1832' (Higman 1988: 11-13).

In parts of Jamaica, on the other hand, there were increases in peasant crops, meaning food produced for internal markets and production of small export crops (requiring less capital), including logwood, pimento (for allspice), ginger, arrowroot, coconuts, beeswax and honey (Sewell 1861: 249). Abandonment and piecemeal sale of former plantations depressed land prices and led to increases in small landholding among former slaves. In 1840, besides thousands of unregistered squatters, there were 2830 registered freeholds of less than fifty acres; by 1845, there were 24,268 small freeholds and by 1861, there were 50,000 (Hall 1978). The invention of an inexpensive one-horse operated coffee-peeling and winnowing machine in 1840, by John Humble of St. Ann, encouraged the growth of the small coffee growing sector (Hall 1978; Sewell 1861: 251).[12] Small freeholds were concentrated not in remote areas, but in central parishes where there was a mixed economy that would support both subsistence farming and occasional wage-work on plantations (Holt 1992; see Figure 2).

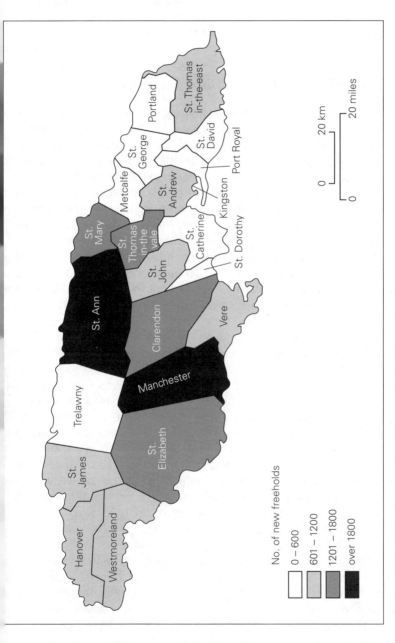

Figure 3   Map of Jamaica showing peasant freeholds, 1840–45

Only during droughts were peasants driven back to the estates in large enough numbers to lower wage rates (Watts 1990: 478). Thus, even without a revolution, Jamaica joined Haiti as one of the prime locations for peasant development in the Caribbean.

The decline of planter political control

The economic decline of Haitian and Jamaican plantations sets these cases apart from other post-slavery societies where plantations remained dominant and independent peasant development was blocked (e.g. the U.S. South or Barbados). Under these economic conditions, the struggle between the planter oligarchy and the plantation workforce is evident in the desperate measures Haitian and Jamaican planters took in trying to shore up their sinking plantations. The degree of control each group exercised over the state apparatus was crucial to maintaining economic dominance; power remained in the hands of the landowning and mercantile elite with only marginal gains in political power for the peasant population. However, the conflict of interests between agrarian crop-growers and merchant crop-exporters would create a fault-line in all post-slavery societies. A key difference between the two islands, of course, was Haiti's independent status, which removed the need to compete with a metropolitan centre for political control and put control of the military in local hands.

In the early decades of Haitian state-consolidation, the republican military traditions of the revolution were institutionalized by the constitution put into place by Dessalines. The revolutionary armies of the French Antilles had been one of the most democratically organized militaries in the world, with Creole officers who were strongly autonomous, antislavery and left-leaning (Stinchcombe 1996: 213); the slave armies of Saint Domingue were perhaps the most extreme form of egalitarian comradeship-in-arms. This generation, which had thrown off European domination, was infused with a strong sense of civic duty and military patriotism, leading it to symbolize the citizen as a soldier, and the soldier as citizen.

Popular figures of African independence and military prowess, like the rebel slaves Makandal, Boukman and General Dessalines himself, served a significant function in marking the transition from slavery to freedom.[13] The armies of revolutionary slaves (and even older bands of independent maroons) stood for African self-determination, black independence and Haitian national autonomy. The first constitution of 1805 envisioned a fraternal brotherhood-in-arms of all men of African descent, and a fundamental aspect of the Haitian nation-building project was the elevation of the black man out of the depths of slavery into his rightful place as father, leader and protector of his own people. Article Nine of the constitution declared that 'No one is worthy of being a Haitian if he is not a good father, a good son, a good husband, and above all a good soldier'.[14] It was a deeply masculinist form of citizenship which did not bode well for a democratic future (Sheller 1997).

Haitians had won their independence, many had obtained small plots of land, and they had created what was nominally, at least, a constitutional republic, yet they lived under the dominion of military chiefs. With the death of Toussaint, the assassination of Dessalines in 1806, and the neutralization of other black military leaders, military symbolism was easily transposed into the state-making projects of post-independence elites who drew on military genres of participation to generate national unity and a sense of common purpose. Military republicanism, which initially served the necessary purpose of building a new state and new citizens from scratch, soon became the *raison d'être* for a state in which there were few civil institutions to balance an overwhelmingly military power. For many Haitian men, citizenship, and with it political participation, took the form of military service. The army, in a sense, became one of the main avenues of political participation for men, as well as a route to land ownership. As soon as the French landowners and British and Spanish occupying forces had been driven out of the island, military leaders seized the land of the former plantations. Pétion nationalized all land, and began to sell it in relatively small parcels of ten *carreaux* (Bellegarde-Smith 1980: 20–49; Linstant 1851, 1: 307–15). Landholding generals quickly dominated government both in the Kingdom of Haiti, which formed in the north, and in the Republic of Haiti in the south.

If Haitian planters enjoyed freedom from colonial rule, however, they were also burdened by a weak and ineffective state, with few governmental institutions and little infrastructure. State control of the Haitian territory was so weak and sparse that it operated only through the most blunt of instruments: military conscription and taxation. Apart from these two basic tools, the state had no other existence (i.e. little bureaucracy, no public services, no public investment, a very localized judicial system). It was only tenuously held together by the loyalty of regional military commands and had little *de facto* control over the Dominican side of the island. Despite an end to the civil war between the north and south, and consolidation of the entire island in 1822, the military remained the most significant branch of the executive government, while the Chamber of Deputies had little power.

The British Consul Charles Mackenzie described the situation in 1827:

> The government that is now established professes to be purely republican, according to the constitution of the 27th December 1806, but in practice it may be said to be essentially military. The whole of the island is divided into departments, arrondissements, and communes. These are all under the command of military men, subject only to the control of the president; and to them is entrusted exclusively the execution of the laws, whether affecting police, agriculture or finance. There is not, as far as I can learn, a single civilian charged with an extensive authority.[15]

Other accounts show, moreover, that the army lacked discipline and pay, with command fragmented among generals with regional followings.

There were very few roads to enable timely communication between regions; there was only one national school of higher education, and no elementary public schools; there was no national bank and weak control of the treasury. Forgery, smuggling and bribery were common.[16] Haiti's big landowners had the political power to pass legislation in their own interest, but had at their command neither the state capacity to enforce these unfair laws nor the capital to protect their investments. Instead, they turned to the machinery of the state to control exports and levy indirect taxes on peasant crops, above all coffee: 'successive Haitian governments were to draw the majority of their revenues from indirect taxes, most of which were collected at the customhouses' (Trouillot 1990: 61; and see Ardouin 1860, Vol. 7).

Jamaican planters, on the other hand, were in theory limited in what they could do by colonial oversight from London, but enjoyed a fairly effective set of institutions and state capacity. The 'Old Representative System' left a good deal of control in local hands; in fact, the 'powers of the [Jamaican] Assembly were vast, those of the executive narrowly limited', for the Assembly not only passed legislation, but also 'levied taxes, supervised their collection, appropriated public money, and audited its own accounts' (Green 1991: 354). The Jamaican Assembly called for a rural code similar to Haiti's during the apprenticeship period (Higman 1995: 11), and after emancipation quickly passed a series of laws designed to constrain the movement and autonomy of former slaves. Specific popular complaints were lodged in 1840, for example, against the Vagrant Act, the Police Bill, the Act for the Recovery of Tenements, the Pound Law, the Registration of Fire Arms and the Fisheries Bill.[17] The Jamaican Assembly enjoyed far more legislative power and autonomy from the Home Government than did Crown Colonies like British Guiana. In Jamaica, '[e]ven during that stormy political and economic period up to 1865 only twelve acts were disallowed (vetoed) by the Crown, out of several hundred passed each year' (McLewin 1987: 68). The Crown did not step in when heavy taxes were levied on small export crops, livestock and wagons; when tough vagrancy laws restricted personal mobility; when toll roads were built on the routes to peasant markets; when high import duties were placed on necessities, but not on luxuries; or when public funds were used to pay for indentured immigration which benefited only big landowners (Hall 1959; Green 1991; Holt 1992).

Nevertheless, the unopposed extremism of Jamaica's planter oligarchy, and its constant conflict with the Colonial Governor and wishes of the Colonial Office, created fault-lines within state institutions that opposition groups could exploit. The best evidence of declining planter political control was the 'mulatto ascendancy' in the Jamaica House of Assembly in the 1840s, when non-whites were increasingly voted into office. Non-white landowners and the Jewish and 'brown' mercantile bourgeoisie began to skillfully play off the planter oligarchy against the colonial government. They coalesced into a voting block known as the 'Town Party' (Heuman 1981; Holt 1992), and were able to gain control of the three-man Executive Committee which carried out executive functions in the House of Assembly on the Governor's behalf. Furthermore, at the local level, increasing numbers of black men were becoming qualified to vote, being elected to parish vestries and serving on juries. The increasing fragmentation of the ruling class and the growing threat from subalterns created precisely the conditions necessary for popular empowerment and possibly greater democratization.

Planters clung to power as long as they could by limiting the franchise with property requirements, overtaxing the peasantry and using public money to import indentured plantation labourers from India and Africa, but they were challenged at every step. In the end, they were only slightly more successful than their Haitian counterparts in stopping former slaves from leaving the plantations, but far more successful in enforcing the legislation they did pass. Not only were they fighting a battle against peasant autonomy, but their control was also being compromised by dependence on both metropolitan and local armies. British naval forces and West Indian militias were necessary to quell popular 'unrest'. The crucial role of the brown population in defending against black uprisings had always been a key aspect of their claim for equal citizenship rights. Planters were no longer the only citizens who mattered in policy decisions. The Sugar Duties Act of 1847, which allowed foreign sugar to enter Britain on the same terms as British colonial sugar, was the final confirmation that sugar planters could no longer dictate imperial economic policy and that the powerful West India lobby had finally lost control in Parliament. Relinquishing Jamaica's two-hundred-year-old House of Assembly to Crown Colony rule (in response to the Morant Bay Rebellion of 1865) was merely a recognition of *de facto* metropolitan control and planter weakness. More ominously, however, it also conveniently abolished democratic representation just at the time when it was becoming accessible to Afro-Jamaicans.

Haiti was far more militarily independent than Jamaica, yet still highly vulnerable to the indirect economic influence and direct military threats of France, Britain, the United States and even Spain. The French persisted in plans to recapture their wayward former colony from the end of the Napoleonic wars onward. Records from the archives of the Ministère de la Marine et des Colonies contain plans to reconquer 'Saint Domingue' by force in 1814, 1817, 1819 and 1822, in addition to more explicit attempts to negotiate French sovereignty with President Pétion in 1816 and with President Boyer in 1823.[18] Although France finally recognized Haitian independence in 1838, it backed the breakaway of the Dominican Republic in 1844, and was involved in secret negotiations for use of the port of Samana. Haiti's initial decades of war-torn state-formation thus tended toward what one observer astutely described as 'republican monarchy sustained by the bayonet' (Brown [1837] 1972). Defensive militarization of a weak state undermined development of civil institutions, and created a crucial difference between Haitian and Jamaican citizen-state relations.

The decline of planter civil control

In contrast to their continuing political power, the social organization, solidarity, and international standing of the planter oligarchies were declining in both islands for a number of reasons. Although Stinchcombe subsumes this set of variables under the heading of 'class solidarity', they, in fact, constitute a distinct set of changes in the make-up of *civil society* in the post-slavery period. Planter class solidarity had in many ways been reinforced by the institution of slavery; without slaves, the distinctiveness of planter culture began to disintegrate, and divisions within the ruling elite began to emerge. Although the Haitian Revolution succeeded in ending slavery and achieving independence, the real winners of the revolution were not the mass of freed slaves, but the old mulatto landowning elites (especially in the south) and the new black generals (especially in the north). This colour divide within the elite undermined class solidarity, a key component of control.

Despite the death or expulsion of most of the white population of Saint Domingue during the revolution and wars of independence, post-colonial Haiti built on the cultural legacies of France, as well as those of Africa. The roots of Haitian civil society lay in the cultural milieu of the French revolution from which the Haitian Revolution and independence arose. As Patrick Bellegarde-Smith argues, 'French colonization had been rejected, but development was to occur within French philosophical traditions', at least for the French-speaking elite who controlled the post-independence government (Bellegarde-Smith 1980: 6). Antebellum Saint Domingue had participated in 'the intellectual culture of the age, and the growth of a spirit of bold speculation in France, had for a long time been operating a silent change in the moral condition and aspect of the colonies' (Brown 1837: 132). Cap Français (later to become Cap-Henry, Cap Haïtien and Cap Républicain, at various times) had been one of the most important centres of philosophical and scientific inquiry in the New World, on equal footing with cities such as Boston and Philadelphia (McClellan 1993).[19]

With the French Revolution, 'the popular doctrines that now began to grow omnipotent in the French metropolis were zealously taught and eagerly adopted in every corner of the earth that was inhabited by a French population'; in revolutionary Saint Domingue, '[c]lubs were formed everywhere, and their influence was spread in a thousand ramifications through every parish in the colony' (Brown 1837: 132, 136-37). The *anciens libres* of Saint Domingue were closely involved in this cultural ferment, and took a large part in the events of the revolution. They sent their own delegates to the Estates General, who successfully proposed full French citizenship for free men of colour in March 1791, and proposed the abolition of slavery in the colonies in 1794. Following the complex events of the Haitian Revolution, however, the Haitian elite was divided between two factions.[20] The *anciens libres,* were mostly '*mulâtres*' who had gained land and wealth before the revolution, while the *nouveaux libres* were mostly '*noirs*' who had risen through the military ranks and been rewarded with land after independence. As David Nicholls argues, these two groups developed competing visions of the nation and how it should be governed, encapsulated in ideologies that came to be known as '*mulâtriste*' and '*noiriste*' (Nicholls 1996).

In the early decades of state-consolidation, elites in both Pétion's Republic and Christophe's Kingdom portrayed themselves as the inheritors of French intellectual and political culture, and took on the responsibility of proving the capacity for self-government and intellectual achievement of the black race. They were engaged in a 'civilising process' of moral education and self-improvement, with an eye to themselves as an example to the world, a beacon of freedom and racial equality. Elite publics were first constructed around the associational ties of regional military hierarchies and membership in the Masonic Order. This official public (articulated in government proceedings, government proclamations and government-supported newspapers) used a language of civic republicanism that drew on the idioms of military fraternity and Masonic brotherhood. It was also restricted to a small, educated, French-speaking elite with complex networks of overlapping ties among themselves, but few ties to the mass of Haitian people.

Freemasonry was one of the few institutions knitting together competing elite factions in post-independence Haiti and the Haitian model of democratic citizenship borrowed heavily from Masonic practices. Freemasonry was a kind of precursor to democratization, for 'in the lodges men also became legislators and constitution makers' (Jacob 1991: 4). They elected their leaders and ruled themselves through means which mimicked (or provided the blueprint for) democratic governance. Masonic practices permeated Haitian political culture of the nineteenth century. Victor Schoelcher wrote in 1843 that there were 23 masonic lodges in Haiti, and 'one derisorily calls the senate the twenty-fourth lodge, since one of the first rules of freemasonry is never to talk politics in their reunions' (Schoelcher 1843: 217–1). The English missionary Mark Bird also reported that many government personnel were members of the Order of Freemasons; 'this institution is so widely extended in Hayti that it has become a distinct feature in Haytian society' (Bird 1869: 186). Bird believed that there were about one thousand Freemasons in Port-au-Prince, and numbers in due proportion to population in each of the second and third tier towns of the country.

The historian Beaubrun Ardouin attributed the custom of the exchange of complimentary addresses between the President of the Republic and the President of the Assembly (a post which he himself had held) at the opening of each session to Masonic experience. '[President] Boyer being the Grand-Protector of the Masonic Order in Haiti, and the president of the Chamber being almost always a freemason like him, one acted thus in the aim of recalling these fraternal relations which were proper for maintaining the harmony between the two powers' (Ardouin 1860, 9: 77n1). Thus, the executive and legislative branches of government were tied together by the fraternal bonds of masonry, and they represented this bond by an 'imitation of what happens within the masonic

lodges' (Ardouin 1860, 11: 5n1). Yet, Freemasonry was clearly an institution that excluded most people from participation, and conferred privi-
lege on an in-the-know minority. The lodge was a 'school of civic
sociability' and self-cultivation for the bourgeois man, and it laid the
foundations for modern civil society (Habermas 1989). However, in creating a new secular citizen, it also presumed that only the literate and
educated 'could be entrusted to act ethically and to think disinterestedly
in the interests of society, government, and improvement' (Jacob
1991: 21). The Haitian sense of civic duty was mixed with an elitist
belief in the natural ascendancy of the best and brightest.

In sum, the north-south split of the country from 1806 to 1820 represented a regional, class and racial fault-line within the ruling groups,
which destabilized subsequent attempts to unify the island (not to
mention the entirely distinctive patterns of racial and class formation on
the Dominican side of the border). Haiti's failure to subordinate the military to civilian control — given this context of foreign destabilization
and civil war — also had a strong negative impact on democratization.
If the relative strength of a state's military prior to democratization
'affects the kind of democracy that emerges' (Tilly 1995b: 377), then
Haiti's revolutionary army certainly constrained Haitian democracy.
Not only did the army remain in power during the period of state consolidation, but its regional divisions also crystallized into competing
factions that vied for control of the state. Military and police repression
of free speech is crucial to explaining how popular political participation was suppressed; this is not to say, however, that militarization
entirely precluded the emergence of democratization movements.

As we shall see in Part Two, the struggle between the ruling mili-
tary-agrarian elite and the liberal bourgeoisie was interrupted by an
intervening group of black middle classes, who claimed to represent the
interests of the peasants and cultivators. The liberal opposition's use of
democratic discourses opened up political space through civil means
such as independent newspapers, which played a crucial role in the
origin of black publics. Newspapers are a crucial civil institution in the
sense that they construct the social networks of communication through
which 'public opinion' is formed. Haitians maintained the French tradition of journalism and publishing and continued to publish many newspapers, some devoted to government proceedings and market news,
others devoted to literature and the arts (see Table 4). As Nicholls
observes, a 'number of weekly newspapers and monthly reviews were
published, but their circulation was small, and the lifetime of many of
them was short. Nevertheless, these journals were read by most of those
who were in a positions to affect the policy of the government, and they
were therefore not without political influence' (Nicholls 1996: 71).

Table 4   Haitian Newspapers, 1804–1860
(Port-au-Prince unless otherwise noted; editors in parentheses where known)

Founded	Title
1804	La Gazette Politique et Commerçiale d'Haïti [paper of Dessalines]
1807	La Gazette Officielle de l'Etat d'Haïti [becomes Royal Gazette]
1807	La Sentinelle, Journal Official d'Hayti [becomes Bulletin Officiel]
1813	Le Télégraphe
1817	L'Abeille Haïtienne (J. S. Milscent)
1818	L'Avertisseur Haïtien (F. Darfour)
1818	L'Eclaireur Haytien ou Le Parfait Patriote (F. Darfour)
1819	Au Temps à la Verité, Aux Cayes
1819	L'Observateur, Aux Cayes (Hérard Dumesle) [ephemeral]
1820	L'Hermit d'Haïti
1821	La Concorde
1821	L'Etoile Haïtienne, Santo Domingo (Caminero)
1822	L'Emile Haïtienne (Caminero)
1824	La Feuille du Commerce (J. Courtois)
1830	Le Phare (D. Inginac & C. Nathan)
1836	Le Républicain (C. Ardouin, A. Bouchereau, E. Nau)
1837	L'Union (T. Bouchereau, C. Ardouin & freres Nau) [to 1839]
1841	Le Manifeste (D. Lespinasse, E. Heurtelou, T. Bouchereau) [to 1848]
1842	Le Patriote (T. Bouchereau, E. Heurtelou and E. Nau)
1842	Le Temps (B. and C. Ardouin)
1842	Compère Mathieu, [becomes Le Journal du Peuple] (M. Lespinasse)
1842	Le Democrate [only lasted a few months]
1843	La Sentinelle de la Liberté [changed to Le Progres, 1844], (E. Heurtelou)
1845	La Moniteur Haïtien, Journal officiel de la Republique (D. Lespinasse directeur 1845–48; T. Madiou directeur 1848–59)

Despite the constitutional guarantee of freedom of the press, writers who criticized the government were put under heavy pressure, sometimes forced into exile and sometimes executed for treason.

In contrast, independent newspapers played a crucial role in the origin of Afro-Jamaican publics. The regularization of postal services and official newspapers helped to integrate colonial populations into the 'imagined community' of the British Empire, and to establish English as the standard language in regions where many other languages were common currency (Anderson 1991). Yet, as Franklin Knight argues, through increasing literacy a 'distinct Caribbean civic culture' emerged in competition with the metropolitan culture, 'aided by the expanding presence of the printing press after the eighteenth century and a growing literate readership for newspapers, books, and pamphlets, the various territories produced a vigorous and perceptive type of literature' (Knight 1990: 157–58). As in early nineteenth-century Britain, editors of provincial newspapers 'wrote not only to inform, but to influence public opinion.... There was evidently a vital link between the writing of politically oriented editorials and making a public declaration of one's viewpoint in a petition. The shaping of public opinion and popular political behavior were thus intimately connected in the persons of newspaper editors' (Bradley 1986: 91–2). This was equally true in Jamaica, if not more so, given the added excitement of a local legislature. Moreover, some newspapers made special efforts to come within the purview of enfranchised small landholders by lowering prices and writing about issues of interest to them (See Table 5).[21]

Jamaica was far more unified than Haiti in the sense that there was a greater array of functioning civil institutions, including an established church, a relatively efficient postal service and even the evidence of successful official censuses in 1844 and 1861. However, the growing presence of nonconformist missionaries in the later years of slavery and early years of emancipation also threatened the solidarity of white planter society. As we shall see in Chapter 6, missionaries often took the side of apprentices and freedmen against the plantation owners, and challenged their control on many fronts (cf. Turner 1982). At the same time, free men of colour and Jews were granted the franchise and other civil rights in 1830, introducing new elements into Jamaican politics (Campbell 1976; Heuman 1981). Here, too, we find an intermediary in the struggle for control between peasant and planter.

Beyond these local-level threats, planter power was also being eroded at the imperial level. The once powerful 'West India interest' in Parliament lost a great deal of its influence following the Reform Act of 1830. Sugar was no longer the most important commodity of the empire, and Britain's expansion into other parts of the world meant that the West Indies were no longer the most important region of the empire (Blackburn 1988; D. Hall 1959). Jamaica, especially, was past its peak, and in terms of investment opportunities could not compete

Table 5   Jamaican Newspapers, 1823–1865
(editors in parentheses where known)

Founded	Title
1823	Public Advertiser
1829	Cornwall Chronicle & County Gazette
182x	Courant (A. H. Beaumont)
1830s	Colonial Reformer
1830s	West Indian & Colonial Freeman
1829–33	Jamaica Watchman and Free Press (Edward Jordon and Robert Osborn)
1830s	Cornwall Courier
1834	Daily Gleaner (& DeCordova Advertising Sheet)
1835–41	Falmouth Post (& General Advertiser) (John Castello)
1838–44	Morning Journal (Edward Jordon and Robert Osborn) [1861–1875]
1839	Baptist Herald and Friend of Africa [later The Messenger] (F. Eberall)
1847	Jamaica Guardian and Patriot (George Rouse)
1840s	Evangelist (George Rouse)
1840s	County Union (Sidney Levien)
1850–53	Colonial Standard and Jamaica Despatch [1864–95]
1850s	Daily Advertiser and Lawton's Commercial Gazette
1854–56	Family Newspaper (George Rouse)
1861–71	Jamaica Guardian (George Henderson [Robert Johnson])
1860s	Standard, (G. Levy and H. Vendryes)
1860s	Trelawney & Public Advertiser (William Clarke)
1860s	Tribune (Isaac Lawton)
1864–65	Sentinel (George W. Gordon; Robert Johnson)
1865	Jamaica Watchman and People's Free Press (I. Vaz; Wm. Kelly Smith)

with new and expanding territories like Trinidad and Guiana. Many planters, in fact, left Jamaica altogether, leaving attorneys (or agents) to run their plantations, thus contributing to the decline of planter control in Jamaica. In this sense, the ascendancy of a new liberal bourgeoisie in Britain had a detrimental impact on colonial agrarian political power.

In sum, in both Haiti and Jamaica, sugar was declining in importance, planter class solidarity was under threat, and the overall power of planters both locally and internationally was weakening. Post-emancipation planters were far less omnipotent than slave masters had been at the peak of the sugar boom, yet they still had a firm grasp on the state. Both governments continued to limit tightly black freedoms after slave emancipation and to resist democratization, contrary to their self-legitimating claims of ensuring and protecting the rights of ex-slaves, and despite concerted attempts to expand black political power. Small, wealthy elites, whether white or *mulâtre*, continued to rule in their own interests, disregarding reputedly cherished democratic institutions, ignoring calls for broader suffrage and stifling complaints about injustice and inequality. By the mid-nineteenth century, increasingly racist ideologies were being used to justify paternalistic white rule in Jamaica (Holt 1992) and legitimize oligarchic mulatto rule 'by the best' in Haiti (Nicholls 1996).

Notes

1   Not only is there a parallel in the political ferment and peasant rebellions of Haiti in the early 1840s and Jamaica in the 1860s, but there is also a generational parallel of the two cohorts who lived through the disappointing first decades of freedom (cf. Mannheim [1928] 1952). This generation reclaimed real freedom in respect of their parents' traumatic struggle out of slavery, a collective history remembered in similar terms and discursively reframed within contemporary social movements.

2   Both Haiti and Jamaica reached their peaks of growth as 'sugar frontiers' between 1750 and 1790. The Saint Domingue Revolution began in 1791, when the colony was the biggest sugar producer in the world; Jamaican sugar plantations were already in decline by the time of emancipation in 1838, but it was still Britain's principal sugar colony. On the economics of abolition, see Eric Williams, *Capitalism and Slavery* (Chapel Hill: University of North Carolina Press, 1944); Barbara Solow and Stanley Engerman, *British Capitalism and Caribbean Slavery* (Cambridge: Camrbrdge University Press, 1987); William Green, *British Slave Emancipation* (Oxford: Clarendon [1976] 1991); and Arthur Stinchcombe, *The Political Economy of the Caribbean, 1775-1900* (Princeton: Princeton University Press, 1996).

3   Surface areas are from Jean Besson, 'Land, Kinship and Community in the Post-Emancipation Caribbean: A Regional View of the Leewards', in *Small Islands, Large Questions: Society, Culture and Resistance in the Post-Emancipation Caribbean*, ed. Karen F. Olwig (London: Frank Cass, 1995), p. 94.

4   The idea of a 'sugar frontier' refers to the timing and regionalization of economic investment in plantations. In the nineteenth century, the costs of plantations always rose with age, while sugar prices were always falling, so new sugar regions ('frontiers') were always being opened at new locations, to keep ahead of the cost/price curve (Stinchcombe, *Political Economy of the Caribbean*).

5   For a good description of changes in sugar-making technology in the nineteenth century, see M. Moreno Fraginals, *The Sugarmill: The Socioeconomic Complex of Sugar in Cuba, 1760-1860* (New York and London: Monthly Review, 1976).

6   Figures are from Franklin Knight, *The Caribbean: The Genesis of a Fragmented Nationalism*, 2d ed. (New York: Oxford University Press, 1990), 370; Michel-Rolph Trouillot, 'Coffee Planters and Coffee Slaves in the Antilles: The Impact of a Secondary Crop', in *Cultivation and Culture: Labor and the Shaping of Slave Life in the Americas*, ed. Ira Berlin and Philip D. Morgan (Charlottesville:

University of Virginia, 1993), 124; and for original statistics, see AN CC9a. 54, Communications Received at The Foreign Office Relative to Hayti, No. 18, Consul General Charles Mackenzie to the Earl of Dudley, 31 Mar. 1828, General Table of Exports from Hayti, 1789, 1801, 1818–26.

7   On Haiti's exports in this period, see Beaubrun Ardouin, *Études sur l'Histoire d'Haïti*, 11 vols. (Paris: Dezobry, Madeleien et Ce, 1860), Vol. 9, 53–4; Alexandre Bonneau, *Haïti: ses progres, son avenir* (Paris: E. Dentu, 1862), p. 38; and David Nicholls, *From Dessalines to Duvalier: Race, Colour and National Independence in Haiti*, 3d ed. (London: Macmillan Caribbean, 1996), p. 69. Also relevant are Dupuy 1989; Lacerte 1981; and Moya Pons 1985.

8   FO 35/1, Wilmot Horton to Mr. Canning, 14 Oct. 1826, enclosing Memorandum of Information from James Franklin.

9   AN CC9a.54, Document 2, Communications Received at the Foreign Office Relative to Hayti, no. 18, Charles Mackenzie to Earl of Dudley, 31 Mar. 1828.

10 Loi sur les Patentes, 26 Feb. 1819, 30 Nov. 1821, in Baron S. Linstant, *Récueil général des Lois et Actes du Gouvernement d'Haïti* (Paris: Auguste Durand, 1860), Vol. 3, 120–40. Sidney Mintz gives a fascinating account of the employment of minimal capital by Haitian market women in the 1950s, reflecting the same hierarchies of wholesale (à grô) versus retail (à détay), revendeuses and dealers in miscellaneous stock. As he points out, 'the market for peasant products is in any case feeble, dispersed, often undependable — and eminently taxable' (Mintz. 'The Employment of Capital by Market Women in Haiti', in *Capital, Savings and Credit in Peasant Societies*, eds. R. Firth and B. Yamey [Chicago: Aldine, 1964], 284). On Haitian women's role in marketing, see also Sheller, 'Sword-Bearing Citizens: Militarism and Manhood in Nineteenth-Century Haiti' in *Plantation Society in the Americas*, Vol. 4, nos. 2 &3 (Fall 1997): 233–78).

11 Many Haitians opposed the treaty, like Félix Darfour, an African-born member of the Assembly, who accused Boyer of 'having sold the country to the whites', for which he was arrested and executed for treason (Ardouin 1860, 9: 186-90; see further discussion in Chapter 5). On government efforts to divide debt payments among communes, see FO 35/3, Charles Mackenzie to Mr. Canning, 28 May 1826.

12 Some freedmen used a rustic hand-operated press: 'I cannot describe their rude wooden implement better', wrote William G. Sewell, 'than by calling it a huge lemon-squeezer' (*The Ordeal of Free Labor in the British West Indies* [1861; reprint, London: Frank Cass, 1968], p. 251).

13 In popular culture, the warrior has long been venerated in Haiti in the figure of Ogou Feray, *lwa* of fire and war, descended from ancient Dahomean gods of warfare. Dessalines, as father of the nation, is today 'served' as an ancestral *lwa* who embodies the indomitable warrior essence of the revolutionary slave freedom-fighter. See Sheller, 'Sword Bearing Citizens'; L. Hurbon, *Voodoo: Truth and Fantasy* (London: Thames and Hudson, 1995); and K. Brown, *Mama Lola: A Vodou Priestess in Brooklyn* (Berkeley: University of California Press, 1997).

14 Constitution Impériale d'Haïti, 20 mai 1805, an II, Art. 9, in Linstant, *Réceuil général des Lois*, 1851, Vol. 1, p. 49).

15 AN CC9a.54, Communications Received at The Foreign Office Relative to Hayti, no. 3, Mackenzie to Lord Canning, 9 Sept. 1827.

16 See, for example, FO 35/3, Mackenzie to Canning, 28 May 1826, on illicit trade.

17 This list is taken from the resolutions of a public meeting held at the Baptist Chapel in Falmouth, 21 Feb. 1840, reported in the *Baptist Herald and Friend of Africa*, Vol. 1, no. 17, 26 Feb. 1840, p. 3. See Chapter 6 on public meetings.

18 Various documents on these efforts appear in AN CC9a.47 and AN CC9a.50-52.

19   This important French colonial city was planned on a grid pattern with four stone houses per block (each of two stories, with metal balconies and a cool inner court-yard), as well as public squares with fountains — prior to its total decimation by earthquake in 1842 (WMMS, Special Series, Biographical, West Indies, Box 588, Autobiography of James Hartwell, p. 55).

20   The revolution itself will not be discussed here, but see the classic interpretations by C. L. R James, *The Black Jacobins* (New York: Vintage [1938] 1989), and Eugene Genovese, *From Rebellion to Revolution: Afro-American Slave Revolts in the Making of the New World* (New York: Vintage, 1979). For more recent analyses, see Patrick Bryan, *The Haitian Revolution and its Effects* (Kingston and Exeter: Heinemann, 1984); Aimé Césaire, *Toussaint L'Ouverture: La Révolution Française et le Probleme Coloniale* (Paris: Presence Africaine, 1981); Alex Dupuy, *Haiti in the World Economy: class, race and underdevelopment since 1700* (Boulder: Westview Press, 1989); and Carolyn E. Fick, *The Making of Haiti: The Saint Domingue Revolution from Below* (Knoxville: University of Tennessee Press, 1990).

21   For an interesting discussion of freedom of the press in Jamaica, see *The Jamaica Watchman*, Vol. 4, no. 43, 30 May 1832, which protested the government clamp-down on press freedoms following the slave uprising of 1831.

Conclusion to part one

Along with the decline of planter control, the other side of the coin of freedom was the increasing degree of peasant agency after emancipation. Did the decline in planter dominance mean more freedom for Haitian and Jamaican freed slaves than for those freedmen who found themselves in more planter-dominated societies? Yes, in so far as former slaves took the opportunity of emancipation to move off the plantations, own their own land, gain control over their own labour, practise their own religious and cultural traditions, educate their children and participate in political decision-making. No, in so far as they still faced limitations on their rights and met encumbrances to full citizenship. In terms of the exercise of specific freedoms, the post-emancipation Caribbean partly continued the trends found by Stinchcombe in the pre-emancipation setting. 'Colored' people enjoyed more freedoms than 'black' people, Creoles enjoyed more freedoms than African-born people, urban inhabitants enjoyed more freedoms than rural inhabitants and specialized workers enjoyed more freedoms than unskilled labourers.

These clear economic and social patterns, however, have seldom been explored in relation to the patterns of political participation and peasant political culture that emerged with them. I argue that peasant agency in the post-slavery period had three components: economic, political and civil. Peasant agency began with control of everyday economic choices and decision-making: decisions about personal mobility, household integrity, land use, allocation of family labour and, for those who also engaged in wage labour, procedures for wage negotiation, collective bargaining and striking. Second, peasant agency concerned demands for political rights and participation in government, including enfranchisement, influence in shaping legislation, just courts, fair taxation and channels for expression and redress of grievances. Third, peasant agency concerned demands for civil rights, above all the key freedoms of association, speech, publication and religion.

Although Stinchcombe's conceptualization of slave agency includes aspects of personal freedom and personal choice, he greatly underplays questions of collective civil liberties and public decision-making. By concentrating on individual rights, grounded in economic and political institutions, his model overlooks the associational and civil rights pertaining to civil society. In post-emancipation societies, these were key concerns in relation to education, religious autonomy, freedom of association and freedoms of speech and publication. Although there was an element of liberal bourgeois support for such freedoms, they also had a certain degree of popular support among former slaves.

Some of the most prominent actors in protest or challenges to authorities in both Haiti and Jamaica were the medium-sized landholders who were part of the peasant class, yet paid taxes, met property-qualifications to vote, participated in local government and became involved in small civil litigation. These middle-peasants, known as 'inhabitants' or 'small settlers' in Jamaica and *habitants* in Haiti, were the 'bones and sinew of the country' (as one group described themselves in a petition). They held positions of leadership in their communities, extended credit to their less wealthy kin and neighbours, and provided employment (in hierarchical relations that could, of course, be exploitative). It was this group that became most involved in politics and demanded democratization, including extension of the franchise, fairer taxation and abolition of fees for registering to vote, petitioning the government or settling court cases. In its most radical guise, members of this class identified with the small peasants and labourers and called for new forms of cooperative association, direct popular sovereignty, land distribution and full racial equality.

As Harding has argued in the case of the United States in 1865, freed slaves were able to seize the tools of democracy to dismantle planter power:

> The men and women who had been legally enslaved just months earlier were now meeting in public not only to discuss the political affairs of the state and the nation, which they immediately claimed as their own, but to challenge the political legitimacy of their former owners, overseers, and oppressors.... They were nominating, debating and voting, reclaiming all the democratic mechanisms for truly democratic purposes (Harding 1981: 293).

So, too, in Jamaica, if to a lesser extent, would freed slaves 'use the master's tools to dismantle the master's house'. Afro-Jamaicans had more latitude for such action than did Haitians not because they had 'learned' more about democracy from British tutors, but because the British state was somewhat more constrained by previous encounters to utilize a civil response to democratic repertoires of contention. Civil control of the British armed forces tied government hands (though not entirely, as we shall see in Part Three), in contrast to the free reign of the Haitian armed forces and the elite cadre of land-owning generals who controlled them.

Both Haiti and Jamaica had a weakened plantocracy and a strongly autonomous peasant culture that stressed majority self-determination, popular sovereignty and broad and equal citizenship for all. Peasants and workers in both countries demanded the franchise, more progressive taxation, equal access to just courts and, in some cases, land distribution. When fissures appeared within the white and brown elites of Jamaica and within the *mulâtre* and *noir* elites of Haiti, black majorities seized the opportunity to reclaim their constitutional rights in two of the most significant post-slavery social movements in the Americas. The central concern of this book is these popular movements and the rulers they were up against. As comparative research on Latin American coffee republics has shown, one must 'avoid the temptation of treating smallholder regimes as the basis for a rural "democracy" in contrast to the oligarchy that characterized planter regimes' (Roseberry, Gudmundson, and Kutschback 1995: 20). Small-scale, commercially-oriented farming was embedded in 'hierarchical social fields' involving merchants and foreign markets, and was not necessarily the basis for democratization. Nevertheless, the emancipatory ideologies of post-slavery peasantries in the Caribbean offered the potential for a radical democratic ideology.

The rest of this book will explore the emergence of peasant agency in Haiti (Part Two) and Jamaica (Part Three), including its economic, political and civil elements. I hope to demonstrate that black publics significantly recast collective narratives of enslavement and emancipation, criticized the continuing existence of racial inequality and slavery throughout the world, critically engaged democratic ideologies and envisioned a democratic diaspora of African-Caribbean, African-American and African freedom and citizenship. Their vision of the future has never been achieved and continues to haunt us. All of the countries that took part in the Atlantic system of slavery, from sea to shining sea, are still engaged in the struggle for racial equality, political freedom and justice. Slaves and their descendants have bequeathed to us an agenda for social change that will continue to shape democratic politics in the twenty-first century.

Part two

Haiti: 'Constitutions are Paper, Bayonets are Iron'

Constitusyon sé papié, bayonet sé fer
Haitian proverb

3 | 'What kind of free this?'

Haiti, placed in the Gulf of Mexico which she is destined to command, is the object of attention of the entire great African family. One day she will head a confederation of all the isles of the American archipelago. It is from southern America, from Haiti, that the intellectual ray that shall enlighten Africa will originate. The great blow that she has hit against slavery has resounded through the entire Universe; the immense space which she has opened up in the order of civilization, in making herself an independent nation, evidently proves her tendency toward the necessary realization of her future (*Le Manifeste*, Vol. 1, no. 19, 8 Aug. 1841).

The revolutionary founding of the Republic of Haiti in 1803 initiated a long-running debate throughout the Atlantic world over how to react to the existence of a 'black republic' at the core of the system of slavery. Haiti's independence set the terms of debate for nearly a century of anti-slavery struggle and shaped international relations in the Caribbean for decades to come. Gripped by fear of contagious slave uprising, Europeans articulated their claims to 'whiteness' and 'civility' in contradistinction to Haitian 'barbarism' through a set of stories that can be collectively referred to as the 'Haytian Fear'.[1] At the same time, however, Afro-Caribbean political activists used the story of Haiti's independence to promote black equality and foster colour-conscious movements for social change. Although European powers worked diplomatically to isolate Haiti, ideological influences, nevertheless, flourished along irrepressible tendrils of regional trade. Networks of subversive people, radical newspapers and contraband trade worked counter to the flows of a global economic system oriented around the Atlantic slave trade.

In their attempts to build transnational alliances, the rudiments of a radical 'Black Atlantic' (as both self-reflexive intellectual project and post-colonial recentring of political identities [Gilroy 1993]) were well in place by the mid-nineteenth century. Thus, instead of treating Haiti and Jamaica as entirely separate 'cases' in an imaginary experiment, I will treat them as linked bundles of relations. As much as they constitute distinct entities with very different historical trajectories, there were also always exchanges of people and information between them, as well as closely related systems of symbolic mapping in which they were each located and related one to the other. As I unexpectedly discovered, some Jamaicans were closely involved in Haiti's Liberal Revolution of 1843, while some Haitians were closely linked to Jamaica's Morant Bay Rebellion of 1865. Both islands also had links to the international anti-slavery movement and to black intellectuals in North America, Central America and Europe. Thus, we must remain attuned to the undercurrent of relationships that enabled the formation of a shared counter-discourse of African identification and Caribbean solidarity.

In his analysis of the white 'terrified consciousness' of Haiti, Anthony Maingot (1996) uses the example of the Haitian Revolution to criticize violent decolonization and praise the gradual 'accomodating' route to black empowerment taken in the British West Indies. He suggests that the white minority in the non-Hispanic Caribbean has not suffered from the same terror of Haiti evidenced among other whites (particularly in the Hispanic Caribbean) because of the successful establishment of 'national norms' through the 'long [non-violent] decolonization process' in the British West Indies (Maingot 1996: 74). Arguing that 'violence is not the only path to liberation' and praising 'liberal pluralism', he concludes that in choosing a 'conservative path to liberation', the leaders of the non-Hispanic Caribbean 'assured the development of a normative context all groups could participate in' (Maingot 1996: 76).

This kind of argument attributes democracy solely to colonial integration, to liberal values and political institutions and implicitly to a British cultural inheritance. It ignores the political strategies that underlay European projections of Haiti as a monstrous and savage place, and it fails to recognize Haiti's positive impact on pan-Caribbean anti-slavery, anti-colonial and democratic movements. By overlooking the long history of ties between Haitians and Afro-Jamaicans, Maingot cannot see the crucial contribution made by Haitian independence to the building of popular democratic ideologies within the British colonies, no thanks to the white (and 'brown') elite who resisted democratization well into the twentieth century. This chapter aims to uncover the racial tactics behind the 'Haytian Fear' and to demonstrate the longstanding political and civil ties between Haiti and Jamaica.

I argue that international reactions to Haiti fed into highly politicized 'racial formations', including competing public discourses of extreme racism among some whites and of racial unity among some people of colour.[2] In addition to depicting the racist underpinnings of French and British diplomatic reaction to Haiti's independence, this chapter also focuses on reactions (both negative and positive) in the nearby British colony of Jamaica where whites were a small minority.[3] By analyzing the symbolic role of Haiti in Jamaican political discourse (as well as actual ties between Haitian and Jamaican political activists), we can better understand the complex interplay of 'racial projects' in the aftermath of slavery. A 'racial project' is 'simultaneously an inter-pretation, representation or explanation of racial dynamics, and an effort to reorganize and redistribute resources along particular racial lines' (Omi and Winant 1994: 56). The narrative of the 'Haytian Fear' served precisely these purposes in two ways: (1) influencing actual social, political and economic ties between the Great Powers and Haiti, and within the Caribbean region; and, (2) shaping symbolic mappings of Haiti in the competing racial discourses of multiple contenders for public opinion.

Diplomatic reaction to Haitian independence

Haiti's radical break with the French colonial system was a unique rejection of the power of whites, sugar planters and colonial rule; it fundamentally challenged the entire basis of the Atlantic slave-economy and the European state-system.[4] Haiti was the first American republic to favour the power of blacks, workers and local self-rule — even if in practice *anciens libres* (usually wealthy mulattoes) retained a good deal of land and power (Stinchcombe 1996; Trouillot 1990). The Haitian Constitution of 1805 specifically banned whites from property ownership, and declared that 'the Haitians will be known under none other than the generic denomination of blacks [*noirs*]',[5] Thus, Haiti became 'a symbol that meant export of revolution...[and] a racial symbol of powerful and rich blacks, black rulers, black generals winning wars' (Stinchcombe 1994: 11). Haiti represented not only black economic autonomy (in the sense of 'free labour'), but also greater black political and civil control than existed anywhere in the Atlantic world.

French and British diplomatic reactions to Haiti were accordingly hostile. As one French foreign minister bluntly put it in a letter to United States President Monroe, 'the existence of a Negro people in arms, occupying a country it has soiled by the most criminal of acts, is a horrible spectacle for all white nations.... There are no reasons...to grant support to these brigands who have declared themselves the enemies of all government' (Farmer 1994: 75; Lawless 1992: 48). Although Haiti was no longer a French colonial domain after 1804, the French government continued to class it as a colony for administrative purposes until at least 1825. Even after official correspondence switched over to the Ministry of Foreign Affairs, the Minister for the Colonies still remained responsible for correspondence concerning settlement of claims by the 'anciens colons' of Saint Domingue and their aggrieved heirs.[6] French Proposals for military reconquest of Haiti continued to be floated up until the 1840s, giving an impression of the strong pressure on the French government by an organized and persistent anti-Haitian lobbying group based on an international network of exile communities.[7]

With the end of the Napoleonic wars and restoration of the French monarchy, France undertook secret negotiations for the return of its renegade colony. Even after making what they thought were considerable concessions to Haitian pride, the French overtures were rejected.[8] As President Alexandre Pétion told them: 'I will never compromise [Haiti's] sovereignty…. The People of Haiti want to be free and independent, I want it with them'.[9] President Jean Pierre Boyer unified the island in 1822, but signed the controversial indemnification treaty in 1825. With the ink drying on these diplomatic niceties, the British government finally felt comfortable establishing official relations with Haiti, 'seen by the British government as a crucial experiment in slave emancipation which should be carefully studied' (Nicholls 1996: 62; cf. Lawless 1992: 44–5). In 1826, they sent Charles Mackenzie, a 'man of color', to report on conditions in Haiti.[10] Despite his politically appropriate colour, Mackenzie judged Haiti a danger to British colonial stability and described the Haitian people as 'young Barbarians'.[11] His *Notes on Haiti* (1830) were thought so harmful to the cause of emancipation that the British Abolition Society sent Richard Hill, a Jamaican free man of colour, to report on Haiti to counter Mackenzie's negative impact (Lawless 1992: 52). Thus began a war of publicity to win the hearts and minds of the European public.

By 1837, with defaults on interest payments and 120 million francs still outstanding on the Haitian debt, the Franco-Haitian treaty was renegotiated. The envoys were implicitly backed by an armed frigate in the Port-au-Prince harbour, as well as by other nearby warships.[12] French attitudes toward their wayward former colony remained racist and patronizing throughout the negotiations. Instructions to the envoys stated that 'it is a case of showing the superiority of the civilized white over the half-savage negro; one must consider the Haitians as big children, pardon them their stupid blunders, and always show them a kind, indulgent face'.[13] A formal report argued that 'civilization cannot operate in Haiti except through the Mulattoes. A Government of blacks would retrograde the country toward a savage state. All the succeeding black chiefs there during a period of more than twenty-five years have been monsters of cruelty. The same tradition of Government will be reestablished, as soon as a black comes to power'.[14]

French Consul General Charles Levasseur lamented 'it is nothing except foreign domination which will reestablish order and work [in Haiti], reconstitute Haitian Society on durable solid foundations.... But when and how will white domination come to bring Civil Society [*la vie Sociale*] to this coarse, lazy and ignorant people?'[15] Racist principles of white rule and African inferiority fueled a fear that black power in Haiti would somehow spill over into other parts of the Caribbean and destroy the carefully balanced system of white domination based on African slavery. Indeed a spate of slave rebellions across the Greater Caribbean was connected, however sketchily, to the direct or indirect influence of Haiti from the 1790s through the first quarter of the nineteenth century.[16] The project of isolating Haiti intertwined with maintaining control over the Caribbean.

Britain and its colonies may have avoided the upheavals of revolution, but still had to live with the consequences of revolutionary ideologies and the threatening example of black independence in Haiti. In the wake of the French Revolution, Jamaican free men of colour began to demand expanded rights, launching a major petitioning campaign in 1823 in concert with the formation of the Anti-Slavery Society in Britain (Heuman 1981). The 'plantocracy', fearful of a revolution like Haiti's, rallied behind the system of white racial domination that upheld slavery. The 1823 campaign met strong opposition and was explicitly linked to Haitian politics when a debate broke out over the political activities of Haitian immigrants in Jamaica, revealing the playing out of the 'Haytian Fear' in Jamaican politics.

Lewis Lecesne and John Escoffery, whose families had been refugees from The Haitian Revolution, were leading activists in the movement for free coloured rights in Jamaica. In 1824, whose families had been refugees from the Haitian Revolution, they were charged with fomenting a 'Haitian plot'. A magistrate made unsubstantiated allegations 'that there was a correspondence kept up with the Government of St. Domingo, not only of late, but ever since the Revolution in 1792; and that there were accredited agents of the Government of St. Domingo in Jamaica'. A newspaper accused them of stirring a rebellion and being 'Agents of Boyer, the Chief of the Brigands of St. Domingo'. Finally, a government committee charged that 'an improper connexion was kept up between Haiti and Jamaica through the medium of certain aliens', and they were promptly exiled.[17]

The Haitian government denied any knowledge of the two men, who made their way to England where they were supported by the Anti-Slavery Society in petitioning the House of Commons to overturn the ruling against them (Heuman 1981: 48).[18] The event lingered in Haitian memory as an insult to their national character and a sign of white prejudice against them. President Boyer proclaimed:

> It is evident that the outrage made against the Haitian charac-
> ter is a deplorable effect of the absurd *prejudice* resulting
> from the difference of colours.... We find it ... in the *pro-*
> *scription* exercised today more than ever in certain countries,
> against men with the tint of Haitians; we find it in the osten-
> sible recognition that some powers have made, while ignor-
> ing our rights, of the republican States recently established in
> central America (Ardouin 1860, 9: 238-39 [emphasis in
> original]).

Boyer here correctly linked the personal prejudice against Haitians and people of African descent to the international refusal to recognize Haitian independence.

The recognition of the new Central and South American republics by Britain and the United States in 1823 was especially galling to the Haitians because Pétion had sheltered Simón Bolívar, providing him with '4,000 guns, 15,000 pounds of powder, a quantity of lead, some provisions, and a printing press' (Logan 1941: 222). To add salt to the wounds, the new Spanish-American republics, at the bequest of the United States, declined to recognize Haiti or to invite its representa-tives to the Pan-American Conference of 1825 (Stinchcombe 1995: 235–38). Amid heated debates over slave emancipation, the shunned Republic of Haiti remained an uninvited guest at diplomatic tables, even though the Great Powers greedily competed to gain the island's forcibly opened trade and coveted resources.

As Stinchcombe suggests, Haiti became a contested object in the foreign policy of the nineteenth-century diplomatic world, functioning 'as a symbol [of slave revolt] in the domestic politics of the imperial countries' (Stinchcombe 1995: 236 [italics in original]). It was 'the first of a number of third world revolutionary societies to become important objects in the politics of the hegemonic or core powers, especially those of the United States, and suffer the consequences of diplomatic isolation and systematic attempts at subversion by those core powers' (ibid: 239). Yet, at the same time, it also became a posi-tive and hopeful symbol of revolutionary social change for those who identified with its racial project. Without recognition as a legitimate state, Haiti had to build international ties through informal and, at times, covert channels of communication that linked it with those who had an interest in abolishing slavery and liberating black people.

Afro-Caribbean reaction to Haitian independence

Contrary to the anti-Haitian developments in foreign diplomacy, for many Afro-Jamaicans, Haiti became a powerful symbol of freedom and African progress, demonstrating the capacity for black self-government. As Julius Scott notes, 'separated from Saint-Domingue by a channel barely one hundred miles wide at its narrowest point, Jamaica lay well within range of even the smallest undecked vessels departing western Hispaniola, and the prevailing westward winds made for a smooth and swift passage' (Scott 1986: 217). As free people of colour sought civil and political rights in the European colonies (calling in some instances for abolition of slavery), and as trade with Haiti became more enticing to Caribbean merchants, non-recognition and diplomatic isolation of the ostracized black republic became increasingly untenable. Haiti had a special meaning for free people of colour, many of whom defended Haitian independence and promoted regional trade. If not always a shining example, Haiti was certainly a barometer and test of Afro-Caribbean progress.

This counter-discourse sought to influence the very terms of public debate about emancipation, freedom, and black equality. As Omi and Winant argue, racial projects serve to 'connect what race means in a particular discursive practice and the ways in which both social structures and everyday experiences are racially organized' (Omi and Winant 1994: 56). Afro-Jamaican efforts to recast the meaning of Haiti — to publicly argue in favour of Haitian independence from a 'black' perspective — represent both a symbolic recuperation and an attempt to change the racist social structures of white colonial societies. Reports of Haiti appeared regularly in Jamaica, above all in the oppositional press owned and edited by prominent men of colour like Edward Jordon and Robert Osborn who were also Members of the House of Assembly in the emancipation period. Their political interests in Jamaican reform dovetailed with an interest in Haitian progress, motivated by a sense of common racial identity (even if 'brown' elites in both countries were not prepared to endorse full equality for the black working class).

There was a constant flow of newspapers and private information passing between the two islands. In 1831, Jordon and Osborn's *Watchman and Jamaica Free Press* printed reports on French negotiations with Haiti, citing Haitian newspapers like *La Feuille du*

Commerce and *Le Télégraphe*. They attacked those 'enemies of freedom' who had vilified Haiti. Britain's abolition of slavery in 1834 and ending of the apprenticeship system in 1838 brightened prospects for inter-colonial trade with Haiti. Haitians warmly welcomed and celebrated British abolition of slavery, observing British Emancipation Day (August the First) as a festive occasion.[19] In the changed situation, Afro-Jamaican merchants promoted open trade with their Caribbean neighbour, articulating an emerging Afro-Caribbean identity and sense of distinct interests counter to the European-controlled world economy.[20]

In 1838 and 1842, Kingston merchants petitioned the government to open trade with Haiti; controlling coastal boat traffic and internal provision markets, these local traders stood to profit most from trade with Haiti. The *Morning Journal*, published by Jordon and Osborn, editorialized in 1838:

> However prudent it may have been considered, to prevent any communication with the black republic, as she is sometimes called, during the existence of slavery, there can be no good reason for still continuing the system of exclusion.... It never was, it never could be the interest of the Haytians to come into collision with Great Britain, by attempting to revolutionize one of her colonies and that colony the brightest gem in the British crown.[21]

By expressing such views of Haiti, the *Morning Journal* became an important link in an emerging network of regional commercial interests amalgamated with a campaign to extend the civil and political rights of people of colour. Intellectual defenders of Haiti were also given a platform in the *Morning Journal*. 'We well know that at one period much dread was entertained for the Haytians, and it was feared they would endeavour to induce our peasantry, then slaves, to follow their example, and secure freedom by violent means', wrote one Haitian commentator, 'and we also know that with some persons the very name Hayti is calculated to rouse old prejudices, and call into exercise the most unkind and un-christian feelings'.[22] Contrary to such views, Linstant argued that Haiti's problems began with the unavoidable violence of revolution and civil war, 'which, out of the oppressions of Negro slavery, brought a nation of free men into the world'.[23]

Meanwhile, President Boyer was himself under pressure to democratize the Haitian political system in the 1830s, as an elite-led liberal reform movement called for greater black participation in government. The liberals also argued that Jamaican-Haitian trade would offer an opportunity to export beef, pigs, maize, grain, salt and wood, not to mention the 'beneficial contact with the English people' it would afford.[24] Mobilizing supportive Afro-Jamaican public opinion, the *Morning Journal* reported a clampdown on freedom of the press in Haiti and criticized Boyer's persecution of journalists, an issue dear to its own heart. In 1842, Dumai Lespinasse, the exiled editor of a Haitian opposition newspaper applauded the *Morning Journal* for its fair treatment of Haitian issues, and thanked the editors:

> Thanks to you, honorable sirs, who have always paid a just tribute to Truth — who have always extended to us your fraternal hands — continue to extend your sympathies and your talents to a suffering and oppressed people — sound the gunshots of the press without cease.... Perhaps the days are not far away when the Republic of Haiti, this mother of African liberty, surmounting the clouds which encircle her, will present herself beautiful and radiant among the nations[;] then, Sirs, you will remember with joy and enthusiasm how you held out your hand in the bad days to this beautiful country destined, I swear it, to become the refuge and the rally point of all Africans.[25]

Given the presence of leading Haitian opponents of the Boyer regime in Jamaica, including Lespinasse himself, it is possible that this remarkable image tacitly refers to material assistance in addition to ideological support. The *Morning Journal* had previously made an explicit statement on the political future of Haiti, asserting that 'the people are becoming dissatisfied with the government — the masses are being made acquainted, not only with their present condition, but also with the necessity which exists for improving it. Hayti is about to undergo another revolution, but it is to be a bloodless one.... Does she not challenge our sympathies and deserve our assistance?'[26]

With such articles appearing shortly before the overthrow of Boyer, the editors were clearly in close association with the Haitian provisional government and their exiled supporters in Jamaica.[27] Britain finally removed restrictions on trade with Haiti in 1843, just as Boyer's regime was falling.[28] In June 1843, the Haitian newspaper *Le Manifeste*, which had strongly supported the liberal revolution, reported that Haitians residing in Kingston, along with 'patriots of that city attached to our cause', celebrated the triumph of the liberal revolution with a splendid banquet. The banquet also raised money for 'one of the editors of the Morning Journal, on account of the constant sympathy of his newspaper for the Haitians and for his strong participation in propagating in Haiti the liberal ideas that brought about the triumph of the revolution'.[29] Thus, there were strong links between Haitian politics and the development of a racially-conscious and democratic public culture among Jamaicans of colour.

The 'Haytian Fear', then, was not simply a chimera of the Anglo-Jamaican imagination; for one thing, there was an increasingly distinct presence in Jamaica of key Haitian exiles who had taken leading roles in the politics of the republic. Although they refrained from any public role in Jamaican political affairs, these exiles were nevertheless an important ideological influence on people of colour (as well as being quietly involved in Haiti's tumultuous politics [see Chapter 8]). Just as the mass of black Jamaicans were beginning to test the limits of their freedom, Jamaican relations with Haiti were entering a period of new possibilities for open communication. When conflict emerged in Jamaica between descendants of slaves and a government that privileged a small propertied elite, what impact would the example of Haiti have on the political ideologies and practices not only of the 'brown' elite, but even more crucially of the 'black' Jamaican peasantry?

The export of black revolution?

Though coming through two different modes of emancipation, Haitians and Jamaicans of the post-emancipation generation made strong claims to being models and exemplars of black political freedom. By the time Jamaica's slaves were freed, there began an unexpected convergence in the projection of Haitian and Jamaican collective destinies on a world stage and an increasing amount of communication between the two islands. By 'demonstrating to the world, that the sons of Africa are capable of exercising the rights of citizens', both Haitians and Jamaicans embraced an African identity, laying the groundwork for the development of Garveyism and later pan-Africanism.[30] Jamaican freedmen addressed African freedom on a global scale by petitioning for an end to the slave trade, criticizing slavery in the United States and supporting a Baptist Mission to Africa. As self-consciously 'black' or 'African' activists seized the new opportunities opened by citizenship rights, popular sovereignty in the Caribbean momentarily seemed possible, perhaps even inevitable. Yet, black citizenship was not a foregone outcome of slave emancipation: democracy co-existed uneasily with large populations of formerly enslaved Africans and their socially 'alien' descendants throughout the Atlantic world. As argued in Chapter 1, other cases show that democratic 'openings' for freed slaves have often been followed by racist reactions.

Given these reactions, Haiti remained an important and contested symbol in post-emancipation struggles, central to the racial projects of various contenders for economic and cultural predominance. Haitians were acutely aware of their special role in the international order, pointedly welcoming both Native Americans and Africans as citizens. As W. Jeffrey Bolster argues, Haiti also served as a magnet to black seamen throughout the Atlantic world because it encouraged free black immigration and harboured runaways. Enslaved sailors 'were regarded as brothers to be liberated and actors in the contest between the dominant hemispheric slavocracy and a nascent black republic' (Bolster 1997: 147-8). When black captives being transported from Maryland to Georgia led a shipboard rebellion in 1826, for example, they reportedly demanded that the vessel's surviving crew take them to Haiti (Harding 1981: 80–1). Most significantly, 'Haitians, African Americans, and West Indians of Color intermingling in Haiti helped create a diasporic black sensibility, which seafarers transported abroad' (Bolster 1997: 152). Thus, Afro-Jamaicans did not stand alone in promoting more positive assessments of Haiti.[31]

As British democratic radicalism momentarily intersected with Haitian radicalism in the 1840s (cf. Blackett 1983), the 'Haytian Fear' duly cast its shadow into the nearby Spanish colony of Cuba via a triangle of links with newly free Jamaica. Like other slave-based empires, Spain had good reason to suspect Haitian involvement in republican or abolitionist movements in its colonies. Haitian influence had been linked to Cuba's Aponte conspiracy of 1812, to an 1837 plot to spark a slave rebellion in Puerto Rico, and in 1842 to a rumour that 'linked political turmoil in Haiti and Santo Domingo to the intrigues of abolitionists in Jamaica' (Paquette 1997). Robert Paquette's careful research on the Conspiracy of La Escalera in Cuba shows that some free coloured conspirators counted on support from Haiti in raising a slave rebellion in Cuba. Following slave uprisings in Mantanzas and Cárdenas in 1843, the conspiracy was brutally suppressed with imprisonment, interrogations, and executions (Paquette 1988).

While Haiti disclaimed any *direct* interference in Jamaica's, or any other colony's internal politics, unrest in Haiti did sometimes spill over into Jamaica indirectly.[32] Colonial Office documents show that awareness of events in Haiti, as well as the influence of Haitian exiles, inspired suspected 'outbreaks'. John Salmon wrote to the Governor in June 1848, 'The negroes are quite aware of the state of Haiti and by many I have been asked if such and such reports were true.... [They used] the expressions "What kind of free this? This the free them gee we. This free worse than slave, a man can't put up with it"'.[33] Here black dissatisfaction with conditions in Jamaica was directly linked to awareness of events in Haiti. Another informant complained that 'recent disorders in Haiti, and the arrival of many colored refugees from that Island on the shores of Jamaica, together with accounts from all parts of Europe of risings of the people against their governments, may have excited a few of the more instructed and clever of the laboring class to indulge in wild and dangerous thoughts.'[34] In later years, the 'spectre of Haiti' was deeply ingrained in the British public imagination and continued to exercise its influence. One woman wrote in despair that 'there is throughout the Island, a secret combination on the part of the black and colored population, against English influence.... We have it sometimes boldly stated in our streets that their object is to get rid of every white inhabitant — and St. Domingo is held up as an Elyseum after which they wish to model Jamaica'.[35] Haiti was, indeed, invoked in anonymous threats: 'We want Robespierres, Dantons and a few other men of that stamp or even of the Haytien kind, then would Jamaica be a happy Island'.[36]

Genovese suggests that Haiti also had a profound influence on black abolitionists in the United States. Especially 'during 1840-1860', he argues, 'many black leaders established contact with Haiti, as well as with Africa, and many more took heart from the revolutionary experience there' (Genovese 1981: 97). Haiti's revolution and black self-government clearly influenced African-American abolitionists like Martin Delaney, David Walker and Henry Highland Garnet (Harding 1981; Stuckey 1987). Garnet's 1843 'Address to the Slaves of the United States' called for rebellion, praising Toussaint L'Ouverture (Monroe 1975). More pacifically, Rev. James T. Holly saw Haiti as the location for a powerful black state to develop and moved there in 1857 to head the Episcopal Church (Holly [1857] 1970). Reeling from the 1850 Fugitive Slave Law, the 1854 Kansas-Nebraska Act, and the 1857 Dred Scott decision, some African American abolitionists supported the idea of free black emigration to Haiti (Blackett 1983).[37] James Redpath's *Guide to Hayti* (1860) promoted the country as a destination for black emigration:

> There is only one country in the Western World where the Black and the man of color are undisputed lords; where the White is indebted for the liberty to live to the race which with us is enslaved; where neither laws, nor prejudices, nor historical memories, press cruelly on persons of African descent; where the people whom America degrades and drives from her are rulers, judges, and generals; men of extended commercial relations, authors, artists, and legislators... The name of this country is HAYTI (Redpath [1861] 1970: 9).

Redpath felt a double interest in the project because it would not only demonstrate 'the capacity of the [Negro] race for self-government', but also surround 'the Southern States with a cordon of free labor, within

Figure 4   Daumier's caricature of Emperor Faustin Soulouque, 1850

which, like a scorpion girded by fire, Slavery must inevitably die'.[38] Thus, it joined a hemispheric racial project aimed at eradicating slavery even in the 'democratic' United States.

   In reaction to these threatening developments, pro-slavery advocates resurrected the 'Haytian Fear', now linked to the idea of black populations 'sinking back' into a state of 'primitive savagery' (Dash 1997; Hall 1996; Holt 1992). Ongoing political unrest in Haiti fueled racist depictions of the failure of black government, exemplified by Thomas Carlyle's vitriolic rant against emancipation. Without the 'beneficent whip' to drive him, he argued, the black West Indian labourer would face a fate far worse than slavery:

[L]et him look across to Haiti, and trace a far sterner prophecy! Let him, by his ugliness, idleness, rebellion, banish all White men from the West Indies and make it all one Haiti, — with little or no sugar growing, black Peter exterminating black Paul, and where a garden of the Hesperides might be, nothing but a tropical dog-kennel and pestiferous jungle (Carlyle [1850] in Hall 1992: 272).

The regime of Emperor Soulouque (1847-1859) especially horrified Europeans. Karl Marx ridiculed Napoleon III in the *Eighteenth Brumaire of Louis Bonaparte,* by comparing his imperial trappings and false power to Soulouque's (Marx 1913). Daumier caricatured the black Emperor as a savage (but finely dressed) cannibal, boiling alive a French journalist (Figure 3; cf. Dayan 1995: 10–13).[39]

In 1862, Alexandre Bonneau, echoing other writers of the period, argued that the mulattoes were 'the necessary conductors of Haitian society; they represent progress in her midst; they are the incarnation of the genius of Europe infused into the blood of African populations.... It is up to the men of colur to try to bring their African brothers closer to civilization' (Bonneau 1862: 100). This 'racial project' continually resurfaced throughout the nineteenth century and into the twentieth, for example, in the infamous memoirs of Sir Spenser St. John, British Consul in Port-au-Prince, whose writing popularized the image of Haitians as savages (Lawless 1992; Farmer 1994: 81; St. John [1889] 1971).

It was not only a revolutionary past or African 'voodoo' that inspired fear and ridicule of Haiti, but more importantly its continuing anti-slavery and anti-colonial stance. 'After the execution of [the insurrectionary abolitionist] John Brown in the United States, in December 1859', points out Nicholls, 'flags in Port-au-Prince were flown at half mast, and the presidential family attended a solemn requiem mass in the cathedral' (Nicholls 1996: 85; Lawless 1992: 43). By the 1860s, Haiti was associated with anti-slavery and anti-colonial struggles across the Americas, from the Dominican War of Restoration (1863–65) to the Mexican struggle against Maximilian (1862–67), and finally the Cuban Ten Years' War (1868–78) (Martinez-Fernandez 1994). In Jamaica, as we shall see in Chapter 8, there were crucial connections between black activists in the 1865 political movement that preceded the Morant Bay Rebellion and certain Haitian exiles attempting to overthrow President Geffrard in Haiti.

Official paranoia regarding Haitian influence and activities was also crucial in Cuba during the two wars of independence, especially because of the major part played by the Afro-Cubans of Oriente (many of Haitian ancestry). As Aline Helg suggests, 'Spanish Authorities continuously brandished the scarecrow of the Haitian Revolution in order to divide Cubans and to prevent separation from Spain. They converted the Guerra Chiquita [of 1879], which was circumscribed in Oriente and led mostly by Afro-Cuban chieftains, into a race war launched under the auspices of Haiti and Santo Domingo' (Helg 1995: 49). Antonio Maceo had indeed called for 'a new republic assimilated to our sisters of Santo Domingo and Haiti'. Spanish authorities alleged that his real aim was 'to establish a separate black state in eastern Cuba with the support of the Liga Antillana...an organization allegedly made up of blacks and mulattoes from Haiti and Santo Domingo' (Helg 1995: 48–54). As Maingot notes, 'fear of "Haitianization" thus hung over Cuban life like a sword of Damocles' (Maingot 1996: 66).

These *intra*-Caribbean relationships are not merely incidental; if anything, Haiti's pariah status eased the underground communication of an oppositional racial project. The 'Haytian Fear' was to some extent invented by paranoid slaveholders, yet Haiti's existence did have an actual influence on the formation of black publics in surrounding territories. The racism that promoted Haiti's isolation also led to anti-racist movements among free people of colour, and may have inspired democratization movements and even anti-colonial movements in some contexts. While exaggerated fears of Haiti ran deep, we should not dismiss Haiti's real significance for the definition of a 'Black' collective identity in the nineteenth-century Americas.

Competing narratives of Haiti were used to construct alternative racial and national maps of the Caribbean. Which 'collective reading' of Haiti (Farmer 1994) various actors adopted depended on their position within relational networks of interaction. From Charles Mackenzie and Richard Hill in the 1820s to the writings of British missionaries like Edward Bean Underhill and Mark Bird in the 1860s, the British (and Jamaican) publics took a keen interest in the development of Haiti.[40] Yet, many Afro-Caribbean people, whether 'black' or 'brown,' rejected the white story line and built their own racial projects around a symbolic alliance with Haiti. They identified with Haitian liberation, military success against European armies, and independent self-rule (even if 'brown' elites in both countries recoiled from the most radical implications of black empowerment). Many whites, on the other hand, believed the terror of the 'Haytian Fear', with its spooky tales of primitive barbarism, savagery and voodoo (a fear that is continually reinforced by the North American media and popular culture). The legacies of both this partial embrace and this fear of Haiti have continued to warp Haitian history. One of my aims in writing this book is to dispel some of those misunderstandings and begin to shed light on the true significance of the contribution of liberated slaves and their descendants to the making of democracy.[41]

Notes

1   On the related history of racist depictions of Haiti in nineteenth-century literature and travel writing, see: Regis Antoine, *Les Écrivains français et les antilles* (Paris: G. P. Maisonneuve et Larose, 1978); J. Michael Dash, *Haiti and the United States: National Stereotypes in the Literary Imagination*. 2nd ed. (Basingstoke and New York: St. Martin's, 1997); Joan Dayan, *Haiti, History, and the Gods* (Berkeley, Los Angeles, London: University of California Press, 1995); Robert Lawless, *Haiti's Bad Press* (Rochester, VT: Schenkman Books, 1992); Paul Farmer, *The Uses of Haiti* (Monroe, ME: Common Courage, 1994).

2   I follow Michael Omi and Howard Winant who define 'racial formation' as 'the sociohistorical process by which racial categories are created, inhabited, transformed, and destroyed' (M. Omi and H. Winant *Racial Formation in the United States: from the 1960s to the 1990s* [New York: Routledge, 1994], p. 55).

3   Specific studies of Haitian diplomatic isolation include Yves Auguste, *Haïti et les États-Unis: 1804–1862* (Sherbrooke, Québec: Editions Naaman, 1979); Alfred Hunt, *Haiti's Influence on Antebellum America: slumbering volcano in the Caribbean* (Baton Rouge: Louisiana State University Press: 1988); Robert K. LaCerte, 'Xenophobia and Economic Decline: The Haitian Case, 1820–1843', *The Americas*, 37: 4 (1981): 449–459; Abel-Nicolas Léger, *Histoire Diplomatique d'Haïti*, Vol. I, 1804–1859 (Port-au-Prince: Impr. Aug. Heraux, 1930); Brenda G. Plummer, *Haiti and the Great Powers, 1902–1915* (Baton Rouge: Louisiana State University Press, 1988) and *Haiti and the United States: The Psychological Moment* (Athens, GA: University of Georgia Press, 1992); and Arthur L. Stinchcombe, 'Class Conflict and Diplomacy: Haitian Isolation in the 19th-century World System'. *Sociological Perspectives*, 37:1 (1994): 1–23. My approach differs from all of these in highlighting regional *Afro-Caribbean* reactions.

4   For analyses of the revolution, see Chapter 2, note 20. On its international impact, see David Gaspar and David Geggus, eds., *A Turbulent Time: The French Revolution and the Greater Caribbean* (Bloomington and Indianapolis: Indiana University Press, 1997); David Geggus, *Slavery, War and Revolution: The British Occupation of Saint Domingue, 1793–1798* (Oxford: Clarendon, 1982), and 'Haiti and the Abolitionists: Opinion, Propaganda and International Politics in Britain and France, 1804–1835' in *Abolition and its Aftermath*, ed. David Richardson (London: Frank Cass, 1985).

5   Constitution Imperiale d'Haïti, 1805, Arts. 12 /14 (Linstant, *Récueil Général des Lois*, Vol. 1, p. 49).

6   Histories of colonial and revolutionary St. Domingue usually draw on AN, Series C9a-b, but the less known sub-series CC9a-c carries on well into the nineteenth century. Large parts of it are made up of correspondence from anciens colons, many of which include not only claims to compensation, but also proposals for reconquest and specific plans for military action.

7   White refugees from St. Domingue moved to Jamaica and the United States and set up corresponding committees advocating Haitian isolation and reconquest (see AN, CC9a-c; Philippe Wright and George Debien, 'Les colons de Saint-Domingue passés à la Jamaïque (1792–1835)', *Notes d'Histoire Coloniale*, no. 168 (Paris: J. Owen, 1976) pp. 188–9; and Hunt, *Haiti's Influence*.

8   AN, CC9a.50, Doc. 3, Report to his Majesty from the Commission to St. Domingue, 1816.

9   AN, CC9a.50, Doc. 1, Corréspondence des Commissaires du roi avec le Gen. Pétion, Nos. 8–10, 25 Oct. 1816, 10 Nov. 1816.

10 FO 35/2, Canning to Mackenzie, 13 Sept. 1826. On earlier British presence in Haiti, see FO 35/1 Horton to Canning, 14 Oct. 1826; and Leslie Griffiths, *A History of Methodism in Haiti* (Port-au-Prince: Impr. Méthodiste-D.E.L., 1991).

11 FO 35/3, Mackenzie to Canning, 6 Sept. 1826; 28 May 1826.

12 AMAE, C. P., Haïti, Vol. 8.

13 AN, A.M., GGII.1, Papiers du Amiral C. Baudin, Mission d'Haïti, 1837–38.

14 AMAE, C. P., Haïti, Vol. 8, Rapport sur la Mission d'Haïti, 1837–38.

15 AMAE, C. P., Haïti, Vol. 8, Levasseur to Ministry, 10 Dec. 1839, pp. 186-95.

16 According to Geggus, Haitian influence was claimed in conspiracies in Jamaica (1791, 1815), Marie Galante (1791), Santo Domingo (1793), Louisiana (1795), Tobago (1801), Trinidad (1805), Puerto Rico (1811), and Cuba (1812). In the United States, it was linked to Gabriel Prosser's 1802 conspiracy, (Egerton 1990; Jordan 1968: 393-6); Lousiana's 1811 slave uprising (Paquette 1997); and Denmark Vesey's 1822 insurrection (Logan 1941: 195). Genovese argues that it 'propelled a revolution in black consciousness throughout the New World' (Eugene Genovese, *From Rebellion to Revolution: Afro-American Slave Revolts in the Making of the New World* [New York: Vintage, 1981], p. 96). Geggus, however, warns that 'one needs to beware of overrating the Haitian example as a factor stimulating other revolts' (David Geggus, 'Slavery, War, and Revolution in the Greater Caribbean, 1789-1815' in D. Gaspar and D. Geggus, eds., *A Turbulent Time: The French Revolution and the Greater Caribbean*, [Bloomington and Indiaapolis: Indiana University Press, 1997], p. 14).

17 *The Public Advertiser*, Vol.1, no. 118, 26 Jan. 1824, encl. in AN CC9a.54. *Papers Relating to the Case of L.C. Lecesne and J. Escoffery,* [1823–1826], pp. 15, 206, 275. See also the *Anti-Slavery Monthly Reporter*, Vol. 1, no. 4, 30 Sept. 1825, pp. 28-32.

18 CO 142/1, *The Watchman & Jamaica Free Press*, Vol. 2, no. 24, 24 March 18[30], in extracts from the Yellow Book on the Lecesne and Escoffery Affair.

19 In Jérémie, for example, a banquet on the First of August toasted the British Nation and the English people (*Le Manifeste*, Vol. 1, no. 21, 22 Aug. 1841).

20 Efforts to form black-owned shipping companies in Jamaica began in the 1840s (Richard Blackett, *Building an Antislavery Wall: Black Americans in the Atlantic Abolitionist Movement, 1830–1860* [Baton Rouge and London: Louisiana State University, 1983], pp. 118–21) and culminated in Marcus Garvey's Black Star Line. See John H. Clarke, ed., with Amy Jacques Garvey, *Marcus Garvey and the Vision of Africa* (New York: Vintage Books, 1974); Tony Martin, *Race First: The Ideological and Organizational Struggles of Marcus Garvey and the UNIA* (Dover, Mass.: The Majority Press, 1976); and Amy Jacques Garvey, comp., *The Philosophy and Opinions of Marcus Garvey, Or, Africa for the Africans*, 2 vols. (Dover, Mass.: The Majority Press, 1986 [first published 1923, 1925]).

21 *Morning Journal*, nos. 18/19, 30 Apr. and 1 May 1838.

22 *Morning Journal*, 10 June 1842, article attributed to [Baron S.] L'Instant.

23 *Morning Journal*, 10 June 1842. Linstant was well known for his prize-winning essay against racial prejudice (Linstant 1841). He addressed the British and Foreign Anti-Slavery Society in 1842 (*Le Manifeste*, no. 41, 28 Jan. 1843), and later published a commentary on the laws of Haiti (Linstant, *Récueil Général des Lois*).

24   *Le Manifeste*, No. 30-31, 28 Sept. 1842.

25   *Morning Journal*, 12 Oct. and 19 Oct. 1842. Elsewhere I have more extensively discussed gender and citizenship in Haiti (Sheller, 'Sword-Bearing Citizens').

26   *Morning Journal*, 13 June 1842.

27   The provisional government also wrote secretly to the Governor of Jamaica asking for military aid, which he declined (FO 35/27, Lord Elgin to Lord Stanley, 16 Feb. 1843, encl. Committee of the People to Lord Elgin, 7 Feb. 1843).

28   FO 35/26, Ministry of Foreign Affairs to Admiralty Office, 28 Mar. 1843.

29   *Le Manifeste*, no. 10, 11 June 1843.

30   *Baptist Herald and Friend of Africa*, Vol. 5, no. 28, 9 July 1844.

31   Recent studies of black seafaring suggest extensive transatlantic networks among sailors and stevedores of African descent (See Julius S. Scott III, 'The Common Wind: Currents of Afro-American Communication in the Era of the Haitian Revolution' (Ph.D. dissertation, Duke University, 1986); and Jeffrey W. Bolster, *Black Jacks: African American Seamen in the Age of Sail* (Cambridge, MA: Harvard University Press, 1997).

32   Refugees of Haitian political turmoil often fled to Jamaica, bringing news with them (e.g., FO 35/28, Ussher to Aberdeen, 21 Apr. 1844).

33   CO 137/299, Salmon to Grey, 25 June 1848.

34   CO 137/299, Pilgrim to Grey, 6 July 1848.

35   NLJ, MS 865, Elizabeth Holt to Underhill, 26 Oct. 1853, p. 2.

36   CO 137/345, Anonymous letter enclosed in Darling to CO, 9 June 1859.

37   For African American emigration projects involving Haiti, see Earl Griggs and Clifford Prator, eds., *Henry Christophe and Thomas Clarkson, A Correspondence* (New York: Greenwood Press, 1968); Loring Dewey, *'Correspondence Relative to the Emigration to Hayti of the Free People of Colour in the United States'* (New York: Day, 1824); James Redpath, ed., *A Guide to Hayti* (Westport, CT: Negro Universities Press [1861] 1970); James T. Holly, 'A Vindication of the capacity of the Negro race for self-government and civilized progress' in Howard Bell, ed., *Black Separatism and the Caribbean, 1860* (Ann Arbor: University of Michigan Press, [1857] 1970).

38   On African-American relations with Haiti in this period, see Fordham Monroe, 'Nineteenth Century Black Thought in the United States: Some Influences of the Santo Domingo Revolution', *Journal of Black Studies*, Vol. 6, no. 2 (December 1975): 15-26; James O. Jackson, 'The Origins of Pan-African Nationalism: Afro-American and Haytian Relations, 1800-1863' (Ph.D. dissertation, Northwestern University, 1976); Auguste, *Haïti et les États-Unis* ; Hunt, *Haiti's Influence*; Plummer, *Haiti and the United States*; Dash, *Haiti and the United States*.

39   An Englishman who met Soulouque in 1850 noted that contrary to European jibes, the Emperor could read, write and speak French, and was 'greatly annoyed at the caricatures of him published in the Paris *Charivari*, and the jokes of the press in general' (Bigelow [1851] 1970: 191). For relatively positive assessments of the Soulouque regime, cf. Murdo MacLeod, 'The Soulouque Regime in Haiti, 1847–1859: A Reevaluation' in *Caribbean Studies*, 10:3 (1970): 35–48; and Nicholls, *From Dessalines to Duvalier*.

40   The copy of Bird's book held at the Bodleian library at Oxford is inscribed 'To Dr. Underhill with the kind regards of the Author. Oct. 6, 1869'; both men had been in Haiti around the same time. As we shall see, it was Underhill's concern for the peasantry of Jamaica that instigated the political movement there of 1865.

41   Many of the ideas and evidence discussed in this chapter appeared earlier in M. Sheller, 'The "Haytian Fear": Racial Projects and Competing Reactions to the First Black Republic' in Research in Politics and Society, Vol. 6, (JAI Press, 1999), pp. 285–303.

Black publics and peasant freedom in Haiti, 1820–1843

If Haiti became a symbol of slave uprising in metropolitan politics and a symbol of black liberation among both free and enslaved Afro-Caribbeans, what was the actual reality of 'freedom' for Haitians themselves? As we have seen in Chapter 2, planter economic dominance declined in post-independence Haiti in so far as landholding was diversified, coffee replaced sugar as the main export crop and ruling class solidarity was fragmented by divisions of colour and region. Politically, however, a small elite controlled an autonomous state over which the majority of the population had little influence and from which they had little protection. Indeed, nineteenth-century Haiti is often described as lacking in intermediate associations, being without a true 'political society', and of experiencing a rift between state and nation. As Michel-Rolph Trouillot argues in *Haiti: State Against Nation* (1990), Haitian peasants are the 'mounn andéyo', the outside people, or what Gérard Barthélémy (1989) calls 'le pays en dehors', the nation outside. It is often said that Haiti lacked (and lacks) a civil society and some have even argued that, 'no matter how one defines politics, in Haiti it has failed.... The pervasive fear, suspicion, and flight engendered by a politics of hostility and indifference have blocked the emergence of a stable society that would encompass large groups of people beyond the family' (Weinstein and Segal 1992: 2).

These views on some kind of failing in Haitian civil institutions are supported by historiographic studies of nineteenth-century Haitian politics. The lack of peasant political participation is one of the central themes of Nicholls' comprehensive study of Haitian political and cultural history (published in 1979):

At no time in the history of the country has there been a significant degree of long-term popular participation in the political process.... Authoritarianism on the part of the government and political irresponsibility or apathy on the part of the mass of the population have gone together in independent Haiti. Only when conditions have become intolerable, or when rival claimants to governmental power have appeared, did the mass of the people intervene and then merely to secure the transfer of power to a new dictator (Nicholls 1996: 245–46).

In certain periods, small and medium-sized peasants did have a more 'positive involvement in public affairs', avers Nicholls, but only with 'transitory' impact. In so far as any democratic ideology existed in Haiti, it seems to have been promulgated by the urban elite, not by peasants. Mintz, in his introduction to James Leyburn's study of *The Haitian People* (1966), likewise verges on dismissing altogether the possibility of peasant political agency. Although admitting that peasants occasionally played a political role in nineteenth-century Haiti, Mintz argues that this was exceptional; in general, they are 'unable to break out of a stagnation that is economic as well as cultural' and are wholly 'apathetic'. 'Seemingly mute and invisible', he further laments, 'apparently powerless, the peasantry of Haiti remind one of Marx's famous dictum that peasants possess organization only in the sense that the potatoes in a sack of potatoes are organized' (Mintz 1989: 270, 297).

The Haitian peasantry, it would seem, is not a good candidate for exemplifying a revolutionary subaltern ideology, democratic or otherwise. What happened to James' Black Jacobins? What can explain this apparent political apathy? Or is it a mistaken appraisal of Haitian political culture? How much do we really know about past instances of peasant political activism, especially in a field where both sources and primary research are thin on the ground? At the very least, further research into the duration and significance of previous peasant political activity is needed if we are to understand the misfortunes of democracy in the first American republic to abolish slavery. Some have explored Caribbean radicalism in terms of the Gramscian distinction between a 'war of position' versus a 'war of maneuver' (cf. James 1998), in which the former involves head-on mobilization and violent conflict while the latter occurs on a more subtle ideological terrain. Are the peasants of Haiti locked into an invisible war of manoeuvre that has simply been overlooked? Others have noted the 'silencing of the past' (Trouillot 1995) and the hegemonic effort to resolve contradictions that leads to gaps and telling silences in dominant narratives or stories (Paige 1998). Are peasant political ideologies in Haiti perhaps lost in the silences of the victor's history?

Stinchcombe takes a stab at explaining Haitian politics by arguing that it resembles other Latin American republics. He suggests that 'black Haiti looked more like a former Spanish colony (except for having a much denser population, so being militarily much more powerful, and speaking French) than like the other slave societies after emancipation' (Stinchcombe 1996: 318). His hypothesis is based on the argument that Haiti's post-emancipation political system resembles the *caudillismo* common to South American republics and the Hispanic Caribbean (Cuba, Puerto Rico and the Dominican Republic). Yet, his description of *caudillismo* as the leadership of charismatic heroes, often arising out of the cattle-ranching *latifundia* so typical of Latin America, simply does not fit the Haitian case. Even by Stinchcombe's own criteria, the three Hispanic cases with which he groups Haiti all had cultural, political and developmental characteristics that were absent in Haiti. They fall into a cluster which he characterizes as 'low' on the slave society scale: they did not experience the sugar frontier until after 1800, sugar never dominated their economies and they had relatively unpolarized racial structures with a 'mestizo' majority. Haiti, in contrast, experienced an early sugar boom, which at its peak dominated the economy, and it was far more of a 'slave society' with strong racial polarization and a black majority. I believe his hypothesis is untenable, and we would do better to try to understand in what ways Haiti's development *is* comparable to other slave societies.

In fact, contrary to his own protestations, Stinchcombe's basic model of variation in planter dominance and peasant agency as the keys to social transformation in post-slavery societies is perfectly applicable to the analysis of Haiti; Haiti is not an exception. In this chapter, I will argue that the apparent apathy of the Haitian peasantry has nothing to do with Haitian social isolation, with a cultural tendency toward *caudillismo*, with the backwardness of peasant subsistence economies or with the lack of social institutions in rural areas. Rather, it has everything to do with the structure of ties between state and civil actors, and, above all, the intervening role of the military in relations between publics and the state. Despite good intentions, republican institutions and a fierce desire for liberty and equality, Haitians created a state de-coupled from its potential citizenry and citizens without access to any channels of political communication. Nevertheless, the dynamic struggle for democratization was still present.

In this chapter, I will focus on the development of peasant agency in post-slavery Haiti, in its economic, political and civil dimensions. My thesis is that although planter power had declined since the era of French colonial control and the sugar plantations were fragmented, a concomitant rise in peasant power was thwarted. Social and political control did not actually pass to the freed slaves who had liberated themselves through revolution. Instead, control of post-independence

Haiti passed into the hands of the military and the small elite which chose to protect its own interests. I suggest that the weak structure of publicity in nineteenth-century Haiti was caused not simply by the military path to emancipation (which, after all, was also taken in the United States), but by the subsequent failure to subordinate the military to civil control. As the Kréyol saying goes, 'constitusyon sé papié, bayonet sé fer' [constitutions are paper, bayonets are iron]; but is the sword always mightier than the pen?

Peasant economic agency

Peasant autonomy depends first on having enough mobility to break out of the master-slave pattern of relations that informed plantation societies in the Americas even after slavery's abolition. Mobility is a key component of freedom. This aspect of freedom was built on the foundations of existing slave autonomous traditions established in what Mintz calls the 'interstices' of plantation society inhabited by 'reconstituted' peasantries (Mintz 1989: 146).[1] In the Caribbean region, the term 'peasant' refers to a whole range of mixed situations involving some access to subsistence plots, but also including occasional wage-labour, marketing, fishing, petty production and/or capacity for migration to areas with greater opportunity for any of these additional activities. British Jamaica and French Saint-Domingue had some of the most well-developed 'proto-peasantries' before the abolition of slavery because of their combination of early, intensive sugar plantations, large size and mountainous landscape. Both were already past the sugar frontier period when slavery was abolished. Both had extremely rugged and isolated interiors, with a tradition of Maroon semi-autonomy. Both had established traditions of land-holding kin-groups, centred in Haiti around the *lakou*[2], and in Jamaica around the yard and provision ground (Mintz 1989: 241; Besson 1995: 77). With the abolition of slavery, the Haitian peasantry after 1804 and the Jamaican peasantry after 1838 were already well on their way to establishing their own communities, kinship structures and semi-autonomous subsistence economies.

Peasant land ownership is one of the most significant measures of peasant civil rights and personal liberties in former slave societies, for with land ownership came control over everyday family decision-making, as well as some degree of economic autonomy. As Carolyn Fick has argued in regard to the Haitian Revolution, a 'personal claim to the land upon which one labored and from which to derive and express one's individuality was, for the black laborers, a necessary and an essential element in their vision of freedom. For without this concrete economic and social reality, freedom for the ex-slaves was little more than a legal abstraction' (Fick 1990: 249). She places the 'ideological origins' of the Haitian peasantry in the struggle for land as expressed in the revolution. In the Northern Kingdom of Haiti, King Henry Christophe maintained the big estates intact and under the control of a few successful generals who formed a new black aristocracy.[3] In the south, President Pétion distributed land to the veterans of the wars of independence who had fought 'to liberate the fatherland'.

His land distribution achieved what Fick calls 'a stabilizing compromise between the hegemonic mulatto elite and the economically dispossessed masses' (Fick 1988: 269). A decree of December 30th, 1809, gave full title to property taken from former sugar plantations, according to military rank: 25 *carreaux* for Colonels, 15 *carreaux* for Battalion chiefs, 10 *carreaux* for Captains to Second Lieutenants, and 5 *carreaux* to non-commisioned officers and soldiers (Lacerte 1975: 81).[4] In 1814, Pétion carried out another extensive distribution of land taken from coffee estates to officers on active service, granting 35 *carreaux* to Battalion or squadron chiefs, 30 *carreaux* to Captains, 25 *carreaux* to Lieutenants, and 20 *carreaux* to Second Lieutenants; land was also distributed in smaller grants to government employees, hospital employees and members of the judicial administration, as a way of paying salaries (Lacerte 1975: 82–3). As Lepelletier de Saint-Rémy put it in 1846, Pétion's parcellization of the old colonial plantations had 'republicanized the soil' (Lacerte 1975: 83–4).

In many respects, Pétion's land distributions were attempts to maintain loyalty in the face of continuing French destabilization and civil war with the north. Yet, it is also important to distinguish hierarchies within the peasant class, which originated in part out of already existing hierarchies within slave communities and in part out of these new land distributions. Clear demarcations developed between 'big peasants' who owned land and often hired labour; 'small peasants' who depended only on family labour; tenants and share-croppers who owned no land, but exercised some indirect control over land and the labour-process; and finally the landless peasants who worked for relatives or bigger landowners in return for subsistence, and sometimes worked for wages on the remaining plantations. Each group had different degrees of economic autonomy and organizational capacities (Mintz 1973, 1979; Isaacman 1993). Land-poor dependents in particular (especially women), who had to share a small piece of family land, were liable to be exploited by '*gros membres*' of the family. These wealthier peasants could use the *lakou* as a pool of agricultural workers, as well as creating political clients of their kin.

Maintaining inalienable 'family land' was one way of counteract-ing these class differences. Family land in Haiti belongs to all descend-ants of the original owner, has sacred meaning and is passed down through generations. Family-oriented Vodou ritual 'plays an important role in maintaining [this] form of social organisation that appeared on the properties granted during the nineteenth century by the Haitian government to soldiers who had participated in the War of Independence' (Larose 1975: 511). Twentieth-century fieldwork in Haiti shows the continuity of the peasant valuation of inalienable family land. In Léogane, for example, the *lakou*, or family yard, was still built around the *démembre*, a special part of the family land with 'its cemetery, its cult house and its trees which are the repositories of the family spirits…. [It] is the basic unit of peasant religion' (Larose 1975: 490–92). As Georges Anglade argues in relation to modern Haiti, rural society is not lacking its own social structures. He rejects the commonplace 'imagery of four million Haitians scattered, alone, autarchic, without organization, living in a heap of disparate beliefs' (Anglade 1982: 135). He describes the infrastructure of neighbour-hoods and 'bourg-jardins' in the plains, valleys, plateaux and moun-tains, converging on the weekly markets, which serve as intersections and 'soldering points' of the peasant social framework. Out of these patterns of trade — already well-established in the early nineteenth century (as seen in the pyramidal hierarchy of license fees in Table 3) — rural society built extensive networks of trade and commerce, but also of kinship and religion, cooperation and collective association.

Contrary to the common image of an unorganized mass of scat-tered peasants, then, the rural working class and small *habitants* have in fact practised their own genres of association and cooperative organ-ization. Barthélémy, likewise, argues that Haitian peasants have devel-oped a self-regulating culture 'outside' of state structures, based on egalitarianism and inter-individual reciprocity (Barthélémy 1989). Collective work structures that can be traced back to the nineteenth century (such as *Sociétés de Travail, Combites, Escouades* and *Avanjou*), all share labour outside of the monetary system, work land collectively, serve as friendly societies and in some cases elect leaders (Barthélémy 1989; Courlander 1960). Barthélémy connects these modern 'collective work structures' to earlier precedents. The visiting Jamaican Richard Hill, for example, described a kind of cooperative share-cropping, observed on his visit to Chateaublond plantation in 1830: 'Their method is to divide themselves by families, and to culti-vate together a part of the plantation, and they receive for salary a portion of the product of that which they cultivate and manufacture in their division, conforming to the dispositions of the rural code'. Hill reported that these groups were self-governing in so far as they 'chose their foremen as a society would elect its president, or a benefit association its secretary or treasurer, not so as to make them work amongst themselves, but as their organ and their representative, charged with keeping an eye on the interests of all, in their arrangements with the proprietor of the soil' (Barthélémy 1989: 40).

These workers' associations — rooted in the plantation work-gangs, but looking forward to modern forms of collective work based on equality, reciprocity and use of the electoral process — contained the seeds of popular political participation. The Haitian historian Ardouin also linked the egalitarianism of revolutionary militias of the 1790s to the self-formed rural cooperatives: 'But what is remarkable is the introduction of the principle of election of all the offices necessary in a rural farm, by the cultivators themselves forming associations' (cited in idem, 93-94). Peasant direct democracy at the local level, then, was founded on the republican egalitarianism of the revolutionary period, and survived throughout the post-colonial period as a major form of rural self-organization. Urban areas also had their own collective work structures. On landing at Port-au-Prince harbour in 1840, the missionary James Hartwell found that 'the wharf was crowded with nearly naked blacks shouting and singing in chorus, who were engaged in landing merchandise'.[5]

Contrary to the stereotyped image of an unorganized mass of peasants, then, various forms of collective labour and land-use characterized both urban and rural production in nineteenth-century Haiti. The rural working class and small landholders practised associational genres including *combites* (groups that worked land together, served as 'friendly societies', and in some cases elected leaders); *compagnies* (more organized fraternities with eleborate symbolic systems of membership and office-holding, originating out of African ethnic affiliations and preserving particular cultures of dance and drum); and *hounforts* (the Vodou temples which served as centres of community ritual and were sometimes clustered into regional networks). These peasant communities, especially in the south, were not lacking in political ideologies that expressed their moral position and sense of injustice. Yet, there were few public outlets for peasant political expression.

Important in peasant leadership 'was a class of independent peasants large enough to be self-supporting and to make small loans to their neighbours, but small enough to be excluded from the ruling elite groups' (Nicholls 1996: 10). In spite of their revolutionary self-liberation, former slaves in Haiti still had to negotiate their freedom, like ex-slaves elsewhere. Fick argues that in post-independence Haiti, popular protest may be seen as an attempt by the ex-slaves, insofar as it was materially possible, to define for themselves and to control in some measure their own working conditions. The demand on the part of some laborers for the five-day work week; the women's demand for equal pay; the refusal of night work on the sugar plantation — all were attempts to impose their independent will upon the restrictions of a system that did not seem too far removed from slavery (Fick 1988: 268).

The state played a major part in influencing these collective settlements, in part by land distribution, but also by the imposition of a system of 'militarized agriculture'.

Former plantation slaves (known as 'cultivators') had few freedoms in the early days of the republic. The 1807 'Law concerning the policing of estates and the reciprocal obligations between proprietors, farmers, and cultivators' stipulated that once a contract was made, a cultivator could not leave his property. Disputes were to be settled in front of a Justice of the Peace (invariably a landowner); and any cultivator who provoked a 'movement' of any kind, by word or deed, would be tried for 'disturbing public order'. Written permission was needed from a plantation manager to travel within a parish (checked by military patrols), and passports were needed for travel between communes.[6]

Like the earlier rural codes of Toussaint L'Ouverture and King Henry Christophe, Boyer's 1826 *Code Rural* provided for the 'protection and encouragement of agriculture' by a strict regime of rural police surveillance and regulation of work contracts and trade.[7] Proclaiming agriculture to be the 'principal source of the prosperity of the state', the Code ordered that all citizens who were not state employees (civil or military) and were not licensed to engage in particular professions, 'must cultivate the land'.[8] Most importantly, it declared that agricultural workers were not allowed to leave the countryside and go to the towns or cities without authorization from a Judge of the Peace, nor could their children be apprenticed in the towns. Mobility was tightly restricted by a pass system, and cooperative ownership of land was outlawed. The longest section of the Code pertained to the duties of the Rural Police, charged with arresting vagabonds, maintaining order in fieldwork, discipline of work-gangs, and oversight of road building.

The British businessman, James Franklin, reported that Gens d'Armes patrolled the rural districts and reported absent cultivators to the local General:

Every Cultivator must remain upon the Estate to which he is attached, or upon his own property, which last is the most common system. When the Cultivator is attached to an Estate to work for wages for a specific time, if he does not work, he is confined by the Police in Jail, and is generally sentenced to work on the public roads, and forfeit any pay that may have been due him. When working upon the public roads, if a Cultivator becomes indolent, his exertion is compelled by the bayonets and sabres of the military guard, whose duty it is to make him work, the whip is never used, but the bayonet or sabre is used in its stead (to prick them).[9]

This system of 'militarized agriculture' begun by Toussaint L'Ouverture, but adopted by Presidents Pétion and Boyer, exemplifies what the Haitian elite wished the state could enforce. The licensing and taxing of marketing, both wholesale and retail, urban and rural, were closely regulated. The Code specifically outlawed collective ownership of farms and worker self-management in 'sociétés' (Art. 30).

Nevertheless, the government seems to have had great difficulty in enforcing certain aspects of the Code, particularly those relating to peasant mobility. There were middle-level farmers and traders (including the female *marchandes)* who had a certain degree of personal mobility and therefore access to more channels of information and inter-regional communication. If the rural and urban working-class population were to some extent excluded from national political debate and public life because of lack of education, illiteracy and restrictions on mobility, they were neither wholly isolated nor completely apathetic. The question of their participation in politics emerged as a central point of contention in Boyer's Haiti. It also came to shape the retrospective interpretations of the events of the Liberal Revolution of 1843 by Haiti's great nineteenth-century historians (who were also central participants). Through the lens of these debates we can begin to see the divergence in elite ideologies between an older generation of conservative big landowners who opposed any democratization, and the younger (more urban, professional and dynamic) Liberals. They opposed President Boyer and argued for a democratic opening (at least in so far as it would favour their own position). It was in the fracture between these two positions that a rural and small town black peasant and artisan voice began to make itself heard.

Peasant political agency

The potential for peasant political agency depends not only on the degree of peasant autonomy in relation to land and economic decisions, but also on the quality of the state-citizen tie, meaning the ways citizens could make claims on the state and the state could make claims on citizens. Peasant political agency can be measured in terms of the degree of input ex-slaves had into the political process and state decision-making itself, as reflected in the interplay of claim-making and state response, both violent and non-violent. From the perspective of the state, instruments for addressing citizens could include communicative means such as constitutions, legislation, proclamations, court rulings and presidential addresses, or coercive means like policing, imprisonment, armed force and martial law. From the perspective of the citizen, repertoires of claim-making ranged from violent riot, direct action and demonstration to holding public meetings, petitioning and voting. If there was great breadth of citizenship in Haiti (apart from whites), there was not a great deal of opportunity for the exercise of citizenship. Given the predominant role of the military in Haiti, political 'space' was very constricted.

When Jean-Pierre Boyer became president following the death of Pétion in 1818, he quickly won control not only of the north, but also of the former Spanish colony of Santo Domingo in the east; the project of national unification began in earnest.[10] With the ongoing threat of French invasion, the military remained the most significant branch of the executive government while the elected Chamber of Deputies had little power. The British Consul Mackenzie described the government as 'a military elective monarchy, in which, though the forms are republican, the whole of the efficient authority of the state is wielded by the first magistrate' (Mackenzie [1830] 1970, 2: 105). Citizenship was defined by the elements of duty, obedience and obligation (what the citizen owed the state), which far outweighed the rights-based element of what the state owed to its citizens. Boyer's proclamations were always issued 'To the Army and the People', often in the form of military 'Ordres du Jour'; the national symbol was a palm tree topped with a republican liberty cap, surrounded with a bristling array of spear-tipped banners, cannon, bayonets and miltary drums (see Figure 4).[11] As the British Consul noted, 'the constitution, as it now exists, is incompatible with the spirit of republicanism, and is so considered by a large number of reflecting people in Haiti' (Mackenzie [1830] 1970, 2: 105).

By 1840, there were approximately 25,000 men in the army and another 40,000 in the national guard, equalling almost one tenth of the entire population, and perhaps close to one quarter or more of the adult male population.[12] Military spending was, not surprisingly, the largest portion of public expenditure in Boyer's budgets (Schoelcher 1843: 278). Beyond their normal military duties, the army also essentially

Figure 5   National seal of the Republic of Haiti

functioned as the local government. Each commune came under the authority of a Commandant de Place and his troops who enforced the law, checked passports and punished offenders, with the help of 'conseils de notables' and 'Juges de Paix', i.e. local landowners. A military spirit pervaded the state, and irrevocably moulded the meaning and practice of citizenship. In this 'republican monarchy sustained by the bayonet', as Jonathan Brown described it, both 'the morale and the materiel of the Haytien government consist in the military spirit embodied in the very minutest of its organism…. [It is] a nation of soldiers…[in which] every man is required to be a soldier and to consider himself more amenable to the commands of his military chief than to the civil institutions of the government' (Brown [1837] 1972, 2: 259). As Boyer himself put it in a proclamation, 'Arms and land, these are our strengths…. Imitate the people of antiquity, and let us be warriors and cultivators at the same time' (Linstant 1860, 3: 42–4).

When the English missionary James Hartwell arrived in Port-au-Prince in 1840, he too reported on the odd state of affairs:

> …[A] ragged soldier at once took charge of us and conducted us first to the colonel commanding the 'Place,' a partly coloured man dressed in a respectable uniform, and then to the Police Magistrate who after various enquiries registered me as an 'Ecclesiastique' and gave me a stamped permission to reside within the territory of the Republic for which I paid a small fee.[13]

Later, he described a member of a rural military guard as 'a man called Captain, no regimental number, no shoes or stockings, with a spur girt on his naked ankle, a sword tied round his waist with a piece of tailors list, and an old straw hat'. These ragged soldiers were ever present in civil life, and were often involved in public events ranging from the reading, cheering or jeering of proclamations, to marching in religious processions.[14] Brown described them as 'a sort of African janizaries, half citizen and half soldier.... Every municipal measure, from the promulgation of a law down to a negro dance, is performed to the beat of a drum. The civil is everywhere subservient to the military power, and the administration of justice in the tribunals of the republic can only be performed at the pleasure of the chiefs of the army' (Brown [1837] 1972, 2: 266–67).

Coercion remained a significant factor in Haitian labour relations after emancipation, but it became a question of what kinds of coercion would be politically sanctioned. Would the rights of 'free' citizenship apply equally to all people? In the long run, most Haitian peasants managed to get their own land and avoid work on the big estates. As one Haitian historian recorded, the peasants had a well-known saying, 'Vous signé *nom* moi, mais vous pas signé *pieds* moi', meaning as the play on the words 'name' and 'feet' imply, you can put my name on a contract, but you can not stop me from going where I want (Ardouin 1860, 10: 23 n.1). But, rural policing and imprisonment were cruel, as Hartwell reported in his autobiography:

> The prisons in this country are in a sad state and the discipline is severe and cruel. Some time after my visit we heard for a considerable time irregular musquetry firing in the direction of the prison. At length we were horrified to learn that the prisoners had risen against their keepers, and that all this time the prison guard of seventeen men had been firing from the walls upon the promiscuous group in the large courtyard. The number of killed and wounded did not transpire (to my knowledge) and little notice was taken of the affair. The people seem used to scenes of bloodshed and are very reckless of human life.[15]

Without protection from arbitrary state violence, political opposition was extremely curtailed in Haiti. The greatest difference between Haiti and Jamaica in this regard was the extent to which the government (or its agents) was willing to use armed force not only against the rural population, but also against opposition politicians. On numerous occasions, as we shall see in the next chapter, the Haitian National Guards were called on to expel deputies from the Chamber or to keep them from entering. The only time such direct coercion of opposition politicians occurred in Jamaica was during the martial law which followed the Morant Bay Rebellion.

The importance of public opinion as a weapon against authoritarianism is exemplified by its thematization in the historical works produced by the two great Haitian historians of the period, Beaubrun Ardouin (1796–1865) and Thomas Madiou (1814–1884), who were deeply involved in national politics and newspaper publication. As Bellegarde-Smith explains of these two writers,

> [they] were diplomats as well as historians. They were also powerful figures in Haitian politics; yet their historical works addressed themselves as much to a foreign public as to Haitians. Their histories and memoirs express concern for national unity and a quest for societal development as generally understood in the nineteenth century. Furthermore, these historians also hoped to address race prejudice outside Haiti by showing the world that Haiti was capable of the kind and level of intellectual achievement they themselves demonstrated (Bellegarde-Smith 1980: 23).

Ardouin is considered an apologist for Boyer, but reserves some criticism for the president's handling of affairs. He served as a senator and was president of the senate during Boyer's presidency, and also edited a pro-government newspaper, *Le Temps*. Madiou was aligned more with the opposition. He became a chronicler of the rise to power of the anti-Boyeriste faction and later served in the government of Emperor Faustin Soulouque. These two sources, augmented by others, document the formation, suppression and fragmentation of publics in Haiti, and reproduce a range of contemporary public texts recording the political language, genres of expression and framing of collective narratives of the various factions.

Indeed, their respective many-volume histories of Haiti are themselves products and records of competing efforts to shape the story of the Haitian nation and influence its trajectory into the future. As Nicholls argues, these major works laid the foundations for an ongoing rivalry between a '*mulatriste*' and '*noiriste*' historiography of Haiti, each with their own heroes and villains (Nicholls 1974, 1996). What Nicholls calls the 'mulatto legend of the past' was a version of Haitian history that aimed 'to encourage Haitians to unite under the leadership of the most patriotic, civilised and technically qualified group in the country, to legitimate the mulatto ascendancy in the social and economic field, and to lend weight to their claim to guide and control developments in the political sphere' (Nicholls 1996: 91–2). Conservative elites elaborated a particular version of democracy that has been identified in other instances of statist autocracy. They 'portrayed the nation-state as a harmonious, integrated community in which competing class interests could be reconciled and smoothed away by enlightened elders ruling with the best interests of the society at heart' (Andrews and Chapman 1995: 20; cf. Paige 1998).

In Haiti, this took the form of comparing the people to children in order to justify 'enlightened' leadership by their wise elders. The ruling elite denied any conflict of interest between classes or colours, even as they argued that the people were not 'ready' to govern themselves (for a similar discourse in Peru, cf. Mallon 1995: 217). Ardouin suggested that Haitians were not ready for full democracy, and like children had to be tutored in politics and gradually given greater rights; this was the conservative ideology of the mulatto oligarchy, who favoured government by the most 'competent' and 'qualified', i.e. themselves (Nicholls 1996: 87-107). In *Le Temps*, this argument was made very explicitly in 1842: 'The boy passes through adolescence before arriving at virility.... A young people...must not make haste more than it should.... It does not suffice for such a people, having adopted certain institutions that old nations could procure for themselves only over the succession of centuries, to then believe that they are in a state to put them into practice right away'.[16] This produced an angry retort from an opposition paper, *Le Patriote*:

> You compare the Haitian Nation to an infant, barely out of diapers; you recommend that he defend himself from the presumption and illusions of adolescence; 'do not make haste more than you should.' And when, then, will we leave this infancy? What! Do you not see that the child has become a man? ...Do you not think, to the contrary, that he should regret his youth, passed in inaction? ...[T]he hour of his manhood has sounded.[17]

These elite debates and the competing versions of Haitian history that they supported are not the end of the story, however. Their silences and contradictions regarding popular participation are telling indictments. Beneath both the conservative and the liberal ideologies, we catch glimpses of a more egalitarian and participatory vision of popular democracy, a strong *counter*-discourse of popular democracy beneath the hegemonic story.

As subsequent chapters will show, democratization movements in Haiti and Jamaica had surprisingly similar social bases, aims and grievances; where they differ was in their capacity to make public claims to which the government would respond in a non-violent way.

With the 'universal respect paid to military rank' in Haiti, and despite its constitutional republicanism, the state developed few modes of addressing citizens as such. The state was institutionally thin, and citizens remained an undifferentiated mass, simply 'the people' or 'the army'. We find few interactions between groups of citizens and representatives of the state. The main archival records are executive proclamations that address the entire people, rather than responding to specific claimants, as is found in Jamaica. And there were no apparent channels through which citizens could address claims or grievances to the state; petitions were rare, and could lead to charges of sedition. There was no question of the Haitian people being 'ready' for democracy. All the principles of democracy were understood and its formulae of elections, a free press, petitioning, etc. were all known, if only partly practised. Yet, full participation by the people was blocked on every front. Contention was pitting those who claimed to represent the black masses against a conservative, mulatto-dominated, aging and defensive agrarian elite. As these competing elites debated the merits of democratization among themselves, they also created opportunities for excluded segments of the black population to take up their own part in these discussions. Few had noticed that peasants were already holding political meetings and practising elections in their rural settings.

Peasant civil agency

Liberation from slavery was not simply about escaping the plantation labour regime; it also crucially concerned civil rights such as the freedoms of speech, of religion and access to education. It is at this point that the bifurcation between 'state and nation', or between state and civil society, as observed by Trouillot and others becomes fundamental. How is it that the peasantry was so thoroughly excluded from civic and political participation? In most post-slavery societies, education is a key component of peasant civil agency because its denial was one of the central deprivations of the system of slavery. Here nineteenth-century Haiti had a poor record. Because there were few priests or missionaries, there were few schools. The continuing lack of schools became a major source of both foreign criticism and local grievance in nineteenth-century Haiti.

To European rulers, it seemed impossible that the slave might advance out of the degradation of slavery without schooling; at the very least, capacity to read the Bible was thought to be necessary to moral development. Although there was a Lycée National in Port-au-Prince, it served only the upper echelons of the elite, many of whom continued their schooling in France (Christophe had also founded a number of elite schools in Cap-Henry early in the century). The education of girls, in particular, was neglected even among the elite institutions (Bonneau 1862). Catholic clergy had largely been expelled or fled during the revolution, attempts to found private schools were discouraged and there were very few Protestant missionaries in the country (Griffiths 1991; Stanley 1992). It was not until 1860 that President Geffrard signed a concordat with the Vatican, allowing French priests to return to Haiti (Nicholls 1996: 117). One of the key elements of reform proposed in the liberal Constitution of 1843 was the introduction of public schooling.

Many elite observers asked, how could the people participate in public debate if they could not read and write? And how could general interests be represented in government if the government only represented a tiny educated elite? The French abolitionist Victor Schoelcher attributed the failure to institute public education to the government's desire to suppress political debate and public opinion: 'When political education also becomes impossible, it renders impossible the formation of public opinion. The Haitian autocrat does not ignore that the people civilize themselves by the press, and he stifles the press, because from the moment his people are instructed, he will no longer be able to rule over them despotically in peace' (Schoelcher 1843: 323). The Methodist Missionary Mark Bird dedicated much of his book, *The Black Man; or, Haytian Independence* (1869), to the argument that education had never been raised to its proper level in Haiti, harming the advancement of the black race in independence and self-government. He asked,

> [w]hat shall we say when an enlightened community in a nation with an enlightened government at its head, for more than sixty years suffer the great masses of their brethren to remain in ignorance?... Under such free institutions as those of true republicanism, the great fact of human equality must not be made an absurdity by the utter inability of two-thirds of the citizens to be Republicans (Bird 1869: 220).

Yet, many of those who harped on education were the same people who saw the Haitian people as young children, still incapable of self-governance. How long would it take to educate them for citizenship?

Madiou blamed President Boyer for failing to prepare the people for citizenship. Because the masses had traditionally known only the leadership of a 'premier chef', he argued, it was the president's obligation 'to lightly guide them toward the practice of their social and political obligations, by giving them a rudimentary knowledge of religion, reading, writing and mathematics, so that they may at least exercise their rights of citizenship, and above all to inculcate in them the dogmas of Christian religion which alone can extinguish those of Vodou' (Madiou 1988, 7: 110). Yet, from 1820 to 1832, Boyer had not done this, nor had he trained the peasantry in agricultural improvements. Nothing had changed, lamented Madiou, since the *ancien regime*: 'three centuries of servitude had formed nothing but asses who were the masters, and the oppressed who had all the vices that their condition entailed: the deceit, the dissimulation, and the mute and implacable hatred which were the only arms of the slave against his oppressor'. As political opposition 'systematically undermine[d] the government', it was simply causing 'grave agitations in the masses, who had not been prepared for the great democratic system which one wanted to bring to the country' (Madiou 1988, 7: 110).

More radical thinkers, however, saw immediate participation in direct democracy as the best route to civic education; claims that the people were not ready simply served to legitimate mulatto domination. Despite the claims of the elite to represent the interests of the black majority, tensions of class and colour were undermining the republican dream of *liberté, égalité* and *fraternité* for black and brown alike. As the American observer Jonathan Brown wrote in 1837, the 'prejudice of color existing among the mulattoes in relation to their fellow-citizens, the blacks, is almost as great as that once entertained by the whites of the colony against the class of mulattoes' (Brown [1837] 1972: 283). Schoelcher was critical of mulatto rule and accused Haitian intellectuals of falisfying history by claiming *noir* and *mulâtre* interests were one and the same. He wrote in 1842, 'The aristocracy of the light skin raises itself on the debris of that of the white skin.... Some young people of color, good and sincere, have avowed to us that in conscience they believe themselves functionally and organically superior to the negroes' (Schoelcher 1843: 236–37). He prophetically warned of revolution if light-skinned *jaunes* did not hand over the reins of power to a black man: 'So long as the normal government of Haiti, a government of the majority, that is to say a black government, is not established, the republic will live a precarious existence, false, miserable, and secretly inquiet. Let a negro appear and all changes direction' (Schoelcher 1843: 241).

In addition to education, freedom of religion would also be a key component of civil rights in all post-slavery societies. Religious autonomy is a major component of peasant civil agency, for through religious institutions, ex-slaves also rebuilt community life and created new modes of civil participation. Yet, even in Haiti, despite its revolution and the powerful political symbolism of the rebel slave, the African religion of Vodou was not tolerated (except during the regime of Emperor Soulouque).[18] Unlike the 'enlightened' Masonic Order, Vodou was persecuted by successive Haitian governments because of its symbolic associations with African 'primitivism', as defined by Europeans. Despite religious tolerance in the early constitutions of Haiti, Vodou was outlawed and forced into hiding. The persecution of *houngans* may in fact have been one of the causes of dissent among the rural black population, although after years of French persecution, they were quite adept at secret worship.

Nevertheless, popular political culture grew from community institutional bases with their own participatory styles. Just as the Masonic Order was an important semi-public locale for the emergence of elite citizenship after slavery, in rural areas, Vodou temples played a similar role in building local institutions for popular participation and community-building. The extended spiritual 'families' of those who 'serve the *lwas*', organized around the *démembre* (the extended family), the *hounfort* (the temple), and in some cases even comprising more extensive *compagnies* (or religious fraternities), became the backbone of peasant associational networks (Hurbon 1995; Hurston 1990; Laguerre 1989; Métraux 1960, 1972). As Serge Larose observes, in the Haitian countryside, 'ritual has not only a psychological function among the deprived, it is also the cultural material through which social relations of production are expressed; it relates to the control by the family of the main economic resource, land' (Larose 1975: 511). Thus, it provided a fabric of local ties and significant relationships that had an overlay of spiritual, familial, economic, recreational and political meanings.

Although the practice of Vodou involved some public elements such as family gatherings, public processions, crossroads ceremonies and pilgrimages, it was largely a religion of secrecy and hidden ritual because of years of persecution (Smucker 1984; Hurbon 1995). One of the few forms of popular collective presence in public space was during religious rituals. Catholic religious ceremonies were one of the main occasions for public rituals, but would have had underlying African-rooted meanings. Protestant missionaries lamented the 'superstitions' of the Catholic population, including the priests, but were particularly troubled by rituals surrounding death, including nine nights of prayer for the dead, with the body laid out in the house, surrounded by laughing, merry visitors.[19] They also noted an event following All Saints Day, known as *Service des Morts*, in which the priest went to the cemetery and sang a libera on the tombs of those whose relatives paid him a dollar. The mass for the dead was in fact closely tied to the practice of Vodou, in which 'death is an event that strikes foremost at the social fabric, that is, the family and community, rather than the deceased individual' (Hurbon

1995: 86). Public Catholic rituals would certainly have been preceded and followed by communal rituals of African origin that had been practised from the days of slavery onward.

There were still other more open forms of popular association, some of which may have had links to particular cult centres. One of the most visible forms of popular association in nineteenth-century Haiti were the 'compagnies' which took part in the annual Carnival; these played more than a festive role for they also embodied symbols of African ethnicity and leadership. As described by Schoelcher, the *compagnies* seem to have first been organized along lines of African ethnicity, and to have kept alive musical and costume traditions from Africa:

> Many of the members of these companies had a rather original costume, entirely composed of eighty to a hundred pieces of madras attached by a point and covering the body, the arms and the legs. Each company has its name, its flag and a king. This king wears a feathered turban as a crown and he is dressed in a rich costume over which is thrown a cloak of satin embroidered all over with gold and silver sequins. It seems that the dance and the group alike are souvenirs of Africa. Most of the companies are even composed of Negroes descending exclusively from such and such nation of Africa and they are proud of having nothing but pure African blood in their veins, without any mixture! (Schoelcher 1843: 299).

What Schoelcher saw as a quaint peasant reunion, however, was tied to deeper structures of peasant association, economic cooperation and political mobilization, structures whose African ethnic-overtones were indicative of a challenge to the Europeanized dominant order. The survival of these companies into the twentieth century enables us to use (cautiously) ethnographic evidence to reconstruct some of their other functions.

Twentieth-century research has shown that carnival *compagnies* were closely tied to other local forms of association and community organization. In his study of Haitian peasant life, the American anthropologist Harold Courlander refers to forms of cooperative labour, known in Haiti as 'coumbites'. These were invitational rounds of shared labour in which the 'rappels' of the drums were central to setting the work pace and serving as the 'newspapers of the people' (Courlander 1960: 116; cf. Herskovitz [1937] 1971). But, there also existed 'a more tightly knit form of coumbite, known as a *société*'. There are close parallels between the Rara bands of the *sociétés* and the *compagnies* described by Schoelcher:

These sociétés are clubs built around mutual work needs and
recreational activities. The Société Congo that appears in the
towns or city streets during Rara days with bamboo or conch-
shell trumpets, drums, flags, and masks, is usually composed of
the men who have joined forces to till the fields. In some
instances, it may also conform roughly to membership in a particular hounfor, or cult center. Unlike the ordinary coumbite,
the société is not a group which meets only at ground-breaking
or harvesting time; it is a permanent organization with regular,
sometimes day-to-day obligations. Week after week it moves
from one man's land to another, doing the tasks that have to be
done.... Coumbites are held not only for agricultural work, but
for housebuilding, and sometimes for the building of a hounfor
(Courlander 1960: 118).

These clubs in effect combined labour cooperatives, religious congregations and social welfare organizations or friendly societies.
Courlander also notes that women formed their own *coumbites* for
tasks such as winnowing, coffee sorting, and weeding. It seems probable that the organized 'compagnies' described by Schoelcher served
these multiple functions as well. The musical instruments such as
drums and the *lambi*, or conch-shell trumpet, were also important com-
municational media in rural areas, where they were (and still are) used
to call meetings, gather *coumbites* and sometimes to send messages.

Other ethnographers have argued that 'numerous institutions
facilitate social cohesion by establishing periodic contacts between the
peasants', including the *coumbite* (Romain 1974: 63). Not only are
neighbours invited to work one family's land together, but a 'president'
and (female) 'presidente' are selected, an orchestra is formed under the
direction of a 'reine-chanterelle', day-care is organized for children,
women prepare and cook food for the entire group and the *houngan* is
called on to keep away the rain. As Jacques Romain points out, this
system 'originally put in place by private and familial intitiative, has
since a certain period evolved towards the form of constituted societies,
such as the Société Souvenance, Société Congo, and Société Real'.
There may even be delegates exchanged between societies, and in some
cases regional confederations. 'The rules of these societies', most
importantly, 'adapted to local particularities, are the object of a plenary
assembly vote. Each member reserved the right to submit and discuss
his point of view, which a majority can freely adopt or reject' (Romain
1974: 65–6). Although these are modern descriptions, the forms of such
societies certainly date back to the nineteenth century, and indicate a
kind of participatory democracy practised at the local level among the
peasantry, with the potential for articulation with the national level.

Elite Haitians who had been educated in France and been exposed to French socialist debates about worker associationalism may well have seen parallels in the African associational practices of the Haitian peasantry. In parallel fashion to the synergies that propelled the Saint Domingue Revolution, the radicalism of European democratic ideologies such as socialism and Chartism in the 1830s and 1840s would take on new resonance in the plantation societies of the Americas. Bourgeois democratic ideologies converged not so much with the artisanal socialism of shoemakers, coopers and printers, as in Europe, but with the African-rooted associationalism of post-slavery reconstituted peasantries. In the next chapter, we will see how these indigenous ideologies sprang forth from the fertile Haitian soil, and took on their own revolutionary aspect.

Notes

1 Reconstituted peasants are slaves, indentees, maroons and other runaways who became peasants 'directly as a mode of resistance and response to the plantation system and its imposed patterns of life'; thus, their very existence attests to both agency and autonomy (David Watts, *The West Indies: Patterns of Development, Culture and Environmental Change Since 1492* [Cambridge: Cambridge University Press, 1990], p. 506).

2 The lakou (from French, *la cour*) is 'a group of interrelated conjugal families, each occupying its own dwelling-unit, and sharing a common yard' (Serge Larose, 'The Haitian Lakou: land, family, ritual', in *Family and Kinship in Middle America and the Caribbean*, ed. Arnaud Marks and Rene Romer [Curacao: University of Netherlands Antilles, 1975], p. 482). This household unit is traditionally patriarchal, and may be polygynous. The family itself is a 'cognatic descent group occupying or originating from a clearly defined piece of land', not an ego-oriented set of relatives.

3 For insight into the Kingdom of Haiti, see King Henry's correspondence with the British abolitionist Thomas Clarkson, in *Henry Christophe and Thomas Clarkson, A Correspondence*, ed. Earl Griggs and Clifford Prator (N.Y.: Greenwood, 1968).

4 One *carreaux* equals 1.29 hectares, or 3.33 U.S. acres (Mintz, 'Employment of Capital by Market Women', p. 257). Although the total distribution of land is difficult to estimate, one Haitian scholar wrote in 1888 that 76,000 *carreaux* had been distributed among 2322 civil and military officers, while approximately 6000 common soldiers recieved grants of 5 *carreaux* each from 1809 to 1825 (Robert K. Lacerte, 'The First Land Reform in Latin America: The Reforms of Alexander Pétion, 1809–1814', in *Inter-American Economic Affairs* [1975], 28: 4: 77–85).

5 Larose, 'The Haitian Lakou', pp. 40, 44.

6 'Loi concernant la police des habitations, les obligations réciproques des propriétaires et fermiers, et des cultivateurs,' 20 avril 1807, an IV, Art. 2, in Linstant, *Réceuil général des Lois*, 1851, Vol. 1, pp. 307–15.

7 AN CC9a.54, *Code Rural d'Haiti*, 1826.

8 Ibid.

9 FO 35/1, General Correspondence, Memorandum of Information from James Franklin re Haiti, enclosed in Wilmot Horton to Lord Canning, 14 Oct. 1826.

10   The Spanish colony of Santo Domingo was ceded to France in the Treaty of Basel of 1795, and on that basis was claimed by Toussaint L'Ouverture, but not controlled. Boyer also faced an uprising in Grande Anse in 1819, led by Goman, but managed to put it down; nevertheless, this remote south-western region remained difficult to control from Port-au-Prince.

11   The red 'Phrygian bonnet' was the 'headgear traditionally worn by emancipated slaves in classical Rome', and adopted by the French Jacobins during the revolution; thus, it had a double significance in Haiti and other French colonies, where it meant both liberty for the republic and liberty for the slave (Richard D. E. Burton, '"Maman-France Doudou": Family Images in French West Indian Colonial Discourse', in *Diacritics* [1993] 23: 3: 71).

12   The French Consul cites sources giving these figures for men under arms, in a population of half a million in the 1830s (plus 200,000 Dominicans), of which three fifths were thought to be women (a gender ratio probably due to high male mortality during the years of revolutionary and civil war, higher male infant mortality, and longer female life expectancy) (Gustave d'Alaux [Maxime Reybaud], 'La République dominicaine et l'empereur Soulouque', detached from *Révue des deux mondes* [15 Apr.; 1 May 1851], p. 195).

13   WMMS, Special Series, Biographical, West Indies. Box 588, Autobiography of James Hartwell, 1817–1902, pp. 40, 133.

14   Hartwell, for example, describes the celebration of the Fête Dieu (or Corpus Christi) as a combined ecclesiastic, military and civil event (ibid, p. 72).

15   Ibid.

16   *Le Temps*, no. 1, 10 Feb. 1842, cited in Jean Desquiron, *Haïti à la Une: Une anthologie de la presse haïtienne de 1724 à 1934*, (Port-au-Prince, 1993), Vol. 1, pp. 191–92 (my translation). On colonial discourses of 'legitimate rulers' and 'childlike subjects', see also Chandra T. Mohanty, 'Cartographies of Struggle' in *Third World Women and the Politics of Feminism*, ed. C. Mohanty, A. Russo, and L. Torres (Bloomington: Indiana UP, 1991), p. 17.

17   *Le Patriote*, Vol. 1, no. 1, 2 Mar. 1842, cited in Desquiron, *Haïti à la Une*, p. 199.

18   Edward Bean Underhill, who visited Haiti in 1860, reported that 'the people are professedly Roman Catholics; but there are mixed with the rights of Catholicism many practices derived from the native superstitions of Africa. Obeahism, Mialism, and snake-worship [sic] are much followed by the ignorant and superstitious people of the plains and mountains. During the reign of the Emperor Soulouque, the Vaudoux, as these people are called, were much encouraged. The palace of the black monarch may be said to have been the centre of these degrading rights, the Emperor and empress themselves being reputed to have held the position of chief priest and priestess among their Vaudoux subjects'. (BMS, *The Baptist Magazine*, Vol. 52, [London: J. Heaton & Son, 1860], enclosing 'Report on the Mission in Haiti' by E. B. Underhill, p. 801).

19   WMMS, West Indies Correspondence, Haiti, Box 206.

5 The army of sufferers: from Liberal Revolution to Piquet Rebellion

The Liberal Revolution of 1843, which overthrew President Jean-Pierre Boyer's faltering regime, was a crucial moment of potential democratization, yet it ultimately failed to consolidate a democratic government. The transition instead led to black protest and peasant rebellion in the south, military coups in the north, and the break-away of the Dominican Republic in the east, reclaiming nearly two-thirds of Haiti's territory.[1] During the revolutionary situation of 1843–44, a popular movement emerged calling for black civil and political rights. They called themselves the 'Army of Sufferers' and were later known as the Piquets because of the sharpened pikes they carried as weapons. The events of this period have often been portrayed as a struggle between black and mulatto factions, which to some extent they were; however, I will argue that this interpretation overlooks additional political issues that were at stake, including a crucial contest between military and civil power. Although there is meagre primary evidence on the Piquet Movement (and no single secondary study of the rebellion), my theoretical framework throws new light on the organizational forms and claim-making strategies of the Piquets.[2]

My argument is that the post-independence political development of Haiti is neither wholly anomalous nor reducible to Latin American *caudillismo*, but forms part of a wider pattern of anti-democratic reaction to slave emancipation that occurred in many post-slavery states of the Americas. The original anti-slavery, anti-colonial and egalitarian premises of the Haitian Revolution did not simply die out, but were crushed. Yet, peasant democratic republicanism lived on in a popular vision of liberty, fraternity and equality, expressed through the Piquet Rebellion and other instances of popular mobilization in defense of the civil, political and social rights of democratic citizenship. The popular vision of democratization expressed during the revolutionary situation of 1843–44 built on the Haitian peasantry's struggle for economic, political and civil agency. It was precisely the threat of this powerful

111

discourse — and the collective action it elicited — that led the liberal faction of the elite to retreat back into their pact with the agrarian-military planters (as Paige's analysis suggests). In spite of their democratic rhetoric, liberals were not prepared for real democracy, especially if accompanied by radical calls for land redistribution and political enfranchisement.

The chapter begins with the growth of civil society in Haiti and the emergence of ideological and institutional contexts for an elite-popular democratic alliance in opposition to Boyer. It then focuses on three phases of the revolutionary situation of 1843–44, mainly played out in the southern department (especially around the major coffee-export region of Aux Cayes). First, there was the Liberal Revolution itself, which ousted Boyer and led to a moment of democratic effervescence, with many possible outcomes. Then, a revolution occurred within the revolution, when a locally influential black landholding family mobilized the smaller landholders and coffee growers of the Aux Cayes region to challenge the racial inequality of the liberal elite and its continuing 'aristocracy of the skin'. Finally, in the third phase, a charismatic peasant leader named Acaau emerged in a religious-political movement in which armed peasants and cultivators seized the initiative, and demanded economic reform, land reform and the protection of their constitutional rights as Haitian citizens.

The press, public opinion and opposition to Boyer

With few channels of communication between citizens and the state, with a stifled press and a tight knit elite, political life in Boyer's Haiti was extremely circumscribed. Despite having an elected Chamber of Deputies, power was concentrated in the hands of the executive. Throughout the 1830s, however, Boyer's leadership was contested by an increasingly vocal group of young men who published their own literary journals and newspapers, advocated social and political reform and depicted themselves as champions of the black majority. Madiou describes in glowing terms the emergence of a new, youthful civil society among the educated elite of the 1830s, among whom he himself could be counted:

> In general, the youth were avid to acquire knowledge; they formed little literary circles where those who felt themselves carried by their natural faculties toward the study of history, economics, or poetry, communicated their productions amongst themselves. Many members of the bar were truly

eminent men. For the first time, journals were created uniquely for the purpose of public utility. A society began to form itself and every family felt well-off from all the work created following the long peace (Madiou 1988, 7: 169).

He went on to describe the frequent balls, cavalcades and 'barbacos' enjoyed by the youth of the capital city. As this younger generation, born after the revolution and well educated, began to exercise their political influence, they found Haiti's supposedly republican institutions were not all they were held up to be. New stories were framed about what it meant to be a Haitian, what it meant to be 'noir', and what it meant to be a citizen.

Most significantly, the whole issue of publicity and the formation and expression of public opinion under a republican form of government became central issues of debate. Young men like Emile Nau, David St. Preux and Dumai Lespinasse began to openly criticize the government. They published newspapers, and ran for public office, pressing for reform. This opposition 'centred in the lower house of the legislature', observes Nicholls, 'regarded itself as liberal and nationalist, arguing for a greater liberty of speech within the country, for increased protection for local industry, and for the development of a truly national culture' (Nicholls 1996: 74). Newspapers were central weapons in this struggle to shape a more liberal political culture, and within them a war was waged over the limits of freedom of speech and the power of public opinion. As one paper observed, quoting Tocqueville, 'there is nothing except a newspaper which can come to deposit the same thought in a thousand minds at the same moment.... Newspapers thus become more necessary to the extent that men are more equal....There is no democratic association that can make do without a newspaper'.[3] First, I will consider the emergence of this oppositional public and Boyer's attempts to suppress it.

The first significant struggle over publicity began with the 'Darfour affair' of 1822, when a controversial newspaper editor, Felix Darfour, tried to present a petition to the Chambre des Communes; the government's authoritarian response set the tone for subsequent battles over civil liberties. Darfour first caught public attention with a newspaper debate over the concept of an African identity for Haiti in 1818. In *L'Eclaireur Haytien ou le Parfait Patriote*, he proclaimed that 'prejudice against the black race was founded on nothing but politics', in so far as Europeans justified the slave trade by 'pretending that these men were of an inferior nature to their own'.[4] He challenged pseudo-scientific racism including measurement of skulls and facial angles, and supported the intellectual ability of both 'noirs' and 'hommes de couleur'; he went so far as to add the title 'Africain' after his name on the masthead of three issues of his paper. His rival in political debate, J. S. Milscent, editor of *L'Abeille Haytienne*, challenged Darfour's assertion of race, arguing instead:

> For a long time I have forgotten that my colour is somber; it suffices me to sense that I can put my ideas in order and combat the quibbles of our detractors; it does not seem fitting to me to adopt a denomination which recalls the difference of my skin. I am a Citizen of Haiti.[5]

He criticized the adoption of the title 'African' by Darfour, the 'Perfect Patriot', asking whether this is because 'there are but a couple of months since he saw Hayti for the first time, or is he waiting for the year and day for writing in Haytian?' (i.e. in Creole). Darfour accepted this point, and dropped the title African, but was now identified as someone who stirred up black unrest against the government.

According to Schoelcher, Darfour (who was born in Africa but raised in Europe) wanted 'to try to awaken his brothers; he wrote, he published newspapers and pamphlets; he agitated and moved their spirits and finished by exposing, in a fiery petition addressed to the Chamber of Deputies, the grievances which the *noirs* had against the government of the *jaunes*' (Schoelcher 1843: 182). The petition was read in a public session and 'the citizens were numerous in the room where the public was admitted' (Ardouin 1860, 9: 182). It was considered so seditious by Boyer and his supporters that Darfour was arrested along with several senators who had backed the public reading of the petition, as well as other opposition members including a judge, the director of the national primary school, and a government notary. Darfour, who opposed European access to Haiti's interior and ports, was accused of spreading the idea that Boyer had 'sold the country to the whites' and of stirring 'civil discord'. In September 1822, he was condemned to death and executed. Several other senators were expelled from the Chamber. Ardouin considered these actions to be the origin of the political revolution against Boyer. By violently and unconstitutionally repressing opposition voices, the President had lost the support of 'public opinion', and 'opinion is the queen of the world' (Ardouin 1860, 9: 200).

Opposition to Boyer continued to build, especially after the July Revolution in France (1830) overturned the Bourbons with whom Boyer had concluded the controversial indemnity deal of 1825. Ardouin explains that the opposition consisted of old enemies of Boyer, enemies dating from his expulsion of the deputies in 1822 (following the Darfour affair), those against the 1825 treaty with France, black immigrants fired with radical anti-white ideas and young men who had come up through the Lycée National. Newspapers played a central role in this movement:

> If the Opposition manifested itself above all in civil society, in conversation, it also found in the capital a kind of organ in a weekly journal founded in 1825, by Mr. J. Courtois, printer, under the title of *Feuille du Commerce*; and this editor was himself one of the opposition, to judge from his turn of mind and by the articles which were published there of his vintage (Ardouin 1860, 10: 108).

A rival paper, *Le Phare*, was founded in 1830 by the son of Boyer's right-hand man, General Inginac. When the young Inginac, who was also married to Boyer's neice, killed a prominent Liberal (a professor at the Lycée) in a duel, the funeral procession became a political demonstration. As they passed the national palace, young men shouted 'Long live independence! Long live freedom of the press! Long live the constitution! Down with despotism, tyranny and tyrants!' (Ardouin 1860, 10: 115). Boyer soon declared the opposition seditious, and in 1831, several men were given prison sentences for articles they published in the *Feuille du Commerce*. Eventually, its editor was imprisoned and the paper 'suppressed'.

The 1832 elections returned a new urban professional class to the Assembly, including lawyers and notaries, surveyors, and civil servants. This Chamber attempted to widen its powers by opening up dialogue with the Executive through presentation of 'addresses' and 'responses' to the executive, which in effect became a forum for political debate by opening up public discussions over government policy. The first Address, probably written by Hérard Dumesle, called for advances in commerce; improvements in science; investments in the arts; provision of public education; and reform of the electoral process and judicial system. Ardouin complained that, 'effectively, public opinion, excited, worked up in all directions by the Opposition, especially since the 1830 revolution in France, felt a vague desire for change, for modification of all things' (Ardouin 1860, 10: 168). When Boyer made proposals for new regulations of elections (giving him power to name lists of candidates for the Senate), he was 'violently' challenged by David Saint-Preux, who was backed by 'the public composed of ardent youth' (Madiou 1988, 7: 299). A committee of the Chamber published its own electoral reform plan in the *Feuille du Commerce,* and composed a collective response to the executive. It was imputed, according to Ardouin, that Saint-Preux had challenged Boyer's plan on the basis that it 'favoured the mulattoes more than the noirs' by tending 'to exclude these latter from the communal assemblies, particularly those in rural areas' (Ardouin 1860, 10: 170n1).

Also at issue in the Chamber was whether it would be open to the public, or sit behind closed doors. The Opposition favoured public debate; as Ardouin notes, 'since 1832 a young public above all had shown itself assiduous at the sessions' (Ardouin 1860, 10: 193). Boyer's supporters fought back by trying to exclude public defenders from holding seats in the Chamber, and finally they simply expelled the most radical members, Dumesle and Saint-Preux, for 'provoking a dissolution of the body politic' through 'corruption of the public mind' (Ardouin 1860, 10: 209). The two submitted a 'protestation' setting forth their position and defending the call for reform and amelioration. Copies of the protest — which called for electoral reform, military reform, better national budgets, public education, support of agriculture and judicial reform — were sent to European 'friends of the negro' like Lord Brougham, Daniel O'Connell and Isambert. It became a rallying point for the progressives, to Ardouin's dismay: 'this protest became the political statement (*le programme*) which he issued to the public, to all spirits ardent or calm who sicerely desired progress, the advancement of Haiti down a civilizing path' (Ardouin 1860, 10: 222).

Despite their expulsion from the Chamber, Dumesle and St. Preux were again returned in the elections of 1838 and even led a majority. The Opposition platform was renewed with a vigorous call for the 'public good' as the moral basis of government. They called for a 'revision of the social pact', declaring, 'May this franchise be appreciated! May it carry you to give to the Chamber that *power of opinion* without which a national representation is nothing but a fiction' (Ardouin 1860, 11: 16 [emphasis in original].) When debates were held in the new Assembly over where 'the power of opinion' lay, the speeches were printed in *l'Union*, a paper edited by 'Emile Nau and other young men of his age' (Ardouin 1860, 11: 39). A 'crowd of citizens, of young men above all, occupied the part of the meeting room reserved for the public' (Ardouin 1860, 11: 61).[6] An attempted assassination of General Inginac in 1838 led to a wave of repression; a wider plot against the government was supposedly discovered, and seventy-five arrests were made and five leaders were executed.[7]

In October 1839, the conflict between the executive and the opposition in the Chamber came to a head. Dumesle, by this time having 'become in some sense a personal enemy of M. Boyer, came to be nominated the president of the Chamber; it was nearly a declaration of war' (Schoelcher 1843: 307). When a garrison in St. Marc revolted, Boyer took the opportunity to crack down on political opposition in what one British observer described as a state of siege. Boyer suppressed the opposition by

> constituting five persons an illegal mob, ordering all persons found discussing politics of the day to be imprisoned, making several arrests, dismissing certain publick employees and threatening others,...placing sentries at the doors of [the Chamber] to prevent the ingress of the members supporting the 'Union' newspaper for having presumed to publish the substance of speeches delivered in the Chamber, and depriving an unhappy Schoolmaster of his licence on suspicion that he had composed some of the said orations.[8]

The dismissed employees included Emile Nau and David Troy, director of the national primary school. 'These two dismissals', according to Ardouin, 'and others which followed them, achieved making opponents of all the young men of the land, with few exceptions' (Ardouin 1860, 11: 96n1). Boyer then formed a 'rump' Chamber of his supporters, who again expelled Dumesle, St. Preux and others, accusing them of plotting to overthrow the government.

Despite these efforts, though, the opposition continued to mobilize. One of the aims of the liberal reform movement was to mobilize the electorate and challenge the 1841 electoral law which had moved the voting age from twenty-one to twenty-five years old, even though the Constitution made the former the 'age of civil majority' for taxation and military service.[9] Like Ardouin, Schoelcher also attributed the resurgence of liberalism in late 1842 to two new opposition newspapers:

> Liberal ideas have made notable progress there, and the vague inquietude that agitated every spirit is beginning to formulate itself, to take shape. The honour for this happy change must be due in great part to a newspaper, the *Manifeste*, which, though only a weekly and able only by great effort to penetrate the interior, has lifted the public spirit during the past year with the firm, courageous, energetically democratic allures of its principal editor, Mr. Dumai Lespinasse, well assisted by Mr. Hertelou (Schoelcher 1843: 323).

Lespinasse, a public defender, was thirty years old in early 1842 when he was elected to represent Port-au-Prince in the Assembly. By 1842, the opposition was increasingly bold and Lespinasse encouraged other young men who supported the opposition to challenge the electoral registers prepared by the local *Conseils des Communes*, and to present themselves as voters at the elections. 'All those of their age felt themselves called upon to rejuvenate, so to speak, "the national representation" in the Chambre de Communes' (Schoelcher 1842: 161–62).

Haiti's opposition newspapers laid the foundations for a bridge between elite liberals and rural smallholders by publicly articulating the political arguments, social means and moral justifications for such an alliance. One way of doing this was through promoting a nationalist consciousness based on anti-colonial protectionism, which suited both local merchants and peasants growing small export crops. The first plank of this platform was the exclusion of whites from property ownership. An 1841 article in *Le Manifeste* defended the constitutional prohibition of foreign proprietors on the grounds that, 'in uprooting the colonial regime and all its attendant evils, it constituted our nationality,' since

> the participation of foreigners in the right of property would be fatal to our political existence. From the day, in effect, when foreigners become proprietors, being capitalists, they will promptly reunite all the big properties in their own hands, by absorbing the small properties; they will be the masters and we the workers — they the exploiters and we the exploited.[10]

Exclusion of whites from the rights of citizenship contributed to a cross-class and cross-colour construction of Haitian national identity, based on protecting the country against renewed foreign domination, whether military or economic.

The young anti-Boyerists also felt it was their civic duty to bring progress to all of Haiti's people, and saw themselves as representing the interests of the black majority; the British Consul Ussher referred to them as 'the democratic party'. In 1842, another opposition newspaper, *Le Patriote,* carried a series of articles on 'Droit Public' that were a sort of primer on political rights. The author explained the democratic system of separate legislature, judiciary and executive as 'the three great wheels which regulate the existence of the social body and for which the motor is the people'. The same piece called for public education, public libraries and savings banks for workers.[11] Schoelcher credited the *Manifeste*, along with the somewhat more moderate *Patriote*, with bringing political education to the citizens of Haiti, a project also being furthered by the establishment of primary schools. 'Already Gonaives, Jeremie, Croix-des-Bouquets, and Petit Goave', he happily wrote, 'have free schools, opened and run by devoted citizens' (Schoelcher 1843: 332). He was very optimistic that schools were being formed and progressive ideas were being discussed in newspapers throughout the country.

Another key tenet of the opposition was the idea of association or cooperation as a basis for the reorganization of labour. An article in the *Patriote* in 1842 cited Saint-Simon, Owen and Fourier, in making its argument that true democracy requires the distribution of land to all, and the pooling of labour, capital and revenue:

> Association, there is the key to the organization of labour…the social programme of the modern republic is association in industry and election in politics…. [W]e do not conceive of democracy without the division of lands; we admit to promoting universal suffrage and the greatest distribution of property… little properties can group themselves around a central common where the buildings and factories necessary for the exploitation of the group's crops can be raised at common expense.[12]

Many of Boyer's opponents had travelled among radical circles in France and Britain, and were familiar with contemporary European debates regarding the working class and social reform. The *Manifeste* sang the praises of a free press (citing Tocqueville), and published articles on the merits of 'association'.

On the eve of the Liberal Revolution, an article entitled 'On the Emancipation of Labour' argued that inequality existed because of the injustice of wealth, the inaccessibility of education and lack of commercial credit for workers:

> Association is thus an indispensable condition of any system of credit that does not repose uniquely on ownership…. [It] is the only way to combat the aristocracy of finance, which tends incessantly to absorb small capitals. It is the only way to arrive not at an equality of wealth, which is impossible, but at a certain equilibrium that prevents those who have more from oppressing those who have less…. [It] protects liberty in the industrial order, just as in the civil and political order.[13]

The emancipation of labour, the author continued, will require equal laws for all, free and equal education, and 'that capital or the instruments of production become directly accessible to [the workers]'. This appears to be the last issue published prior to the revolution, and it indicates the more radical wing of the intelligentsia.

The progressive elite was also engaged in forging links between its efforts at reform and what was perceived as popular consciousness and aspirations. One young mulatto sugar planter and processor James Blackhurst (probably an American or West Indian immigrant) practised his radical politics by living among his workers 'fraternally' and holding meetings with them in a 'regime of association'. 'Mr. Blackhurst does not forget that he is a citizen', wrote Schoelcher, 'he dreams of a noble regeneration for his country, and is already known as a member of the most extreme opposition.... [O]nce a week he assembles the most intelligent men of his workshop (*atelier*), and gives them a lecture (*conference*) which reacts on the others' (Schoelcher 1843: 269). This political practice exemplified the aim of the young radical opposition to try to build alliances with the black working class. It was at this anti-authoritarian intersection of educated liberalism and popular association that democracy in Haiti became a possibility.

The Liberal Revolution

The mobilized opposition swept the elections of 1842, but Boyer garrisoned twelve armed regiments in the capital. When the deputies tried to meet, 'he stationed at the door of the House a guard of 180 men with strict orders to admit those men only who were declared supporters of the Government. The remainder, about 30 in number, were, on presenting themselves for admission, rudely repulsed by the guard and compelled to retire'.[14] Those excluded in 1839, along with their supporters, were not allowed to take their seats. Altogether almost one third of the deputies, including most for the capital, all from Santo Domingo, and most of the representatives of the south were forced out.[15] These events were being closely followed in Jamaica; the *Morning Journal* published Boyer's Proclamation of March 28, 1842:

> Haytiens!...The electoral assemblages became in some districts the centre of new machinations — the promoters of dissent confederated together. By dint of intrigue — by dint of audacity, they checked the freedom of the election, and our good citizens saw with alarm the return of these men whom the Fifth Legislature had expelled in 1839.... Citizens! Be calm and peaceful — repel the perfidious suggestions of those who would lead you astray.[16]

At this very moment, however, the country was also entering a major financial crisis, brought on in part by Boyer's desperate attempts to buy the army's loyalty.

In early 1842, it became apparent that Haitian paper money (liberally printed by the government treasury whenever needed) was depreciating so rapidly that the whole monetary system would have to be overhauled and all the money pulled out of circulation and replaced with hard currency. Although import duties were collected in Spanish currency, this was ear-marked for debt repayments to France; army and civil officers were paid in Haitian dollars, originally pegged to the Spanish dollar, but now worth less and less. One scheme was to redeem the paper money in exchange partly for Spanish dollars and partly for Treasury bonds; the Government rejected, this, though, because it would have involved a temporary suspension of payments to the army. As the British Consul Ussher noted, 'Discontent and perhaps disaffection might arise, and as the present Government depends almost entirely on the support of the army, they could ill afford to paralyze such an arm of strength; the more particularly, as it is on the eve of meeting the most decidedly hostile Chamber of Representatives that have ever sat in Haiti'.[17] To make matters worse, it was revealed that some of the government were speculating on the depreciation of its own notes, while others, entrusted with destroying old notes, had secretly reissued them. The country was not only awash in worthless paper money, but public trust was by now completely destroyed.[18]

Revolution was near at hand. 'There is', as the historian Ardouin put it, 'for every government which is attacked by public opinion, a solemn moment which it must know how to seize in order to bring opinion back to itself; if it lets this occasion escape, it is lost. Unhappily for the country, such would be the destiny of that of Boyer' (Ardouin 1860, 11: 218). The missionary Bird also observed that the formation of true and open public opinion had been suppressed in Haiti, but its invisible working could not be entirely suppressed. 'The leading idea of a true Republic', he argued, 'is that the people govern'; however,

> in Hayti the leading idea, up to the present time, has been
> that the executive governs. Under really Republican institu-
> tions, the people discuss political questions, both privately
> and publicly, as being their own special interest and concern,
> relating quite as much to them, and even more, than to the
> executive; but in Hayti, for more than 60 years, it has been
> supposed that conversations on political questions or open
> discussions, would be dangerous, and therefore are not
> tolerated (Bird 1869: 423).

Following Boyer's crackdown on the elected representatives of the people, the liberal opposition formed the secret Society for the Rights of Man and the Citizen, which in September 1842 signed a call to arms and catalogue of grievances that came to be known as the Manifeste de Praslin. Madiou describes how this revolutionary manifesto was secretly circulated among the opposition in Aux Cayes, Port-au-Prince,

Jérémie and other towns. Small groups communicated among themselves, swore adherence and formed secret revolutionary societies.

The revolutionaries were also aware that they had to mobilize the
peasant farmers to their cause, so they brought their project directly to
the people by holding meetings in rural districts. According to
Ardouin, the revolutionaries elaborated their ideas in conjunction with
small farmers in 'patriotic banquets':

> The opposition contrived meetings, which they made in the
> country on the habitations of the small proprietors, to better
> indoctrinate them. With speeches, with toasts, they excited
> the desires of these peaceful citizens in favour of the new
> order of things which they hoped to found, by promising
> them above all a more advantageous sale of their produce,
> and the purchase of foreign goods at a price below their
> actual value (Ardouin 1860, 11: 235–36).

Madiou wrote less negatively that the opposition, especially in the
south, tried to make their doctrines known in the countryside by
holding reunions 'on diverse habitations in the principle centres of
population, there giving banquets attended by the principal cultivators;
they put before their eyes the perspective of a better future: the education of their children, better prices for their crops, abundance' (Madiou
1988, 7: 421). Small coffee-growers and regional exporters seem to
have been united in this movement. The diplomat Ussher received a
letter from Jérémie indicating that small landholders and cultivators
had been convinced to support the opposition. 'The Country people
are, it appears, highly dissatisfied at the low price of Coffee and having
been led to believe that it proceeds from the mismanagement
of the Government, they have taken side, I am told, with the
Opposition'.[19] The movement also took advantage of a fire that swept
through the mercantile district of Port-au-Prince on the 9th of January,
1843, to gather urban supporters by publicly accusing the government
of failing to provide public fountains with the water that might have
extinguished the flames (Madiou 1988, 7: 434).[20]

With popular support for Boyer at its lowest ebb ever, the secret
Society sent a message to Hérard, their chosen leader in Aux Cayes,
that the moment was opportune to take up arms. Word of the imminent
revolution was spread among their 'coréligionnaires politiques', as
Madiou calls them, and Hérard himself wrote to the 'Giron of Jérémie'
to ensure their support. It is significant that at this early stage in the
revolution, Hérard himself was fearful of a popular uprising; he recommended 'above all that no cultivators be introduced into the ranks of
the national guard, which must be composed only of proprietors, sons

of proprietors, farmers, and under-farmers, etc.'.[21] This fear of an uprising of the cultivators indicates the extent to which this was an elite, not a popular, movement, despite claims to the contrary. The revolutionary faction in Jérémie, in particular, feared a popular uprising; as Madiou observed, 'it is evident that they wanted to overturn the government, all the while maintaining the people in order and in agricultural labor…[saying in effect] stay calm, keep working, we will take care of your interests' (Madiou 1988, 7: 443). Nevertheless, what began as an elite movement had to mobilize rural supporters to succeed against Boyer's armed forces. This fragile alliance succeeded temporarily, but its underlying inequality was soon exposed in the face of a mobilized peasantry.

The revolutionaries gathered at Praslin, Hérard's property outside of Aux Cayes in January 1843. They contacted General Borgella, the regional army commander, to seek his support. He declined, and issued an order declaring Hérard a traitor. The men at Praslin set out toward Grand Anse, the mountainous south-western part of the country, knowing that Borgella would be sending troops after them. Allies in Jérémie were contacted and on the 31st of January, they formed a 'committee of the popular government' which issued its first circular dated '40th year of Independence and 1st year of the Regeneration'. Once again, though, elite fear of a black uprising was paramount; they advised their supporters 'to cooperate with the local authorities and the rural [police] officers on the necessary means for maintaining order, assuring public tranquility, and mobilizing the work of the countryside…. [E]ncourage the *habitants* to persevere in their labor…. [T]hey must have entire confidence in the efforts that we are making to ameliorate the people's condition' (Madiou 1988, 7: 443). Even Madiou recognized the hypocrisy of this fearful elite. Their efforts succeeded, however, as Hérard's 5000 insurgents marched into Jérémie and were 'welcomed openly by the leading citizens'.[22]

The locally-stationed 17th and 18th regiments joined the new popular government in Jérémie. On February 3rd, over three thousand men crowded the *place d'armes* to cheer as two generals were sworn in as members of the provisional government. An act was passed (and signed by over 300 men), stating the people's grievances against Boyer for 'lacerating the social pact, attacking the inviolability of the national deputies, and annihilating public and individual liberties' (Madiou 1988, 7: 445). They justified their actions in a letter to the Governor of Jamaica, whose support they sought. They had 'appealed to Arms', they wrote, 'to claim their rights which the Authorities had endeavored to violate by the intended arrestation of some distinguished citizens, for no other cause than the expression of liberal opinions'.[23] They claimed to have six thousand armed supporters and — after marching through the country — eventually reached Port-au-Prince with twelve thousand.

When government troops sent from the capital met the revolutionary army in the south, many soldiers refused to fight and whole regiments deserted *en masse* to the provisional government. The descriptions of this largely peaceful, yet revolutionary situation are quite remarkable. According to one British officer,

> all the Soldiers having refused to fire upon their countrymen and, when repeatedly urged to advance by their Commandant, they went over in a body, and recommended the General if he valued his life to make the best of his way back to Head Quarters; indeed, it appears that the Rebels act only upon the defensive and have not in any instance been the aggressors; they have no uniform and many go unarmed, the leaders only wearing a sash or girdle, and on the two parties meeting, the Deputies step out and harangue the Loyalists, and it would appear to some purpose, as desertion amongst the ranks of the latter to a considerable amount invariably follows. This extraordinary mode of revolutionizing a Country with scarcely any of the attendant scenes of Bloodshed, rapine, and violence (so common in such cases in European Civilized Countries), the ultimate success of which cannot be doubted, will present a case almost unparalleled in History and place the character of the Negro in a more exalted station in the scale of civilization than it had hitherto been deemed capable of attaining to.[24]

Other accounts of the revolution confirm this method of conversion of the troops and mass desertion. The 11th and 14th regiments 'went over to the patriots' without a shot fired, while the 4th lay down, pretending to be shot, until their general fled (Madiou 1988, 7: 468). Bird also reported that the soldiers refused to fight the insurgents. When shot upon, 'the national guard immediately shouted "Vive le Comité populaire!" and went over to them, followed by a considerable number of the government troops; the rest of the President's army fled and each one saved himself as he could'. Bird blamed Boyer's loss of popularity and the affection of his army on the fact that he had 'ruled more as an absolutist sovereign, than as simple President of a Republic', as the people wanted.[25] His colleague Hartwell wrote that the 'Haytien Revolution of 1843 is no ordinary movement of the kind, nor does the term revolution present the requisite idea to the mind; nearly bloodless and accompanied by no enormities, the revolution asks in behalf of the Son of the African his place in religious, intellectual, and civil society'.[26]

Thus, it was the resurgence of a black-identified democratic movement along with Boyer's loss of military loyalty that led to his downfall. The degree of popular support for his overthrow is reflected in the fact that women were central protagonists in several key events of 1843. In February, General Borgella, supreme commander of the armed forces in the south, issued an order that he would act against all people making seditious remarks, 'even against women who sought to induce the soldiers and the officers not to fulfil their duties. The women, in effect', commented Madiou, 'composed in Aux Cayes a powerful propaganda in favour of the revolution' (Madiou 1988, 7: 455). Women in Léogane, 'while singing, dragged from fort Ça-Ira into the town, two cannon of very high caliber, and placed them in a battery facing the plain of Dampuce'. Two shots from these weapons killed thirty of Boyer's men, probably one of the highest death tolls in a single event of the entire revolution (Madiou 1988, 7: 468). On the 12th of March, urban women played a pivotal role. Madiou reports that after the loss of the battle in Léogane, Boyer ordered a battalion of national guardsmen in the capital to join the battle on foot. 'The battalion began to march, but as soon as it arrived at Morne-à-Tuf, it was stopped by an innumerable multitude of women.... [Boyer] was assailed by a new disturbance of women, who followed him and cursed him, abusing him in the most scathing manner' (Madiou 1988, 7: 468). Bird reports that, 'some of the mothers of those who had been killed in the Leogane affair... assembled before the Palace, and besides bitterly reproaching the President, gave vent to their feelings of hatred to his Government, &c., &c.; this led him to desist, and probably conclude that all was lost' (Bird 1869: 226).[27]

After this 'manifestation', as Baudin calls it, Boyer 'lost hope', wrote a final act of abdication, and embarked on a British ship to Jamaica, refusing one offered by the French (Madiou 1988, 7: 468). Following his departure, mobs invaded the National Palace, breaking everything, tearing trees from the garden, defacing portraits of Boyer and his family, and most upsetting to Madiou, 'throwing the archives to the wind' (Madiou 1988, 7: 472). A week later, Hérard led the popular army on a triumphal march into Port-au-Prince, now renamed Port-Républicain. They were welcomed 'with delirious enthusiasm', wrote Madiou, with three nights of 'meals, banquets, balls, fraternal embraces, [and] illuminations'. White flags were flown and white feathers worn in men's hats as a sign of adhesion to the Revolution; a review of 17,000 troops was organized (Madiou 1988, 7: 473). Ussher reported that Hérard was 'idolized by the lower orders and soldiery, over whom he seems to maintain an extraordinary influence, as I have not heard of one single act of violence or disorder committed by the uncivilised and starving masses that support him'.[28]

The forms of government remained democratic and constitutional, as a formal transfer of power was planned. On the 24th of March, an Act was passed, signed and published, setting forth Boyer's crimes and announcing a provisional government. It was installed on the 1st of April 1843, during public celebrations of the anniversary of Alexandre Pétion's birth, at which the National Guard paraded, proclamations and acts of the new government were read and one hundred and one salvos were fired; the crowd were said to number over 10,000.[29] Debate quickly began over what kind of government to form and what procedures should be followed in forming it. As Lepelletier de Saint-Rémy put it, 'one knew not how much the Haitian population was acutely moved by the spirit of democracy'. With Boyer's removal, all was revealed:

> From this moment, political passions became the day in the press with the impetuosity of a torrent which has broken its dikes. It was, as never before, the case of saying: Democracy flowed full to the brim. And what democracy! The shock of ideas the most heterogeneous, the alliance of principles the most contrary, of American federalism and the unitary tendencies of '93; the sovereignty of the people replaced by the sovereignty of the commune; at last all the intellectual extravagance of a young people, untried and long hampered in the legitimate manifestation of their voices (Saint-Rémy 1845: 681).

Some writers in the radical press called for radical democracy, while others took a more conservative position. Writing in *Le Manifeste*, Saint-Rémy charged that:

> Representative government which is nothing other than government of indirect election is a train of intrigues formed by a few guardians against a few minors[;]...in France it is the government of the *right sort*, it is the domination of the material interest of the bourgeoisie over the worker, over the labourer.... [I]n England it is the domination of the gentleman or of the rich capitalist over the urban worker; it is the haughty arrogance of Lord Palmerston over Sir O'coneel [*sic*]. [D]emocratic or popular government is the inverse of representative government; here the people always make heard their strong voice, magnanimous and always intelligent; despite their apparent ignorance, they have the good sense of their own interests.[30]

Others argued over the form of municipal government. Some advocated an American-style system of town meetings headed by selectmen and generated from the bottom up, while others advocated a more French-style centralized system in which the central executive directed the formation of local administrations along with indirect election of mayors. 'One spoke only of the free and independent commune', wrote Madiou, and 'as for clubs, one was passionately fond of them; it was said they were all that is beautiful, grand, positive; they were the foyer of enlightenment and of patriotism' (Madiou 1988, 7: 486). Ardouin argued that the Liberal Revolution succeeded because it mobilized popular opinion in favour of reform, whereas Boyer had turned his back on the people, especially those in the South whose representatives had been expelled from the Assembly.

The new government would be based on open debate, the expression of public opinion, a free press and freedom of association. One newspaper suggested that meetings were the best means to extend political participation:

> Once the people have been seized by a passion for political affairs, once they have been imbued with the necessity of following the workings of government and have understood all the power of well-formulated public opinion against the invasions of power, *les meeting* [italicized English in original] or political reunions shall become the great occupation of the national elite, the rendezvous of the enlightened, the intelligent and the capable, and the good that will flow from all these public discussions will forevermore be immense.[31]

Even Inginac, in self-exculpatory memoirs published from exile in Kingston in 1843, attributed Boyer's downfall to his failure to 'consult' liberal public opinion. Inginac claimed that he himself promoted liberalism, but that Boyer would not listen and instead fell back on the force of the army. If Boyer had listened to him, Inginac claims, 'he would have opened all matters of public interest to free discussion...he would not have believed that in relying on the masses, he had sufficient force to disdain the opinion of his enlightened fellow citizens' (Inginac 1843: 109).

In the meantime, however, it was only a small group of educated lawyers, newspaper editors and teachers who were turning up at the 'popular clubs'. The aspiring revolutionaries were finding it difficult to mobilize the people at whom all of this democracy was directed. 'In the final battle of the mulatto government against the mulatto opposition', observed Maxime Reybaud, 'the masses, feeling themselves cajoled on one side and then the other, were remaining nearly neutral' (d'Alaux 1860: 55). Madiou makes it clear that during the interim period of the revolutionary transfer of power, there were a number of competing factions with different aims. There were those who had signed the Manifeste de Praslin and backed Hérard; there were those in Jérémie who were old enemies of Boyer, his family and his partisans, but who were not particularly sympathetic to the black cause; and there was a more radical black faction emerging in the countryside around Aux Cayes and Grand Anse, who wanted a black leader. As primary assemblies met in May and June 1843 to choose the electoral colleges, each of these factions jockeyed among themselves for position.

From February 1843 to March 1844, the revolution seemed to elicit only minimal popular support, as the electoral assemblies tried to hammer out a new constitution. There were 26 *arrondissements electoraux* (divided into 68 communes), but they comprised a total of only 620 electors to choose the 124 members of the Assemblée Constituante, which would write and approve the new constitution (Madiou 1988, 7: 488; cf. FO 35/26). As Saint-Rémy observed, 'The work of the new elections was long and difficult; the presence of two castes in the electoral committees brought about conflicts and agitations which were raised at times to the proportions of civil war' (Saint-Rémy 1845: 672). Already within a month of Boyer's overthrow, radical editors like Dumai Lespinasse and Emile Nau were complaining that Hérard was liberally giving out military offices, when he should have been reorganizing and reducing the army (Madiou 1988, 7: 489). Against the more radical implications of an elite-popular democratic alliance, Hérard and the army seemed to be fomenting a populist state-military alliance. The democratic alliance that had briefly bridged differences of colour and class was beginning to buckle under the strain of the revolutionary situation; colour discrimination would be the final straw.

Black mobilization and the Piquet Rebellion

When the peasantry of the south, under the leadership of the black land-owning Salomon family, turned against the provisional government, it became clear that the elite ideology of racial equality did not represent the reality experienced by black *habitants*. The south had always been a stronghold of *affranchi* power and land ownership, even in colonial days, and big coffee plantations had been maintained here after independence; thus, class solidarity of the *ancien libres* was probably stronger here than elsewhere in the country. Yet, it was also a region in which many black soldiers had been given land grants by Pétion (see Chapter 2). The disturbance began when the primary electoral assembly in Aux Cayes split between a mulatto faction supporting Edouard Grandchamp and a black faction supporting Salomon jeune.[32] Neither obtained a clear majority, but in the end Grandchamp won and excluded many black men. Madiou writes that the 'elite of the black population of les Cayes' rallied around Salomon jeune and sent a petition complaining of colour discrimination to the provisional government (Madiou 1988, 7: 506–20). The petition, signed by seventy men, charged not only that Boyer had oppressed the 'black class', but also that this 'cancer' of the 'prejudice of caste' continued to destroy the unity of the nation: 'in this Haiti conquered at the price of the blood of both *noirs* and *jaunes*, Boyer has succeeded in establishing a veritable aristocracy: he had made the coloured class the dominator of the black class' (Madiou 1988, 7: 503).

The format of these initial exchanges between the provisional government and aggrieved blacks is significant because it shows an initial attempt to act through civil, public means, e.g. meetings, petitions, resolutions, public manifestoes, etc. Likewise, the state initially responded to these claims through civil channels of communication. The provisional government sent an official delegation to Les Cayes to investigate the charges, and Salomon demanded annulment of the primary election, full participation of blacks and that the government extirpate 'caste prejudice'. He asserted that 'the country is a common heritage, that it is by all and for all; that it was conquered by the black and the brown' (Madiou 1988, 7: 516). He prepared a long 'exposé', reproduced in full by Madiou, who called it a remarkable document. At its heart is this claim:

> The unjust are those who recognize as citizens only the businessmen, merchants, professionals, capitalists, etc. and who say they were revolted to see men with black skins, tanners, coopers, cultivators by profession, come to vote concurrently with them in the assemblies of the 15th and 16th of June; the unjust are those who do not want to conceive that in Haiti the *nègres* and the *mulâtres* are equal and constitute but one; the unjust are those who want to ignore that we all owe our independence to a *nègre*, to the great Dessalines who reigns in our hearts and to whom reparatory justice will one day raise altars (Madiou 1988, 7: 512).

Finally, Salomon concluded, 'we are the poor pariahs that they seek to disinherit from the patrimony conquered by our fathers, reddened by their precious blood. We want to be equal to all, we want to see the aristocracy of skin disappear from our society…. [W]e declare it to the nation [and] to the entire world'.

A government delegation managed to bring the two sides together, and a concordat was signed and approved by the provisional government. It momentarily seemed that democratic channels of communicative claim-making had preserved peace. In the meantime, though, Hérard, who was leading troops in the east and was not in direct communication with the capital, received the original petition and ordered the arrest of its signatories. By resorting to a military response, he broke a fragile democratic compromise between the two factions. As arrests began, the Salomons left Aux Cayes in the night, 'meeting on the habitation of Castel père, and reuniting the cultivators at the sound of bells and the lambi. They announced that they had escaped from Aux Cayes because of the persecutions the mulattoes exercised against the blacks. The cultivators responded to their appeal, armed themselves with rifles and pikes of hardwood, and organized themselves into cavalry and infantry' (Madiou 1988, 7: 521). Government troops were quickly sent against them, and reports came to the capital of an uprising in the south, put down by General Lazarre. The Salomon army, 'composed of approximately three hundred-or-so rifles and five hundred-or-so hardwood pikes', was pardoned and the Salomons were ordered to turn themselves in to the provisional government. They later left for exile in Jamaica.[33] This would not be the end of their political influence, however, for the questions of colour and class discrimination still hung in the air and black citizens, both rural *habitants* and urban artisans, still demanded democracy.

The *Patriote* reported the 'deplorable news' of Salomon's uprising, rhetorically asking, 'Would one speak to us of an aristocracy of caste and of privileges of skin, here where the principle of election is desired by all, here where the majority forms the basis of all nominations to public functions?'[34] The paper sighed in relief when the nine hundred rebels, mostly armed with long wooden pikes, or 'piquets', were peaceably dispersed. Its paternalistic outlook emerged more clearly as it called for a 'moralisation of the masses', who were 'today that which they were yesterday, without enlightenment and without morality; to teach them, to moralize them, to procure their well-being, that is what there is to do for them'.[35] British Consul Ussher wrote to the Admiralty,

> An element of discord has displayed itself which threatened
> to deluge the country with blood. It is nothing less than the
> hatred that exists between the negroes and the mulattoes….

[T]he Chief Offices of state have generally found their way into the hands of the mulattoes. The negroes perceiving only the difference of colour in this arrangement, fancy themselves an oppressed and aggrieved race and evince a strong determination to assert their supposed rights.[36]

Ussher feared further unrest and asked the Admiralty to have a British ship call in at Haiti in case of a black 'counter-revolution'. Any revolution that came, though, would not be against democratic reform, but in favour of greater democratization — a notion as distasteful to English merchants as to the Haitian landowners and military.

A new Constitution was finally written and approved by the constituent Assembly on the 30th of December, 1843, ten months after Boyer's flight. It called for the first purely civilian government in Haiti, and for a four-year presidency elected by a wide electoral assembly. The three powers were to be separated, and the legislature divided into a Commons and a Senate. Representatives in the Commons were to be elected for three-year terms by the primary assemblies in each commune, with numbers determined by population. The voting age was twenty-one, while representatives had to be twenty-five and own property. Each department was to have six Senators (who had to be thirty years old and own property) elected by electoral assemblies for six-year terms. The constitution maintained the right to citizenship of all people of African or Indian heritage, and continued to ban white property ownership. Local governance was to be based on direct election every two years, to form the Municipal Committees, Municipal Councils and Communal Councils; these were to hold public sessions and publish budgets and accounts (Janvier 1905: 38–9). The new constitution opened with a long section on civil and political rights, and public law. It ensured inviolability of the home and the sanctity of property; the right of each to express his opinions in all matters, to write, print and to publish his thoughts; equality of all religious cults; free public primary schooling to be gradually phased in; the right to peaceful assembly and freedom of association; the right of petition; and the right to use any language, except in the case of acts of public authority or judicial affairs (Moïse 1988, Appendix 1, Constitution de 1843). It was similar to the United States Constitution and Bill of Rights in many respects, but it outlawed slavery and gave broad and equal rights to all male citizens.

One of the barriers to popular political participation was the language divide between French and *Kréyol*. We know from missionary reports that most Haitians did not speak or understand French. Government documents such as proclamations and *Ordres du Jour*

were always written in French (occasionally with Spanish translata-
tion), and therefore had to be orally translated for most of the populace
to understand them. Disturbances were reported in Port-de-Paix following municipal elections in July 1843 after illiterate voters accused
the scribes who had written out their votes of cheating them.[37] The
newspaper *Le Progrès* reported that at Petit-Goave,

> the constitution having been read article by article, without
> omission, each article was explained in Creole to the numer-
> ous listeners who called for it and seemed at times to
> demand it. Arriving at articles 8, 24, and 25 [excluding
> whites from property and protecting existing claims to prop-
> erty], some *habitants* very well said that it was not thus that
> they had been made to believe. They had been told that the
> big properties would be rehabilitated to such as they were in
> the *ancien regime* and that in consequence they would lose
> their properties.[38]

In other words, opponents of the revolution had misled the small landholders against the revolution until its aims were translated into Kréyol
for them.

Soon, however, it became apparent that the interests of peasants
and small landholders were not being represented by the 'enlightened'
political elite. The long awaited constitution was not to everyone's
liking, and new fissures began to appear. Most alarmingly, conflicts
emerged between civil and military authorities, and between the new
legislature and President Hérard, backed by the army. Following the
ceremony in Port Républicain to install Hérard as President, according
to Ussher,

> [The new Constitution] was publicly read in the presence of
> a great concourse of the people and the Army. At its conclu-
> sion the great majority of the officers present came forward
> to the Hustings with loud cries of 'En bas la Constitution! En
> bas les Préfets!' and it was with some difficulty that Hérard
> was able to pacify them and persuade them to have recourse
> to a more legal method of protesting against such portions of
> the constitution with which they were dissatisfied.[39]

When national guardsmen refused to obey newly elected municipal
authorities in some areas, discord between the legislature and the
President erupted. 'Hérard has all along expressed his dissatisfaction at
the ultra democratic principles of the new Constitution', Ussher noted,
'which he considered ill adapted to the habits of the people, and is
secretly pleased to observe a similar feeling exhibiting itself in the

Army. A short time ago, in the North, three regiments, under a General Thomas, openly protested against several articles of the Constitution, those in particular relating to Municipal Institutions'.[40]

The conflict, then, was not simply between black and mulatto factions, as many historians have argued, but between those committed to constitutional democracy as the best route to black equality versus those committed to statist militarism as the best route to power (allied with conservative big landowners and traditional local powerholders who feared democratization). Some elements of the army were drawn to their origins among 'the people' and supported the democratic revolution, while others (especially officers it seems) were drawn to their bread-and-butter position and supported a reprise of military authority. Military autonomy thus drove a wedge between the bourgeois/peasant democratic republican alliance, both by offering some poor blacks a route to power within the army, and by planting seeds of fear of 'the masses' among the elite. It was the inability of civilians to wrest control of the state from the military that ultimately destabilized Haitian democratization.

As the patronizing French Consul General Maxime Reybaud (writing under the pen-name Gustave d'Alaux) put it: 'when the new regime was consolidated, when so much fracas had ended at nothing more than to give a few thousand epaulettes to the mulatto youth of the Hérard party, the "black people" understood that one had decidedly forgotten them, and looked to the four cardinal points to see if anyone would not present themselves to give them their "revolution à li"' (d'Alaux 1860: 55). Claiming to represent the true black interest, the Salomons appeared in the south, Dalzon in Port-au-Prince, and the black generals Pierrot and Guerrier in the north, followed by the final straw — break-away of the Dominican Republic in the east. Together, these coups and civil wars destabilized Hérard's regime, leaving it open to a more serious peasant uprising. This time, however, the movement was not led by landowners, but by a political-religious leader who dressed like a peasant.

Throughout March and April of 1844, President Hérard was leading up to 30,000 troops against the Dominican independence movement, which had declared itself in Santo Domingo in February (cf. Hoetink 1982). The poorly provisioned Haitian army met with a number of defeats against smaller guerrilla-style forces at Azua and other locations, and Hérard declared that deserters would be shot. Meanwhile, his cousin Hérard Dumesle had been left in charge of Port Républicain, as Foreign Minister, and was sending unpopular press-gangs through the city. A presidential proclamation blamed the Legislative Assembly for the Dominican insurrection. The next day, according to Ussher, 'the Chambers were taken possession of by a military force, the Municipality closed, and both legislators and civic authorities ordered to shoulder their muskets and join the Army, where they might more effectually serve the Country'.[41] Ussher was especially concerned by reports that the Dominican rebels were negotiating with the French to become a protectorate; the French fleet was stationed nearby, and they were thought to have offered two to three million dollars in exchange for use of the northern port of Samana. They may even have had designs on invading Haiti itself.[42]

Although the Salomon uprising of August 1843 had been defeated and the Salomons sent into exile in Jamaica, once the Dominican Republic declared its independence, the opportunity was again seized to attack Hérard, whose press-gangs and closure of the National Assembly were resented. Military unrest in the north became a plot to make the black General Guerrier president of the Republic; this movement was supported by a new rebellion in Aux Cayes. Ussher reported, 'There is no doubt that the present movement in the South is the revival of the insurrection headed by Salomon in August last and connected with the Dalzon affair in this City in September, that is to say a war of caste, of negroes against mulattoes'.[43] Two weeks later, though, it emerged that the initial reports had been exaggerated:

> [T]hree fourths of the most respectable inhabitants fled to Jamaica and other places, spreading exaggerated reports of outrages committed at Aux Cayes. Nothing of the kind appears hitherto to have taken place.... Jérémie was also taken possession of on the 12th inst. by a large body of blacks, under a Colonel Desmoulines who pretends to act under divine inspiration. As at Aux Cayes, the respectable inhabitants fearing outrages, embarked and fled to this City, but no excesses appear to have been committed.[44]

'The North has declared its independence,' reported Bird, 'and offered the Presidency to General Gue[r]rier. The Southern citizens are marching on the capital, and declare that they will treat with none but General Guer[r]ier (a black man) and the citizens in the Capital have positively refused to march to join the President's army'.[45]

In early May, the aged war hero General Guerrier was proclaimed President both in the north and in Port Républicain, after 'a conspiracy was got up in his favor by several respectable Citizens, who considered the election of a black chief as the only means of restoring tranquility to the Republic'.[46] The citizens of the capital joined in proclaiming Guerrier president not by an election, but 'in the open air, with loud acclamations'.[47] Both groups of supporters published manifestos announcing the coup, with signatures of, respectively, 300 and 150 leading citizens (including Beaubrun Ardouin). The deposed President escaped immediate violence, but was put under house arrest. This apparent black victory, however, was not a guarantee of democratic participation, and the peasant uprising *in favour* of the revolution continued in the south. As Reybaud put it, half in fear, half in mockery,

> Guerrier, like Pierrot, like Dalzon, like Salomon, was only a *noir*, but now came in the south a *nègre*, the humanitarian negro and handsome speaker from the school of Jean François. He was called Acaau, 'general in chief of the reclamations of his *concitoyens*,' he had gigantic spurs at his naked ankles, and, followed by a troop of bandits mostly armed with sharpened pikes being short on rifles, he wandered about, in the interest of 'the unhappy innocents' and for 'the eventuality of national education,' as the towns were depopulated in terror at his approach. Acaau was the special spokesman in the 'name of the rural population, wakened from the slumber in which it had been plunged' (d'Alaux 1860: 56).

As Leslie Manigat argues (and Nicholls agrees), the Piquet movement 'was the fruit of the conjunction of interests between big and medium black proprietors and small peasant *parçellaires*, equally black' (cited in Nicholls 1996: 276n68).

A former member of the rural police, Jean-Jacques Acaau led the revolt of the 'army of sufferers' affirming 'respect for the Constitution, Rights, Equality, Liberty'.[48] In spite of the fact that Acaau's proclamations asserted that 'it is not, nor can it be a question, in any circumstance, of a war of colour', elite commentators at the time, including both Madiou and Ardouin, interpreted his actions as a 'caste war'. Acaau was reported to be raising a forced 'loan' and confiscating property from mulatto merchants in Aux Cayes to pay his poorly armed troops; he was also said to have shot or imprisoned women and children.[49] In a number of proclamations printed in the newspapers, he called for the return of the Salomons from exile, the reinstatement of the disbanded Twelfth Regiment, and an end to martial law, and he blamed the new government for failing to live up to its promises.[50] Ussher observed that Acaau 'is a man of some instruction for a negro, has great influence over his followers which he has acquired by Obeah [*sic*] practices, and affects the dress of a labourer'.[51] Reybaud described him as a bandit:

> Following the black reaction of 1844, the bandit Acaau came barefoot to the wayside cross of the parish, dressed in a

species of canvas packing-sheet and wearing a little straw
hat, and there publicly vowed not to change his clothing until
the orders of 'divine Providence' were executed. Then,
turning towards the negro peasants convened by the sound of
the *lambi*, Acaau explained that 'divine Providence' ordered
the poor people, first to chase out the mulattos, second to
divide up the mulatto properties (d'Alaux 1860: 111).

He was backed by a religious leader named Frère Joseph, who clarified
that what was meant were not colour distinctions alone, but distinctions
of class or status. The famous phrase is worth repeating in its full form:
'The rich Negro who can read and write is mulatto; the poor mulatto
who cannot read nor write is Negro' (d'Alaux 1860: 112). The link to
literacy is often skipped when a shortened version of this quote is cited
(cf. Trouillot 1990; Nicholls 1996), yet it is crucial in regard to civil
agency. Haitian peasants knew that literacy was a status boundary
excluding them from civil and political participation. Thus, the Piquet
movement had more aims than simply the seizure of mulatto property.
Reybaud himself compares their ideology, in retrospect, to that of the
European movements of 1848, calling it 'negro communism':

'Unhappy innocence' plays, for example, the same role in
the proclamations of Acaau as 'the exploitation of man by
man' in certain other proclamations. 'The eventuality of
national education,' this other chord of Acaau's humanitarian
lyre, corresponds visibly to 'free and obligatory instruction',
and in so far as he reclaims in the name of the cultivators,
who are the *workers* down there, 'reduction in the price of
foreign merchandise and augmentation in the value of their
crops', the black socialist has certainly found the clearest and
most comprehensible formula for this problem of the white
Acaaus: reduction of work and increase of salaries (d'Alaux
1860: 115 [emphasis in original]).

Reybaud consoled himself that 'black communism would run aground
like white communism on the extreme morcellization of property'. It is
clear that the Haitian peasantry identified their enemies in class as well
as colour terms. Theirs were the hybrid peasant/proletarian aims of
other post-emancipation social movements in the Caribbean. Their
grievances were not simply against mulatto power, but against abuses
of martial law, violations of the constitution and the subversion of
democracy.

Other peasant leaders associated with the movement included
Dugué Zamor and Jean Claude (who were former soldiers), Jeannot

Moline, Antoine Pierre, Augustin Cyprien and a woman, Louise Nicolas, who is credited by some historians with organizing the movement (Bellegarde-Smith 1990: 70). A Methodist missionary in Jérémie described the 'army of sufferers', in which there 'were a great many men armed with sticks of different sorts of wood; they sharpened the edge, and applied poisonous gum to it, so that any wound which might not be dangerous, would through the poison become so. The sticks were from 8 to 10 feet long'.[52] The Piquets defeated government troops in battles at Les Cayes, Jérémie and l'Anse-à-Veau; Acaau's control of the south 'from Aquin to Petit-Goave', forced the government to accept the necessity of a black president. Acaau's followers were somewhat mollified by the election of a black President, and he sent in his submission to Guerrier, if two conditions were met: banishment of Hérard and suspension of General Lazau's command of the south. Hérard was exiled to Jamaica and Acaau was elevated to General of Division and Commandant of the arrondissement of Aux Cayes, despite grave doubts among the elite about his actions and intentions.[53]

Eventually, however, it became clear that this was only a ploy to contain his influence; the government gradually eroded Acaau's followers with 'bribes and threats', according to the British Vice-Consul, undermining his supporters until he was left barricaded alone in his house. The *armée souffrante* was finally defeated, and the south was brought back under the control of 'the mulatto general Fabré-Nicolas Geffrard and the black general Jean-Baptiste Riché, both of whom later became president of the republic' (Bellegarde-Smith 1990: 70). Acaau finally went to negotiate with President Guerrier, whom he apparently trusted, in Port Républicain; on his arrival, 'the mob followed him shouting, and would have massacred him in the street, but he moved quickly on a good mount'. He was arrested and brought before a court martial, but sentenced to only five years in prison and loss of his military rank because 'they want tranquillity among his black followers in the south'.[54] General Salomon, along with his family, was recalled from Jamaican exile by President Guerrier; but rather than support the Piquets, the Salomons are judged to have 'used their influence in the South to contribute to the neutralization of the Acaau movement in 1844' (Moïse 1988, 206). The Salomons, according to Manigat, had 'acquired the reputation of adversaries of the men of color, for having denounced what they called the aristocracy of the skin.... From this epoch already, Lysius Salomon jeune appeared with the double face of black leader and of porte-parole of the peasant masses of the south' (quoted in Moïse 1988: 206). Salomon became a Senator, signed the less democratic constitution of 1846 and was an influential minister under Soulouque. He never sought the democratization for which the

Piquets had fought, but became an important advocate of a 'noiriste' position in Haitian political thought. The democratic window of opportunity was slammed shut.

Although Hérard had gone into exile in Jamaica, he and his supporters still attempted to overturn the government; he sailed for Haiti in an armed schooner in May 1845, but after an aborted coup, many from his party were arrested and some executed.[55] As Bellegarde-Smith points out, the outcome of the Piquet Revolt was not only the cynical 'politique de doublure', in which an apparent black leader was really controlled by powerful mulattoes behind the scenes, but also 'an extraordinary outpouring of reactionary literary justification for elite control' — including the major histories of Haiti written by Ardouin and Madiou, both of which favoured cultural assimilation of blacks to 'Western' norms under elite tutelage (Bellegarde-Smith 1990: 70, 56). Writers like Lepelletier de Saint-Rémy argued that '[t]he new society no longer awaits its salute from these terrible civilizers, the slaves of yesterday. Barely knowing how to read, and marching proudly in pursuit of abuses, in all the rude franchise of a primitive despotism, the black race had a role to fulfil in as much as the intervention of brutal force was necessary: today that force must unite itself with intelligence, and for that the black race must return to the second rank' (Saint-Rémy 1845: 683). He recommended the introduction of more whites to Haiti, for 'without the contact of whites, nothing will grow, nothing will develop, and the law which proscribes them from a country decrees barbarity' (Saint-Rémy 1845: 684).

This failure to unite the radical intelligentsia and the peasantry destroyed the Haitian democratic republican project, and contributed to the subsequent emergence of Faustin Soulouque as Emperor, who rejected republican institutions and eventually unleashed violent repression on the liberal mulatto faction. This was not the triumph of blacks over mulattoes, but the triumph of statist autocracy over the potentially democratic alliance of radical segments of the bourgeoisie with peasants and cultivators. Yet, the Piquets would continue to influence Haitian popular politics for decades to come. Lysius Salomon was again banished to Jamaica by President Geffrard, who succeeded Emperor Soulouque; when his older brother attempted an insurrection against Geffrard in 1862, he was caught and executed along with a dozen others. This sparked a series of 'piquettiste movements' in January 1865, in 1866-67 and 1868 (Moïse 1988). The most important insurrection was that of Salnave in Cap Haitien, from May through November 1865, which nearly became a civil war between north and south.[56] We shall see below the significance of these events in relation to the contemporaneous Morant Bay Rebellion.

Salomon became president of Haiti in 1879, yet we know much less about the fate of the Piquets, the followers of the peasant-leader Acaau. As Moïse writes:

> One has spoken of the manipulation of the peasants (Cacos in the North, Piquets in the South) and of the cynical use of the question of colour by fractions of the bourgeoisie and by politicians in their battle for power. Beyond these incidents of the political struggle, it is time to reflect on the specificity of the peasant movements. The *piquettiste* wave of 1868 was the third since 1844. Each time, the interventions came in periods of sharp political crisis within the ruling classes, provoking reactions of panic not only among the bourgeoisie of the South, but also among those of the West. If the agrarian claims (*revendications*) of the piquets appear clear and precise, their political claims, their mode of organization, and their methods of struggle, are not well known. *Piquettisme* still awaits its historian (Moïse 1988: 169).

The documents that come directly from Acaau suggest some clues to the Piquets' political ideology and organization. They attempted to use democratic means of political address, publicizing and justifying their claims in proclamations and in newspapers such as *Le Manifeste*, and claiming to uphold the democratic constitution of 1843. They mobilized supporters through public gatherings, with religious leaders and some spiritual content to the message. They symbolically utilized the dress and language of the peasantry, to show in actions the kind of equality and participation they were speaking about in words.

The failure of democracy at this conjuncture, then, should not be interpreted as the result of ideological incoherence arising out of a reactionary and disorganized pre-modern setting. The timing, form, and stated grievances and demands of the Piquets all suggest a class and colour conscious movement, with democratic aims and a clear critique of landowner-merchant domination and unmitigated control of the state. We can call this a democratization movement because it carried on in the tradition of the anti-colonial and anti-slavery movements of the late eighteenth century, and represents the farthest 'left wing' of democratic republicanism, despite its location outside of the metropolitan core. Its failure to achieve a democratic outcome goes back to the militarization of the Haitian state, and the continual suppression of public means of communication and contention. The Haitian peasantry was neither unaware of democratic ideologies, nor particularly enamoured of *caudillos*; however, the structural conditions of political communication between citizens and the state in post-colonial Haiti favoured armed groups over civil associations. The bitter paradox of Haitian history is that its successful revolutionary struggle to overcome slavery left the new republic with all the tools for democracy but one, and that the most fundamental — subordination of the military to civil control.

Notes

1   On the Dominican War of Independence, see Frank Moya Pons, 'The Land Question in Haiti and Santo Domingo: The Sociopolitical Context of the Transition from Slavery to Free Labor, 1801–1843', in *Between Slavery and Free Labor: The Spanish-Speaking Caribbean in the 19th Century*, ed. Frank Moya Pons and Stanley Engerman (Baltimore: Johns Hopkins University Press, 1985); Nicholls, *From Dessalines to Duvalier*, 79–82; FO35/28, British Consul Ussher to Foreign Office; FO 35/29, Republica Dominicana, various documents, 1844.

2   There is no single monograph focusing on this period, but most interpretations refer to a conflict of colour leading to a 'politique of doublure' in which black presidents became front men for the mulatto elite. See, for example, Nicholls, *From Dessalines to Duvalier*; Michel-Rolph Trouillot, *Haiti: State Against Nation* (New York: Monthly Review Press, 1990); and Patrick Bellegarde-Smith, *Haiti: The Breached Citadel* (London and Boulder: Westview Press, 1990).

3   *Le Patriote*, no. 51, 4 May 1843.

4   *L'Eclaireur*, no. 1, 5 Aug. 1818. Cf. Nicholls, *From Dessalines to Duvalier*, 7.

5   *L'Abeille*, no. 3, 1 Sept. 1818.

6   A generation gap was important, but the opposition bristled at charges of youthful over-zealousness: many were in their 30s, while Boyer's supporters were old enough to have fought in the War of Independence (*Le Patriote*, no. 43, 21 Dec. 1842).

7   AMAE, C.C.C., Port-au-Prince, Vol. 4, Consul Cerfberr to Secrétaire d'État, no. 12 (10 May 1838) and no. 15 (10 June 1838).

8   FO 35/21, Captain Courtenay to Viscount Palmerston, 24 Oct. 1839.

9   *Le Manifeste*, Vol. 1, no. 26, 26 Sept. 1841.

10   *Le Manifeste*, no. 38, 19 Dec. 1841, enclosed in FO 35/24, Vice Consul Ussher to Lord Aberdeen, 21 Dec. 1841.

11   *Le Patriote*, no. 34, 19 Oct. 1842.

12   Ibid.

13   *Le Manifeste*, Vol. 2, no. 41, 29 Jan. 1843.

14   FO 35/25, Ussher to Lord Aberdeen, 20 Apr. 1842.

15   *Le Patriote*, no. 7, 13 Apr. 1842.

16   *Morning Journal*, 13 June 1842.

17   FO 35/25, Ussher to Lord Aberdeen, 5 Mar. 1842.

18   The crisis was compounded when a powerful earthquake destroyed Cap Haitien on the 7th of May, 1842, killing about six thousand people. There was no government response and the ruined city was pillaged by armed gangs from the countryside (FO 35/25, Ussher to Lord Aberdeen, 17 May 1842).

19   FO 35/27, Ussher to Admiralty, 25 Jan. 1843, encl. in Admiralty to FO, 22 Mar. 1843.

20   The fire hit the business district where the market women, or *marchandes*, kept shops. They were 'nearly all burnt out and, possessing no other security than their good faith, are utterly unable to fulfill even a portion of their engagements',

according to Ussher. Losses arising from their debts to foreign mercantile houses were estimated at $840,000 (FO 35/26, Ussher to Lord Aberdeen, 14 Jan. 1843).

21 Hérard aîné to Honoré Féry, président du comité de Jérémie, 15 janvier 1843, in Thomas Madiou, *Histoire d'Haiti*, ed. Michlle Oriol [Port-au-Prince: Henri Deschamps, 1988] Vol. 7, p. 436. Charles Hérard was a cousin of Hérard Dumesle, editor, poet and senator, who became Foreign Secretary after the revolution (Nicholls, *From Dessalines to Duvalier*).

22 FO 35/26, Ussher to Lord Aberdeen, 15 Feb. 1843.

23 FO 35/27, Lord Elgin to Lord Stanley, 16 Feb. 1843, enclosing Committee of the People (Provisional Government, Jeremie) to Governor of Jamaica, 7 Feb. 1843.

24 FO 35/27, Commander Robert Sharpe, H. M. *Scylla*, to Admiralty, enclosed in Admiralty to Foreign Office, 21 Apr. 1843.

25 WMMS, West Indies Corr., Haiti, Bird to Secretaries, 14 Mar. 1843 (sent via H. M. *Scylla*, the ship that carried Boyer to Jamaica).

26 WMMS, West Indies Corr., Haiti, Hartwell to Secretaries, 6 Dec. 1843 (from Port-au-Prince, now 'Port Républicain').

27 According to another version, the wives, mothers and sisters of the National Guard blocked their route when they were called out. When Boyer appeared, they insisted 'that they would not let go the soldiers unless he put himself at their head'. (AN, Archives Marines, GGII.1, Baudin Papers, letter of 29 Mar. 1843).

28 FO 35/26 Ussher to Lord Aberdeen, 4 Apr. 1865. This is as close to a description of a charismatic *caudillo* as one finds in Haiti at this time, but it was exceptional if compared to the long presidencies that preceded and followed it.

29 *Le Manifeste*, Vol. 3, no. 1, 9 Apr. 1843.

30 *Le Manifeste*, Vol. 3, no. 1, 9 Apr. 1843.

31 *Le Manifeste*, Vol. 3, no. 2, 16 Apr. 1843.

32 Madiou reports that Salomon's mother was a black marchande, and that racial tensions were exacerbated when a young 'fille de couleur' turned down his marriage request (Madiou, *Histoire d'Haiti*, Vol. 7, p. 521). Colour distinctions were closely tied to patterns of class and status distinction through marriage choices. For an interesting comparison, see Verena Martinez Alier, *Marriage, Class and Colour in Nineteenth Century Cuba*, 2nd ed., (Ann Arbor: University of Michigan Press, 1989).

33 *Le Manifeste*, Vol. 3, no. 21, 3 Sept. 1843.

34 *Le Patriote*, no. 13, 10 Aug. 1843.

35 *Le Patriote*, no. 17, 14 Oct. 1843.

36 FO 35/29, Ussher to Admiralty, 18 Oct. 1843, encl. in Admiralty, 23 Jan. 1844.

37 *Le Manifeste*, Vol. 3, no. 16, 23 July 1843.

38 FO 35/28, *Le Progrès*, 7 Mar. 1844, encl. in Ussher to Earl of Aberdeen, 6 Mar. 1844.

39 FO 35/28, General Corr., Ussher to Lord Aberdeen, 5 Jan. 1844.

40 FO 35/28, General Corr., Ussher to Lord Aberdeen, 23 Feb. 1844.

41 FO 35/28, Ussher to FO, 5 Apr. 1844.

42 General Pedro Santa Anna became the first President of the Dominican Republic. See FO 35/28, Ussher to FO, 22 Aug. 1844; 21 Sept. 1844; 23 Oct. 1844; 23 Dec. 1844; and FO 35/29, Documents *Republica Dominicana*, 1844.

43 FO 35/28, Ussher to Lord Aberdeen, 7 Apr. 1844.

44 FO 35/28, Ussher to Lord Aberdeen, 21 Apr. 1844. With this flight to Jamaica and unrest over the next four years, news of black uprisings in Haiti filtered through to the Afro-Jamaican peasantry and influenced their actions and attitudes in 1848.

45 WMMS, West Indies Corr., Haiti, Bird to Secretaries, 7 May 1844.

46   FO 35/28, Ussher to Lord Aberdeen, 7 May 1844.

47   WMMS, West Indies Corr., Haiti, Bird to Secretaries, 7 May 1844.

48   FO 35/28, Ussher to Lord Aberdeen, 2 May 1844, encl. 'Ordre du Jour' of J. Acaau, 23 Apr. 1844.

49   FO 35/28, Ussher to Lord Aberdeen, 2 May 1844, encl. Lt. C. Jenkins to Cpt. Elliot, 27 Apr. 1844.

50   *Le Manifeste*, Vol. 3, no. 52, 26 May 1844.

51   FO 35/28, Ussher to Lord Aberdeen, 24 May 1844. Acaau's peasant dress is also suggestive of the figure of the Vodou *lwa* related to agricultural work, Cousin Azaka, who appears as a peasant, in a straw hat, and protects the interests of the rural labourer (Laennec Hurbon, *Voodoo: Truth and Fantasy*, trans. L. Frankel [London: Thames and Hudson, 1995], pp. 79, 99).

52   WMMS, West Indies Corr., Haiti, Bauduy to Secretaries, 24 May 1844.

53   FO 35/28, Ussher to Lord Aberdeen, 24 May 1844; and 23 June 1844.

54   FO 35/28, Vice-Consul Thompson to FO, 23 July 1844; 8 Aug. 1844; 21 Sept. 1844.

55   WMMS, West Indies Corr., Haiti, Bird to Secretaries, 8 Apr. 1845.

56   Geffrard was supported by the British, but the rebels in the Cap tried to tempt the U.S. into supporting them by offering the Mole St. Nicolas in exchange. The revolt failed after the British fleet bombarded Cap Haitien on November 9 1865, losing one ship (Claude Moïse, *Constitutions et Luttes de Pouvoir en Haïti (1804–1987)*, Vol. 1 [Quebec: CIDIHCA, 1988], 146); and see Conclusion below.

Part three

Jamaica:
'Colour for Colour'

'[He] said to the people without they come together, and go down to Morant Bay in lump, to let the white people see there was plenty black in the island, it was no use at all, and cry out that they don't mean to pay any more ground rent again; and after twenty-seven years in freedom the outside land was given to them a long time, and the white people kept it to themselves. That is what I heard him say'.

(JRC, Part 2, 1866, p. 165, Evidence of William Anderson on a public speech by James McLaren, a leader of the Morant Bay Rebellion).

6 | Black publics and peasant freedom in post-emancipation Jamaica

The 'Liberty Tree' that appears on the Haitian national symbol — adopted for a tropical context from the French revolutionary Liberty Tree — also makes an appearance in Jamaica's emancipation celebrations. John Woolridge of the London Missionary Society described the 'First of August' festival of 1839, in which a public examination of one hundred children was witnessed by an assembly of their parents, bringing a tear to their eyes. After buns and lemonade, they watered the coconut palm that they had planted the year before as a symbol of liberty.[1] Another missionary wrote that his congregation also 'planted a cocoanut tree, the emblem of liberty — this had been pulled up since, by some of the gentlemen in the neighbourhood, we have replanted it, and as one of the people remarked, "they pull up we tree, but them can't take away we August"'.[2] In addition to the evident importance of education, such struggles over symbols indicate the deeper significance of non-economic factors in marking the transition out of slavery and building a new society.

We have seen above how the decline of planter domination in Jamaica allowed for the emergence of an elite, literate, oppositional public among free men of colour. This indigenous Jamaican public developed its own newspapers to influence public opinion, utilized petitioning to make claims on the government regarding the rights of free people of colour even prior to the abolition of slavery, and, more controversially, gave support to Haiti as a self-governing black republic. As Gordon K. Lewis argues, the 'old groups of planter, merchant monopolist, and white colonial official were gradually superseded both in economic power and social status, by the new groups of creole cultivator, peasant farmer, and native politician' (Lewis 1968: 72). This chapter moves on to the development of plebeian publics in the post–emancipation period and explores the claim-making styles of self-consciously fashioned 'black publics'. The emergence of popular political participation in Jamaica will be analyzed according to the same framework used in the case of Haiti: the tri-partite development of peasant economic, political and civil agency.

My overall aim is to show that there were multiple publics in Jamaica, some with a strongly 'Black' or 'African', though still 'British' identity. In contrast to Haiti, there were well-established channels of communication between peasant-citizens and the state, both at the local and metropolitan levels; moreover, there were numerous ties between Afro-Jamaican publics and the wider British public. Yet, Afro-Jamaicans did not 'learn' democratic political culture from British tutelage. Rather, they seized on structural opportunities to push forward their own vision of freedom. On the one hand, they adopted elite forms of political communication such as public meetings and petitioning in an effort to expand peasant control and defend their freedom. This widening of democratic repertoires was mediated by Baptist missionaries who helped their congregations make the transition from slavery to apprenticeship, and then to freedom. On the other hand, there were also potentially more violent undercurrents of labour protest and 'riotous bargaining' always threatening to break out.[3]

The British abolition movement was a major component in the emergence of a new national field of public opinion in Great Britain (Tilly 1995a). Abolitionists were especially effective in mobilizing public meetings, petitioning, forming corresponding societies and inventing other symbolic forms of expressing public opinion, such as boycotts of slave-grown sugar. As Drescher argues, '[i]n developing a whole range of agitational techniques and symbolic forms, [anti–slavery] primarily expanded the tactics and the social base of non-violent public opinion' (Drescher 1982: 47). Colonial populations were well aware of the powerful impact of these repertoires of contention on political decision-making, and of the involvement of their own missionaries in them. It is not surprising, then, that these methods of agitation were taken up by ex-slaves in their push for civil and political rights. Yet, there were also points of departure where Afro-Jamaicans drew on their own culture, styles of communication and unique relationship to the colonial state to develop new political practices. British repertoires of contention could not be lifted *in toto*, but had to be reworked from the position of the former slave in relation to a colonial wing of the state.

This chapter traces the rise of peasant agency and the development of plebeian publics in post-emancipation Jamaica. It begins with economic agency as seen in the forms of mobility, labour bargaining and labour protest that developed from the period of apprenticeship to the mid-1840s. The next section focuses on peasant political agency, from voting, public meetings and petitioning to forms of riotous bargaining. The final section considers peasant civil agency, from religious and voluntary associations to the increasingly autonomous subaltern publics that emerged out of the African-rooted traditions of the Native Baptists and Myalist Revival. Each of these features of publicity in Jamaica will be important to understanding the emergence of the Underhill Movement and the Morant Bay Rebellion which followed it.

Peasant economic agency

Although our focus is the post-slavery period, it is important to keep in mind that labour bargaining in Jamaica began during slavery and gathered momentum during the apprenticeship period. Even workers with no rights could attempt collective protest, work-stoppage or group 'petit marronage' (in effect walk-outs) from the semi-industrial sugar plantations, all of which required some degree of organization.[4] Various forms of slave resistance and rebellion have been recognized as important precedents (within constricted circumstances) for later strategies of labour bargaining (Bakan 1990; Craton 1982; Cross & Heuman 1988; Hart 1980, 1985). Mary Turner, for example, found in her study of collective action by Jamaican slaves:

> Collective withdrawal of labour, the presentation of grievances and the use by owners and managers of mediation were methods developed by 1770. Group action by slaves with particular grievances was also used, notably by women, and secured positive results. Skilled and confidential slaves pioneered these processes and the head men...emerge as instigators and, by inference, organisers of group and collective action (Turner 1988: 26).

Indeed, one of the most significant findings to emerge from comparative evidence is that not only wage workers, but 'all categories of worker in the Americas practiced forms of collective labour bargaining customarily associated with industrial wage labourers' (Turner 1995: 1). Collective action in the post-emancipation period clearly had roots in this earlier organizing by slaves. Abigail Bakan also argues that 'a persistent ideology of class resistance has characterized the Jamaican labour force from the period of slavery, through the period of post-emancipation peasant development, and into the era of modern working-class activity' (Bakan 1990: 4).

The British Parliament finally passed legislation to abolish slavery in 1834 and instituted a period of 'apprenticeship'.[5] One of the most immediate changes was in the sphere of justice. Judicial oversight of the operation of apprenticeship by Special Magistrates (instead of the earlier system of Justices of the Peace who were invariably planters) created a somewhat fairer structure for adjudication of labour disputes, not least by removing the legitimate use of violence from the hands of former masters and overseers, and placing it in (supposedly) more objective state institutions. Although discipline remained harsh, plantation workers for the first time had contractual terms of labour and the right to complain of their treatment before a relatively neutral judge. It is evident that many apprentices took up this right immediately, even if complaints were met with imprisonment in the work-house, with its hated treadmill (Holt 1992; Sewell 1861; Sturge and Harvey 1838). There was also a great deal of public attention focused on this 'great experiment', and both pro-slavery and anti-slavery organizations in Britain sent their own investigators to report on conditions in the West Indies. The Quaker abolitionists Joseph Sturge and Thomas Harvey, who travelled through Jamaica collecting accounts from apprentices, brought one apprentice, James Williams, to England as a first-hand witness to abusive treatment of apprentices.[6] Despite continuing semi-bondage, then, apprentices had a far more public 'voice' than had slaves.[7]

In Jamaica, as in Haiti, claims to land were one of the most important points of post-emancipation political contention, and even the tiniest plots of heritable but inalienable 'family land' became cherished symbols of freedom, passed down to all descendants through unrestricted cognatic kinship networks (Besson 1979, 1993, 1995). Even during slavery, plantation workers had carved out traditional use rights to particular houses and provision grounds, stamping their own conceptual schemas on the built environment (Higman 1988).[8] 'Such land rights', argues Besson,

> were not only of economic significance, providing some independence from the plantations and a bargaining position for higher wages when working on them, but also symbolized freedom, personhood, and prestige among the descendants of former slaves.... [Family land was] a dynamic cultural creation by Caribbean peasantries themselves in resistant response to the plantation system' (Besson 1993: 22, 27).

Widespread evidence shows that ex-slaves in Jamaica did not immediately flee the estates, but struggled to maintain customary 'use rights' they had won, however marginal. As Douglas Hall argues, the 'movement of the ex-slaves from the estates in the immediate postemancipation years was not a flight from the horrors of slavery. It was a protest against the inequities of early "freedom"' (D. Hall [1978] 1993: 62).

Struggle to control land and labour created the context for the negotiation of freedom, and out of this bargaining rose distinctive citizenship identities and black publics. A vibrant peasant political culture emerged from both plantation workers' protest activities and the associational life of cultivators' villages, giving impetus to movements promoting land distribution, cooperative marketing, friendly societies and ambitious programmes for political reform. Baptist churches facilitated negotiations over labour contracts by organizing public meetings of apprentices to respond collectively to unfair practices and protest 'class legislation' by planters. In Haiti, these issues, identities and movements were far less clear not because they did not matter, but because they did not have the institutional channels with which to activate collective identities and press public claims. There was no 'transmission belt' to translate collective protest into public policy.

Extensive disputes in the immediate aftermath of emancipation over labour issues such as wages, hours of work and rent of houses and provision grounds on the sugar plantations, became the context for public debate over alternative directions for the post-slavery economy in Jamaica (Wilmot 1986). The first meetings of apprentices were organized by missionaries in reaction to rumours circulating among planters in the spring of 1838, that fieldworkers intended to stop working in August. The terms of apprenticeship differed for fieldworkers ('praedials') and skilled and domestic workers ('non-praedials'), with the latter scheduled for full freedom on the 1st of August, 1838, and the former expected to wait until 1840. These initial meetings seem to have been organized to quell any unrest at its source and demonstrate good faith on the part of the soon-to-be free. As reports of one meeting organized by the Baptist Reverend Walter Dendy show, the aims were initially conciliatory:

At a MEETING of about two thousand Apprentices at Salter's Hill Chapel, St. James...the following resolution was unanimously adopted: Having heard a report has been circulated that the praedial apprentices in the parish of St. James will not work after the 1st August next; we, the Members and Congregation of Salter's Hill, under the pastoral charge of the Rev. Walter Dendy, Baptist Missionary, RESOLVE — That this report is a false and malicious Libel upon us, as we never had such thoughts or intentions; but we are willing to work as usual for our Masters, so long as the present law continues in force, although we would rather be free: and that a copy of this resolution be forwarded to Sir Lionel Smith, Governor; Lord Glenelg, Colonial

Secretary; and to the Rev. John Dyer, Secretary of the Baptist
Missionary Society.[9]

Public meetings like this one provided a forum for popular expressions
of hopes and desires for the future; despite its aims of reassurance, it
was obviously difficult to restrain the desire for full freedom. The
phrase 'although we would rather be free', sandwiched into this assurance to obey the law, belies the prevailing aspirations. It is also
significant that the apprentices felt compelled to protect themselves
publicly from libel and felt entitled to send their resolutions to the
highest levels.

A meeting attended by 'between 3 and 4000 of the praedial
apprentice population' at the Baptist Chapel in Montego Bay on the
12th of May, 1838, likewise proffered contradictory messages of both
appeasement and challenge. The resolutions adopted were summarized
in the *Morning Journal* as declaratory of 'the determination of the
apprentices industriously and peaceably to pursue their course in obedience to the laws of the land, and agreeably to the word of God, and
the instructions received from their pastors'. Yet the actual printed proceedings show that the deacons, members and congregation used much
stronger language:

> Resolved 3rdly — That whenever it suits the wisdom and
> policy of our legal Rulers to grant us a perfectly equal and
> just participation in the laws, we shall hail the day as one of
> our brightest in human prosperity; and although we feel that
> we are entitled to all the immunities of free subjects without
> distinction, yet we are determined not to be betrayed by the
> schemes of our adversaries into acts of insubordination; but
> to pursue our course industriously and peaceably.[10]

Though eschewing violence and insubordination, the resolution makes
clear the popular sense of frustrated entitlement. The meeting also
reached out to a wider political audience, resolving to send its resolutions not only to the Governor, the Colonial Secretary and the
Secretary of the Baptist Missionary Society, but also to several famous
abolitionists: the Marquess of Sligo, Lord Brougham and Joseph
Sturge. They also wanted their proceedings published in Jamaican
newspapers, as well as British ones (*The British Emancipator* and *The
Patriot*). These meetings, staged with an international audience in
mind, went far beyond local grievances.

The *Morning Journal* also reported that Rev. Thomas Burchell
told a meeting of apprentices in Montego Bay, 'I have thought that you
yourselves should communicate, by a public meeting, you[r] senti-

ments to the Governor, to the Colonial Minister, and your friends here and in England'.[11] Thus, even before full emancipation, the classic British forms of political communication and claim-making — public meeting and petitioning — were being extended to the entire Afro-Jamaican population, with missionaries serving as brokers between isolated rural populations, local newspapers, officials and wider metropolitan publics. These missionaries, many of whom had led efforts to abolish slavery, and some of whom were opposed to apprenticeship, found themselves caught between ex-slaves and ex-masters as they tried to mediate between estate managers and workers to help ensure a fair transition to wage labour. As Swithin Wilmot notes, missionaries 'mobilized the mass of ex-slaves; [and] provided them with a constitutional forum in chapels and open-air meetings, to show their dissatisfaction with the Acts' passed by the planter-dominated legislature' (Wilmot 1977: 111). In addition, the earlier example of free people of colour using circulars, meetings and petitions to lobby for their rights had also laid the necessary groundwork for this broadening of political participation.[12]

When the campaign to end apprenticeship for both praedial and non-praedial workers on the 1st of August, 1838, was successful, announcement in July of full freedom was accompanied by public meetings and lavish celebrations; hereafter, the First of August became an annual public holiday. A report in the *Morning Journal* in July noted that Governor Smith had addressed a crowd of about two hundred 'negro headmen' from the balcony of the Court House at Halfway Tree in Kingston, 'setting forth the duties that would devolve on the free apprentices'.[13] The crowd listened respectfully and cheered him, then made their own speeches heard by the Governor. Some apprentices raised subscriptions for gifts to their 'benefactors' and formed delegations to present them. The selection of 'delegates' and the role of headmen in such public events attests to the already well-developed leadership structures among the apprentices, based on the status distinctions and work-gang hierarchies of the plantations. Some headmen were Baptist class leaders, and it may have been through them that the Baptist churches mobilized such good turnouts for their meetings.

As freed people stopped work to celebrate their emancipation, meetings were attended by crowds overflowing out of the small chapels in which they gathered. In some cases, these meetings involved delegates from various estates, who presumably reported back to local gatherings on the results of the meetings. Reports indicate that these meetings were not simply celebratory; they also dealt with pressing concerns and turned almost immediately to questions of justice. Just a few days after emancipation, 'some thousands of the Apprentices of Hanover' met at the Baptist Chapel in Falmouth:

> At the meeting on Thursday night there could not have been less than two thousand five hundred persons present: most of these were delegates from the majority of the estates in this parish; many of them came from St. James's. The rapturous bursts of applause which followed the observations of the several speakers sounded like music to our ears —- 'Justice to Jamaica' and 'Justice we will have', seemed to be the wish and the determination of everyone present: the meeting was altogether one which we shall not easily forget.[14]

These freedmen were prepared to mobilize and claim their rights. Only seven years on from the deadly repression that had followed the 'Baptist War', injustice would have been strong in the minds of the people of St. James. Justice was not easily won, though, and worker solidarity would be crucial in opposing the power of planters.

Even before apprenticeship ended, planters were holding their own meetings to discuss setting a fixed scale of wages; collusion in setting low wages and restricting labour mobility were already well in place by the time apprentices were ready to enter the labour market. With the apprenticeship experiment abandoned, sugar plantation workers quickly turned their attention to the fair negotiation of wage rates and ground rent, including organized strikes in demand of higher wages across many parishes. There is widespread evidence that newly freed plantation workers effectively utilized collective bargaining in the immediate post-emancipation period to wrest concessions from estate managers (Turner 1995; Wilmot 1984). This appears to have been most effective in St. Mary's parish, where all work was stopped for several months in what newspapers designated a 'strike'. In other areas, workers negotiated contracts based on wages of 1s. per day, but only if certain conditions were met. Newspaper reports indicate that some people were willing to work for the one shilling a day offered by most planters, but others were holding out for 2s. 6d.[15] In what came to be known (perhaps not without irony) as the 'Oxford and Cambridge terms', one shilling per day was accepted by first class workers if they were guaranteed rent-free houses and provision grounds, special pay for skilled workers, provision of medical services and watchmen for the remote mountain grounds. The terms also allowed workers to work only four days per week outside of crop harvesting time; this was an important concession because it allowed time for wage-workers to cultivate their own provision grounds and possibly market the produce. This agreement was reportedly adopted by forty-one properties (Wilmot 1984).

Where satisfactory labour contracts were not negotiated, however, workers turned to the new modes of claim-making that they had learned as apprentices. By the end of the first month of full emancipation, newspaper editors who were initially sympathetic towards labourers' wage demands were becoming increasingly concerned with the continuing stoppage of work, and there was growing anger towards missionaries, especially Baptists, who were accused of encouraging the strike for higher wages. The *Morning Journal* angrily wrote:

> We cannot believe, that any minister of religion would advise the people to sit down in idleness for three months, and waste so much valuable time, or to stand out for the exorbitant rates of wages, which some are demanding.... Still there is no denying that the stand for exorbitant wages is general, and the refusal to resume work such as to justify the opinion that the plan was preconcerted. The evil is not confined to two or three parishes, or to particular parts, or districts of a parish, but to nearly every parish in the island, and to all parts of them.[16]

In response, the planters and attorneys held their own meetings to represent their case to the governor. One meeting in St. David complained of 'the continued indisposition of the lately emancipated apprentices to labour, and the unsettled and unsatisfactory state of the affairs of the parish'.[17] Dawning realization of the power of organized workers led planters to attack the missionaries who were helping the people negotiate contracts. Collective bargaining between workers and estate managers was no longer confined to the plantations, but had taken on the character of a public debate over the terms and conditions of freedom.

One local example conveys the degree of tension between emancipated plantation workers, missionaries, planters and local officials in these initial months of hammering out 'free' contracts. On the very first weekend following full emancipation, the Falmouth area was hit by a widespread work-stoppage and an armed disturbance involving the famous anti-slavery Baptist Missionary, Rev. William Knibb. After Knibb spoke to meetings of labourers on obtaining fair wages, some white magistrates in Falmouth 'conceived the foolish and hazardous project of burning Mr. Knibb in effigy', the rumour of which was transformed into a planned attempt to murder him. Knibb's followers 'armed themselves with cutlasses, muskets, bills, and those who could not procure more deadly weapons, with sticks, and group after group of them proceeded out of the town towards Piedmont to guard him in'; they only dispersed after he collected their weapons in his carriage, met with the planter magistrates in Falmouth and showed the crowd that they were on perfectly good terms.[18] Most estates, however, 'still refused to go to work, unless their demand for high wages were conceded'. Then another rumour spread that Knibb was shot, 'and the people ran together; and from all parts armed bodies of negroes began to march upon Falmouth, threatening destruction of all the Whites, and Mulattoes, and to all the properties. "Buckra begin the war", said they "and now we will make them see St. Domingo"'.[19] Hundreds of people entered Falmouth armed with bludgeons, threatening to burn the town and the plantations, and uttering 'extremely hostile and treasonable language', according to local newspaper accounts. The crowd was finally quieted by a Stipendiary Magistrate who convinced them that Knibb was alive and well. This was an effective example of bargaining by riot in which fatalities were avoided, but planters and magistrates were nonetheless directly challenged; it also shows clearly that the Haitian Revolution was vivid in popular memory.

Peasant political agency

Baptist missionaries helped to organize scores of public meetings, in which freed slaves were encouraged to make speeches, to draw up resolutions that could be printed in the newspapers and to send petitions making their views known to the government and to the British public. As early as November 1838, seething dissatisfaction with labour conditions was being channelled into peaceful meetings and political petitioning among Baptist congregations, including demands for a broader franchise. It had been quickly grasped that there would be no progress in workers' social and political rights so long as former slave-owners continued to legislate for them. The increasingly defensive editors of the *Morning Journal* commented disapprovingly on politics in Trelawny under the headline 'Our Black Brethren':

> We perceive in an extremely ill-humoured article in the Falmouth Post of the 21st, that it is the intention of the lately enfranchised 'to hold county and parochial meetings, for the purpose of petitioning Parliament to pass those just and equitable laws for the government of the colony.... [A] statement of the wrongs which the negroes yet endure will be forwarded to their ever-vigilant friends, the Anti-Slavery Society. A request will be made for *an extension of the elective franchise*, to those who pay a certain rental for houses and lands, and when it is remembered that in this

parish there are no less than 40,000 inhabitants *chiefly blacks*, among whom at present there are not as many as 40 possessing the right of returning representatives to serve them in the popular branch of the Legislature, the Post feels that so reasonable a request will meet with immediate attention from the ministers of the crown [italics in original].[20]

The *Morning Journal* then sneered sarcastically, 'But why make two bites of a cherry? Why not request *Universal suffrage* at once, and the vote by ballot [emphasis in original]'. Despite having championed the civil and political rights of the free coloured population only a few years earlier, the editors of the *Morning Journal* were clearly not ready for popular democracy.

The planned meetings were held in Baptist chapels in January 1839. The *Falmouth Post* printed the resolutions passed on the first of January by a meeting chaired by Rev. Walter Dendy at which '[u]pwards of 3000 persons were in the chapel, and numbers standing outside who could not get admittance'.[21] The resolutions complained of the almost total exclusion of ex-slaves from political representation, and called for the framing of 'more just and equitable laws' whether by enfranchisement or by direct intervention by the Crown. The meeting also formed the 'Falmouth Auxiliary Anti-Slavery Society' to advance abolition in North America and other parts of the world. Not only were Jamaican freedmen placing their grievances at the level of the national system of legislation, but they were asserting their international solidarity with the continuing anti-slavery cause. An even bigger meeting in Kingston later that month prepared a petition signed by around 6000 people, taking a firm stand against the House of Assembly (which had lately been challenging the Governor's authority). The resulting address to Governor Smith expressed 'unqualified disapprobation' as 'British subjects' at the Assembly's 'contumacious behavior' towards the Crown. Native Jamaicans, in other words, were claiming a greater entitlement to the name of 'British subjects' than the disloyal planters in the House of Assembly. Who had the right to make decisions about the future of Jamaica? Many freed slaves immediately claimed that right as their own.

By June 1839, labour conflict was still unsettled in many areas, and Governor Smith had an official proclamation on the subject printed in the island newspapers and posted on public buildings in town squares throughout the island:

> Whereas it has been represented to Her Majesty's Government, that the Agricultural Population of this Island labour under considerable misunderstanding as to a supposed

right on their part, to the Houses and Provision-Grounds which they were permitted to occupy and cultivate, during Slavery and Apprenticeship: AND WHEREAS such misunderstanding, wherever it exists, is calculated to produce great evil both to the said Labouring Population and to the Proprietors of the Soils of this Island: I DO HEREBY make known that I have received instructions from Her Majesty's Secretary of State for the Colonies to assure the Labouring People, in Her Majesty's name, that such a notion is totally erroneous, and that they can only continue to occupy their Houses and Grounds upon such conditions, as they may agree upon with the Proprietors of such Houses and Grounds, or their lawful agents in this Country.[22]

In response, labourers again held meetings at Baptist chapels to discuss the 'rights and privileges' of the people. At a meeting chaired by Rev. Knibb in Falmouth, the separation of rent from wage payments was debated, with several labourers speaking. Edward Barrett,[23] a labourer on Oxford Estate and Deacon in Knibb's church, argued that 'we want to pay our rent by itself, and receive our wages under another agreement', while Alexander Stevenson argued that if anyone was confused about who owned what property, it was the overseers, or 'Bushas' who took all the estate property for their own use, living in the big house, taking supplies freely, and feeding their horses. 'It is not us who expect our master's houses and grounds; it isn't we who are looking for any new laws; it is the white people who want everything for themselves'.[24] A note of anger was creeping into popular public meetings, as workers recognized the violation of their rights.

Political power would be necessary to curtail the schemes of the planters, and such power would require independence from the sugar plantation's tight control over land and labour. Mobility itself was a key component of freedom. A newly mobile population was challenging planter control, not only on the plantations and in the House of Assembly, but also in the public spaces of the towns. As Rebecca Scott notes, 'one can ask to what extent juridical freedom, and the physical mobility that accompanied it, helped to make broader alliances possible' (R. Scott 1988: 426). Mobility began with movement off of the sugar plantations, as freedmen bought their own small plots of land.

An early form of self-determination among freed men and women began in the free villages founded by missionaries on land bought from former plantations or the backlands of large estates, and broken into smaller plots to be sold to freedmen (see Figure 2 in Chapter 2). These villages involved a fairly significant number of people: 'Between 1838 and 1844, a period of six years, [at least] 19,000 freedmen and their families removed themselves from the estates, bought land, and settled in free villages' (Mintz 1958: 49). The villages were autonomous and to some extent self-governing at the local level, with many costs and tasks shared among the settlers; the experience of community self-government in free villages laid the groundwork for citizenship identities and subsequent participation in civil and political rights movements. As Walter Rodney noted in the similar context of British Guiana, to live in a village was to open up the possibility of participating in a political process which was by no means totally under planter control. Village self-administration

> provided an opportunity of escape from the tyranny of the plantation in Guiana much like the physical movement of black freedmen to the mountains of Jamaica.... When the Times of London described the proprietors of Guiana's communal villages as 'little bands of socialists', this was in effect a reference to the cooperative self-government characteristic of those villages (Rodney 1981: 128).

As in Guiana, the Nonconformist churches in Jamaica 'provided an important bridge between the middle classes and the working people, especially in rural areas'; within these safe settings, workers' associations and Friendly Societies contributed to the development of workers' solidarity outside of the plantation sector (Rodney 1981: 146, 162-65). Cooperation, autonomy and new collective identities emerged at the village level and contributed to new kinds of political consciousness-raising. A new peasant political culture (and sense of both economic and political agency) quickly formed, combining the protest traditions of slave communities with the exercise of new freedoms.[25]

Despite local elite resistance, Nonconformist missionaries put the mass of Jamaican labourers in contact with the political networks of a wider British public of reform-minded activists. Public meetings not only offered a visually powerful way of demonstrating physical majorities that were not represented in the island legislature, but they also fostered personal empowerment through participation in this wider public. The Baptist church in particular was crucial to realizing the mass public meeting as an effective means of popular claim-making in post-emancipation Jamaica. The Baptist-led public meetings that accompanied emancipation enabled the exercise of greater self-assertion and decision-making powers within ex-slave communities; participants also cultivated new organizational and leadership skills that would be applied to later popular mobilizations. In the meetings, held at chapels according to strict procedural rules, participants learned about calling a speaker to the chair, moving and seconding resolutions, raising subscriptions, forming delegations to draw up and formally present resolutions, publishing proceedings in local and metropolitan newspapers and circulating and signing petitions. Many church members also gained experience in public speaking, church elections (of elders, churchwardens, deacons, etc.) and general participation in the internal governance structures of the churches.

Overall, Baptist chapels organized at least five major public meetings in 1838 involving thousands of labourers, besides holding numerous local emancipation celebrations. In 1839, there were several public meetings held at the Baptist chapel in Falmouth, and others at chapels in Kingston, Bethel Hill and St. Ann's Bay, with many locales forming auxiliaries to the British and Foreign Anti-Slavery Society. In 1840, there were over fifteen recorded meetings, including the 'Jamaica Anti-Slavery Convention' held at the Spanish Town Baptist Chapel in March, and several meetings to found the African Missionary Society of the Baptist Church. At such meetings, correspondence from Britain was read out and delegates were appointed to go to London and New York, for the World Anti-Slavery conventions to be held in May and June.[26] Meetings continued throughout the decade, many attended by two thousand or more people. There was an especially heated series of meetings in 1844, following parliamentary proposals to remove tariff protection from sugar and the government decision to subsidize indentured immigration.

Many of these meetings drew up petitions that were submitted either to the Jamaican House of Assembly, or in some cases to Parliament in Britain. Common grievances included complaints that legislation and taxation favoured planters and disadvantaged labourers and small landholders, especially public expenditures on indentured immigration and in support of the established church. A religion-infused 'civic culture' enhanced by literacy education in many ways empowered emancipated slaves as free citizens despite the recognized 'colonizing' effects of missionary movements (cf. Comaroff and Comaroff 1991).[27] As Gordon Catherall argues, Baptist missionaries 'provided an experimental framework in which to work out some practical definition of freedom with involvement.... [They] provided a necessary environment for the training of citizens', thereby 'rebuilding civil society' in ways comparable to the Gandhian village communities of India, or the Christian base communities of Latin America (Catherall 1990: 271–72).

At the same time, the re-emergence of African religious idioms and practices presented an ongoing resource for more radical resistance to colonialism (Stewart 1992; Chevannes 1994). Support for Africa,

Africans and the continuing anti-slavery movement were major areas of public interest among Jamaican ex-slaves. An anti-slavery meeting held at Bethtephil Baptist Chapel in 1840, for example, resolved that they 'consider it to be their bounden duty to use every means in their power to expose and put down the slave-trade and slavery, as carried on in Africa, and in the boasted lands of freedom, the United States of America'.[28] Increasing resentment of white racism led to dissension within the Wesleyan Methodist and Baptist churches in Jamaica, as black congregations recognized the limitations of white pastorship and sought to select their own leaders and preachers. Even more radically, grassroots 'revivalism' promoted Afro-Christian leaders and practices; by blurring the boundaries between Christian and African-rooted religious beliefs, the Revival movements challenged the entire basis of European religion. Also of significance for popular participation was the part played by Afro-Jamaican women both in promoting a popular 'voice' within the missionary societies, and in forming their own religious networks and followings (Sheller 1998).

A special case for peasant political agency must be made in regard to women. In both Haiti and Jamaica, women were responsible for local marketing and they covered great distances bringing rural produce to the market centres, and urban and imported goods back to the country. Their mobility, access to credit and centrality in networks of communication gave market women a greater degree of autonomy than other peasant groups. Yet, women were excluded by definition from equal citizenship; they could not vote or hold public office, and had no officially recognized claim to political participation.[29] The modern status of citizenship was originally closely tied to bargaining between states and subject populations over the obligation of military service (Tilly 1994). Thus, it is not surprising that male slaves often gained freedom as an incentive or compensation for military service (i.e. during the Haitian Revolution, the Latin-American Wars of Independence, the United States Civil War and the Cuban Ten Years' War). Military service gave men a claim on the state not available to women. Though still excluded by property qualifications from voting or holding office, Afro-Caribbean men at least had a legitimate claim on equal political rights. Nevertheless, Afro-Caribbean women did play a significant role in several major political events.[30]

Non-white women were a permanent presence in the public spaces of towns because of their central role in marketing agricultural produce, as well as their concentration in domestic service jobs in urban areas. An 1844 census of Kingston found a total population of 14,350 males and 18,543 females, while the 1861 island-wide census found that in all the towns of the island there was a total of 36,805 females, compared with only 26,378 males.[31] Thus, women played an important part in the development of a politically active Afro-Jamaican public in two ways: first, they facilitated flows of information between town and country; and, second, they filled the streets and squares during popular political mobilizations or demonstrations. As I have argued elsewhere (Sheller 1998), women's political leadership was not simply due to sheer numbers on the lowest social rungs. Rather, it was their special economic and social position as a link between town and country, between markets and fields, and between the state and the families it tried to control. Market women, or 'higglers', brought produce from the country into the towns and carried news and information to rural districts in the process. In largely non-literate societies, women's concentration in the market towns advantaged them in gathering oral information, while their economic and familial ties throughout the countryside enabled them to disseminate news more quickly than official channels.

The importance of internal marketing networks as channels of political communication during the period of slavery has been recognized by a number of historians. There has been less discussion, however, of the ongoing significance of these networks after emancipation, when Jamaican markets continued to be run largely by women, with only minimal regulation of their organization.[32] Whereas many studies have concluded that the street was the locale of masculine 'reputation' in the Caribbean, with women relegated to the home, the fenced-in yard or the 'respectability' of the church, there is in fact much evidence that urban working-class women dominated the life of the streets.[33] As Rhoda Reddock has noted for Trinidad & Tobago, 'For most women the street was their arena of activity. They worked there, were entertained, quarreled, fought, and even ate there. The Victorian adage that women should be seen and not heard was not applicable here, and the strict division between public and private life was not yet instituted among the working classes'.[34] Given their numerical predominance in urban public spaces, black women played a special part in public disturbances and riots, where they often made up the majority of participants in contentious gatherings.

Above all, it is clear from police reports that black women played a highly visible part in the streets and rioting 'mob', often suffering retaliatory police attack. Not only were women's public activities a constant challenge to the security of the class, racial and gender identities of the white male elite, but working-class public culture often transmuted into direct verbal challenges to the authorities, sometimes turning into violent riots. Many examples of 'violent language' recorded in the British records were spoken by women, whether during slavery and apprenticeship, or in later court-house scuffles and 'riots'; when violence occurred, working-class women were often at the forefront, brandishing not only insults and provocation, but quite often weapons as well. By the 1850s, those words and weapons were increasingly turned not only against overseers and plantation personnel, but against the actual representatives of the colonial state: policemen, court-houses, militias, even magistrates. At this level, we discover one of the main differences between Haiti and Jamaica, for any popular mobilizations were quickly met with armed force in Haiti. The Haitian military moved with impunity, whereas in Jamaica rights of association, speech and publication were to some extent protected, at least in so far as one could protest at their withdrawal.

Peasant civil agency

As in Haiti, newspapers were a key component in the development of a democratic alliance in opposition to the political domination of big landowners. Some publications in Jamaica were specifically targeted at the population of freed slaves. A Baptist weekly newspaper was started in Falmouth in September 1839, with the explicit purpose of empowering freedmen and aiding Africans. *The Baptist Herald and Friend of Africa* proclaimed in its opening editorial that '[we] have long felt the desirableness of having a cheap publication by which the labouring population might be instructed in a knowledge of those rights and privileges which belong to them as free men, as well as in those duties they owe to each other and to the community, now they are invested with the name of British subjects'. The same issue also advertised the 'free village system' in Trelawny, with 'sundry pieces and parcels of LAND which will be sold in LOTS to suit buyers among the labouring peasantry', in Sturge's Town, Castle Town, New Birmingham, Calabar, Hoby's Town, and Shady Grove.[35]

The paper claimed to be the cheapest in the island (6s. 8d. per annum, later reduced to only 6s.), and by 1844 reported a circulation of over one thousand per week, 'chiefly in the parishes of St. Thomas in the Vale, St. Mary, St. Ann, Trelawny, St. James and Hanover'.[36] It was not only strongly against foreign slavery, but also took some very pro-labour stands in comparison to most of the Jamaican press. In August 1844, following attempts to lower wages to 9d. per day, an editorial stated that 'we give it as our decided opinion, that labor here is worth 1s. 6d. per day. Our advice to the peasantry therefore, is to insist on present prices, and on no account, to work for less.... Let them resist [the wage reduction] *at once*, and *universally*'. In February 1845, it printed 'Advice to the Peasantry. From what is going on, we strongly advise the laborer not to enter into any agreement with the Overseer or Attorney, unless that agreement be in writing; and not to sign any paper except in the presence of some friend who can read, and in whom he has confidence'.[37]

Less militant whites tried to build civic culture by organizing philanthropic associations (see Table 6 for a summary of Jamaican voluntary and welfare associations). Some institutions were founded with the explicit aim of educating and 'bettering' the working classes. In 1842, the *Morning Journal* published an article under the headline 'Reunions of the Working and Middle Classes', promoting the formation of clubs modeled on the Leeds Parliamentary Reform Association, to diffuse 'sound political information to the working class, and to promote a kindlier feeling between them and other classes'. As the author went on to explain, '[W]hat is needed is, that any change which must come, in the fulness of time, in an ever-progressive society, should be approached not as a matter of bloody contest, but as a matter of co-operation, or if you like of bargain'.[38] Along the same lines, local agricultural societies were formed in almost every parish in the early 1840s. They arranged lectures and demonstrations, offered practical advice on better techniques and new technology and sponsored fairs or contests each year in which monetary prizes were offered for the best examples of produce, livestock and workmanship. The island-wide Royal Agricultural Society was founded in 1840, and the Royal Society of Arts in 1854 (the two were amalgamated in 1866).

'Industrial education' societies were founded to promote better agricultural practices and introduce new technologies, such as the St. James and Trelawny Society for the Promotion of Industrial Education, founded in 1843 (Hall 1959: 30). Perhaps influenced by French socialism and British Christian Socialism (Lewis 1983), there were several attempts to establish marketing cooperatives in this period; most, however, were unsuccessful. The most ambitious cooperative production and marketing scheme in the 1840s was Special Magistrate Alexander Fyfe's proposed Metcalfe Central Sugar Factory and Timber Company (1846), which never got off the ground.[39] In a later scheme, the St. David's Joint-Stock Co. and Society of Arts was established in 1857, 'to regulate by means of co-operative labour, certain schemes of cultivation upon such lands as the Company might be able to purchase' on the basis of shares of five pounds raised from individual investors (Hall 1959: 202). Such projects, however, were aimed more at bigger landowners, not smallholders and labourers.[40]

In Jamaica there were also far more schools than in Haiti in part because the British government financially supported education as a

Table 6   Voluntary Associations and Societies in Jamaica, 1823–1866

Founded	Name (Founder)
1823	The Bienfaisance Society (Lecesne & Escoffery)
1828	The Kingston Benevolent Society (Rev. T. B. Turner)
1838–39	Society for the Protection of Civil and Religious Liberty
1839	Falmouth Auxiliary Anti-Slavery Society & other auxiliaries to BFASS
1839	Jamaica Education Society (Baptist Western Union)
1840	African Missionary Society of the Baptist Church
1840	Royal [Jamaica] Agricultural Society (& various parish branches)
1841	St. Thomas in the East & St. David's Savings Bank
1842	Trelawny Savings Bank
1842	St. Thomas in the Vale Savings Bank (T. Witter Jackson)
1841–42	Kingston Mechanics Institution
1843	St. James & Trelawny Society for Industrial Education
1843	Baptist Benefit Society
1854	Royal Society of Arts
1855	Trinity District Mutual Aid Society, Westmoreland
1856	The Mutual Improvement Society, Kingston (Gardner)
1857	The Provident Society, Kingston (Gardner)
1857	St. David's Joint-Stock Co. & Society of Arts
1859	Kingston & St. Andrew Ladies' Reformatory & Industrial Association
1859	The Falmouth Association for Moral & Social Improvement
1850s	Industrial School, Mount Holstein, St. George (Rev. G. Rouse)
186x	S. J. Walcott's Industrial School, Richmond Estate
186x	Hanover Society of Industry
1864	The Benefit Building Society (Model Home Department) (Gardner)
1864	Mercantile Agency Association, Black River (Barrett)
1865	Freedman's Aid Society-Joint Stock Association (Brydson & Plummer)
1865	The Underhill Convention (Rodney & Burton, St. Ann's Bay)
1865	The New Belvedere Society
1866	The Royal Incorporated Society of Arts & Agriculture

means to 'moral reformation' of the slave, while missionaries themselves saw education as a key aspect of faith, conversion and moral
development. In particular, between 1835–45 the government awarded
an annual subsidy of up to £30,000 to the non-denominational Mico
Charity.[41] The Baptists instituted a Jamaica Educational Society as soon
as slavery ended, and by 1839, they reported a total of 16,313 students
in day and Sunday schools (mostly in Cornwall and Middlesex).[42] A
compilation of missionary statements for 1841 shows 21 teachers
attached to the Wesleyan Methodist Mission, 22 with the Church
Missionary Society, and 71 with the Baptist Missionary Society; the
total number of school children was estimated to be between 25,000
and 31,800.[43] These schools taught both girls and boys, and about one
third of the teachers were women. Many Jamaicans expressed the desire
to educate their children, and some were clearly proud of their children
who were literate. As in the United States, ex-slaves were willing to
spend what little money they had on building schools, paying school
fees and buying clothing for their children to attend school (Du Bois
[1935] 1992).

The economic restructuring associated with the emancipation of
an enslaved rural labour force (along with the continuing process of
decline of an old sugar colony faced with falling sugar prices), led to a
more mobile and town-based popular culture in Jamaica. While some
former slaves could survive by growing provisions for the local village
markets — selling coffee, pimento, arrowroot, sugarcane, fruit and
vegetables, as well as handicrafts (Sewell [1862] 1968: 248–49) — or
even for export, the local economy was inadequate to support the entire
population. As Elizabeth Petras suggests, after about 1840, Jamaica's
'mechanics, foremen, skilled workers, and artisans steadily abandoned
the agricultural sector and moved into the towns' (Petras 1988: 49).
However, 'in the urban centers, they found no incipient industry that
could employ them. Thus, they became members of the first urban
floating labor reserve…. By 1850 a geographically mobile urban sub-
proletariat was distinguishable in Jamaica' (Petras 1988: 49, 52).
Thousands of such workers left Jamaica between 1850 and 1855,
recruited to work on the Panama Railroad that was being built across
the isthmus by a U.S. joint-stock company. They were offered enticing
wages of 3s. 2d. per day, with promises of food and medical attendance, but many died in Panama, where worker mortality was
extremely high (Petras 1988).

A distinctive working-class consciousness was apparent as early
as 1842, as seen in this article written by a self-described 'Mechanic'
in *The Morning Journal*:

To the Mechanics of Jamaica. Fellow Craftsmen. Most of you, it may be presumed, in common with myself, have experienced many drawbacks in our varied avocation, for want of an institution where mutual sociality and communion of sentiment and ideas might be unrestrictedly and beneficially enjoyed.... A mechanic's society would not only be of essential service to the master, but particularly to the labouring operative, whose present very prescribed knowledge or total ignorance of practical mechanics in most instances, renders him intolerably intractable to his master.... What is there to prevent the formation of such a society among us, where we might have the advantage of at least a well stored library, if not of popular lectures, with our museum and school of arts and sciences?[44]

With his plans for a Kingston Mechanic's Institution, this worker was aware of an international labour movement; he also planned to 'open a connecting correspondence with the "London Mechanics Institution", through whose paternal means we might derive every assistance possible in establishing a library, museum and school'.[45]

There were also attempts, especially in the 1840s, to found Savings Banks for the 'poorer classes' in order to encourage 'habits of thrift'. At a public meeting in Morant Bay in 1841, inhabitants of St. Thomas-in-the-East and St. David resolved:

That the establishment of a Savings Bank...would be productive of great benefit to the community; and especially to the labouring Classes, as affording them a safe and convenient investment for their surplus earnings, and good interest for the deposits they may make; and as tending toward their moral improvement, by checking their too frequent inclination to useless and extravagant expenditure, and encouraging industrious and frugal habits.[46]

The bank was to be opened in the Old School Room at the Court House on Saturdays. It was soon found, though, that the labourers were not very enthusiastic about putting their money into elite-run savings banks: 'the labouring population of the parish are not yet aware of the principles on which such an institution is conducted'.[47] For most labourers with a stake in family land, there was no better bank than a fattening pig.

In the 1850s, many associations were created with the needs of the working class in mind. The Trinity District Mutual Aid Society, for instance, was founded in Westmoreland in 1855 and aimed at 'persons of the labouring class'; for a small subscription, it offered medical attendance, disability payments and old age support.[48] A London Missionary Society report mentions several societies connected with the Kingston Station, including a Mutual Improvement Society founded in 1856 with over 300 members, offering lectures and a periodical for 4s. a year; and a Provident Society founded in 1857, which insured for sickness and death for 1s. 6d. a month. They also formed a Benefit Building Society in 1864, which built model homes and gave grants for renovation of dilapidated buildings.[49] Besides joining voluntary associations, freed men and women often volunteered their labour to complete collective projects in the community or to support a missionary.

Edward Holland of the London Missionary Society wrote that his congregation was donating both cash and labour to build a new chapel. He linked this to the prevailing low wages: 'In one instance I had the Father, Mother, daughter and two sons — the whole family for the week... As they are so ill requited for their labor on the neighbouring Estates since the introduction of the Hill Coolies who work for 6d. per day and their food, they prefer laboring at their Chapel'.[50] This kind of voluntary labour could involve single families, but it could also draw on the contributions of large gangs. Holland reported in 1847 that he had planted 'a small patch of canes' to support his family, and a young man in his congregation 'cheerfully consented' to bring his work fellows to harvest it: 'he came accompanied with seventy-six others and ground away until the day began to dawn — three of the number remained to boil the liquor. Besides that they planted all my provisions, corn, and gave upwards of 600 days labour to the new chapel, free of expence'.[51] For low-paid agricultural workers, cooperative labour had significant returns not only in terms of the expectation of future help in digging or harvesting one's own grounds, but also in some instances as a kind of barter replacement for cash payments.[52]

Missionaries clearly hoped that civil institutions such as churches, schools, friendly societies and savings banks would build a sense of community; former slaves, however, already had their own ideas of community, and their own public networks. Unlike Haiti, 'native' religions were tolerated to some extent in Jamaica, at least in the form of 'Native Baptist' practices. A crucial part of changes in public life in post-emancipation Jamaica was the emergence of distinctive 'African' and 'black' identities. Baptists played an important part in raising consciousness about the ongoing struggle against slavery throughout the world, and the need for Jamaican solidarity with Africa; perhaps, they did not realize quite how strong the symbolic meaning of Africa could become. At the chapel in Falmouth in 1842, for example, a commemorative monument was placed above the pulpit with an inscription, 'By Emancipated Sons of Africa, To Commemorate the Birth-Day of their Freedom, August the First, 1838'; it included the prophetic psalm verse: 'Ethiopia Shall Soon Stretch Out Her Hands Unto God'.[53] What did Africa mean to Afro-Jamaicans? And how did the collective identity of being a 'son of Africa' dovetail with the identity of being a 'British subject'?

During emancipation celebrations at Kettering, at which a 'large map of Africa... [was] suspended behind the speaker's chair', Edward Barrett of Oxford Estate significantly summed up the debts owed Africa:

'The set time had come' when Africa was required payment for the wrongs she had suffered; and he trusted they would shew their gratitude for their own freedom, by trying to send the Gospel to their Fathers and Mothers in Africa. Black, White, and Brown — all were interested in Africa. Let none say they had nothing to do in the work. For the white ladies and gentlemen, who were not related to Afric' people, had received much of their property, from those who got it out of the blood of Africa.[54]

This consciousness of being African, and of owing some repayment to the people of Africa, was partly fostered by the abolitionist wing of the Baptist church, but it also reflected a deeper Afro-Jamaican sense of identity. Missionary churches themselves began to come under fire from Afro-Jamaican publics realizing their own power and resources. As Barrett makes clear, those people back in Africa might be their own fathers and mothers; for others, they were symbolic ancestors. This African identity was one of the bases for an alternative political culture that increasingly broke free from the Baptist churches which had helped to incubate it.[55]

Christianity was not the only spiritual resource to be called upon by the 'children of Ethiopia'. The missionary vision of a Christian public was melting into an autonomous and powerful Afro-Jamaican public, and Jamaicans were beginning to assert (and seek public recognition for) their African cultural identities in new ways. If Baptist missionaries had started out in the role of mediators, they had become clearly aligned on the side of the peasantry, against the planter. The Baptist churches became central locales for the emergence of black leaders and black publics out of slavery, as they did in other post–emancipation contexts, for example in the United States (Higginbotham 1993, 1997), or in Guyana (Rodney 1981). The alliance between white

missionaries and black congregations in Jamaica would be effective for
some time, but it would eventually lead to dissentions within the
churches, as increasingly autonomous black congregations turned their
attention to the churches themselves, which also became objects for
reform and democratization. By the 1840s, it was apparent that there
was a vast social chasm between white missionaries and black congregations. If petitioning, public meeting and formation of voluntary societies were engagements within the terms of the existing civil and
political system, the emergence of Afro-Christian religious revivals
provided a more radical challenge.

In Jamaica, the practices known as Myalism and Obeah, with
African origins, were the root of subsequent 'syncretistic' Afro-
Christian religions, many of which came to be associated with crucial
peasant political movements (Chevannes 1994; Post 1978; Schuler
1991; Stewart 1992; Turner 1982). These 'roots' religions were the
fundamental basis for post-emancipation community formation
throughout the Caribbean (Bastide 1978; Chevannes 1994; Métraux
1960). Practitioners of Myal, both male and female, were not only
community leaders — gathering a 'flock' of followers, advising them
on personal affairs, spiritually guiding them, and healing illnesses —
but were quite often Baptists as well. As Barry Chevannes explains,
Myalism took root mainly in Baptist congregations because the Baptist
class and leader system 'provided greater autonomy and freedom for
Myal to refashion the symbols and teachings of Christianity into its
own image, to snatch the "Christian message from the messenger"'
(Chevannes 1994: 18). Moreover, as Robert J. Stewart argues, 'Black
religion, in its unique and several Jamaican syntheses of African and
European elements, provided communities of cultural cohesion and
spiritual motivation for political protest' (Stewart 1992: 122–23). Thus,
in examining structures of popular religion in Jamaica, one is also
examining the resources and ideologies for political mobilization. 'The
Myal tradition,' suggests Monica Schuler, had a *this-world* orientation
that 'formed the core of a strong and self-confident counter-culture. It
guaranteed that none of the evils of the postslavery period would be
accepted passively, but would be fought ritually and publicly' (Schuler
1991: 301).

This *public* component, I suggest, was fundamental to the political and civil agency fostered by these religions. There were two major
Afro-Christian Revivals (or Myal 'outbreaks'), in post–emancipation
Jamaica, in 1842–43 and 1860–61. The Revival of the early 1840s
occurred mainly in St. James and other western parishes. White
observers were dumbfounded by the rate at which the revival 'sponta-
neously' spread, but it was an indication of the hidden word-of-mouth

networks through which news travelled in the black community. Waddell wrote that the 'wild outbreak of Myalism, in 1842, ... [was] one of the most startling events in the history of Jamaica missions, and showed how deeply rooted the old heathenism of their race still was among the negroes'. Others described how a group at Flower Hill said they were 'sent by God...to purge and purify the world, they had the spirit, and were Christians of a higher order than common'. They performed public rituals of purification:

> After these fanatics had spent several days extracting the supposed pernicious substances from the houses and gardens of their own class, with singing and dancing, and various peculiar rites[...], we found them in full force and employ- ment, forming a ring, around which were a multitude of onlookers. Inside the circle some females performed a mystic dance, sailing round and round, and wheeling in the center with outspread arms, and wild looks and gestures. Others hummed, or whistled a low monotonous tune (Waddell [1863] 1970: 187–89).

Some groups seized chapels and prayer-houses 'for their heathenish practices', opened graves and disrupted prayer meetings with violent spirit 'possessions'. Myal rites were a radical expression of self-determination, demonstrating grassroots control of religion; they also indicate the exercise of 'popular justice', as communities tried to solve collective problems by rooting out harmful Obeahmen and digging up the 'wanga' or evil charms that these sorcerers had planted.

These public ceremonies indicate one kind of subaltern public bringing its 'hidden trancripts' into the light of day (J. C. Scott 1990). 'What is significant about revivalism as it developed from the early 1860s', argues Stewart, 'was that it was increasingly open, indepen- dent, and self-confident in a way that Obeah could never be and that Myalism had only been previously during periodic "outbreaks"'. It broke the walls of the churches, as it were, and took to the road' (Stewart 1992: 147). Beyond overtly political claim-making directed at the government, I suggest that these religious forms of peasant agency must be theorized as part of the emergence of black publics. As Stewart suggests, in some instance 'impromptu revivalist services served the same purpose as many political marches and street demon- strations today' (ibid: 147; cf. Schuler 1991). 'To a far greater extent than most people realize', argues Chevannes, 'Myal and its later mani- festation, Revival, have shaped the worldview of the Jamaican people, helping them to forge an identity and a culture by subversive participa- tion in the wider polity' (Chevannes 1994: 20–21). Baptist churches had once provided safe locales in which to develop communities after slavery and practise repertoires of democratic participation, but former slaves were beginning to develop a new sense of collective agency and to create their own subaltern publics. As mobilization outran the confines of churches, black leaders emerged, expressing grievances in new ways and making new demands.

Notes

1   LMS, Box 2, Woolridge to Directors, 2 Aug. 1839. The event also raised £20.
2   LMS, Box 2, W.G. Barret to Directors, Four Paths, 15 Aug. 1839. Whether Jamaicans recognized the revolutionary origins and Haitian resonance of their symbolic tree is unclear.
3   As John Bohstedt has argued in regard to England and Wales, riots 'were social politics in the sense that they tested rioters' and magistrates' resources of force and persuasion, affected the policies of local authorities and the distribution of goods and social burdens, and took place within calculable conventions' (John Bohstedt, *Riots and Community Politics in England and Wales, 1790–1810* [Cambridge: Harvard University Press, 1983], 4–5).
4   I follow James (1938) and Fraginals (1976) in referring to plantations as 'semi-industrial' in so far as they concentrated a workforce in partly factory-like conditions and thus created 'proto-proletarians' (cf. Mintz, 'Slavery and the Rise of Peasantries').
5   The actual campaign to abolish slavery, on which there is an extensive historiography, will not be discussed here. See Chapter 1 for an overview.
6   Williams' narrative was presented in the House of Lords, and used in the formal parliamentary enquiry that contributed to the early ending of praedial apprenticeship. See 'A Narrative of events since the First of August, 1834', by James Williams, An Apprenticed Labourer in Jamaica', bound with *Lord Brougham's Speech on the Slave Trade in the House of Lords*, 29 January 1838 (London: J. Rider, 1838); cf. *Morning Journal*, Vol. 1, no. 2, 11 Apr. 1838.
7   It should not be forgotten that the community of freed slaves living in England in the late eighteenth century also played a crucial part in the abolition movement, including public speaking tours and well-known narratives by Ottobah Cuguano and Olaudah Equiano. Thus, began a black diaspora public. See Henry L. Gates Jr., ed., *The Classic Slave Narratives* (New York: Mentor, 1987); Peter Fryer, *Staying Power: Black People in Britain Since 1504* (Atlantic Highlands, NJ: Humanities Press, 1984); Gretchen Gerzina, *Black London: Life Before Emancipation* (New Brunswick: Rutgers University Press, 1995); Douglas A. Lorimer, 'Black Resistance to Slavery and Racism in Eighteenth Century England' in *Essays in the History of Blacks in Britain*, ed. J.S. Gundara and I. Duffield (Aldershot: Avebury, 1992), pp. 58–80.
8   Land-use studies of plantations in the U.S. also suggest that 'slaves carved out landscapes of their own' (John M. Vlach, *Back of the Bighouse: The Architecture of Plantation Slavery* [Chapel Hill: University of North Carolina Press, 1993], *x*).
9   *Morning Journal*, no. 11, 21 Apr. 1838.
10 *Morning Journal*, no. 34, 18 May 1838.
11 *Morning Journal*, no. 36, 21 May 1838.
12 On the development of petitioning among the free coloured and free black populations, including tensions between the two groups, see Sheila Duncker, 'The Free

Coloured and their Fight for Civil Rights in Jamaica, 1800–1830' (MA thesis, University of the West Indies, March 1965).

13 *Morning Journal*, no. 93, 26 July 1838.

14 *Morning Journal*, no. 101, 4 Aug., 1838.

15 This was a standard rate for hired labour during the apprenticeship period, and was based on the previously used 'valuation' of slaves who wished to purchase their own freedom. There were twelve pence to a shilling, and twenty shillings to a pound.

16 *Morning Journal*, Vol. 1, no. 116, 22 Aug. 1838.

17 *Morning Journal*, Vol. 1, no. 125, 1 Sept. 1838.

18 LMS, Box 2, John Vine, First Hill, Rio Bueno P.O., 4 Sept. 1838.

19 Ibid.

20 *Morning Journal*, Vol. 1, no. 196, 23 Nov. 1838.

21 *Falmouth Post*, Vol. 5, no. 1, 2 Jan. 1839. Dendy supported popular political participation, chaired meetings and organized petitions over the next two decades.

22 *Morning Journal*, Vol. 2, [no day] June 1839.

23 Edward Barrett — who probably helped negotiate the 'Oxford and Cambridge' terms — was a labour leader who accompanied Knibb on a trip to England in 1840. He spoke to a meeting at Exeter Hall on the subjects of slavery, Christian conversion and his desire to found a mission to West Africa (*Baptist Herald*, Vol. 1, no. 40, 5 Aug. 1840 and Vol. 5, no. 32, 6 Aug. 1844).

24 *Falmouth Post*, Vol. 5, no. 24, 12 June 1839.

25 Cf. Julie Saville's similar description of 'neighbourhood leagues' in South Carolina, which emerged out of freed slaves' military societies (Julie Saville, *The Work of Reconstruction: From Slave to Wage Laborer in South Carolina, 1860–1970* [Cambridge: Cambridge University Press, 1994], p. 180).

26 This summary is based on my collection of public texts, but for this period a crucial source is the *Baptist Herald and Friend of Africa*, which claimed to be the cheapest paper in the island and to issue nine hundred copies weekly. See especially Vol. 1, nos. 8, 11, 16, 17, 19, 24, 25 and 40 (covering 1839–40) for specific reports.

27 As Elsa Brown argues for the U.S., 'Central to African Americans' construction of a fully democratic notion of political discourse was the church as a foundation of the black public sphere' (E. B. Brown, 'Negotiating and Transforming the Public Sphere: African American Political Life in the Transition from Slavery to Freedom', in *The Black Public Sphere*, ed. Black Public Sphere Collective [Chicago: University of Chicago Press, 1995], p. 114).

28 *Baptist Herald and Friend of Africa*, Vol. I, no. 11, 15 Jan. 1840.

29 For a longer discussion of the origins of the sexual division of labour in Haiti, and its relationship to concepts of citizenship, see Sheller, 'Sword-Bearing Citizens'. On women's political participation in Jamaica, see Sheller, 'Quasheba, Mother, Queen'; and Heuman, 'Post-Emancipation Protest in Jamaica: The Morant Bay Rebellion, 1865' in Turner, *From Chattel Slaves to Wage Slaves*, pp. 258–74.

30 There is a growing body of research on women and politics in the Caribbean; see, for example, Janet Momsen, ed., *Women and Change in the Caribbean* (London: James Currey, 1993); Marietta Morrissey, *Slave Women in the New World: Gender Stratification in the Caribbean* (Lawrence, KS: University of Kansas Press, 1989); Rhoda Reddock, 'Women and Slavery in the Caribbean: A Feminist Perspective', *Latin American Perspectives*, Issue 44, 12:1 (Winter 1985): 63–80; and R. Reddock, *Women, Labour, and Politics in Trinidad and Tobago* (London: Zed

Books, 1994); Verene Shepherd, et al., *Engendering History: Caribbean Women in Historical Perspective* (Kingston: Ian Randle; London: James Currey, 1995); *Feminist Review*, no. 59, ed. Patricia Mohammed, 'Rethinking Caribbean Difference'(Summer 1998).

31   Census figures are from *Baptist Herald and Friend of Africa*, Vol.5, no. 33, 13 Aug.1844, p. 259 and Barry Higman, ed. *The Jamaican Censuses of 1844 and 1861* (Kingston: University of the West Indies, 1980); the overall female population in 1861 was 6,521 white, 42,842 brown, and 179,097 black.

32   On women's role in markets as crucial networks of communication during slavery, see Sidney Mintz and Douglas Hall, 'The Origins of the Jamaican Internal Marketing System', *Yale University Publications in Anthropology*, no. 57 (New Haven: 1960); Olwig, *Cultural Adaptation*; Mary S. Turner, *Slaves and Missionaries: The Disintegration of Jamaican Slave Society, 1787–1834* (Urbana: University of Illinois, 1982); Janet Momsen, 'Gender Roles in Caribbean Agriculture' in Malcolm Cross and Gad Heuman, eds., *Labour in the Caribbean* (London: Macmilan, 1988), 141–58; and Robert Olwell, '"Loose, Idle and Disorderly": Slave Women in the Eighteenth-Century Charleston Marketplace' in David Gaspar and Darlene Hine, eds., *More Than Chattel: Black Women and Slavery in the Americas* (Bloomington and Indianapolis: Indiana University Press, 1996), pp. 97–110.

33   On the reputation/respectability debate see Peter J. Wilson, *Crab Antics: The Social Anthropology of English-Speaking Negro Societies in the Caribbean* (New Haven: Yale University Press, 1973); Diane J. Austin, *Urban Life in Kingston, Jamaica: The Culture and Class Ideology of Two Neighborhoods* (New York: Gordon and Breach, 1984); Besson, 'Reputation and respectability reconsidered: a new perspective on Afro-Caribbean peasant women' in Momsen, ed., *Women and Change in the Caribbean*, pp. 15–37; Carolyn Cooper, *Noises in the Blood: Orality, Gender and the 'Vulgar' Body of Jamaican Popular Culture* (Durham: Duke University Press, 1995); and Richard D. E. Burton, *Afro-Creole: Power, Opposition and Play in the Caribbean* (Ithaca and London: Cornell University Press, 1997).

34   Rhoda Reddock, *Women, Labour and Politics in Trinidad & Tobago, A History* (London: Zed Books, 1994), p. 81. A similar point has been made regarding the working women of San Juan, Puerto Rico (Felix V. Matos-Rodriguez, 'Street Vendors, Peddlars, Shop-Owners and Domestics: Some Aspects of Women's Economic Roles in Nineteenth-Century San Juan, Puerto Rico, 1820–1870' in Shepherd *et al., Engendering History*, 176–96).

35   *Baptist Herald and Friend of Africa*, Vol. 1, no. 1, 14 Sept. 1839, p. 2, p. 1.

36   *Baptist Herald and Friend of Africa*, Supplement to Vol. 1, no. 57, 2 Dec. 1840, and New Series, Vol. 1, no. 12, 20 Mar. 1844.

37   *Baptist Herald and Friend of Africa*, Vol. 5, no. 35, 27 Aug. 1844, p. 274; and Vol. 6, No. 7, 8 Feb. 1845, p. 52.

38   *Morning Journal*, Vol. 1 [No. 136], 28 Jan. 1842.

39   Fyfe was still running advertisements in 1847 for a Jamaica Central Factory Co., to establish central sugar processing factories linked to estates by tramways. Its capital was to be £300,000, raised in 6000 shares of £50 each, 'liability of Shareholders limited to amount of Shares subscribed for' (*Morning Journal*, 15 Apr. 1847).

40   The concept of the joint-stock company (with legal personality and freely transferable shares) existed in English law from 1844, but was extended by the Limited Liability Act of 1855, the Joint Stock Companies Act of 1856. The *sine qua non*

for such companies was the idea of a public of shareholding investors afforded full publicity of information, including the publication of annual business accounts.

41 See C. Campbell, 'Social and Economic Obstacles to the Development of Popular Education in Post-Emancipation Jamaica, 1834–1865', in Beckles and Shepherd, *Caribbean Freedom*, op. cit., p. 262–68.

42 *Baptist Herald and Friend of Africa*, Vol. 1, no. 22, 1 Apr. 1840, 3rd Report of the Jamaica Educational Society.

43 *Baptist Herald and Friend of Africa*, Vol. 2, no. 12, 24 Mar. 1841; and Vol. 2, No.13, 7 Apr. 1841.

44 *Morning Journal,* Vol. 1, no. 2[14], 5 Jan. 1842, p. 3.

45 This was a vision of skilled artisans forming a craft union, but did not extend to the mass of unskilled workers. The first formal union in Jamaica, to my knowledge, began in Kingston in 1843. A General Meeting of journeymen printers demanded a nine-hour day, special rates for overtime and limits on night work (*The Morning Journal,* 9 Mar. 1843). Agricultural labour would not be unionized for many decades.

46 *Morning Journal*, no. 211, 1 Jan. 1842; there was also a Trelawny Savings Bank and a St. Thomas in the Vale Bank (*Morning Journal*, 4 Mar. 1842).

47 *Morning Journal*, 4 Mar. 1842.

48 The Trinity District Mutual Aid Society, Westmoreland, Est. 1855: Rules and Regulations (Kingston: R. J. de Cordova, 1855).

49 LMS, Box 9, Gardner to Directors, Kingston Decennial Report, 22 Jan. 1866.

50 LMS, Box 5, Holland to Directors, 29 July 1845. As we shall see below, the introduction of 'coolies' was a major bone of contention between planter and peasant.

51 LMS, Holland to Directors, 24 Mar. 1847.

52 Holland was a Waywarden in charge of collecting road taxes and realized that the 'readiness of the people [to donate labour], arises…from the fact, that for the last three years I have done a good deal to ease them in the payment of their Taxes…. I manage to obtain the liberty for them to settle their accounts with work instead of money'.

53 *Baptist Herald and Friend of Africa,* Vol. 3, no. 7, 16 Feb. 1842, p. 46.

54 *Baptist Herald and Friend of Africa,* Vol. 5, no. 32, 6 Aug. 1844, p. 250.

55 Both the verse above, from Psalm 68, and the argument for reparations to Africa are strong elements of the Rastafarian faith, which almost certainly has its roots in this original post-emancipation peasant culture of resistance (Chevannes 1994).

7 | Popular democracy and the Underhill Convention

This chapter documents the emergence of a more democratic public culture in Jamaica in the 1840s and 1850s, which I argue contributed to the popular mobilization that culminated in the Morant Bay Rebellion in 1865. The strength of this popular democratic movement unintentionally led to the reactionary consolidation of an elite anti-democratic pact between conservative planters, liberal merchants and the colonial state. Just as in Haiti after the Liberal Revolution, just as in the United States after the Reconstruction Era, and just as in later Central American politics, a potential democratic opening was met with an authoritarian backlash. What is most interesting about the Jamaican experience is the extent to which the well-developed networks of civil society allowed for the elucidation and articulation of a semi-peasant semi-proletarian democratic ideology. Not only were the dominant groups unable to suppress it entirely (for it remains in the archives for all to see), but it also continued to inform radical Jamaican politics well into the twentieth century.

This interpretation of Afro-Jamaican political ideologies is based on two modes of analysis. In the first two sections, I document the emergence of black publics and focus on the major instances of 'riot' or violent political protest in post-slavery Jamaica. In addition to these instances, however, I have also collected approximately sixty 'public texts' produced in processes of political contention from the 1830s to the 1860s, including petitions, resolutions from public meetings, printed reports of speeches made at public meetings, anonymous letters of threat and placards or posters. The major sources are government archives, missionary archives, local newspapers and contemporary memoirs and histories. In this regard, this is neither a random sample nor a complete catalogue of all public texts from the period, but represents a theoretically guided search for instances of popular claim-making during moments of intense public debate. In spite of the recognized limitations of colonial archives as sources for subaltern history (cf. Isaacman 1993), I believe that these public texts offer a key resource in a number of respects.

First, they record the actual rhetorical genres and political discourses of those involved in framing and writing them; in this sense, there is a web of symbolic meaning that indicates connections of memories, ideas and arguments over time. Second, they leave a trail of connections indicating the actual channels of political communication and the brokers through whose hands it passed (e.g. literate members of the community, missionaries, newspaper editors, local colonial officials, the Colonial Office in London, eventually into local or metropolitan archives). Third, through the temporal pattern of one document in response to another, the set as a whole reflects the actual give and take of political communication over time. They embody the available repertoires of political communication and dynamic contention that constrained and enabled particular types of political agency and state response. Starting with the social tensions of the 1840s and culminating in the Underhill Movement of 1865, this chapter charts the emergence of popular democratic ideologies in Jamaica. However, to understand the political space in which British subjects operated — so different from Haiti's — we must first turn to the contours of more violent interaction between black publics and the colonial state in Jamaica.

Democratic politics and riotous bargaining

Political space in Jamaica was surprisingly open to peasants, semi-proletarians and the urban poor, at least in comparison to Haiti. Jamaican small landholders and some urban artisans were in fact highly involved in politics, including yearly elections of vestry members, less frequent elections of the House of Assembly and, for those who could not vote, participation in public meetings, petitioning and occasionally more violent demonstrations or riots. As Heuman has suggested,

> The traditional accounts of the freed slaves in postemancipation Jamaica provide little hint of their role in politics. It has been suggested that most of the freed slaves left the plantations, set up communities in the interior of the island, and had little to do with local political institutions. Historians have therefore concluded that politics as well as the franchise were largely in the hands of the white planter class. Recent research suggests that this view fails to take account of more complex developments after the abolition of slavery. Specifically, it overlooks the political role of the peasants and small farmers (Heuman 1981: 117).

As the enfranchisement that came with freehold land ownership increased in Jamaica, black and brown men (if not women) became qualified to vote in greater numbers (even if still extremely limited in comparison to the population as a whole). As William Green points out, 'West Indian governments were dominated by elected assemblies, and narrow franchises served as the cornerstones of white oligarchic power.... In the 1863 election for the Jamaican Assembly only 1,457 votes were cast out of a population numbering above 440,000' (Green [1976] 1991: 176–77). Nevertheless, by 1859, there were seventeen non-white members of the House of Assembly out of a total of forty-seven (Sewell [1862] 1968: 254). When Edward Vickars (one of only two black Assemblymen) won the Spanish Town seat, his black supporters paraded him victoriously through the streets of Kingston; but changes in the electoral law in 1859 meant that he was unable to regain it (Wilmot 1994).

As in Jacksonian America, electoral politics began to take on a more raucous character, spilling over into outdoor public spaces (cf. Ryan 1990) and including what Heuman describes as ruffianism and intimidation. After a clerk of the vestry was killed in an election riot in 1851, for example, the *Falmouth Post* referred to those involved as 'a low, unruly mobocracy', and berated the 'unwashed constituency' (Heuman 1981: 118–19). At times, the line between rowdy meetings, mobs in the streets and actual riots depended largely on the actions and reactions of police, militias, courts and government officials. Both Heuman (1981) and Holt (1992) have carefully studied electoral politics in this period, demonstrating the emergence of a 'colored', Jewish and black voting block known as the 'Town Party' and representing more mercantile interests than those of the planters' 'Country Party'. I will instead focus on the less studied popular life of the towns, from which the so-called 'mob' emerged.[1]

If Afro-Jamaican publics first took shape among Baptist congregations in the rural milieu of plantations and free villages, the social tensions of the mid- to late 1840s produced an increasingly autonomous and racially conscious black public. Efforts to build trust between workers and employers had progressed little in the first decade of freedom; at the same time, the alliance between Nonconformist missionaries and estate labourers was also increasingly brittle. The Sugar Duties Act of 1846 and a broader economic crisis in 1847 led to the failure of eighteen West Indian merchant houses in Britain, as well as the West India Bank, based in Barbados (Hall 1959: 91). In this situation, the Country Party pushed to have the Jamaican House of Assembly done away with so that they could exercise full control over plantation labour. 'The Merchant or Town party, on the other hand', argues Hall, 'sought to increase the power of the Assembly by... asserting all the ancient claims to rights and privileges' (ibid: 98). It was this tension between the two factions that created a crack in the facade of planter power in which popular politics could take hold.

By 1848, a sharp political crisis and strained labour relations led to a 'spirit of disaffection', evident in racially defined grievances and in some instances a black-centred political ideology. A collection of Colonial Office documents entitled 'Apprehended Outbreak in the Western Parishes, 1848', indicates the new mood. One man wrote to Governor Grey from Savanna-la-Mar in June 1848:

> I for my own part of late perceived a spirit of bitterness, wanton insolence, and daring provocation rapidly gaining growth among certain classes of the community; and a hatred and impatience of order and restrictive law, '*White Man's*' or '*Buckra law*,' openly evinced among our working population, betokening a vast change in the popular mind.... [A]s in 1831 there are again symtoms [*sic*] of insurrectionary movement, directed towards expelling the white inhabitants from this colony, at least in this parish [emphasis in original].[2]

Attached to his report was a memorandum stating that there had recently been a large meeting of the Baptists in Savanna-la-Mar, and 'that whether intended or not by its promoters, was evidently conducted as an exhibition of physical force... above 2500 negroes attended!' This large group intimidated the non-black population by galloping up and down the streets, rudely splashing them. From the day of this meeting, 'a marked change for the worse has been almost universally observed among the peasantry — discontent — debate — field consultation — and wanton rudeness being the symptoms'. The image of 'field consultation' suggests that meetings were being held on rural sites, independent of any white interference; peasants were controlling their own meeting formats outside of missionary influence.

Other reports from Westmoreland indicated extensive preparations going on for the August 'Drumming, Dancing and John canoeing'; workers with sullen characters 'allied to passive resistance'; Baptists getting labourers to sign resolutions and to pay up their taxes (in order to claim voting rights). Some observers linked the unrest to abuse of the Home Government by planters, who had spoken openly of transferring allegiance to the United States, raising fears of re-enslavement. Others, as noted previously, stated that 'the arrival of many colored refugees from [Haiti] on the shores of Jamaica, together with accounts from all parts of Europe of risings of the people against their governments, may have excited a few of the more instructed and clever of the laboring class to indulge in wild and dangerous thoughts'.[3] It was clear to such commentators that 'intelligence of what goes on in Haiti may excite a few reprobates amongst the black population to indulge in wicked thoughts and audacious language'. It also shows that the unrest went beyond local grievances and labour disputes; it is evidence of a popular public with an awareness of international events and a critical appraisal of the practices of an unrepresentative colonial government.

Political participation by labourers and peasants was leading to a critique not only of the planters, but also of the very terms (and security) of the freedom they were supposed to be enjoying. As Mallon has shown for nineteenth-century Mexico and Peru, '[t]he contradiction between promise and practice became a central tension in the historically dynamic construction of national-democratic discourses and movements, providing the space for struggles over their practice and meaning[;]... peasants and other rural folk took up the challenge of national-democratic discourse and attempted to create their own version of a more egalitarian practice' (Mallon 1995: 9). A more militant political discourse of replacing 'Buckra Law' with real freedom and justice was emerging. It drew on the elite liberal discourse of rights, fairness, justice and political representation, but went beyond it in a more critical appraisal of what real equality and real freedom would look like.

In response to the feared outbreak in 1848, the Governor sent police reinforcements from Kingston, and printed a Proclamation that was given full publicity. It is a good example of the colonial state's mode of addressing citizens, similar in some ways to modes of address in Haiti, but laying far more emphasis on the guarantee of rights along with the obligations of the citizen. As a kind of lecture on freedom and the rights and duties of citizenship, it is worth quoting at some length:

> The Freedom, which was given to the Negro People of Jamaica, was given without recall or reserve, and the rights of the Laborers of that Race now stand on the same foundations as those of the Planter or Proprietor, or those of the People of England, and are a part of the Constitution of the Empire. The Crown, to which the allegiance of all its Subjects is equally due, will afford to all equally the protection of the Laws, and will secure to all the enjoyment of their rights, and especially that first and greatest and most precious of all rights — their personal freedom.... Whilst this

Warranty and Assurance of their Freedom, and their Rights, is willingly given to the Negro People of Jamaica, it is required of them that they shall conform to the Laws, of which those Rights form a part: That as good Subjects of Her Majesty they will abhor and prevent the employment of Violence or Threatening Language to others, and that in the enjoyment of the perpetual and Constitutional Liberty which is gladly recognized as belonging to them, they will abstain from all Riotous and Rude Behaviour, which might alarm the minds of Peacable Persons; and will endeavour, by Soberness and Steadiness of Demeanour, and by Prudence of Conduct and of Language, to shew that they are worthy to sustain the Character of freemen, and to be the Fathers of Free Families.[4]

Yet, the 'Negro People' had been exercising their rights and trying out the guarantees of their freedom for over ten years, with little success. Many began to turn to more forceful means of political contention and claim-making.

In the post-emancipation period, the black and brown populations were growing, while the already relatively small white population was shrinking (see Table 7). This newly mobile population began to challenge planter control not only on the plantations, but also in the public spaces of the towns. As noted above, non-white females outnumbered males throughout the post-emancipation period, and formed the majority of the population of the larger towns and ports. William Sewell estimated in 1860 that Jamaica had approximately 65,000 children between the ages of five and fifteen; 20,000 labourers of both sexes working on the estates 'who may still be regarded as a laboring class'; about 10,000 working as domestic servants; about 3000 working on road building; a number of merchants, mechanics and tradesmen; and the remainder of the non-white population who were small proprietors, yet who worked on the estates for wages when they could (Sewell [1862] 1968: 254).

The colonial vision of male-headed rural households left the government unprepared for the politics of urban Jamaica where a semi-proletarian population displaced from the declining plantations was gathering. A new urban political culture was emerging on the streets of Kingston and other large towns in the mid-nineteenth century, and women were instrumental in its formation. Protest involved the entire community, and emerged out of the popular justice of the street and the market, locales populated by women as well as men. Swithin Wilmot has begun to trace women's participation not only in plantation labour

Table 7   Jamaican Population by 'Colour' and Sex, 1844 and 1861

		'White'	'Brown'	'Black'	'Total'
1844	male	9289	31,646	140,698	181,633
	female	6487	36,883	152,430	195,800
	subtotal	15,776	68,529	293,128	377,433
1861	male	7295	38,223	167,277	212,795
	female	6521	42,842	179,097	228,460
	subtotal	13,816	81,065	346,374	441,255

(based on Census Figures from Higman 1980)

protests, but also in urban 'riots'. Even when so-called riots arose out of religious or cultural issues, the following examples show that they were always political in so far as they demonstrated black physical power and numerical strength against representatives of the state. In a clash with police over the treatment of recaptured (and indentured) Africans in Falmouth in 1840, a woman named Mary Clarke was singled out by police: 'She abused the Police frequently and we were obliged to put her back. She always retreated with reluctance, and came back again... Mary Clarke was conspicuous from first to last... . She damned the police and asked what right they had to interfere with people in the street'. Here the street is claimed as a public space, to which the people had a 'right'.[5]

After Christmas riots in Kingston in 1842, the *Morning Journal* reported that when the usual John Canoe festivities were banned by the mayor, and a man was arrested simply for playing a violin, angry women assembled:

> But so soon as the people saw that one of their body who had violated no law, who had acted contrary to no order, had been taken by the police, they assembled in numbers, 4–5ths of them women. The crowd was great, but it consisted chiefly of defenseless women. Then was it that the police committed an outrage upon the people which was unparalleled. Seeing the people thus assembled, instead of recommending them quietly to disperse...[t]he police attempted to ride the people down — and then had the people recourse to brick-bats; then, as he was informed, began the uproar.

The police were driven back and eventually opened fire on the crowd, killing three people, including one pregnant woman, and wounding several others. Although the imagery of 'defenseless' women was capitalized on by this writer, these urban crowds were in fact far more threatening than the small groups of women who had once challenged plantation personnel. As James Scott suggests, 'large, autonomous gatherings of subordinates are threatening to domination because of the license they promote among normally disaggregated inferiors.'[6]

During the Westmoreland Tollgate riots of February 1859, tollgates and tollhouses on the main roads were pulled down after petitions to have them removed were ignored. Over one hundred warrants were put out and thirty-one people were bound over to appear at the Circuit Court. During the hearing, the petty court was surrounded by a 'large mob collected principally of Females and boys,' who threatened witnesses and interrupted the proceedings. The Circuit Court meeting in Savanna-la-Mar had to be adjourned when crowds estimated as up to 10,000 people, 'male and female', filled the streets. A group of over 1800 people attacked thirty policemen, stoned the police station, broke windows and vandalized its interior. As the Custos put it, 'every person, male and female, amongst the laboring population, are now sympathising with the parties concerned in this movement and from all I can learn labor is at a standstill on the estates'.[7] Because women were the backbone of the internal marketing network, shifting goods between the countryside and the towns for tiny profits, added tolls were particularly burdensome to them.

In July 1859, another riot broke out during a court case in Falmouth. The 'Rabble' freed prisoners from the lock-up, assailed both police and magistrates and stoned the houses of officials. Finally, they attacked the police station and battered in every window; twenty-two policemen holed up inside opened fire, killing two women and wounding others, one of whom later died; the deaths were ruled to be justifiable homicide. Trials of the rioters revealed that women were prominent, including Emily Jackson, Mary Hoad, Margaret Anderson, Wilhemina Peterkin, Jessy Simpson, Isabella Campbell, Mary Frackis, Adelaide Benarm, Elize Lyon, Rebecca Saffery, Maria Chippendale and Mary Campbell. The crowds involved were described by some witnesses as 'principally female'. Emily Jackson was singled out in the report of the inspector of police, who stated that, 'Emily Jackson was also most prominent, she was armed with this stick and flourishing it, she was very violent. She and Sutherland appears to be leadings [*sic*] the whole mob. The riot began with her that morning and she was one of those rescued in the first attack and rescue at the Cage in the morning'. Further reports indicate that she had to be forcibly removed from court after shouting that, 'Da Buckra commence the war and they must take all them get. This is nothing, before the week is out you will see the whole of the Maroons down here and they will make them fly'. Her father was said to be a Maroon himself.[8]

Charting the transformation of black publics, 1838–1865

Official reports of 'riots', however, are not a reliable source for gauging popular grievances, demands or political ideologies. By utilizing the database of public texts, we can arrive at a better assessment of the actual grievances and political discourses of Afro-Jamaicans in this period. The shift in political culture that I have been tracking in terms of increasing urbanization and independence from missionary influence is also evident in the collection of public texts. These can be divided into two main periods of intensive political contention. The first period is the immediate post-emancipation period from 1838–1844, which, as we have seen in the previous chapter, was a time of great political turmoil. Aside from the rumours of 1848, the second major flurry of public meeting, petitioning and other forms of claim-making occurs in the 1858–1865 period, following changes in the electoral laws that began to disenfranchise the black population, which had until then been making gradual inroads into formal political representation. The comparison of these two periods points to an overall shift towards more independent black publics, with their own leadership, genres of communication and political ideologies.

The public meetings of the 1838–1844 period were almost invariably organized under the auspices of the Baptist missions. The meetings were often held in Baptist chapels, and the resulting petitioners usually identified themselves as representing the members of a particular Baptist congregation. In the 1858–65 period, in contrast, there are very few references to Baptist organizations or congregations, and increasing identification in more generic terms such as 'inhabitants' or simply 'a public meeting'. Meetings in this later period also tended to be held either on an official basis in local court houses, or on an unofficial basis, in and around the villages where people lived. There is also an evident shift in regional activism away from the western parishes of Cornwall, where the Baptist Western Union was strong, and towards Kingston and the eastern parishes of Surrey, where the Baptist mission was weak and the Native Baptists were more prevalent. There were also some crucial shifts in the kinds of grievances that were expressed and the demands that were made.

Matching our previous framework of analysis, the following discussion will be divided into a consideration of economic, political and civil grievances and demands. In relation to the first area, there was a shift in the public texts from the concerns of a plantation labour force in the 1838–1844 period, to the concerns of a small peasantry and urban informal sector in the 1858–65 period. Where early petitioners identified themselves most often as 'freedmen' and 'laborers', the later groups of petitioners often identified themselves as 'peasants,' 'small settlers' and 'mechanics'. Indeed, a whole new language appears in relation to 'the masses' or the 'mass of the people', which was not evident in the earlier period. Where the early petitions are concerned with labour bargaining with the large estates and issues of political representation, the later petitions are concerned with a broader range of issues more relevant to a community that has escaped the plantations. There is also a distinctive new concern with economic depression, poverty and the 'poor sufferers', a discourse clearly linked to the decline in the Jamaican economy.

In general terms, there are five main peasant or smallholder concerns related to land and economic rights. First, peasants require access to land and secure land tenure either on an individual or a familial basis. Second, they require access to capital or credit in order to accumulate tools, seeds and storage facilities with which to work. Third, they require the capacity to process their agricultural produce in order to add the greatest value to it before sale. Fourth, they need the capacity to transport crops to market on a regular basis, with appropriate information available on when and where the best prices might be found. Finally, they require some political representation of their interests in order to have some influence over economic policy such as taxation and tariff levels. Each of these areas creates particular problems and sets of grievances or political demands.

The problem of insecure land tenure can lead to demands for land distribution and access to state-owned lands. Problems of capitalization tie into grievances concerning the advance of credit on crops, share-cropping arrangements and problems of debt peonage, and lead to demands such as the formation of savings banks, the formation of credit associations or the abolition of indentured labour. Processing concerns relate to the role of middle-men in monopolizing profitable export processing, and may lead to demands for cooperative investment in central processing plants, shared storage facilities and marketing associations. Transport issues may be linked to grievances over investment in roads, taxation of transport, retail and wholesale licensing fees and the role of exploitative speculators. Finally, influence over economic decision making is connected to a range of demands concerned with levelling the playing field between big and small landholders, and creating a favourable economic climate for independent peasant production (including the abolition of subsidies for indentured labour). Aspects of each of these economic concerns and demands appear in the petitions of the 1858–65 period.

A second set of trends concerns the political grievances and demands expressed in these texts. Here we have already seen that there were calls for enfranchisement and political representation almost as soon as slavery was abolished. However, in the 1838–1844 period, popular public claim-making led by Baptist missions, tended to target local colonial government and to be sent out to British philanthropists and 'friends of liberty'. In 1858–1865, the petitioners were more likely to petition the Queen directly and to broker their political activities through local non-white political and religious leaders, rather than through white missionaries. In the struggle with planters over political control, political demands also become more explicit and detailed. Having started out in terms of a general grievance against 'planter government' and the continuation of slavery, by the 1850s, there are specific concerns with taxation, injustice, class legislation, immigration of indentured labour, and 'planter oppression'. Disenfranchisement becomes a central concern after 1858, and the public texts begin to demand protection (and extension) of political rights such as the franchise, greater participation in decision-making at the local level of vestries and more control over expelling corrupt officials. By 1865, this becomes a call for an official enquiry into the economic and political conditions of Jamaica.

The third set of trends concerns the emergence of civil rights as a key locus of political claim-making. Here the key demands are for freedom of association, freedom of the press and a right to education. In this category, we could also include more 'identity oriented' demands concerning public recognition of issues of importance to the labouring population of African descent. These include requests for government celebration of the First of August Emancipation Day as a public commemoration, and for the support of Africans in other parts of the world (including demands for the abolition of slavery in the United States). There are also more explicit discussions of the need for people to sign petitions, to demonstrate and to print their resolutions and petitions in newspapers not only within Jamaica, but also in Britain and even the United States. There is an increasing polarization of collective identities such as rich and poor, white and black, merchant and mechanic, showing a political consolidation and framing of a distinctive collective identification.

One other significant change is evident in popular claim-making between these two periods. Whereas in the earlier period, every document was transcribed by a white missionary and usually put into his own words, the later texts make evident in their actual language that they were written by Afro-Jamaicans. The growing autonomy of black publics, in other words, is seen in the simple fact that they began to have members of their own communities write down their collective grievances and demands nearer to their own words and shaped by their own Creole forms of expression. At a Baptist meeting in 1841, for example, Joseph McLean observed:

> White people often said that a black man could never make a speech, because he had got no education; but, although he could not use the same fine words, he could make the people understand him, and that was good enough. It was not the fine words, but good sense that makes a good speech, and if a black man spoke good sense, and his hearers all understood him, his speech would be just as good as a white Gentleman's, with all his fine language. Some people said Massa, others said Master, but both meant the same thing, and he wished to know if the people couldn't understand Massa as well as Master.[9]

By the 1850s, there seems to have been a new sense of agency among less formally educated people that they too could make speeches and 'put their hand to paper'. Not only are there more petitions written in a local Creole idiom, but there is also an increasing frequency of anonymous letters of threat dropped in front of courthouses and the private houses of government officials.

Before turning to the Underhill Movement itself, it will be useful to examine some significant petitions that preceded it. When the new electoral law was passed in 1858, requiring a ten-and-a-half shilling registration fee to be paid by all voters, black publics were ready to protest against it. The first petition on this issue came from a meeting held at Easington Court House in Saint David, a parish in the hills on the outskirts of Kingston that had a number of black vestrymen. In a petition to the Queen, this group charged that by this law 'a serious injury is done to the class of your Majesty's subjects, who were emancipated from slavery, and invested with the rights of British Freemen'. Their grievance is linked specifically to the political power of planters:

> By the operation of this clause, therefore, the entire political power of the Island is left in the hands of an exceedingly small minority of fellow Citizens, most of who belong to that class who but too recently owned our bodies and souls and who seem loth and backward to accord to us the equality of political rights secured by the British Constitution, alike to

all classes. That the masses of this colony should be trained
so as to participate in the legislation of the Country seems in
all account desirable.[10]

This issue also created the occasion for one of the first big public meetings organized by George William Gordon. In February 1859, he
chaired a meeting at the Old Court House in Kingston to protest the
Electoral Law, from which a petition was produced with over five
hundred signatures.[11] This petition added the point that the 'numerous
body of electors, consisting principally of the lately emancipated
people…are the bones and sinew of the country, having a permanent
stake in its fortunes'. It also made reference to partiality, injustice and
class legislation. Several of those who moved resolutions at this
meeting — Rev. Robert A. Johnson, Rev. James Roach and Robert
Wiltshire — were Native Baptists and went on to participate in the
Underhill Meetings of 1865.

The best testimony to the existence of a subaltern counterpublic
consisting of small landholders and labourers emerges out of two 1859
petitions representing five parishes in the rural vicinity of Kingston.
These eloquent memorials, each with over one thousand signatures on
blue thin-lined paper, were rejected by Governor Darling on the spuri-
ous grounds of 'doubts as to their genuineness and authenticity'.[12]
Additional correspondence indicates that there was an organized corresponding committee mobilizing meetings across the parishes and
raising subscriptions. The Custos described the people involved as
'more a class of yeomanry than in the ordinary sense of the word a
peasantry. Possessing freeholds ranging from 1, 2, 5 to 15 and 20 acres
some of them, many can read and write, whose names have been
used'.[13] The 'testimonial of attachment' to the Queen from her 'loyal
and Devoted Subjects, Mechanics and Peasantries' — who later refer
to themselves as 'your sable subjects of Jamaica, of African descent'—
opens with an elaborate profession of loyalty to demonstrate 'how
much we prize and value our privileges as free people'.

The petition first lays out political complaints about the laws
'enacted to deprive us of the rights of trial by jury, and prevent our
voting at elections unless we pay a fee of Ten shillings and six pence
and hence we see oursleves deprived of the last vestiges of our political liberty and consequently delivered over to the hands of our most
inveterate enemies'. It then moves on to economic grievances and fears
of being 'reduced to starvation and slavery'. It reports that planter
complaints of lack of labour arise 'from the nonpayment of the labourers, the unjust and cruel conduct of the planters toward the people' and
demands an end to indentured immigration until 'an enquiry be made

as to the necessity of immigrants being actually required, and the provisions that are made for them, and means adopted to prevent their being murdered by the cruelties of their employers'. The petition concludes with a hope that the Governor will attend, on behalf of the Queen, the First of August Jubilee planned in commemoration of the twenty-first anniversary of their emancipation from slavery.

The second, and much longer, petition to the Governor comes from 'us the small settlers that are Mechanics and Peasantries, and, who as a people [are] suffering under pecuniary disadvantages, oppressed by partial and heavy taxation, rights disregarded and trampled on, and as a crowning act our privileges are now about to be wrested from us'. It describes the legislation over the previous six years as 'retrograde steps to a refined state of slavery or something akin to it'. It refers in particular to laws concerning dues and licenses on livestock, market fees and the indirect taxation of import duties. They then provide a striking political and religious analysis of racial inequality and class oppression:

> Here we see ourselves prevented from improving our circumstances, and for no other crime but because we are african descendants, and being such we are likened to the beasts of the field, therefore every oppressive means must be employed to trample and reduce our aspiring manhood.... It does not appear that these men believe in the supremacy of a just God. If they did they would acknowledge that God is no respector of persons, that he governs rich and poor, planters and peasantries, white and black....

The petition then refers to threats against them, penalties for representing their grievances and imprisonment, ironically called 'the Jamaican Planter's school for teaching Her Majesty Sable Subjects morality and civilization'. Nevertheless, they attest, 'We believe ourselves British subjects... and not all the planters and our enemies may do will ever sever us [Her Majesty's] sable subjects of Jamaica from our attachment to her Person and Government'.

The petition goes on to complain of poor roads to peasant settlements, unfair taxes on livestock, tollgates and various other fees. In a radical assessment of indentured immigration, they observe that the 'blood of immigrants, Europeans, Asiatic and Africans have stained the streets, roads, and hedges of the country[;] they have been murdered by the very men who are now seeking to obtain immigrants and it is to obtain their ends that laws and oppressions are introduced and our extermination sought after'. They conclude with three requests: that the Governor attend their public celebration of the Jubilee of

freedom; that there be an official investigation into the condition of
Jamaica; and God's blessings on the Governor and his family. This
final prayer echoes an earlier passage in which the petitioners describe
how 'To us it is a great deal to have something which we can call our
own.... All our necessities are derived from the soil; the Mechanic, or
the peasant, who owns a hut and a few acres of land, feels himself con-
tented being certain of a home and food... These are the essentials at
which we have aspired, and which Gracious Providence have crowned
with success'. Not only did Governor Darling ignore the straightfor-
ward request to attend the Jubilee, but he cast aspersions on the petitions altogether. The only official response was a circular sent to the
Custodes of each parish and printed in the newspapers, announcing the
forgery of the signatures and denouncing the covert agitation by
Fletcher and 'other incendiaries' charged with stirring false grievances.

Over the next several years, a combination of drought and economic recession brought on by the U.S. Civil War made conditions the
worst they had been since slavery's abolition (Hall 1959). The large
unemployed population of the towns became especially apparent (and
threatening) to the ruling elite. Working in an 'informal' economy of
higglering, domestic work, washing, sewing and little documented but
ever-present prostitution, urban women were especially vulnerable to
economic downturns. As the Custos of Kingston reported in 1865,
'Out of a population of 27,000 persons in Kingston, nearly one-half
have nothing to do. Great hulking men and women may be seen in the
different yards all day long, basking in the sun and picking each
other's heads, alternating the singing of psalms with ribald and
obscene songs'. Baptist missionaries described the 'very precarious
existence' of Spanish Town's tradesmen and other residents in 1865,
including 'nearly 1,000 domestics, not half of whom were employed;
772 seamstresses, who got occasional work before the August and
Christmas holidays; 422 laundresses, who were nearly all out of work;
and 163 fishermen and fisherwomen'. The town 'was pauper-stricken,
with large numbers seeking relief'. Out of this urban milieu emerged
the politicized population who participated in the Underhill Meetings
and petitions of 1865.[14]

The Underhill Convention and democratic participation

The most intensive cycle of public meetings in post-emancipation
Jamaica took place in 1865, in a series of events known as the
Underhill Meetings. Edward Bean Underhill, secretary of the Baptist

Missionary Society, had long taken an interest in Jamaican emancipation.[15] In January 1865, he wrote to Edward Cardwell, Secretary of State for the Colonies, following reports in England about starvation and poverty among the Jamaican peasantry. His letter referred to the distress of the people consequent on the lack of paying work, drought and heavy taxation, as well as their grievances concerning lack of justice and the denial of political rights. He recommended an enquiry into the legislation of the island since emancipation, and suggested the formation of marketing associations for the small freeholders. A copy of this letter reached Governor Eyre, from the Colonial office, in February. In March, a circular echoing the same grievances was sent out by the Baptist Missionary Society to all the Custodes, judges, magistrates and clergy of all denominations; it was also published in the *Jamaica Guardian*. Given the emerging public debate, Eyre had copies of Underhill's letter printed and circulated throughout the island, and asked missionaries and other local officials to respond to the accusations — presumably with the intent of disproving them.[16] His plan appears to have backfired, however, when circulation of the letter became the catalyst for public discussions in every parish about the state of the island. His official request for reactions 'gave to the subject unexpected importance', according to Underhill. 'It became at once the topic of heated discussion in every class of the community' (Underhill 1895: 13). As the black Rev. Samuel Holt explained at a public meeting in Montego Bay, 'We all felt the hardship of the times but we did not know what was the cause; we did not know what the rumbling was till every one ask, have you read Dr. Underhill's letter? Then we know what all the disturbance was, and the rumbling that bring us here today'.[17]

Baptist ministers gathered dozens of pages of evidence and submitted an eighteen-page summary report calling for a government Commission of Enquiry into the state of the island. Their own investigations substantiated Underhill's report of starvation and nakedness among the peasantry. This was blamed on low wages and high prices, stemming from a number of causes. A recent drought had forced more people to seek estate work, while less sugar was being grown since prices were low, both tending to drive down wages; there was also an increasing use of indentured African and Indian labourers, as well as more use of low-paid women's and 'children's gangs'. People also complained to the missionaries of unfair taxation, laws biased towards the big planters and lack of justice in the courts.

Governor Eyre's report on the condition of the island, when he transmitted the responses to the Underhill letter, blamed the peasantry for their impoverishment: '[It] owes its origin in a great measure to the habits and character of the people, induced by the genial nature of the climate, the facility of supplying their wants in ordinary seasons at comparatively little exertion, and their natural disposition to indolence and inactivity, and to remain satisfied with what barely supplies absolute wants'.[18] To this explanation he added other short-comings, including: 'idleness, apathy, pride, improvidence, night-revels, gambling, social disorganization and open profligacy'. At the Colonial Office, Henry Taylor added his own notes to the report, stating 'I believe the question to be at bottom merely a question of whether the Negroe is to be industrious according to the industry of other Countries or according to the standard of industry which he has set up for himself in Jamaica'. Citing Machiavelli and Adam Smith, he added that the 'Negroe Race is I think by temperament volatile and sanguine more than others and he will not exert himself to provide against rare contingencies'.[19] The Colonial Office response to the Baptist minister's report was that 'it does not appear that [the people] are suffering from any general or continuous distress from which they would not be at once relieved by settled industry'.

Although public discussion of Underhill's letter began among Baptist missionaries, it quickly spread as public meetings were called. The Attorney General for Jamaica Alexander Heslop described in dismay how 'the people went to these Underhill meetings, and they made speeches and passed resolutions, and this is what particularly struck me at the Kingston meeting, which is sort of a head-quarters; they formed a corresponding committee to correspond with the people in the other parishes, and got up similar meetings in the country upon that agitation'.[20] To his alarm, they 'formed themselves into a permanent society called "The Underhill Convention", with branches all over the country'. As Eyre noted when he transmitted the resolutions from the public meeting organized by George W. Gordon in Kingston in early May, the fifteenth resolution 'calls upon the descendants of Africa throughout the Island to form Societies and hold Meetings, and co-operate for the purpose of setting forth their grievances. There are always a number of political demagogues ready to stir the people to a belief of imaginary wrongs'.[21] That this group was addressing the 'descendants of Africa throughout the island' was especially alarming to the government, since it suggested a political identity that went beyond simply being generic British subjects. By now the blundering Eyre realized that 'Dr. Underhill's letter will be productive of much evil to this Colony by unsettling the minds of the Peasantry and making them discontented;' yet, it was he who had made it public, so he had only himself to blame.

Evidence on the Underhill Conventionists comes in part from their own resolutions and in part from additional correspondence collected by the Royal Commission that investigated the Morant Bay Rebellion, which followed on its heels. The Convention formed following a meeting at Rev. Edwin Palmer's Baptist chapel on Hanover Street in Kingston, in April 1865. Related public meetings were held at Savanna-la-Mar (Westmoreland) in April; at Kingston, Lucea (Hanover), Montego Bay (St. James), Four Paths (Clarendon & Manchester), and Spanish Town (St. Catherine) in May; at Mannings Town (St. Mary) and Easington (St. David) in June; at Saint Ann's Bay (St. Ann) in July; and, finally, at Morant Bay (St. Thomas in the East) in August. All of these meetings produced resolutions that were usually printed in local newspapers and sent to the Governor; some also sent formal petitions or memorials to the Governor or the Colonial Office.[22] Thus began a popular movement 'for the expression of public sentiment on the part of the Freedmen ... [who were] not without able expounders of their rights, men risen from their own ranks... fully capable of appreciating their civil rights, and of standing before an audience to advocate and defend them' (Underhill 1895: 23–4). In addition to these formal public meetings, numerous informal meetings seem to have taken place in smaller villages. In St. Thomas in the East, especially, meetings were led by Native Baptists Paul Bogle and James McLaren, at which there was reported to be talk of an uprising, and people were asked to swear oaths on the Bible (Heuman 1994: 80–83).

The organizers of the Underhill Meetings clearly saw this as an opportunity to challenge elite publics by mobilizing Afro-Jamaicans to speak for themselves. George W. Gordon's radical newspaper, the *Jamaica Watchman and People's Free Press*, gleefully reported in early June that 'the Underhill Convention has been triumphantly successful in its operation.... Since the Kingston meeting, despite the malignity of our contemporaries, meetings after meetings have taken place in other parts of the island'. Most importantly, the *Watchman* explicitly described the meetings as a public challenge to the elite:

> The several Custodes of parishes have been designedly duped into a contradiction of the actual condition of the people of the island. Little could they have expected that the slumbering people would have been awakened...and rise 'en mass' and give the emphatic contradiction to their cooked up statements to his Excellency the Governor for transmission to the authorities in Great Britain. If the people of Jamaica do not speak now, when will they do so again. For years have they tamely submitted to the iron yoke of oppression; they have been taxed; taxed again and again...until

now, bidding defiance to the pressure of an oligarchical
dynasty, and now the fire has been kindled in them, they
have at last given utterance to the words of distress.[23]

Aware that ultimate authority rested in Britain, Gordon's supporters
recognized that they could circumvent local power-holders by appeal-
ing directly to the Colonial Secretary (as Gordon himself had done
on several occasions in the past), to British Parliament, to the Queen
and, perhaps, most importantly, to the British public. The Underhill
Meetings would give voice to an *alternative* public — an African,
poor, black, urban working class and rural peasant public.[24]

The acting Chairman and the Secretary of the Underhill
Convention were Thomas Rodney and Joseph Burton. The *Jamaica
Guardian* published a letter that Rodney and Burton were circulating in
July 1865, which was seen as evidence of political agitation (and was
passed on by Governor Eyre to Cardwell). It indicates the close relationship between British and Jamaican public opinion and networks of
communication, since the Jamaican meetings were orchestrated in
direct response to public debate in England:

> As there is now a discussion in England on the subject, with
> a view to elicit the truth, whether or not the labouring people
> of this colour are distressed in circumstances, and the
> *enemies of the negro race, and opposers of their advance-
> ment, are busy both with their tongues and pens to bring into
> disrepute and falsify the statements regarding the rampant
> distress and oppression of Jamaica and to censure the
> conduct of Doctor Underhill, the Baptist Missionaries and
> others,* in bringing the same before the British public, let us
> seize the present favourable opportunity to furnish our
> Philanthropic friends there with the necessary details of this
> fact, in order to straighten them in their advocacy on our
> behalf. But the Only Way *by which you can do this is to
> convene a public meeting and then to propose and pass
> certain resolutions expressing your distressed and oppressed
> condition* [italics in original].[25]

This evidence of the self-conscious creation of an adversarial print-
public representing the viewpoints of 'the negro race' shows an awareness of political opportunities and an ability to organize meetings with
much larger aims than the mere expression of immediate grievances.
The target of the public resolutions was not only the local government,
but a wider public; the aim, to furnish British supporters with first-
hand evidence and 'straighten them in their advocacy'.

The Governor's response to the Underhill letter might not have been so inflammatory had it not been so widely publicized; however, in April, just as Underhill's letter was gaining notoriety, Eyre made a second miscalculation of public opinion. The first petition of 1865 to the Queen from a popular gathering was sent from the parish of St. Ann in April, prior to the first Underhill meetings. The 'poor people of St. Ann' asked the government to secure them a quantity of land, and then 'we will put our hands and heart to work, and cultivate coffee, corn, canes, cotton and tobacco, and other produce. We will form a company for that purpose, if our Gracious Lady Victoria our Queen will also appoint an agent to receive such produce as we may cultivate, and give us means of subsistence while at work' (Underhill 1895: 277).[26] An answer came back from the Colonial Office, drafted by Henry Taylor, and seized on by Governor Eyre as an opportunity to nip the movement in the bud. In July, he had fifty thousand copies of the response printed, 'distributed and posted in every district of the island'.[27] The poster, entitled 'The Queen's Advice', stated:

> The prosperity of the labouring classes, as well as of all other classes, depends in Jamaica and in other communities, upon their working for wages, not uncertainly, or capriciously, but steadily and continuously, at the times when their labour is wanted, and for so long as it is wanted; and that if they would use this industry, and thereby render the plantations productive, they would enable the planters to pay them higher wages for the same hours of work than are received by the best field labourers in this country; and, as the cost of the necessaries of life is so much less in Jamaica than it is here, they would be enabled, by adding prudence to industry, to lay by an ample provision for seasons of drought and dearth; and they may be assured, that it is from their own industry and prudence, in availing themselves of the means of prospering that are before them, and not from any such schemes as have been suggested to them, that they must look for an improvement in their conditions (Semmel 1968: 43–4).

If Underhill's letter had not already stirred people to join the public debate, this insensitive and inappropriate official advice, posted across the island, certainly did. The extensive outdoor publication of the Queen's Advice sparked off a struggle over the discursive framing of Jamaica's problems. Poverty meant one thing if the labourers were lazy and improvident, quite another if they were deprived of fair wages, 'oppressed' by the planters and unjustly treated by the local government.

The Custos of St. Elizabeth reported that the Queen's Advice was 'represented here as a "false make up". The People never see the gazette and few have heard of Mr. Cardwell's letter'. Even more alarmingly, the parish was 'distressed by rumours of intended disturbances by the Negroes: among them the resisting the payment of taxes and the appropriation of lands to their own use is said to be their every day conversation.... I am told the chat among the negroes is "Buckra has gun. Negro has fire stick"'.[28] One minister was hooted out by his congregation after reading the Queen's Advice. In St. James, there were rumours of a possible refusal to pay taxes, and anonymous letters of threat to merchants and planters. The Governor became concerned about an outbreak in the Western parishes, and had two vessels of war sent around the western coast, firing blank shots along the way.[29]

The Baptist ministers in St. James (Revs. Henderson, Dendy, Reid, Hewitt and Maxwell, who all took part in the Montego Bay Underhill Meeting), wrote to Eyre to decline to circulate the Queen's Advice, saying it had no meaning to the people in their part of the island, who had 'social and political grievances', not economic ones. Governor Eyre was infuriated by this insubordination:

> It is quite clear that if the Ministers of Religion residing amongst an ignorant, debased and excitable colored population, take upon themselves to endorse and re-iterate assertions such as those in Dr. Underhill's letter, to the effect that the people are starving, ragged or naked; that their addiction to thieving is the result of extreme poverty; that all this arises from the taxation being too heavy; that such taxation is unjust upon the colored population; that they are refused just tribunals and denied political rights, then such Ministers do their best not only to make the laborer discontented, but to stimulate sedition and resistance to the laws and constituted authorities.[30]

Eyre was already trying to rein in public discussion with threats of sedition charges; freedom of association and free speech were becoming particularly worrisome to the beleaguered colonial government. By this time, however, the organization of Underhill Meetings was already beyond the control of Baptist Ministers. Having taken on a far more popular character, an extensive political movement was beginning to consolidate Afro-Jamaican grievances and to call for democracy, accountability and justice across the island.

A placard printed at the newspaper office of George William Gordon (and reproduced in the paper) challenged poor people to publicly demand their rights:

We Call On **You** to come forth, even if you be naked, come forth and protest against the unjust representations made against you by Mr. Governor Eyre and his band of Custodes.... People of St. Thomas ye East, you have been ground down too long already. Shake off your sloth, and speak like *honorable* and free men at your meeting.... Remember that 'he only is free whom the Truth makes free.' You are no longer Slaves, but Free men. Then, as Free men, act your part at the meeting [emphasis in original].[31]

This use of a poster was a kind of mimetic appropriation of the official form of address exemplified by the Queen's Advice. This one was found posted on a tree in the Morant Bay area, where popular meetings were being held in the summer of 1865, to which we now can turn.

Notes

1 There are surprisingly few full accounts of political protest in post-emancipation Jamaica, given its thorough documentation in the archives, but see Heuman's, '*The Killing Time': The Morant Bay Rebellion in Jamaica*, (London and Basingstoke: Macmillan Press, 1994), esp. pp. 38–43; Abigail Bakan, *Ideology and Class Conflict in Jamaica: The Politics of Rebellion* (Montreal and Kingston: McGill-Queen's University Press, 1990); Lorna E. Simmonds, '"The Spirit of Disaffection": Civil Disturbances in Jamaica, 1838–1865' (M. A. thesis, University of Waterloo, 1982); Swithin Wilmot, '"Females of Abandoned Character"? Women and Protest in Jamaica, 1838–65,' in *Engendering History*, ed. V. Shepherd, pp. 279–95.

2 CO 137/299, Evelyn to Grey, 12 June 1848.

3 CO 137/299, Evelyn to Grey, 6 July 1848, encl. letter of T. F. Pilgrim.

4 CO 137/299, Apprehended Outbreak in the Western Parishes, Proclamation of Governor Charles Edward Grey, 14 July 1848. His choice of Bastille Day may have been deliberate.

5 *The Baptist Herald and Friend of Africa*, Vol.1, no. 31, 3 June 1840. Mary Clarke ended up among the three women and six men sentenced to three months in prison for rioting; Wilmot has found that women were also prominent in several tax riots in the 1840s, and in election riots in the 1850s (Wilmot, 'Women and Protest', pp. 286–9).

6 *Morning Journal*, Vol. I, no. 215, 7 Jan. 1842; Scott, *Domination and the Arts of Resistance*, p. 65. A similar violent struggle between police and 'the mob' over banned Christmas parading occurred in Montego Bay in 1841, when an African drum known as a 'Joe Wenda' was confiscated by a magistrate (*Morning Journal*, Vol. 1, no. 211, 1 Jan. 1842). A report by the Central Board of Health, presented to the legislature in 1852, reveals official views of popular urban life, in which the private sphere was as much a threat to 'public order' as the streets and markets. See *Report by the Central Board of Health of Jamaica* (Spanish Town: F. M. Wilson Printer, 1852).

7 CO 137/344, various enclosures in Darling to CO, 25 Mar. 1859.

8 CO 137/345, Darling to CO, 9 Aug. 1859, enclosing Kitchen and Castle to the Governor's Secretary, 2 Aug. 1859; CO 137/346, Darling to CO, 10 Nov. 1859.

9   *Baptist Herald and Friend of Africa*, Vol. 2, no. 36, 8 Sept. 1841, p. 271.

10   CO 137/343, Darling to CO, 24 Feb. 1859, Petition from Saint David's, 15 Jan. 1859, with 10 Feb. 1859 Governor's notes. Darling admitted that the Assembly had introduced the legislation to 'operate as a great discouragement of the exercise of the Franchise, by the more numerous and humble Freeholders', but he still defended it.

11   CO 137/344, Darling to CO, 12 Mar. 1859, enclosing Resolutions of Meeting in Kingston, 23 Feb. 1859, and Petition of Freeholders and Taxpayers.

12   CO 137/345, Governor's Despatches, Darling to CO, 9 June 1859, enclosing two petitions from Rev. Charles M. Fletcher (of Rodney Hall Post Office, St. Thomas ye Vale), to the Queen and to the Governor, both dated 18 Mar. 1859. Rodney Hall was the site of an attempted popular savings bank, one of whose founders was the Stipendiary Magistrate T. Witter Jackson, a well-known spokesman for popular rights (cf. *Morning Journal*, 4 Mar. 1842; and Heuman, *The Killing Time*, 68).

13   CO 137/345, Darling to CO, 9 June 1859, enclosing S. Rennales to Darling, 7 April 1859 and Davis to Rennales, 2 May 1859. Although the government claimed the signatures were not genuine, they are in a wide variety of hands and very few are marked with an 'x'; approximately 160 of the names are women's.

14   PRO 30/48/44, Cardwell Papers, Evidence of Louis Q. Bowerbank; Baptist report quoted in Douglas Hall, *Free Jamaica, 1838–1865: An Economic History* (New Haven: Yale University Press, 1959), 213; WMMS, Box 199, Edmondson to Directors, Apr. 20, 1865.

15   On a visit to the West Indies in 1859, Underhill also visited Haiti to report on the small Baptist mission there, begun in 1845 and consisting of just one congregation in Jacmel (E. B. Underhill, 'Report on the Mission in Haiti', *The Missionary Herald*, 801, enclosed in *The Baptist Magazine*, 1860, no. 52; cf. Brian Stanley, *The History of the Baptist Missionary Society, 1792–1992* [Edinburgh: T & T Clark, 1992], p. 93).

16   The letter exists in the form of small handbills that were posted in public (NLJ, MS 106, Underhill Letter, copy of CO 137/3.98, Underhill to Cardwell, 5 Jan. 1865).

17   CO 137/391, Eyre to Cardwell, no. 137, May 1865.

18   CO 137/391, Eyre to Cardwell, no. 128, 6 May 1865.

19   CO 137/391, Henry Taylor note, 8 June 1865, attached to Eyre to Cardwell, no. 128, 6 May 1865.

20   *JRC*, Part 2, Evidence of Alexander Heslop, 330–31.

21   CO 137/391, Eyre to Cardwell, no. 132, 17 May 1865.

22   The original series of resolutions appears in CO 137/391, Governor's Despatches, Eyre to Cardwell, nos. 132, 136, 137, 142, 148, 172 and 174.

23   *Jamaica Watchman and People's Free Press*, 5 June 1865.

24   Women were also involved in these meetings. At the Underhill Meeting held at Lucea Court House in Hanover, for example, it was reported that over one thousand persons were present, with 'a good sprinkling of crinolined and handkerchief-turbaned females' in the crowd (CO 137/391, Eyre to Cardwell, 19 June 1865, encl. extract *Falmouth Post* [n.d.]).

25   CO 136/392, Eyre to Cardwell, 17 July 1865, encl. *Jamaica Guardian*, 15 July 1865.

26   Grand Jurors of the St. Ann's Circuit Court commented on the memorial: 'We have ascertained that it emanated from but a small portion of our labouring people residing in the district of Ocho Rios, and was concocted by some idle persons living about the villages — that it was prepared without the knowledge or consent of their Ministers, to whose churches they profess to be attached, nor did the

memorial bear the signatures of such Ministers, [n]or [was it] vouched for by any persons of respectability' (CO 137/392, Eyre to Cardwell, no. 183, 21 July 1865, encl. extract from newspaper).

27 CO 137/392, Eyre to Cardwell, no. 189, 24 July 1865.
28 CO 137/392, Eyre to Cardwell, no. 189, 24 July 1865, encl. Salmon to Eyre [n.d.].
29 CO 137/392, Eyre to Cardwell, no. 198, 7 Aug. 1865.
30 CO 137/392, Eyre to Cardwell, 22 Aug. 1865, encl. letter from Baptist Ministers.
31 *Jamaica Watchman and People's Free Press*, 21 Aug. 1865.

8 'Little agitators, small speechifiers, and embryo cut-throats'

Black publics and the Morant Bay Rebellion

In the months prior to the Morant Bay Rebellion , James McLaren, a 22-year-old Native Baptist with close ties to Paul Bogle, spoke at several unofficial public meetings.[1] One of his speeches was paraphrased in the evidence given to the Jamaica Royal Commission by William Anderson, a young black estate labourer:

> 'Why cause me to hold this meeting; myself was born free, but my mother and father was slave; but now I am still a slave by working from days to days. I cannot get money to feed my family, and I am working at Coley estate for 35 chains for 1*s*., and after five days working I get 2*s*. 6*d*. for my family. Is that able to sustain a house full of family?' and the people said, 'No.' Then, he said, 'Well, the best we can do is to come together, and send in a petition to the Government; and if they will give up the outside land to *we*, we shall work with cane, and cotton, and coffee like the white. But the white people say we are lazy and won't work.' When he said that the people said, 'We have no land to work.' He said, ... 'if the outside land was given up to them to work, they should pay the taxes to the Queen ... they did not want anything from the white people, they would try to make their own living themselves; but they would not give them the land to work, neither give them any money; how then were they to live?' And when he said that he said to the people without they come together, and go down to Morant Bay in lump, to let the white people see there was plenty black in the island, it was no use at all, and cry out that they don't mean to pay any more ground rent again; and after twenty seven years in freedom the outside

198

land was given to them a long time, and the white people kept it to themselves. That was what I heard him say [emphasis in original].[2]

McLaren became a central protagonist in the rebellion, and was executed under martial law. What can this 135-year-old document, preserved in the British Public Record Office, tell us about freedom, democracy and citizenship in Jamaica?

James McLaren's speech can serve as a microcosm of the problems we face in trying to understand slave emancipation as an ongoing process of contentious negotiation and citizen-state communication. As a paraphrased speech, not an original, this document first raises the question of where we find the voices of slaves and their descendants in the historical record. Seldom are there 'direct' sources of writing from a largely illiterate population; much of what we know is based on records kept by others, second or third-hand stories or oral histories and transcribed narratives. The very fact that McLaren's words have been preserved reflects the insistence of interested publics back in Britain that the rebellion and its suppression be publicly investigated through an official enquiry, and that an open report of the evidence be placed before Parliament. It is precisely the absence of such documents in Haiti that points to a significant difference between the two cases. The Haitian government, far less constrained by democratic accountability and transparency, left fewer points of entry for democratic claimants and fewer records for the historian. In Jamaica, the numerous two-way ties between freed people and the British government made both sides adept at addressing the other.

This document must also be situated in relation to a whole series of other public meetings that produced printed speeches, resolutions and petitions, drawing on similar themes and actions. A number of internal features stand out in this paraphrased speech, some of which suggest that it presents a standard genre of popular public speaking, if not an exact replica of the words and structure of the original (given Anderson's goal to incriminate McLaren). It begins with a personal story in which McLaren compares his present condition to that of his parents during slavery. He describes his work and wages, eliciting an audience response by putting the argument in the emotional context of the community as a whole and evoking a participatory confirmation of his words. Having established an experiential bond, McLaren then calls on the people to join together and petition the government for the 'outside' land (marginal plantation land that had always been used by slaves for their provision grounds). As soon as this strategy is proposed, however, he points out its ineffectiveness, since white people will neither pay them the wages they demand nor give them the land they want. Once the dilemma is starkly posed and the issue effectively framed, he is able to direct collective anger into a new plan of action: a targeted demonstration in Morant Bay to let the white people 'see' their numbers and hear them 'cry out'. His moral justification is that for twenty-seven years they had been denied land that should have been theirs following emancipation.

A crucial aspect of this speech is its effort to tell a particular story, to frame a shared account of the disappointing experience of freedom. As social movement theorists suggest, framing is 'the conscious and strategic efforts by groups of people to fashion shared understandings of the world and of themselves that legitimate and motivate collective action' (MacAdam, McCarthy and Zald 1996: 6). Beyond framing, however, I want to suggest that McLaren is also drawing on the *polyvocality* of speech. Not only is he selecting from a multiplicity of stories with which his audience is already familiar (e.g. about their families' struggles out of slavery, about the injustice of employers, about oppression by white people), but he is also contesting the well known 'official' versions of these same events (e.g. about the great boon of freedom conferred by the British people, about the importance of sugar plantations for all classes of the community, about progress through working steadily and saving for the future). These official narratives lurk between the lines, but so too do the stories of the people: each line drips with a weighty infusion of accumulated indignities, grudges, grievances, tall tales, hopes and memories.

The exchange hinges on the problem of how to make white people *hear* this story, and beyond that, how to make the government act to redress the grievances. It is significant that twenty-seven years after emancipation there was still a strong feeling among former slaves and their children that they had been (and still were) treated unfairly, and should have been given land in return for their years of forced and unremunerated slave labour. The struggle to communicate (to one's enemies as well as one's allies) compelling understandings of past, present and future were central to the events of 1843 in Haiti and 1865 in Jamaica. The suggestion of going down to Morant Bay 'in lump' to 'cry out' becomes crucial in the context of the rebellion; it implies not necessarily a violent action, but a peaceful march or demonstration of some kind. George W. Gordon made a similar reference in 1863: '"Coming events cast their shadows before us". In St. Thomas in the East the people are desirous of coming down here in a body to demand redress, but I have told them that that would not do, because they would not be heard at the bar'.[3] The idea of coming in a body to demand redress suggests a Jamaican version of the

English demonstration; in the colonies, though, the line between demonstration and riot was thin, in part because of armed responses by untrained police and volunteer militias. The words of McLaren and Gordon certainly did foretell events to come in St. Thomas in the East, when the people did come down from the hills. Understanding why this peasant mobilization differed from similar peasant mobilizations in Haiti, and how state reactions to such mobilizations differed in the two cases, will bring us a long way toward understanding the varying constructions of citizenship, freedom and democracy in the post-emancipation Caribbean.

The best single description of the events of October 1865 is Heuman's account in *'The Killing Time': The Morant Bay Rebellion in Jamaica* (1994), based on a careful examination of the evidence collected by the Jamaica Royal Commission. As he points out, some previous studies of the period have minimized the aims of the rebellion, depicting it as a march or riot that went badly wrong because of the government's over-reaction (Curtin 1955; Hall 1959; Campbell 1976). Others have linked it to grievances throughout the island, and to a broader culture of resistance among some of the peasantry; they consider it a premeditated and planned rebellion (Green 1976; Robotham 1981; Bakan 1990; Holt 1992). Heuman's argument falls within the latter category, showing that the outbreak 'was a rebellion, characterized by advanced planning and by a degree of organization'. My findings also support this conclusion. Significantly, Heuman also points out that St. Thomas in the East was predominantly a sugar parish with 'some of the richest properties in Jamaica', and was 'one of the most politically divided parishes in the colony' (Heuman 1994: 63). Those political divisions undermined planter control.

In addition to considering the internal features of the rebellion, I will also set it in the context of specific networks of activists both within and beyond Jamaica, in order to better understand its relation to wider Afro-Caribbean political movements, political identities and genres of claim-making. This chapter focuses mainly on the events leading up to the rebellion, the networks of activists involved, the popular grievances that were expressed just prior to the rebellion and the government's reaction to these claimants. I will not spend a great deal of time on the details of the rebellion itself, as these have been thoroughly summarized by Heuman. However, I will devote extra attention to the wave of political contention that preceded the rebellion, and to the role of George W. Gordon and his supporters in organizing the Underhill Movement. In contrast to all previous accounts of the rebellion, in the conclusion that follows, I will also focus attention on the Haitian exiles who were politically active in

Jamaica at the time, and will consider their influence on the network of Afro-Jamaican activists in and around Kingston and Morant Bay.

On the 7th of October, 1865, James Geoghagan shouted out in the Morant Bay Court House that the defendant in a case of trespass should not pay the costs of 12*s* 6*d*. He was ordered out of the court, and when he did not go quietly, the judge ordered his arrest. A police-man reported that he said to Geoghagan: "'You come here to cheek me always in this Court", and as Geoghagan was going out of Court, his sister, called Isabella Geoghagan, came up directly and said, "Come out of the Court, let us go down in the market, and let us see if any d—d policemen come here if we don't *lick* them to hell"'.[4] Her chal-lenge clearly demonstrates the sense of female control over the market as a public space in which, unlike the courts, popular justice could prevail; it was a threat backed by force, for an armed mob indeed rescued James from police. Involved in the rescue was a Native Baptist leader named Paul Bogle and his followers from a small village known as Stony Gut.

Following the events in the Court House that day, the police were ordered to arrest those involved; but on their arrival at Stony Gut, the black policemen were captured and forced to swear oaths to 'cleave to the black'. This outright resistance seems to have pushed Bogle's group toward immediate armed action, although there is much evi-dence that they had been swearing people to loyalty and preparing for violence prior to this date. On the 11th of October, people from Stony Gut began an organized, armed march into Morant Bay, where the vestry was meeting under the leadership of the Custos Baron von Ketelhodt. As Heuman summarizes,

> On that day, several hundred black people [both men and women] marched into the town of Morant Bay, the capital of the predominately sugar-growing parish of St Thomas in the East. They pillaged the police station of its weapons and then confronted the volunteer militia which had been called up to protect the meeting of the vestry, the political body which administered the parish. Fighting erupted between the militia and the crowd and, by the end of the day, the crowd had killed eighteen people and wounded thirty-one others. Seven members of the crowd died. In the days which followed, bands of people in different parts of the parish killed two planters and threatened the lives of many others (Heuman 1994: *xiii*).

In response to the rebellion, the government imposed martial law and brought in British and Jamaican forces, as well as the irregular force of the Maroons (who lived high in the nearby Blue Mountains). In the process, 'nearly 500 people were killed and hundreds of others seriously wounded. The nature of the suppression led to demands in England for an official enquiry, and a Royal Commission subsequently took evidence in Jamaica on the disturbances for nearly three months' (Heuman 1994: *xiii*). Governor Eyre was eventually rebuked for the severe repression, and dismissed from his post; however, efforts to try him on criminal charges in England were unsuccessful (Semmel 1963; Hall 1995).

Economic, political, and civil grievances in 1865

As Robotham (1981) argues in regard to the Morant Bay Rebellion, economic grievances alone do not explain a political movement; nevertheless, they are important. At the heart of peasant grievances in this period were a series of economic issues related to wages, land tenure, access to markets and labour rights. As Holt points out, the grievances of the Jamaican freedmen included 'proletarian issues such as higher wages and better working conditions on the estates along with peasant issues such as lower taxes and more land. The mixed character of their grievances reflected the hybrid character of the Jamaican peasantry' (Holt 1992: 300; cf. Bakan 1990). The 1865 resolutions and petitions usually reflected a combination of these proletarian and peasant grievances, along with urban issues relevant to 'mechanics', seamstresses or small traders. As seen in the previous chapter, a hybridity of rural and town life characterized the Jamaican 'peasantry,' many of whom engaged in occasional wage labour and regularly attended markets, courts, churches and public meetings in the towns.

As with earlier popular meetings, questions of land, rent and fair wages were at the centre of the Underhill Meetings, and are reflected in the petitions and speeches that came out of the meetings. A good example is the petition from African indentured labourers in Vere, who organized their own meeting, stating:

> That we are in great distress and Poverty on account of not getting sufficient work to do so as to enable us to maintain our familys, some of our children were at school, we are compelled to take them away, as we cannot afford to purchase clothes to send them there, some of us our members in the church, and cannot attend the worship of God for want of clothing for our self and family, and we are in a state of

> starvation.... The estates give us little work but what we earn
> weekly cannot purchase sufficient food to suffice us for the
> week, as what work they give us to perform for a sixpence is
> worth two shillings and sometimes we labour for nothing, for
> when Friday comes, which is our pay day, there will sure to
> be some fault or the other found with the work, and then our
> pay is stopped....[5]

This petition was reportedly written by 'Alexander McClymont, an
engine driver out of berth who does small writing jobs for any remu-
neration he can get'. Eyre's cover letter charged that the statements of
the labourers were incorrect, and 'that some of the signatures have
been attached without the knowledge or consent of the persons
named'. Once again his claim of 'designing persons' using the petition
'to serve their own purposes' was used to dismiss the grievances.
Rather than respond to the claims, Eyre tried to block political communication on a procedural technicality.

An essential aspect of peasant economic agency was the attempt
to improve economic conditions through cooperative efforts (as we
have noted in Haiti). From the perspective of Jamaican wage labourers, this included organized work stoppage, strikes and collective bargaining. For small landholders or peasants, it also included other
forms: cooperative labour (morning digs, etc.); self-help or friendly
societies (to help in sickness or death); collective landowning or marketing associations; local credit or savings associations. Many of the
speeches recorded from Underhill Meetings made direct demands
either for fair wages *or* some form of land distribution, representing
the dual strategy of wage labour and peasant subsistence/commodity
production. Some politicians supported schemes of land distribution
and the formation of various kinds of marketing cooperatives to help
peasants benefit from their own labour. Dr. Underhill himself argued
that the government should encourage the growth of small export
crops 'by the formation of Associations for Shipping their produce in
considerable quantities', and 'by opening channels for direct transmission of produce without the intervention of Agents, by whose exer-
tions and frauds the people now frequently suffer'.[6] In fact, in a letter
of 1864, he commended one such association that was already in
operation at Black River. 'I think more could be done in coffee than is
done at present', he wrote. 'Then there is ginger, nutmegs, and other
spices, arrowroot, and the like. Then if the people could put their
produce together and ship it in one good lot, as the Black River people
are doing under Barrett, it would come into the market under
favourable conditions'.[7]

Just prior to the Rebellion, there were several efforts under way to improve economic conditions for the small settlers in Jamaica through the practices of 'association' or 'combination', as alluded to by Dr. Underhill. Newspapers such as *The Sentinel* ran editorials on the desirability of labour associations. In March 1865, an editorial argued that Dr. Underhill's suggestions for associations hinted at 'the means which might be taken to advance the people of this country, develop our numerous — but latent resources, and help forward the social amelioration of the masses of this country'.[8] Again, in April, the paper argued with reference to shipping associations that there was an even 'more important field':

> It cannot be said that the principle of association is unsuited to Jamaica.... We have, all over the island, vast tracts of uncultivated land, of great fertility. Surely, there is nothing to prevent these from being cultivated on the principle of association! Why should Sugar Estates be dismantled and abandoned, to revert to the original wildness of Nature, when there are plenty of people to keep them in cultivation, and who, we are persuaded, would gladly engage to do so were proper inducements held out to them?[9]

At a meeting held in St. David, it was suggested that an Island Agricultural Loan Bank or Joint Stock Company be formed. 'The gathering also called for the establishment of a committee known as the Central Communicating Committee "to correspond with the yeoman throughout the island on subjects of agriculture and other branches of native industry"' (Heuman 1994: 53; cf. Hall 1959).

Few in the government, however, were prepared to support cooperatives, let alone hand over property; many whites found any 'combinations' among blacks extremely threatening. Critical reports were submitted to the Governor just after the rebellion concerning a joint-stock association being attempted by three men in St. Elizabeth. The Custos, John Salmon, reported that they were holding meetings of 'the inhabitants and small settlers black and colored', where the people were 'informed that the growers of produce are imposed upon and cheated'.[10] Building on ideas that had been around since emancipation, their plan was to form a 'commercial and agricultural association' (underwritten by £5 shares). It would not only sell Jamaican small agricultural produce direct to English buyers, but would also bring affordable manufactured goods back from England to sell cheaply to association members. Correspondence describing the plan gives us the best idea of its aims:

> Our joint-stock association...was to be managed by
> Englishmen brought here for the purpose; the basis of the
> whole affair is cotton planting by the small settlers. Neither
> Brydson nor myself expected any compensation from the
> scheme save the dividend on our shares.... Our main object
> is to get the people to plant cotton, and we would have had
> the means of the cotton supply association at our disposal.
> Then to establish model farms, industrial schools, savings
> banks throughout the island; but our scheme was looked on
> as too gigantic to be good.[11]

Salmon complained that the association would 'materially injure
general society', as the Members were to pledge 'not to dispose of any
oil nuts, oils, coffee, ginger or other produce to any white person'.
This, he thought, would foster distrust; furthermore, the small settlers
might be cheated by these 'men of straw who have no capital and no
character entitling them to conduct such an undertaking even if it were
legitimate and honest. It is so barefaced an attempt as not to be mistaken for a piece of rascality'. When Governor Eyre submitted the
question to Attorney General Heslop of whether such an association
was legal, Heslop determined that it was perfectly legal, but observed
that like the similar schemes of Fourrier in France, and Robert Owen
in England, the best argument against it would be its own failure.
Indeed, part of the importance of this plan was its connection to a
broader worker's associational movement (also prevalent in Haiti, as
we have seen), and its ties to international efforts to promote economic
opportunities for freedmen and socially responsible investment by
British anti-slavery publics.[12]

Land tenure disputes also intensified in the summer of 1865, as
reports began to circulate that a disturbance of some sort would occur
in the western parishes in August. John Salmon found many people
'distressed by rumours of intended disturbances by the Negroes:
among them the resisting the payment of taxes and the appropriation of
lands to their own use is said to be their every day conversation'.[13] In
Black River, he reported, 'the People allege that they have been
informed that the Queen has sent out a large sum of money to be laid
out in the purchase of lands to be divided among them and that the
Custos has kept it for himself'.[14] It seems that these rumours were
probably connected to the Plummer-Brydson project. 'Squatting' was
common on the numerous abandoned estates and Crown-owned land
throughout Jamaica; some landless peasants clearly took a radical
approach to occupying their own land outside of the law. When owners
tried to clear squatters off their land, it often resulted in protracted civil

court cases and sometimes in violent conflict. Governor Eyre reported on one such case to the Colonial Secretary in 1865:

> … at a place called 'Hartland' where a large body of black people amounting it is said to 600 or 700 have for years past taken violent possession of a property of 3000 acres and set all attempts of recovery by the lawful owners at defiance — arming themselves with firearms, threatening to kill any one who goes near the place, barricading up the road and shooting at a man who had given some evidence against them. This is *within three miles of Spanish Town*, and it is confidently asserted that there are living on this property black people who have never been into the town or to any European settlement *for years*…. [T]here are a *large number of similar cases* throughout the country and much trouble and possible bloodshed may be entailed in settling them. Nothing will persuade the black people that they are not unjustly treated in being called upon to retire from lands that they have occupied and cultivated for some years even tho' they have no title or claim whatever. It is a singular fact that all the most troublesome people in the country are what may be termed the small settlers who own or occupy lands and who are not necessitated to labor for hire and do not do so except occasionally to suit their own convenience or the wants or views of the moment [emphasis in original].[15]

Although this report was filed after the rebellion, it indicates a situation that had gone on for some time and in other parts of the island. It also indicates the typical government response, and echoes the views of Colonial Office officials like Henry Taylor. The court cases that led to the conflict at Morant Bay in October 1865 also arose from disputes over trespass near the Native Baptist village of Stony Gut.

Beyond these economic grievances, charges of political corruption, injustice and social oppression were also central to the popular claims made during the Underhill Movement. Issues of land ownership were closely related to conflicts over local decision-making. Local electoral politics were the most important basis for black participation in formal politics. Each parish was divided into several 'vestries' tied to the established churches. These elected bodies, with local budgetary powers,

> consider and draw up the estimates of all parochial expenditures, ways, and means; whilst sub-committees from those vestries…perform the duties of the Boards of Health,

> estimate the costs of repairs of the public roads, not being main roads, and assist in the supervision of their repairs, and they form estimates of the cost of repairs of their numerous parochial buildings (Price 1866: 1).

These were all key local concerns, and black electors increasingly gained a voice on these vestries, and in some cases even controlled them. George Price, the Custos of St. Catherine, was unusually sympathetic toward the aim of full black political participation; he wrote that one vestry in his parish was 'composed of coloured men, and another in the mountains almost entirely of black men, mountain settlers'. He defended their participation and praised 'the demeanour of the black members of those boards, their courtesy and orderly conduct, respect towards the chairman and each other, and manner of addressing the boards... even the good sense and justice of their arguments' (Price 1866: 2–3).

The conflict of planter control versus peasant agency was evident in the failure of local politics. Looking back at the 'Tragedy of Morant Bay' in 1895, Dr. Underhill referred to a litany of injustices that had contributed to the movement:

> ... the acknowledged inefficiency of the courts of law; the failure of justice for the lower orders; the laxity, untrustworthiness, and improprieties of public boards; the gross and unblushing bribery and corruption practiced at elections by the upper classes; the licentiousness and gross perversions of the truth...; the scandalous abuses, want of integrity and shortcomings in the management of public institutions; the laxity, the perjury, the defalcations, and the frauds committed under the shelter of the laws; the disgraceful bickerings and jobbery of the members of the Assembly (Underhill 1895: 9–10).

Sydney Levien, editor of the *County Union*, also made an explicit connection between the 'riot' in Morant Bay and wider issues of social injustice and misgovernment:

> What does the riot speak of — happening where it has — in a district where, because a magistrate represented the people as dying in the lock-up without attendance and without food, he was dismissed [from] the magistracy? ...A Government that sows the wind must expect to reap the whirlwind; and a Government that spends thousands upon thousands on prisons and penitentiaries, yet cares not to educate the people, must expect a semi-barbarous population.[16]

Levien was also known for his outspoken criticism of the system of indenture that had replaced plantation slave labour, and which had become a subject of political protest among the peasantry. He had been tried for libel after vividly criticizing the horrific condition and treatment of Indian indentured labourers:

> One must see — as those who live in Montego Bay cannot close their eyes to — these wretched, hungry, houseless and outcast spectres picking up in the street a chance bone, or any putrid offal they may fall in with, to realise the sufferings they hourly undergo from want of sustenance.... Mothers hugging shrunken abortions of human nature to their parchment dugs from which no nutriment can flow — pale fever-stricken children for whom God in his mercy might well cancel a cruel existence — darken our doors and there mutely plead against the murderous enactment of a Statute Book that brought them here to undergo the slow torture of the death to which they are inevitably doomed.[17]

The 'Coolies' themselves had little opportunity to protest their treatment, though some tried.[18] Rev. Henry Clarke likewise wrote that 'the mere fact of [a Coolie's] having complained to me against an overseer is a complete bar on his being employed on any other estate.... A long experience has taught me that it is impossible to get justice in this country for the poor, either native or foreign, against an overseer'.[19]

Jamaican public affairs were in a sorry state by many accounts, and it was largely the black peasants and indentured workers who suffered the consequences. Prior to the Underhill Movement, there were many complaints concerning the poor condition of roads and the tendency to build roads only to the big estates, and not to the areas where small peasants farmed. The Stipendiary Magistrate T. Witter Jackson (a popular judge who was controversially moved out of St. Thomas in the East by Governor Eyre just prior to the rebellion), reported in 1859 that in St. David's parish, the roads leading up to the coffee estates in the hills where 'a fair proportion of coffee is cultivated by the lately enfranchised people upon their new settlements', were nearly impassable.[20] The Fletcher petitions of 1859 had also referred to the poor roads; as road building was controlled by local Vestries, it was an issue closely related to charges of corruption and lack of justice for the poor at the local level. In the battle between white plantation owners and small peasant farmers, control over road building was an issue that was at once economic, political and civil: who would control the public thoroughfares that shaped the social space of Jamaica?

Among other causes, Price blamed the unrest of 1865 on what he called the 'Tramway Swindle', and the role of Governor Eyre and the Colonial Office in it. Few other studies of the Morant Bay Rebellion have considered the importance of this scandal in discrediting Eyre and one of his major allies, Baron von Ketelhodt, especially in the eyes of black taxpayers and freeholders; in fact it was crucial to the emergence of the Underhill Meeting Movement. This complex public scandal occupied the press for more than a year. At its core was an irregular transfer of a major public road into private hands to build a Tramway at public expense:

> The road in question is the only road leading from Kingston and Spanish Town, westward to the principal coffee districts of the island, and was of the last importance to the negroes, both for the conveyance of their produce to the market, and of their imported goods to their homes, and to the towns in the interior. The illegal and unconditional surrender, therefore, of such a road, and of the monopoly of its traffic, to any one, and especially to the public officer charged with its care, for his own private benefit, could only cause great anger and excitement amongst the people (Price 1866: 26).

In 1863, about eight miles of the Tramway were laid down, but never completed; they fell into disrepair, with iron rails sticking up from muddy ditches, and soon 'horses were being killed, carts broken, and the road became all but impassable, having but just previously been about the best in the island' (Price 1866: 49). Meanwhile, a high toll was still being collected from anyone who braved the journey. Price argued that the men attacked at Morant Bay, like Baron von Ketelhodt, had not only created local conflicts, but were also at the centre of wider governmental irregularities involving the Governor, including the Tramway scandal and another scandal at the public hospital.

Even fairly conservative newspapers criticized Eyre and the unsatisfactory state of public affairs created by the Tramway and Public Hospital scandals:

> All feel that the public credit is damaged by the tramway swindle, and fear to trust one farthing of the public money in any public enterprise, which shall be overlooked by the Government. The House is dispirited because its character has been aspersed, and a system more military than constitutional adopted by the Colonial Office, to require the transmission of all complaints through the Governor himself, prevents them from clearing it up. Public officers are

dejected because whilst the Governor exercises despotic control over them, their voice cannot reach those who may call him to account except through himself.[21]

'The refusal of the constituencies and the Assembly to be parties to transactions such as Mr. Eyre and his Government approved of', Price argued, 'or to place more money at their disposal, has caused the black electors to be disfranchised, and the Assembly to be annihilated' (Price 1866: 120). In both 1859–60 and 1863–64, the black electorate successfully voted against the party of government. It was the spectre of this increasing black control of the legislature that led Eyre to argue for abolition of the House of Assembly as early as 1863 (in his government correspondence), but especially after the rebellion.

The operation of local vestries and courts also became key focal points of black grievances over equal participation and equal justice for all alike, poor and rich, black and white. Several newspapers observed how justice had failed. In March 1865, the lead editorial in *The Sentinel* complained:

> Every department of our social and governmental system, is falling into a state of disorganization; and an undefined presentiment leads one, and all to feel that mischief is in the air…. [I]f we turn to our courts of law, we find the most disgusting partialities, and instances of justice turned aside; of law strained to suit a purpose; of packed juries and all the rest. The utmost insecurity prevails, and men appeal to the law for justice with fear and trembling.[22]

Apart from the few Stipendiary Magistrates who were appointed and remunerated by Parliament, most Jamaican courts were administered by local magistrates, usually planters. Juries, too, were overwhelmingly biased against the poor black litigant, and even Eyre admitted that the Clerks of the Peace were 'wholly irresponsible and uncontrollable'.[23] Bringing a case to court could also be very expensive. The court fees often far outstripped the original damages awarded in petty cases. Rev. Robert Parnther, for example, stated that the people had 'complained to me of the injustice in the courts, at times when they have been there to seek for justice, that they had not obtained it… they have often told me of the troublesomeness and uncertainty of having justice done to them and that it was not worth their while to do so, because they were sure to fail'.[24] There was a strong incentive for poor people to seek justice outside of the formal court system (Heuman 1994). There is evidence that 'in many districts, the black people simply gave up taking any cases into court and instituted a private court system composed of their own community leaders, who were usually religious leaders, to handle disputes among themselves' (Stewart 1992: 132).

As Underhill Meetings began to publicly address all of these grievances, planters began to worry. On the 10th of July, 1865, an editorial in the conservative *Colonial Standard and Jamaica Despatch*, complained that Underhill's letter had 'furnished pretexts to the worst class of agitators and demagogues, political and religious, with which the community is infested'. These he described as

> [the] village politician, the stump orator, the little agitator, the small speechifier...the disappointed scoundrel, the embryo cut-throat, the ambitious leader of illicit trainbands and secret associations.... Our peasantry... are being taught to distrust those above them, and to look upon the upper classes of society, and the employers of labour, in the light of merciless vampires who grow fat upon the blood and sinews of the labouring classes, and aim at nothing but re-enslaving and oppressing the latter.

The editor was not far off the mark when he went on to refer to 'class warfare.' But who was responsible for stirring up the peasantry or had they stirred themselves?

George William Gordon and his supporters

Who exactly attended the Underhill Meetings? The meeting at Montego Bay, convened by advertisement and held in the Court House, included not only the Custos, the local representative, several Baptist ministers, merchants and newspaper publishers, but also 'a dense mass composed of the shopkeepers, middle class, labourers — a meeting of such mixed elements as only the great pressures of the times, with the interest felt in the great social question to be discussed, could by possibility have got together'.[25] The meeting at Four Paths in Clarendon was a less official one, according to the Custos, held in the Baptist Chapel, and 'attended by four and five hundred persons of the Labouring Classes.... I could not hear of any person of position or education being present'.[26] The meeting at Lucea in Hanover was reported in the *County Union* as 'the most turbulent and disorderly one, ever witnessed in the Court House', with a lively public debate:

> Mr. Browne was interrupted several times in his introductory address and angry conversations were carried on by different

parties in several parts of the hall, who seemed to pay little or no attention to what was said to them from the platform.... The audience roared like inmates of bedlam! Clenched fists were lifted above the crowd and seemed to threaten annihilation of any one who would dare to assert that the picture of poverty was capable of being overdrawn.[27]

As for the meeting at Manning's Town Court House in St. Mary, the Custos reported that 'with two or three exceptions it entirely consisted of Common trades-people and labourers', though they were 'well dressed'.[28] In St. David, the Custos reported that the meeting 'was convened at the request of Mr. Samuel Clarke and others who delight in Political Excitement, and attended by their followers. The better disposed and industrious portion of the Inhabitants and small freeholders were not present'.[29] It included black Baptist pastors like Rev. Robert Palmer, as well as political activists like the shoemaker Thomas Hardy.

Many meeting attendees were political supporters of George William Gordon. While the meetings in Cornwall were associated with a somewhat more elite group of Baptist missionaries, those in Kingston and Surrey revolved mainly around Gordon's clique. In fact, to understand their origins, we must take a closer look at the political network that Gordon had built up at least since the 1859 meetings against the electoral law. A better picture of the ambitious bridging of oppositional middle-class and black smallholder networks in Jamaica during the Underhill Movement can be gained by tracking joint attendance by some of the most important activists at a series of public meetings, from 1862 to 1865. Table 8 shows all of the people who were named in newspaper reports, on resolutions or in petitions as participants at more than one of the meetings for which fairly complete lists of participants are available (ten in total). They are then cross-referenced with each other in a person by event matrix, rearranged to show two major blocks, one centred around Kingston and Spanish Town, the other centred around St. Thomas in the East, including Morant Bay, Stony Gut, Church Corner and nearby St. David. It becomes evident that the main link between these two blocks was George William Gordon, who served as a kind of political broker. Gordon was the most influential organizer of Underhill Meetings, personally chairing the meetings in Kingston and Saint Ann, but also closely associated with those who organized the meetings in Spanish Town, St. David and Morant Bay. Table 9, a person by person matrix, brings out Gordon's central prominence in this cluster of activists, some of whom shared other personal or professional ties with him.[30]

Table 8 Attendance at Public Meetings in Jamaica, 1859-1865; Person by Event Matrix

	Span. Town Uhill	St. Ann Uhill Mtg	Kings Taber Mtg	Kings 1859 Mtg	Kings Uhill Mtg	St. Thos. 1862	St. Thos. Uhill	St. David Uhill	Stony Gut Mtg	Church Corner Mtg
J. McLaren									X	X
P. Bogle									X	X
G. B. Clarke							X			
W. F. March						X				
W. Grant						X			X	
S. Clarke					X		X	X		
W. Smith					X	X				
R. Palmer					X	X		X		
R. Wiltshire				X	X			X		
G. W. Gordon		X	X	X	X	X	X			
E. J. Goldson	X		X		X					
Kelly Smith	X		X		X					
J. H. Crole		X	X		X					
J. F. Roach			X	X	X					
J. Sergeon				X	X					
E. Brown				X	X					
J. Burton		X								
T. Rodney		X								

Table 9 Attendance at Public Meetings in Jamaica, 1859–1865; Person by Person Matrix

	PB	GC	WM	WG	SC	WS	RP	RW	GG	EG	KS	JC	JR	JS	EB	JB	TR
P. Bogle		*	1	1	1		1		1*								
G. B. Clarke	*		1	1	*	1	1		1*								
W. F. March	1	1		1		1	1		1*								
W. Grant	1	1	1				1		1								
S. Clarke	1	*				1	2	2	2	1	1	1		1	1		
W. Smith		1	1		1		2	1	2	1	1	1		1	1		
R. Palmer	1	1	1	1	2	2		2	2	1	1	11	1	1	1		
R. Wiltshire					2	1	2		2		1	1	2	2	2		
G. W. Gordon	1*	1*	1*	1	2	2	2	2		2	2*	3*	3	2	2	1*	1
E. Goldson					1	1	1		2		3*	2	2	1	1		
Kelly Smith					1	1	1	1	2*	3*		2	2	1	1		
J. H. Crole					1	1	11	1	3*	2	2		2	2	2	1	1
J. F. Roach							1	2	3	2	2	2		2	2		
J. Sergeon					1	1	1	2	2	1	1	2	2		2		
E. Brown					1	1	1	2	2	1	1	2	2	2			
J. Burton									1*			1					1*
T. Rodney									1			1				1*	

each cell = how many political meetings each pair jointly attended

* = presence of some other significant tie (professional, financial or kinship)

Gordon's strategy had always been to seek maximum publicity in all of his political activities, whether as a representative in the House of Assembly, a church warden, a lay preacher, a commissioner of the peace or a newspaper editor. He was enmeshed in a number of different public networks, and occupied a special position in the overall structure of publicity in Jamaica. First, he published *The Watchman and Jamaica Free Press* and *The Sentinel*, at a time when newspaper offices often served as centres of political discussion and places for the exchange of ideas and information. 'Public opinion' was a highly contested terrain in Jamaican politics, and editors of oppositional newspapers were regularly brought to court, and sometimes had their presses seized. Gordon himself argued in the Assembly in favour of a free press:

> Read the northside press and you will find public opinion expressed there. Public opinion is a great lever, and cannot easily be changed, and is not easily formed either. The public is a discriminating body, and takes a long time before it gives a verdict; but that verdict is now ready, which is, that the Lieutenant-Governor [Eyre] is not entitled to the confidence of the public, and that his remaining here must be detrimental to the interests of the island (Price 1866: 129).

Indeed, during Eyre's government, opposition newspapers became targets for repression. In 1864, Eyre had complained of 'the Kingston Newspapers, owned, controlled and edited entirely by coloured persons or Jews';[31] in July 1865, he filed a report to the Colonial Office on these opposition newspapers and their editors. 'The real truth', he confided to Cardwell, 'is that the entire Press of the Colony is in the hands of a very few persons and those for the most part are either Jews or coloured persons — classes that have been generally for the last two years in violent antagonism to me from one cause or another'.[32] The cumulative effect of these despatches was to discredit both the opposition and the Jamaican press in the eyes of the Colonial Office; not surprisingly, one significant response to the rebellion was the new limits set on freedom of the press. Besides Levien, the editors of *The Watchman and Jamaica Free Press*, William Kelly Smith and Emanuel Joseph Goldson, were also arrested under martial law.

Gordon also stood out for his fiery rhetoric in the House of Assembly. In 1864, the *Morning Journal* mischievously published an excerpt from one of his speeches, which verged on sedition:

> I regret, Mr. Speaker, that I am out of order: but when every-day we witness the mal-administration of the laws by the

lieutenant-governor we must speak out. You are endeavouring to suppress public opinion — to pen up the expression of public indignation — but I tell you that it will soon burst forth like a flood and sweep everything before it. There must be a limit to everything — a limit to oppression, a limit to transgressions, and a limit to illegality! ...When a governor becomes a dictator — when he becomes despotic, it is time for the people to dethrone him, and to say, 'we will not allow you any longer to rule us'.[33]

The speech, meant for the floor of the House, seemed in the glare of the public press to be inciting rebellion. Usually Gordon's disparate social ties allowed him to separate different publics. Thus, he presented one public 'face' in the House of Assembly, another in his Kingston Tabernacle, another in the newspapers and another still in St. Thomas in the East, where he was a Church Warden and connected with the Native Baptist group led by Paul Bogle. As public debate intensified in the early 1860s, he became infamous for his public speaking and appeals to the peasantry.

A number of contemporary observers described Gordon's unusual public presence among the people. The Custos of Kingston testified that

George William Gordon was a most eccentric character. He was gifted with great powers of speech, and by no means lacked natural talent. His speeches were strangely mixed up with Scripture quotations, and he generally carried in his pocket a Bible, which he often quoted from. He was ready at all times to preach, and went from parish to parish holding forth in the various conventicles and native Baptist chapels.[34]

Indeed, in each social arena, he faced several publics at once: the official public of 'white' Jamaica, the oppositional public of 'coloured' Jamaica, the oppositional public of Britain, and the subaltern public of 'black' Jamaica. One way in which Gordon had built his popular support was through the practice of economic cooperation. Gordon's friend the Rev. Duncan Fletcher wrote in his personal recollections that

Mr. Gordon's proprietary adventures arose chiefly from a lofty and laudable desire to provide little farms or freeholds, as cheaply and conveniently as possible for his liberated brethren. I know that he also formed, and to some extent executed, a system of mercantile enterprize, by which the enfranchised small settlers could obtain, in full, the current market prices for the produce of their industry (Price 1866: 33).

This would seem to indicate not only cooperative land ventures, but also some form of marketing association designed to avoid the loss of profit to middle-men.

Gordon played a central role in mobilizing popular attendance at the Underhill Meetings, building a bridge between a black Jamaican public and oppositional publics in Britain, who could influence Parliament and the Colonial Office. A key feature of his unique position was a bitter personal enmity between himself and Lt. Governor Eyre. When Eyre took over from Governor Darling in 1862, he became embroiled in Gordon's attempts to reform the jail at Morant Bay. Gordon wrote to the Governor's Secretary complaining of the lack of hospitals, alms-houses or debtor's prisons in Jamaica, as well as the unsanitary conditions of the local prison. Eyre's response was to have Gordon removed from his positions in several parishes as a Commissioner of the Peace. Gordon protested his removal from the Commission in these terms:

> [It] is as insulting as it is *unconstitutional, unworthy, un-english* and *undeserved*, and I truly regret that Her Majesty's Representative in this Island could indulge in such unbecoming and unmerited personal insults, and become so great a Partizan as to mix up private feelings with public duty.... The Commission requires that equal justice should be done to the *Poor* as well as the *Rich*, but in Jamaica it appears that a premium is held out to inhumanity, cruelty and corruption! [emphasis in original].[35]

Gordon then asserted that he would bring Eyre's behaviour in this matter 'before the tribunal of an English public in order to shew the *enormities* of this Country, and the manner in which the Government is administered'. Even the Colonial Office had to rebuke Eyre for ignoring Gordon's pertinent evidence on the abuses at the lock-up; but Eyre defended his decision by attacking Gordon:

> I believe Mr. Gordon to be a most mischievous person and one likely to do a great deal of harm amongst uneducated and excitable persons such as are the lower classes of this country. His object appears not to be to rectify evils where they exist but rather to impress the Peasantry with the idea that they labour under many grievances and that their welfare and interests are not cared for by those in authority.[36]

Following Eyre's actions, some of Gordon's supporters in St. Thomas in the East petitioned the Queen in support of him. Written in beautiful calligraphy on fifteen inch cream-coloured paper, the petition was accompanied by a cover letter addressed directly to the Duke of Newcastle (Secretary of State for the Colonies). It clearly indicates a distrust of the Lieutenant Governor, who was usually the first channel through which to transmit petitions; thus, the petition was an attempt to go over his head on a local matter. As in the Fletcher petitions of 1859, Gordon's supporters express profound attachment and loyalty to the Queen, and 'deepest feelings of gratitude' to 'Almighty God' for the blessings of emancipation, twenty-eight years before. The petition then states:

> That your Memorialists consider that the proceedings against Mr. Gordon were irregular, unconstitutional and altogether unwarrantable, and that his removal from the Magistracy is a wrong to himself and a grievance to the People…. That the principles involved in this matter are *Serious* to us as a people, and we pray that Your Gracious Majesty may be pleased to institute an enquiry to remove the wrongs from which We are suffering [emphasis in original][37]

The petitioners refer to themselves as the 'Emancipated Classes, and others'. Their claims were clearly grounded on an assertion of membership in the British empire, and morally grounded in English law and constitutionality. The call for an enquiry echoes that of 1859, and adumbrates that of 1865. Eyre's cover letter dismisses the petition, saying that the 'signature of the Chairman may I think fairly lead to the presumption that it was a meeting of the lower and uneducated classes… it was neither a very numerous or influential meeting'.

This meeting of Gordon's supporters was held at the Native Baptist chapel in Morant Bay (after the Custos refused to call a public meeting in the usual location, the courthouse). They moved that their resolutions be published once in each Jamaica newspaper, and be sent to the London *Times* and other English papers, as well as to Lord Brougham, Lord John Russell, John Bright and 'other friends of the cause of Liberty'. They were evidently experienced in petitioning and the manipulation of international publicity. Surprisingly detailed information on their social position is provided by a highly critical report prepared by P. A. Espeut, a Member of Assembly and large landowner in the parish.[38] Under the title 'An Analytical Report of Mr. George W. Gordon's so-called Public Meeting', Espeut vehemently attacked the men who supported Gordon. Describing each one's colour, personal background and occupation, such as mechanic, carpenter or petty shopkeeper, he singled out the 'small lawyers' for special derision. He describes William Grant, for example, as: 'Mulatto, a petty saddler at Morant Bay, another kind of character which particularly infests the small communities of the island, viz. one who acts as what is termed "a half inch lawyer" and advises the ignorant to put themselves against the Law'. William Foster March, the secretary of the meeting, is described as:

> Mulatto, illegitimate son of the late Foster Henry March, Attorney at Law, Kingston.... He was for some time in his Father's office, and has acquired a little knowledge of Law, gains a wretched livelihood by going about the country advising the lower orders of the people on law matters, provoking litigation, preparing documents and otherwise acting as what is called in this country, 'a Negro house lawyer' of no principle or character, so bad his father turned him out of his house and office[;] ...lives in the Negro Huts about the country and has no position whatever and only of influence for evil among the lower orders.... He can scarcely put half a dozen words together of good English either in writing or speaking, and never could have uttered the Speech attributed to him.[39]

March was actually a reporter for some of the opposition newspapers, and worked as a clerk for Gordon. Both Grant and March participated in the Underhill Meetings.

Espeut finally completed his rant against the Gordon supporters by generalizing their local activities to a whole 'nest' of such characters:

> the town of Morant Bay and its immediate vicinity is like many other small towns both in this Island and elsewhere, but perhaps pre-eminently so in this Island, the nest of a set of characters whose principal occupation is that of *half inch lawyers* and village politicians, some of them possessing scarcely means of livelihood and others with no visible means of subsistence, but professing to be Mechanics in a small way, while the town and its vicinity are also the hotbed of prejudice against *white persons in particular* and all respectable persons in general, their position in society being regarded by the characters alluded to as the greatest *crime* of which they could be guilty [emphasis in original].[40]

A second meeting was held in Morant Bay in October, when the published resolutions complained that 'it was no part of the Lieutenant Governor's duty to proceed to discharge the offices of *Prosecutor, Jury* and *Judge*, and to punish for the alleged offence'.[41] Despite rebuking Eyre for including Espeut's remarks in his correspondence, someone in the Colonial Office noted on the margin of the resolutions that, 'it is evidently the production of some ignorant men and it is impossible to make anything of it'.[42] This depiction of an anti-elite political ideology conveys both the social networks and the political symbolism of this popular opposition, emerging from an educated group who mediated between peasants and the state. It was these literate and outspoken 'organic intellectuals' in Jamaica whose 'agitation' and 'electioneering' so threatened the white establishment, and whose organization of Underhill Meetings led to the greatest local public criticism of British colonial rule up to that date.[43]

Gordon also had close political and religious ties with Bogle's group at Stony Gut, near Morant Bay. Gordon had his own Native Baptist chapel in Kingston, known as the 'Tabernacle', in which Bogle served as a Deacon. Bogle also acted as Gordon's 'election agent' in St. Thomas in the East, helping to register voters and get them to turn out for elections (Heuman 1994: 64–6). In March 1863, the small settlers organized by Bogle helped elect Gordon as a Member of Assembly for St. Thomas in the East, and in July of that year, he was also elected to the parish vestry and as a churchwarden (Heuman 1994: 66). However, in early 1864, the Custos Baron von Ketelhodt had Gordon ejected from the vestry while his position as a churchwarden was challenged on the basis of his identification with the Native Baptists. Yet, the people of the parish continued to return Gordon as a vestryman in parish elections in 1864 and 1865 (Heuman 1994: 67). The conflict resulted in a highly publicized court case between Gordon and Ketelhodt, which took various twists and turns throughout 1865, and was still scheduled for retrial when the rebellion broke out in October. It was these ties with the black people of the parish, and enmity with the white officials, which drew government ire upon Gordon following the involvement of Bogle in the Morant Bay Rebellion.

St. Thomas in the East was especially infamous for its lack of justice for the poor and complaints about the judicial system were common in the period prior to the Morant Bay Rebellion. Heuman argues that the administration of what justice there was was particularly corrupt in St. Thomas in the East, leading people to establish alternative courts. The group around Bogle 'were heavily involved in the organization of these courts. In practice, these courts issued summons, tried cases and exacted punishments. They also appointed or elected their own barristers, lawyers, judges, justices of the peace, police and clerks' (Heuman 1994: 73). The Custos of Kingston alluded to the mock courts in evidence he gave to the Royal Commission. Ketelhodt also observed that, 'Paul Bogle had always been counted a great man, and looked up to by the other people, and that they generally took their squabbles to him to adjudicate'.[44]

Although Gordon was not proven to have any direct involvement in the rebellion, his words, ideas and public activities were seen as inciting rebellion. Witnesses such as Rev. Samuel Ringold Ward, a Black American Independent Baptist Minister, blamed Gordon and his supporters for causing the Rebellion. In a damning pamphlet entitled 'Reflections on the Gordon Rebellion', he wrote:

> The origin of the Jamaica Rebellion of October 1865, was nothing more nor less than the seditious and treasonable teachings of George William Gordon and his subalterns; in various ways and places upon various occasions. In St. Anns, St. Dorothy, Vere, Kingston, St. Thomas in the East; in Parliament, by letters, placards, harangues, by means of various agents and sub-agents, by political stratagems, Vestry broils, party bickerings, and secret cabals; by specious misrepresentations and downright lies, all designed and tending to unsettle the minds of the lower classes, and to teach them to disregard and undervalue the authorities of the land form the Governor down to their employers.[45]

Ward, in fact, had been given permission by Ketelhodt to hold a public meeting at the Morant Bay Court House, to try to counter Gordon's influence there (Heuman 1984: 77).

Shortly after the uprising Gordon was arrested in Kingston, which was not under martial law, and transported to Morant Bay. Prohibited from communicating with family or friends, or presenting witnesses in his defence, he was summarily tried by court martial, found guilty and hanged. Apart from Gordon's ties to Paul Bogle, there is no evidence that other people involved in the Underhill Meetings had anything to do with the Morant Bay Rebellion. A few of Gordon's supporters were present in 1865 when Bogle called an Underhill Meeting in Morant Bay. (Baron von Ketelhodt refused them permission to use the Court House, and the meeting had to be held in the open air on the 12th of August, well after most of the other parish meetings.) Paul Bogle spoke at the meeting, and led a deputation to Spanish Town to present the parish grievances to the Governor; they were disappointed when Eyre refused to see them (Semmel 1962: 45). Yet, Bogle's presence at this meeting does not indicate that others knew of the plans being made at Stony Gut. An anonymous letter to the Custos of Kingston during the period of martial law even stated as much. 'It is true that these men are to hold their Underhill Conventional meetings', stated the unknown writer, 'but men like Kelly Smith, Vaz, Roach, Goldson, Harry are not negroes of a rebellious character, nor would they excite or advise ignorant men like the lower orders of St. Thomas ye East barbarians.... Take care if these black men, who are keeping themselves respectably, are disgraced'.[46]

Following the rebellion, the phrase 'mock courts' would better apply to the drumhead courts and month-long reign of terror that were unleashed under cover of 'martial law'. Underhill charged 'that at least 430 persons were shot or hung in retaliation during the existence of martial law...many sufferers were entirely innocent of any crime whatever; that a thousand dwellings were wantonly and cruelly burnt; and that certainly not fewer than six hundred persons were scourged in a most reckless manner, with the greatest barbarity, at Bath, with cats having piano wire inserted in the lash' (Underhill 1895: 52–3). Even as these events were unfolding, though, various publics were competing to narrate them. Contesting the official reports in the newspapers, in the dangerous context of martial law, one group sent an anonymous letter to the Custos of Kingston giving their account of events:

WE tell you of what happen in St. Thomas in the East; that the governor sent to shot every man and woman, old and young, and to burn down every house. That it is a damn shame to see, but God will save them from the second death the innocent ones them, Lord save them. This Governor send men to shot without law, not to seek for the rebels alone and the riotors ... our best black men are going to shot. Well, Sir, it is but one death, as Mr. G. W. Gordon is gone, the poor man's friend, for in the House not a man remember the poor man. Well, we will burn down the town to the ground, and kill you and kill ourselves if you don't bring back every man you take away from Kingston... . We, as black and brown, and poor whites so we don't care for burn lose lives, so bring them back and let them go. You will laugh at my writing, but I don't care. Death, death for all....[47]

Threats such as this fed into the general white fear of a black uprising and reinforced the belief in the 'Gordon-Haytian' doctrine — social revolution from below. To fully examine this charge, the conclusion of this book will delve into the swirl of murky connections between Haiti and Jamaica that existed in the underworld of Kingston in 1865, among the 'little agitators, small speechifiers, and embryo cut-throats.'

Notes

1 Evidence from McLaren's father suggests that his son was literate and sometimes served as a lay-preacher or exhorter of prayer in the Native Baptist chapels around Morant Bay (*JRC*, Part 2, Evidence of John McLaren, p. 246); cf. Heuman, *The Killing Time*, p. 80–83.

2 *JRC*, Part 2: Evidence of William Anderson, p. 165; cf. Heuman, *The Killing Time*, p. 82.

3 PRO 30/48/44, Original Evidence of the Jamaica Royal Commission, Extracts from English Newspapers, 53.

4 JRC, Part 2, Evidence of John Burnett, p. 229. In other parts of the report, the name is spelled 'Geoghegan', but I keep this spelling for consistency. Women were again prominent during the events at Morant Bay, as both Wilmot (1995) and Heuman (1994) have documented, and my own research confirms (Sheller 1997).

5 CO 136/392, Eyre to Cardwell, 5 July 1865, encl. Petition of African labourers, Vere.

6 NLJ, MS 106, Underhill Letter, 5 Jan. 1865.

7 BMS, 'Extracts from Correspondence with Missionaries in Jamaica, On the Disturbances, by E. B. Underhill, 1864 to 1866', Underhill to Dendy, 1 Dec. 1864.

8 *The Sentinel*, 28 Mar. 1865.

9 *The Sentinel*, 15 Apr. 1865.

10 CO 137/394, Eyre to Cardwell, 7 Nov. 1865, enclosing Salmon to Eyre.

11 From 'Jamaica: Its State and Prospects', Anonymous (London, 1867), p. 13.

12 This race-conscious joint-stock association foreshadows the idea behind Marcus Garvey's Black Star line, which had similar aims and came under similar attack (Clarke and Garvey, *Marcus Garvey*). Following the formation of a Freedman's Aid Society in the United States after the Civil War, a British and Foreign Freedman's Aid Society was also formed to promote projects to benefit former slaves in the British colonies. ('Jamaica: Its State and Prospects', [London, 1867]). After the Morant Bay Rebellion, however, all workers' meetings were banned and such projects were linked to 'agitators.'

13 CO 137/392, Eyre to Cardwell, no. 189, 24 July 1865, encl. Report of John Salmon.

14 CO 137/392, Eyre to Cardwell, no. 198, 7 Aug. 1865, encl. Report of John Salmon.

15 PRO 30/48/42, Eyre to Cardwell, [Nov.] 1865, 56. As Barry Higman notes of this period, 'squatters were often unable to obtain freehold tenure and one of the principal objectives of the government survey office established in 1867 was the identification and eviction of such squatters' (Higman, *Jamaica Surveyed: Plantation Maps and Plans of the eighteenth and nineteenth Centuries* [Kingston: Institute of Jamaica, 1988], 286).

16 JRC, Part 2, *The County Union*, 17 Oct. 1865, 199.

17 Reported in the *County Union*, Vol. 16, no. 26, 1 Apr. 1864. Levien was arrested during martial law after the Morant Bay Rebellion, but eventually released. For further details on indentured immigration, see Hugh Tinker, *A New System of Slavery: The Export of Indian Labour Overseas, 1830–1920*, 2nd ed. (Lonson: Hansib, 1993); David Northrup, *Indentured Labor in the Age of Imperialism, 1834–1922* (Cambridge: Cambridge University Press, 1995); and David Dabydeen and Brinsley Samaroo, eds., *India in the Caribbean* (London: Hansib, 1987).

18 The remarkable story of one East Asian migrant exists in the petition of Muni Sarni (a.k.a. Thomas Laurence). Converted to Methodism, he came to Jamaica under indenture in 1846; in 1859, he became immigration agent for the govern-

ment, travelling to London and Calcutta, where he helped sign up 5000 new contract labourers. His petition describes their terrible treatment, his ostracism by his own people and being black-balled from the plantations after complaining (see WMMS, West Indies Corr., Jamaica, Box 204 [misfile], 'Petition of the Coolies', 8 Oct. 1864).

19 *Jamaica Papers*, no. 1, Rev. H. Clarke to Mr. Chamerovzow, 6 Jan. 1866, 31–4. Clarke was also prosecuted in 1862 for 'libel on the Government and on the planters as a body, for saying in the newspaper that the coolies were "cheated, starved, flogged, and murdered"'. The case was dropped when many of his charges were substantiated.

20 CO 137/346, Governor's Despatches, Darling to Newcastle, 8 Sept. 1859, encl. Half-yearly Agricultural Report of T. Witter Jackson.

21 *Colonial Standard & Jamaica Despatch*, 8 Feb. 1865.

22 *The Sentinel*, 24 Mar. 1865. This paper was edited by Robert A. Johnson, a coloured member of Assembly, who also edited *The Watchman and Jamaica Free Press* (Heuman 1981).

23 CO 137/368, Lt. Gov. Eyre to Duke of Newcastle, no. 113, 24 Nov. 1862.

24 *JRC,* Part 2, Evidence of Rev. Robert Myret Parnther, 44.

25 CO 137/391, Eyre to Cardwell, no. 137, May 1865, encl. *County Union*, 23 May 1865.

26 CO 137/391, Eyre to Cardwell, no. 142, 6 June 1865.

27 CO 137/391, Eyre to Cardwell, no. 148, 19 June 1865, encl. *County Union*, 23 May 1865.

28 CO 137/391, Eyre to Cardwell, no. 172, 10 July 1865, Report of Custos Alexander Lindo.

29 CO 137/392, Eyre to Cardwell, no. 174, 12 July 1865, encl. Custos Georges to Eyre [n.d.].

30 This compilation of information is based on names or participants and signatories reported in the following sources: CO137/344 Darling to Newcastle, 12 Mar. 1859, encl. Resolutions of Kingston public meeting chaired by G. W. Gordon and Petition to the Queen; CO137/367 Lt. Gov. Eyre to Newcastle, 8 Sept. 1862, encl. Memorial to the Queen from St. Thos-ye-East, resolutions of a public meeting at Morant Bay on 27 Aug. 1862; CO137/368 Lt. Gov. Eyre to Newcastle, 3 Dec. 1862, encl. Cheyne to Newcastle copy of Resolutions from a meeting at Morant Bay on 13 Oct. 1862; CO 137/391 Eyre to Cardwell, 17 May 1865, encl. Resolutions from the Kingston Underhill Meeting; *Jamaica Watchman and Free Press*, 5 June 1865, report of Public Meeting at Kingston Tabernacle chaired by G. W. Gordon; CO 137/391 Eyre to Cardwell, 7 June 1865, encl. Resolutions of Spanish Town Underhill Meeting; CO 137/392 Eyre to Cardwell, 12 July 1865, encl. Resolutions from St. Davids Underhill Meeting chaired by Samuel Clarke; *Jamaica Watchman and People's Free Press*, 28 Aug. 1865, Resolutions of Saint Ann's Bay Underhill Meeting, chaired by G. W. Gordon; JRC, Part 2, 1866, Evidence of William Anderson on speech of James McLaren [at Church Corner?]; Papers relating to the Disturbances in Jamaica, Part 1, no. 28, Eyre to Cardwell, 8 Nov. 1865, encl. 1, Petition of James Dacre and others, Stony Gut, 10 Oct. 1865.

31 CO 137/376, Lt. Gov. Eyre to Duke of Newcastle, 20 Feb. 1864.

32 CO 136/392, Eyre to Cardwell, 8 July 1865.

33 CO 137/376, Eyre to Duke of Newcastle, no. 73, 25 Feb. 1864, encl. extract from *Morning Journal*, 25 Feb. 1864.

34 PRO 30/48/44, Cardwell Papers, JRC, Evidence of Lewis Q. Bowerbank, 2.

35   CO 137/367, Gordon to Hugh W. Austin (Governor's Secretary), enclosed in Lt. Gov. Eyre to Duke of Newcastle, no. 41, 8 July 1862 and no. 52, 24 July 1862.

36   CO 137/367, Lt. Gov. Eyre to Duke of Newcastle, no. 56, 7 Aug. 1862.

37   CO 137/367, Memorial to the Queen from St. Thomas in the East, 4 September 1862, enclosed in Eyre to Newcastle, no. 80, 8 Sept. 1862.

38   CO 137/367, Report of P. A. Espeut, encl. in Eyre to Newcastle, no. 84, 23 Sept. 1862.

39   CO 137/367, Report of P. A. Espeut, encl. in Eyre to Newcastle, no. 84, 23 Sept. 1862.

40   CO 137/367, Report of P. A. Espeut, encl. in Eyre to Newcastle, no. 84, 23 Sept. 1862.

41   CO 137/368, Eyre to Newcastle, 3 Dec. 1862, encl. Cheyne to Newcastle, Nov. 1862.

42   When government correspondence concerning Espeut's report was included among papers laid before Parliament in 1865, there were clear Colonial Office instructions that the offensive report and the Governor's references to it be omitted (see PRO 30/48/2). If anything, this served to protect Eyre from charges of a long-standing vendetta against Gordon, for whose execution he was personally responsible (cf. Heuman, *The Killing Time*; and Bernard Semmel, *The Governor Eyre Controversy* (London: Macgibbon and Kee, 1963).

43   In other parts of Latin America, Mallon has found a similar mediation role for local intellectuals and village lawyers, known as *tinterillos* (Mallon, *Peasant and Nation*, p. 12); and cf. Robert Paquette, *Sugar is Made with Blood* (Middletown, CT: Wesleyan University Press, 1988), p. 94.

44   PRO 30/48/44, Evidence of Louis Q. Bowerbank.

45   Samuel R. Ward, *Reflections Upon the Gordon Rebellion* [Pamphlet, n.p., n.d.] 4. See also his evidence in JRC, Evidence of Samuel Ringold Ward, pp. 555–6.

46   *Papers* 1866b, Part 1, Eyre to Cardwell, 20 Oct. 1865, encl. 49.

47   *Papers* 1866b, Part 1, Eyre to Cardwell, no. 22, 7 Nov. 1865, encl. 43, p. 125.

Conclusion: the Morant Bay agitators — a Haytian conspiracy?

Fear of the Haitian example was a powerful 'story line' in elite views on popular organizations and political movements in Jamaica, especially when the phrases 'black cleave to black' and 'colour for colour' became the slogans of the Morant Bay rebellion. Prior to the uprising, Jamaica's white newspapers and governmental correspondence spoke commonly of the 'Gordon-Haytian' doctrine, a vague supposition that Gordon was promoting an anti-colonial, anti-white rebellion along the lines of the Haitian Revolution, and in keeping with the traditional white fear of Haiti noted in Chapter 3. Gordon had in fact been known to indulge in the imagery of revolution in some of his writings and speeches. In a letter of his published in *The Sentinel* in April 1865, he suggested, rather ominously:

> When Charles Ist of England refused to abide by the laws to which he had become a party — a revolution ensued and he was beheaded! When the Sovereign of the French disregarded the popular elective rights there was a revolution, and he had to abdicate and fly from the Kingdom! If in Jamaica our laws are to be disregarded, by those who are bound to conserve them...how long may good order be expected to continue?[1]

During the court martial at Morant Bay, it was also charged that he had told the people at a public meeting to 'do as the Haytians do', though he adamantly denied it. As Catherine Hall has suggested, the 'double spectres of Haiti (where the blacks had driven out all the whites), and of the Indian Mutiny...were ever present in both the Jamaican and the English consciousness, shaping expectations and raising hopes and fears' (C. Hall 1992: 282). In the aftermath of Morant Bay, references to Haiti and to the recent 'Indian Mutiny' peppered the evidence and shaped British perceptions of the events. Heuman, too, suggests that the '1831 rebellion as well as the Haitian Revolution continued to serve as models of protest' in Jamaica (Heuman 1994: 40).

Is it possible that there actually was a transnational conspiracy among politically disaffected groups of Jamaicans and Haitians in

227

1865? There had certainly been many Haitian exiles in Jamaica over the years, and some had gone so far as to express political views in the public newspapers, as we have seen above, but were any involved in actual political conspiracy with black Jamaicans? The evidence for this is slim, and in many cases seems to have been fabricated for purposes of repression. Though, as William Green concludes in his analysis of the Morant Bay era,

> Although there was no organized conspiracy to transform Jamaica into a second Haiti as Eyre and a large portion of the white and coloured population believed, the Underhill meetings and the agitation of 1865 had produced a strong sense of solidarity among the black population and afforded them a conspicuous leadership which they had not previously possessed (Green 1991: 390).

It seems very unlikely that Haitians in Jamaica had any interest whatsoever in supporting a black rebellion of any kind there. On the other hand, Haitians did involve some black Jamaicans in their own political intrigues, and more generally offered an example of an independent black state, perhaps thereby contributing to a greater sense of political agency. It is conceivable that some black Jamaicans may have moved towards a radical anti-colonial stance, inspired by the Haitian example.

Haitian exiles in Jamaica in the 1860s were certainly involved in efforts to overthrow the government of President Fabré Geffrard, which was at that time supported by the British government. As early as 1862, Lt. Governor Eyre was monitoring the activities of General Lysius Felicité Salomon, who had arrived in Jamaica following the fall of Soulouque. The Governor informed the Colonial Office that Salomon was not involved in any plots against the existing government of Haiti, although one had occurred shortly before his arrival in Jamaica.[2] In a speech to the Haitian Senate, President Geffrard claimed that besides enemies within, there was another centre of agitation 'on foreign shores, formed of men who, in their own country, were divided in politics, and hated each other, but [were] now being animated by the same one purpose of fabricating calumnies and falsehoods, and of furnishing ammunitions, arms and money to the disaffected at home' (Bird 1869: 401). Bird, describing this coalition, confirmed that Soulouque's party in Jamaica had joined forces with more recent exiles associated with General Sylvain Salnave. He noted that 'the large exiled party of Soulouque, at the fall of the Empire in 1859, were now in sympathy, and unitedly contributed immensely to the general embarrassment; in truth, the elements now at work, both in and out of the country, were powerful and threatening' (Bird 1869: 399).

The coalition against Geffrard was animated by a nationalist and potentially 'noiriste' outlook. It included Salnave, a populist northern army chief (who became president in 1867), and General Salomon, (of the black land-holding family in Aux Cayes, who challenged mulatto control during the liberal revolution in 1843), who served as a diplomat and minister of finance under Soulouque prior to his exile in Jamaica, and went on to become leader of the *Parti National* and eventually President of Haiti (1879–88). Authorities like the Custos of Kingston suspected these Haitian emigrés of setting a bad example for the Afro-Jamaican 'lower classes':

> For some time past the ex-Emperor of Hayti, Soulouque, and members of his family and adherents have resided in Kingston, as also, latterly, some of those who have left Hayti under President Geffrard's rule — as General Lamothe and Salomons, etc. These persons lived in a good deal of style, and externally appeared orderly and well-conducted. I believe that the presence of these refugees in Kingston has had a prejudicial effect on the minds of some of the lower classes in and about Kingston, as many of them appeared to be under the impression that the wealth of these persons had not been acquired by legitimate means, and they argued that if black men could acquire wealth and live in that style, they might do the same.[3]

Was the presence of these major actors of the Haitian opposition linked in any way with political agitation in Jamaica prior to the Morant Bay rebellion? At the very least, they must have inspired some degree of emulation, as Bowerbank suggests; more importantly, they were involved in military activities during their stay in Jamaica.

Supporters of Salnave were known to be purchasing arms in Jamaica in the spring of 1865, and possibly gathering supporters. The end of the Civil War in the United States created an illicit market in leftover arms and munitions from the defeated Confederacy. During the enquiry into the Morant Bay Rebellion, a former Confederate Lieutenant, H. B. Edenborough, wrote a letter to the British Secretary of State for the Colonies — later forwarded to Governor Eyre in Jamaica — claiming to have evidence 'connecting certain Haytian negroes with the rebel Gordon'.[4] Edenborough claimed that in June 1865, Gordon came to him along with a 'bright mulatto' whom he introduced as a General, and they negotiated to purchase a clipper-schooner along with breech-loading rifles, nine shooting pistols, hand grenades, small torpedos and ammunition and gunpowder. He also described their plans to pick up several refugee Haitian generals, touch at the Mole St. Nicholas and then land them in Jamaica near Black River. He also claimed that they referred to a 'new West India Republic', by which he thought they referred to the Dominican Republic, which was in the midst of a War of Independence against Spain. The charge was never substantiated, but it was repeated both in the Jamaican press and before the Royal Commission. After the unproven charges were quietly dropped following the enquiry, however, it emerged that the real negotiator had not been Gordon at all, but a Haitian supporter of Salnave named Andain (Harvey and Brewin 1867: 21). Although unconnected to Gordon, the activities of the Haitians were both contrary to the terms of Jamaican asylum and opposed to Britain's pro-Geffrard foreign policy.

Likewise, attempts to link some Gordon supporters with revolutionary doctrines were equally unsupported. A secret society was supposedly discovered in the parish of St. Ann shortly after the Morant Bay Rebellion and, according to the *Falmouth Post*, its leader and seven members were arrested:

> Intelligence has reached us that Mr. Rodney, the chief promoter, and seven members of a secret association, recently founded in the above parish under the title of the 'Liberation Society,' have been arrested.... The very appellation of it smells of conspiracy and treason, since its obvious meaning seems 'the liberation of the island from the existing government,' and since its head, Mr. Rodney, appeared to be a proselyte of the Gordon-Haytien doctrine, and a supporter of the Underhill letter. Societies of this description, which aim at rebellion and miracle, must be suppressed by the strong arm of the law.[5]

Thomas Rodney was in fact Acting Chairman of the Underhill Convention, as noted above, and along with Joseph Burton had helped to organize the Underhill Meeting at St. Ann's Bay, chaired by G. W. Gordon.[6] Local whites considered Rodney and Burton 'turbulent dangerous characters', and suggested they be arrested, though there was nothing to connect them to the Morant Bay Rebellion.[7] Other black politicians also came under suspicion for speaking out in support of the disenfranchised and for organizing public meetings. Samuel Clarke, a black vestryman, was described by the Jamaica Committee as

> a freeholder in the Parish of St. David's, where he enjoyed considerable influence among his coloured brethren, because of his ability to speak for them and protect them from injustice. He had in this way become especially obnoxious to the

planters or estate attorneys.... During the summer prior to the riot at Morant Bay Mr. Clarke had taken the chair at an Underhill Meeting, in St. David's, and formed one of the deputation to Governor Eyre to present him with copies of the resolutions for transmission home. He also spoke at the Underhill Meetings in Kingston and St. Thomas in the East.[8]

Clarke was also known as someone who 'acted as a 'lawyer' on behalf of the people, especially in the petty courts' (Heuman 1994: 154), and his activities had brought him into conflict with the Custos. During suppression of the Morant Bay Rebellion, Major General Forbes Jackson reported that Bogle and other rebels had ties to 'rebel leaders' like Samuel Clarke. 'The demagogues', he wrote, 'were in the habit of holding night meetings previous to the late election of a Coroner for the Parish...and I was informed by a blackman that it was then and there decided that whoever might be proposed by the whites should be strenuously opposed by the Blacks'.[9] Samuel Clarke was executed under martial law at Morant Bay for the use of seditious language at Underhill Meetings; he had been seen going into Gordon's office in Kingston on the day of the rebellion and his brother was married to Bogle's daughter.

Some popular political associations, on the other hand, *were* connected with armed drilling, military exercises and secret oaths. The formation of secret societies raises the question of what happens to a subaltern public if it is not given legitimate means of organization and expression. There is evidence of numerous semi-clandestine and secret societies among Afro-Jamaicans, in Kingston and in other parishes, some of which were practising militia-style drilling in 1865. Two months before the Morant Bay Rebellion, *The Colonial Standard and Jamaica Despatch* reported elite fears in the west:

It is beyond doubt that in several parishes, and notably in Kingston, considerable numbers of the humbler classes have enrolled themselves into companies, that they wear distinguishing uniforms, attend regular drill, and instruct themselves in every variety of military exercise. There are societies among the same classes, holding secret conferences and using private passwords and signs.[10]

In a report to the Governor written after the Morant Bay Rebellion, the Custos of Kingston indicated that reports on drilling by the 'lower classes' in the newspapers were true, and that his inspectors had found that 'a number of them met almost daily in a private yard at the west end of the city, and were regularly drilled; that they went by the name of 'Sham Volunteers'; that they had two companies organized, and were about raising another one at the east end of the city; that they had also a staff of generals, colonels, adjutants, doctors, &c'.[11]

Although there was nothing illegal in popular groups organizing into drill bands, the government was especially concerned that the members of the 'Sham Volunteers' in Kingston had held several 'balls or evening parties under the title of the Belgradia or Belvidere Society'. The Custos considered these social activities, along with the wearing of expensive uniforms in the public streets, to be objectionable, and asked them to desist. Like the rich Haitian Generals-in-exile, black 'lower classes' holding public celebrations and wearing uniforms threatened 'public order'. A letter printed in the *Jamaica Watchman and People's Free Press,* from a member of this society (signed simply 'A Negro'), indicates that one of the purposes of the 'New Belvedere Society' was to commemorate emancipation. On the eve of the First of August, the members 'gave an entertainment to commemorate the 27th year of emancipation in this Island' at which 'creditable speeches' were given, remembering the days of slavery and celebrating their deliverance from its evils, but also chiding others for overlooking the significant date.[12] The event indicates the importance of public commemoration and remembrance for the construction of a black political movement, and echoes the sentiments of the mechanics and peasantries who had requested the Governor's attendance at their 1859 Emancipation Jubilee. The symbolism of emancipation and the sanctity of the First of August, however, were part of a conceptual network not shared with the majority of whites in Jamaica, and seemingly of little significance to the government or official public.

Other more menacing groups were also arming themselves. During martial law, secret bands of 'Revivalists' in other parishes were accused of involvement in the Morant Bay Rebellion. One Justice of the Peace wrote to his local police office in Malvern in November, 1865, that:

> On Monday last I was informed that there were a large number of spears or lances at a place called the Buildings, near Round Hill, and a number of persons, male and female, keeping secret meetings, and have been doing so for a long time past.... After the search was made a large number of these spears were found, also a large quantity of stones, a loaded gun, and a paper signed Bogle, with several unintelligible sentences.... I believe the police apprehended 12 or 14 persons, and conveyed them to Black River...[who belong] to the same band or society called 'Revivalists'.[13]

Similarly, a Mr. Finlason reported in November that at some Revivalists' meeting-houses were found 'some hard wood spikes about seven or 8 feet long and well sharpened[;]...the police took with them about three dozen of the sharpened iron-wood sticks, and...left as many as would load a mule cart in the house'.[14] Perhaps, these groups were inspired by the methods of the Haitian Piquets; in any event, they were reminiscent of the worst Anglo-Jamaican fears of a Haitian 'race war'.

Although there is little evidence of an actual 'Haytian conspiracy' *in* Jamaica — i.e. a plan for violent overthrow of the government and expulsion of the whites — it is certainly probable, or at least very plausible, that some Jamaican political activists were involved in the plans for the overthrow of Geffrard in nearby Haiti. Even more compelling than either Gordon's rhetoric of revolution or white rhetoric of the black menace is concrete evidence of connections between some of Gordon's supporters and certain of the Haitian exiles in Jamaica who were clearly organizing support for Salnave's campaigns against Geffrard. Two associates of Gordon's and key organizers of some of the 1865 Underhill Meetings, were Emanuel Joseph Goldson and William Kelly Smith. There is evidence that they were in contact with General Salomon and General Lamothe, who were key links in the coalition planning an overthrow of the Haitian government of Geffrard at the time of the Morant Bay Rebellion. The Haitian exiles had got so far as to fit out a schooner with ammunition and had sailed for Haiti in October 1865, but had returned to Port Antonio in Jamaica, supposedly because of bad weather, but more probably because of a Spanish blockade of Hispaniola.[15] Geffrard's speech in the Haitian Senate implied that shipments of ammunition and arms had got through previously. Some of the Jamaican political activists in opposition to the Eyre government appear to have also been involved to some extent in these plans for a new black government in nearby Haiti.

Custos Bowerbank suspected Goldson and Kelly Smith of involvement in some sort of conspiracy (and was responsible for their deportation to Morant Bay under martial law), as he reported in his evidence to the Royal Commission:

> Subsequently I heard from the inspector of police, as also from the Haytian Consul, that certain notoriously disaffected citizens of Kingston, especially a person of the name of Wm. Kelly Smith, was in frequent communication with General Salomons, a friend of General Lamothes; and the inspector of police told me that Joseph Emanuel Goldron [*sic*] had stated to him that he and Kelly Smith intended going to

Hayti with General Lamothe.... They both of them had attended the Underhill Meetings held in Kingston and Spanish Town. They had both taken an active part at such meetings, and Kelly Smith was the secretary of the Underhill Convention.[16]

Goldson and Kelly Smith represented not only the development of a black political base and indigenous leadership, especially in Kingston, but also the emergence of a wider black Caribbean identity. It was these men and their associates who took an active part in organizing Underhill Meetings in the eastern parishes.

Goldson, whom Bowerbank describes as 'a very intelligent, shrewd black man', had in fact been a senior sergeant of police in Kingston, but was discharged in 1862 for improper conduct. Nevertheless, he reportedly continued to exercise great influence over the mostly black police force, and still had allies in the Corporation of Kingston. Both Goldson and Kelly Smith indicated to the authorities that they would desist from organizing the peasantry and stirring up agitation against the government if they themselves were given respectable positions in local government.[17] Whatever their political motivations and ideologies were, they are the clearest link between Gordon's supporters, Underhill Meetings and Haitian political intrigues. Shortly after the Morant Bay Rebellion, government officials reported to Governor Eyre that 'we arrested Kelly Smith and Goldson this morning on an affidavit made that they were constantly in communication with George W. Gordon at the Watchman office. We are also ordering certain Haytians to quit the country on the 25th (not Soulouque), as we find they are in communication with Kelly Smith'.[18]

What makes these speculations more than mere character defamation is the support lent them if we turn to the newspaper edited by Kelly Smith in association with Gordon, *The Jamaica Watchman and People's Free Press*. In the summer of the Underhill Meetings, it carried a number of articles on political events in Haiti. In an article of August 7th, 1865, the lead editorial went out of its way to dispel rumours that Jamaicans were involved in the opposition against the Geffrard government, and it criticized the Governor's enquiries into the activities of General Lamothe. At the same time, however, it referred to several Haitian newspapers and gave one of the most detailed accounts in the Jamaican press at the time of current events in Haiti. The article was particularly disparaging of the British role in the affair, referring to the British consul's deal with Geffrard as dishonorable:

> The public are already aware, that a Provisional Government has been established at Cape Haiti and that Françoise Joseph

directs the affairs of the insurgents. Geffrard's army made several attempts to regain possession, but were repulsed by the Cape Haitians. The remnant of the army returned and reported at Port-au-Prince the results of their expedition, and which induced President Geffrard to enter into some dishonorable arrangement with the British Consul under the plea of 'protection' to the British Subjects at that place. In conformity with this statement, on the 4th day of July last, Her Majesty['s] ship Lilly arrived at Cape Haiti, and landed three hundred Europeans, including a number of Marines with rifles in hand, alleging that their visit was to protect English property from being destroyed by the insurgents with two pieces of Artillery. The Cape Haitians, seeing these strangers parading in the public thoroughfares, became amazingly incensed, and deputed their General Salnave to enquire whither are they come.[19]

Eventually, two British ships joined the force and were fired on from Fort Picolet. A Haitian newspaper, the *Bien Public*, was also said to have reported a schooner, *Fashion*, turning back to Kingston without seeing the coast of its intended visit. This was probably the ship reported to Governor Eyre by the British consul, who believed it was sent from Jamaica in support of the Haitian insurgents. The *Watchman* claimed to doubt any such doings, but concluded that, 'It cannot be doubted, that President Geffrard's power is on the *wain* (*sic*), and that he is adopting every method to keep up his tottering government [emphasis in original]', which, indeed, would have fallen had it not been for British intervention at this time.

The British force was actually responsible for bombarding Cap Haïtien and dislodging the 'provisional government' of Salnave from its stronghold there, thus allowing Geffrard's hitherto unsuccessful troops to enter the city (Bird 1869: 396). Finally, on August 21st, 1865, the *Watchman* printed an even more direct statement on its views of political events in Haiti, views that were distinctly contrary to British foreign policy (which was backing Geffrard, as was made clear in other Jamaican newspapers):

Can President Geffrard express his ignorance of the history of his own country, and of the habits and disposition of his people? Was it wise on the part of a Ruler of the Country to depart from a sacred compact entered into between himself and his people, that of his holding office for three years? Secondly, contrary to the Constitution, the unwise President Geffrard recommended the introduction of Europeans to be

> place on the same footing, and to enjoy the same rights and
> privileges of Haitien born subject[s] — These two move-
> ments have rendered him totally unpopular, and nothing can
> satisfied [*sic*] the people but his immediate removal. We
> mention these facts not in the spirit of party men, but in sym-
> pathy, and with anxious desire for the permanent prosperity
> of the Island; but, we deprecate much the improper mode
> adopted in the city of publishing exaggerated statements,
> concerning the affairs of Hayti, only with a view, perhaps, of
> misleading exiles whilst other persons having family con-
> nexions there are misled.[20]

This unprecedented attack on British foreign policy, on the Jamaican
press and, most radically, on Geffrard's plan of introducing Europeans
'on the same footing' as Haitian subjects, represents a thoroughly independent black public opinion in Jamaica, and indicates the ideological
milieu that contributed to the government's violent reaction to the
Morant Bay Rebellion. After the outbreak of the rebellion at Morant
Bay, there was a strong suspicion of Haitian involvement, especially
after their armed ship was stopped in Port Antonio during the rebellion,
well within range of aiding the rebel forces — although there was no
indication that this had been their intention. Governor Eyre ordered all
of the Haytian exiles to be arrested, and they were soon after ordered to
leave the island. At the very least, they had clearly been supporting
overthrow of a ruler in Haiti who was considered a British ally.

We do not know whether the views printed in *The Watchman* were
actually Kelly Smith's, or some other writer's, nor do we know
whether G. W. Gordon endorsed them in any way. However, it does
appear from Bowerbank's reports that Kelly Smith, along with
Goldson, was in close contact with the exiled Haitian generals, one of
which was Salomon. The regimes of both Salnave (1867–69), who
took over after a finally successful coup against Geffrard, and of his
supporter Salomon, were known for their populist nationalism and promotion of 'noirs' over the *mulâtre* elite. These certainly would have
been the kinds of ideologies that Salomon was espousing during the
mid-1860s, and he may have had some influence on the Jamaican
black political activists. This is not to say that the circle around
Gordon were in any way 'Haitian revolutionaries', but that they did
have a developed racial ideology that was sympathetic to the Haitian
model; this was certainly picked up on by white observers like Espeut,
Bowerbank and Eyre.

The Jamaican government attempted to control information on
events in Haiti, fearing that such news would inspire further bloodshed

in Jamaica. During the hysteria of suppression, the Governor sent this warning to the editor of the *Tribune*:

> His excellency the Governor having noticed in your paper of this day's date a statement purporting to be an account of the destruction of Her Majesty's ship 'Bulldog' by the Haytiens, which is altogether a perversion of facts, and calculated to do extreme injury in this colony by misleading the black population into the supposition that people of their own race have been able to destroy one of Her Majesty's ships of war, I have to request that this statement be contradicted in tomorrow's paper.... [Y]ou must exercise a discreet caution in publishing news, and not give to the public unauthorized statements such as that referred to.[21]

In fact, the Haitians had sunk a British ship, and it was the truth of this that the government feared, not the rumour. Following the suppression of the rebellion, Governor Eyre defended himself to the Colonial Secretary by arguing that 'it must be borne in mind that the success which attended the efforts of the Haytians against the French, and more recently of the St. Domingans against the Spanish, afforded examples and encouragement which from the vicinity of those republics to Jamaica, were constantly before the peasantry of this country' (cited in Green 1991: 390n24).

The crucial symbolic role of Haiti and the actual role of Haitian exiles should not be dismissed simply because the white and coloured elite misinterpreted its significance. By pursuing the notion that there were many linkages between Jamaican and Haitian publics, I have discovered a fascinating and little noticed aspect of the Morant Bay Rebellion: the possible intermeshing of Jamaican and Haitian political activists and black oppositional ideologies. Memories of the Haitian revolution offered a compelling vision of African freedom. News of Haiti and the direct example of Haitian exiles in Jamaica served as models of black independence. Haitian successes against European powers suggested the strength of an Afro-Caribbean military. Direct involvement in the political affairs of Haiti enabled the elaboration of an autonomous Caribbean-centric political culture. It is hard to say in what direction Jamaican democracy would have gone had Gordon lived, had the House of Assembly not been abolished, had black publics not been suppressed.

In 1870, a coalition of Jamaican missionaries, merchants and landowners founded a monthly newspaper, the *Queen's Newsman, A Monthly Newspaper, Specially Designed for Circulation among the Peasantry of Jamaica*. This paper was a patronizing attempt at 'the enlightenment and instruction of the Labourers on our Estates — the mechanics and artizans who are employed in our country workshops — the small settlers, penkeepers and provision growers in the interior of the Country and on our Mountain slopes', including the growing population of 'Coolies' from British India. News summaries in the first issue professed to be written 'in a style so simple as to be understood by the most illiterate of the people', and among these was one on Haiti. It provides a remarkable example of a clumsy attempt at shaping popular public opinion from above, as if speaking to children:

> In this island of Hayti (which is not more than two days' sail from Jamaica) the people have been quarreling and fighting, and killing one another, in a very dreadful way, for many months past; but now they are beginning to feel wearied of this wickedness, and the mischievous effects of neglecting business and provision grounds to fight about politics.... They are in great want of money, just now, and very few will trust them, just because they are not a steady and industrious people. What a blessed thing it is to live in a country like Jamaica, where all is peaceful, and the peasantry not so easily misled, and disposed to follow such evil courses. In Hayti they have very few Missionaries to instruct and advise the people. How grateful we should feel to the Missionaries in Jamaica, for the good counsel they give us.[22]

If anything, this 'little narrative' — apparently a reference to what Moïse called the 'Piquettiste wave' of 1868 — demonstrates the great gulf between elite publics and popular political opinion, which at times seemed to move in diametrically opposed and mutually exclusive networks of understanding. Those networks did not die out, however, with the suppression of popular publics and democracy in Jamaica.

It is not without significance that a man named Marcus Garvey moved a resolution to give thanks to British philanthropists at the Saint Ann's Bay Underhill Meeting, chaired by G. W. Gordon.[23] Marcus Mosiah Garvey, famed founder of the Universal Negro Improvement Association, was born in the parish of St. Ann in 1887. His father, also named Marcus, is surely the man who attended this Underhill Meeting in 1865 (cf. Wilmot 1994). Family histories of 'Pa Garvey', preserved by Amy Jacques Garvey, recount that he was descended from Maroons, was a stonemason by trade and at home had a room where 'he had a collection of books, magazines, and newspapers. He was called "the village lawyer", because he was well informed and advised the townfolk.... Pa Garvey went to funerals or big rallies, but his Bible was well marked, as he studied it so as to argue about the Scriptures'

(Clarke and Garvey 1974: 29–30). He was also a Freemason, according to Wilmot, and clearly had an influence on his eleventh child, his namesake, who went on to lead his people.

The family held on to stories of Paul Bogle, also recounted by Amy Jacques Garvey. She remembered how Pa Garvey brooded over the Maroon betrayal of Bogle, but the oral history is telescopically condensed into older stories of Maroon betrayals of slave rebellions: 'In the 1665 slave rebellion [*sic*] the Maroons decoyed the brave rebel leader Paul Bogle and captured him for the English authorities; perhaps that was why Pa Garvey brooded so much as he looked back on the history of his people' (Clarke and Garvey 1974: 30). This story, which dates from the early twentieth century when Pa Garvey was still alive, can be compared to another Maroon account of the Morant Bay Rebellion, recorded by the ethnographer Martha Warren Beckwith in 1929. She recounts a 'lively account of this event from an Accompong Maroon':

> 'Pa Bogle and Garden [i.e. Gordon] were in St. Thomas in the east. Pa Bogle was a black man. He refused to pay the people and the minister went to talk to him and he cut out his tongue. So the parson sent to the governor and the governor sent to Missus Queen — whether Queen Mary or Queen Victoria I don't remember — and they sent for the Maroons. The Accompong Maroons didn't get the letter. Moore Town Maroons got it. Moore Town Maroons, they harsh, especially one named Old Brisco — that was the baddest of all. First they killed Bogle — shoved the bayonet right through him! Killed Garden too. After that they killed out the whole district — leave nothing, but one old woman and a ram goat and one rooster cock!' (Beckwith 1969: 185–86).

In this account, not only is there no brooding over the event, but there is a sense of pride in the Maroon's treaty relationship with the Queen, and their fierce warrior tradition. The Garvey family clearly took a different view, and recognized the problematic nature of the Maroon 'betrayal' of their race (cf. Campbell 1988). Marcus Garvey, both the older and the younger, struggled with the conflicting meanings of being black, being of African descent and being British.

Amy Jacques Garvey also noted that when young Marcus was trained as a printer, he heard stories in the back room of his godfather's book shop 'about the old slave days, plantation stories and slave rebellions. He admired leaders such as Cudjoe, Tacky, Sharp, Quaco and Bogle, who came down from Stony Gut warning his people: "Remember your colour and cleave to the blacks"' (Clarke and Garvey

1974: 32). His father was not only a direct link to the days of Bogle, but also (as one small fragment from Gordon's newspaper suggests) a participant in the Underhill Movement and someone who kept alive the network of 'village lawyers' even after government repression. Marcus Mosiah Garvey, with experience of working as a printer and inspired by his father and by black newspaper publishers like Robert Love, was a direct inheritor of the subaltern public of the Underhill Movement, with its radical networks among the 'pariah intelligentsia'. He too suffered government harassment for his activities and ideas. Just as Mallon has found in Mexico and Peru, alternative popular visions were 'repressed politically and militarily, [but they] were never exterminated. They remained part of local political culture, emerging time and again during periods of unrest and political fluctuation' (Mallon 1995: 141).

In considering the long-term prospects of democracy after slavery, it is crucial that one focus not on colonial inheritances and cultural backgrounds, but on the interactions between popular claimants and states. If the British colonial state offered more opportunities and means for public claim-making, it nevertheless learned more about democracy from Afro-Jamaicans than it ever taught them, for democratization occurs through collective learning processes, not elite tutelage. Focusing on political communication and contention highlights the deep history of democratization processes within societies that are often thought to have become 'modern democracies' only with the aid of British or United States imperialism. The democratic practices of the former British West Indian colonies, for example, have often been attributed to their inheritance of the 'Westminster system' and their peaceful 'tutelage' under British leadership (Payne 1993; Maingot 1996). The arrival of democracy in Hispanic regions has often been understood as an achievement of United States military intervention, as it similarly has been understood in Haiti recently. What is missing from such accounts is the crucial link between popular contention and political participation in making democracy possible in the post-slavery era.

If the Haitian republic lacked well-functioning democratic institutions, protection of citizens and means for public claim-making, this does not imply that it was culturally incapable of, or socially unprepared for, democratic governance. Nor was colonial Jamaica (not the most democratic place) a colony barren of democratic practices. The objective of this book is to demonstrate that peasant agency was far more extensive in post-emancipation Jamaica than has previously been shown, and that popular movements for democratization were not without significant impact in the history of Haiti. In both cases, there were serious attempts to implement democratic reforms by extending the franchise, encouraging wider participation in electoral politics, and protecting black rights and freedoms, but these efforts were blocked by small ruling elites who controlled big armies. It was in part the failure of the liberal bourgeois elements of the elite to break from their more authoritarian agrarian rivals that contributed to the radicalization of peasant politics. In neither case could it be said that peasants were unaware of democratic ideologies; in fact, in some instances they were willing to fight and die for democratization, seen as the legacy of freedom won for the descendants of African slaves in the Haitian revolution.

Beyond liberal representative democracy, however, the radical Caribbean vision of democracy included cooperative land ownership, associational modes of economic organization and demands for wider influential participation by all classes in government decision-making. It is also important to remember that subaltern groups do not bargain only for resources or inclusion in the polity; they also seek to publicly assert their own collective identities, stories of their history and solutions to the problems they identify. In other words, beyond the individualism of liberal democracy, peasant democracy involves a collective subject and collective aims. In both Haiti and Jamaica, collective identities extended beyond the confines of the nation to encompass a transnational African diaspora, including links between these sister islands of the Greater Antilles, as well as symbolically important links to Africa.

Elite reluctance to implement real democratization produced similar peasant rebellions in Haiti in 1844 and in Jamaica in 1865, despite their differing starting points and political conditions. Both rebellions occurred in regions with mixed economies of declining big plantations, owned by whites or 'mulattoes,' and expanding smallholding by blacks. Both movements emerged out of elite-led liberal reform movements, which in the end could not carry through with democratization. They also both involved oppositional leaders, Gordon and Salomon, who spoke for the black masses, but again were surpassed by peasant mobilizations beyond their control. Both movements were headed by charismatic 'native' religious leaders, Bogle and Acaau, with some education and prominence in the local community. Both involved a mixed class/colour ideology of fighting for the rights of the descendants of slavery. Both were reacted to by elites in terms of a 'war of the races' and both had a major impact on the subsequent reorganization of government. Nowhere, as far as I know, have any of these parallels previously been noted.

There are also some major differences between the two events, above all in relation to the balance of power and the kind of state that the rebels faced. In Haiti, the radical democratic political ideology among peasants had its origins in the republican revolutionary tradition, the post-independence land distributions, the obligations of military citizenship and the inspiring anti-slavery and anti-colonial stance of the 'Black Republic' in the international arena. While it is easier to trace democratic ideologies to the literate oppositional networks who published newspapers and books, made passionate arguments in the Chamber and claimed to stand for black equality of rights, I argue that there was also wider popular support for democratization. The peasants who participated in the movement led by the Salomons supported a broadening of representative democracy to include blacks, while those in the Piquet Movement seem to have supported an even more radical programme of democratization backed by land reform and substantive social change. Because Haiti was in the midst of a revolutionary situation, with a fractured state and a serious threat of nation-wide popular insurgency and civil war, the Piquets were in a relatively strong position, and were able to influence the selection of a black president. Once demobilized, though, their leader was arrested (because landowning elites, whether black or brown, feared his radical aims of land distribution), their demands for democratization were ignored and a shift to military authoritarianism closed the democratic window of opportunity.

In Jamaica, the evidence of a democratic political culture among black peasants is even stronger because they had so many more channels through which to express their claims, and leaders adept at reaching both the government and wider publics. By tracing the development of the distinctive networks and symbolic discourses of black publics in Jamaica from the emancipation period up to the Morant Bay Rebellion, I have highlighted an increasingly autonomous peasant political culture which broke away from the missionary churches and developed its own political language, ideology and modes of claim-making. Despite repeated attempts by this black public to use democratic genres of political communication to initiate a debate over reform and enfranchisement, government officials repeatedly ignored its claims and grievances. This government stone-walling, combined with a direct attack on the popular leader George William Gordon, the miscarriage of justice in St. Thomas in the East, and long-standing local grievances about wages and land, provoked one group of small settlers from Stony Gut to resort to violence. What may have begun as demonstration or riotous bargaining ended in outright rebellion.

Unlike the Piquets, however, the Morant Bay rebels were in an extremely weak position and up against a quickly unified government with the extensive capacity for repression within a British Governor's grasp. Governor Eyre used this opportunity to unleash an extreme form of martial law on the entire populace of the region, amounting to state terrorism: not only the rebels, but also many other people not involved in the rebellion were hunted down and killed; entire communities were decimated and burned; and the political allies of the peasantry were arrested and in many cases executed. This reaction not only quelled popular political expression, broke up organizations and suppressed the opposition press, but it also led to the abolition of the House of Assembly, thereby ending a long tradition of elected representative government in Jamaica, and quickly erasing any possibility for black political influence. The 'Governor Eyre controversy' that resulted from the brutal repression of the Morant Bay Rebellion marked a turning point in the hardening of British attitudes towards its colonial subjects (Semmel 1963; C. Hall 1992). It also contributed to the more explicit elaboration of the notion of tutelary democracy that would also be applied in other parts of the British Empire to retard the implementation of full rights for colonial subjects. Thus, the very analytical tool that has been used to explain lack of democratization in the Caribbean is in part a product of the process of repression that produced that lack in the first place. In so far as the British self-image of civilized superiority rested on their role of emancipating slaves and teaching 'natives' the culture of democracy, any form of peasant political agency was anathema. Self-liberation such as that in Haiti could only lead to savagery, in this view, given the absence of white tutelage.

Former slaves were ready for democracy from before the first day of emancipation, but democracy was not ready for them. To ignore three decades of political organization and contention by Jamaican freed men and women would only be to compound this silencing of black publics; to attribute political apathy to the Haitian peasantry would be to ignore the constraints under which they lived. Peasant political activists — with far-reaching ties to anti–slavery organizations and publicity projects in Europe and America, as well as to regional African-American and African-Caribbean political networks — posed a significant threat both to European models of paternalistic elite governance and to the new kind of post-plantation state that developed in the Caribbean. In other Latin American contexts, similar ideologies have been referred to as 'popular liberalism' (Mallon 1995; Roseberry, Gudmundson, and Kutschback 1995), and similar 'oppositional cultures' have been recognized as the precursors to twentieth–century uprisings of peons and tenants, culminating in some instances in full-blown revolutionary movements. Haiti is not an historical anomaly, but is the first 'coffee republic' in which competing elites turned 'the state into a machine that would suck off the peasant surplus, which was becoming more difficult to obtain through mere ownership of the plantations' (Trouillot 1992:

163). In the struggle of 'state against nation', as Trouillot (1990) calls it, black publics and the oppositional views they represented were the disappearing middleground.

Comparative analysis of these political configurations is gradually leading towards a far more complete understanding of the parameters of peasant political mobilization, and an appreciation of both its strengths and its limitations. The time is surely ripe for comparisons of peasant politics between the Caribbean, Central America, Africa and other post-plantation regions of the world. The particular process of *de*-democratization that occurred in Haiti and Jamaica is not unique to the Caribbean, but appears also to have occurred in other 'liberal states' in Latin America where independent post-plantation peasant development occurred (cf. Roseberry, Gudmundson and Kutschback 1995). With the demise of the plantation system and the emergence of an independent peasantry in those Caribbean and Central American regions amenable to the expansion of small-scale commercially-oriented farming (particularly coffee-growing), a 'post-plantation' type of state emerged. Paige has picked up on the process of democratization by social revolution from below in the late agro-industrial period of these states in the Central American context. This study of black publics and peasant rebellion in Haiti and Jamaica contributes to an earlier genealogy of the emergence of peasant radicalism in the Caribbean.

Although Jamaica remained a colony, controlled from London, it too was vulnerable to some of the same tendencies of peasant political radicalization because of its relatively autonomous House of Assembly, its declining plantation system and its self-sustaining independent peasantry. Even here where an emerging bourgeoisie had all the 'tutelage' that the British Empire could provide on the enlightened and rational merits of liberal democracy, dependent development of a commodity export economy pushed it back into the ideological arms of agrarian authoritarianism whenever democracy threatened to break out.

Having moved beyond the notion of tutelary democracy in Jamaica and peasant apathy in Haiti, we can begin to see how these Caribbean cases fit into the bigger picture of political contention in post-plantation democratic states. In both Haiti and Jamaica, the rapid expansion in the breadth of citizenship entailed by slave emancipation was gradually counteracted by a restriction in the equality of citizenship, a lessening of binding consultation with citizens and a selective exposure of some citizens to arbitrary violence. This pattern should be familiar to students of the postbellum U.S. South. A fuller understanding of the backwards steps taken along the democratic path of development might help us to better theorize both the limitations of existing liberal democracies, and the chances for democratization actually lasting in newly democratized states, including Haiti. At the same time, we can also begin to see that there were processes of democratization occurring at the sub-national level in many regions of the Americas, as several scholars have found in Mexico (Mallon 1995; Womack 1969): at the level of the work-unit, at the level of the village, at the level of the municipality or affecting whole regions. Just as capitalist development is uneven, so too is democratic development. Besides national actors and national constitutions, we must look at regional actors, regional practices and regional publics (for a European example, cf. Somers 1993).

International comparison also suggests that a wider history of the political experience of Caribbean semi-peasant/semi-proletarians is badly needed. From the movement for the rights of free people of colour in Jamaica in the 1820s to the underground political world of Kingston in 1865, the apparent convergence of some Haitian and Jamaican political projects and identities should warn us against assuming that highly-mobile and multilingual Caribbean peasants were isolated from wider currents of political thought. With a constant flow of exiles and newspapers, visitors from Europe and inter-island travel, there was far more overlap in the conceptual worlds and concrete ties of Haitians and Jamaicans than has previously been recognized. Long before the current fashion for studying 'new' transnational identities, the peoples and histories of 'national' entities intertwined and interacted with each other. Another fascinating story awaits telling in the connections between Haiti and oppositional black publics in the United States, both before and after slave emancipation; or the story of similarly important ties between Haiti and the province of Oriente in Cuba. Also relevant are the continuities of oppositional publics, from Paul Bogle to Marcus Garvey and Bob Marley, from Jean-Jacques Acaau to the current leaders of Haiti's peasant movements. Finally, we must ask more questions about how working-class and peasant women contributed to these popular movements in countries where they were (and still are) the majority of the population. It still remains to explain how systems of sexual domination, overlaid with racial and class inequalities, constrained black women's political participation, yet also inadvertently enabled their access to subversive publicity in post-slavery societies.

This is the crucial challenge for post-emancipation studies: to understand how slaves and their descendants contributed to the processes of democratization that reshaped the nineteenth-century states involved in slavery and the slave-trade. If Afro-Caribbean resistance from the beginning revealed the limitations of the claimed democratic ideals of liberty, equality and freedom for all, then all of us have benefited from their efforts to unmask domination. Democracy was not bestowed by Europe on its colonial periphery, but was bestowed to us in the modern West by the struggles of colonized and enslaved peoples to liberate themselves and to change the world in which they lived. Realizing this requires us to elaborate a new Atlantic history, a history centred on the Caribbean core, emphasizing the agency of slaves and freed people (including women), and highlighting their critique of the limitations of modern democracy. This book, then, is not about 'backward' people on small islands in a forgotten place and time; it is about the meeting of seemingly immovable structures with forces of irresistible human agency in places far more central to the making of the modern world than their contemporary marginalization would suggest.

Notes

1   *The Sentinel,* 27 Apr. 1865, letter from George W. Gordon.
2   CO 137/367, Lt. Gov. Eyre to Duke of Newcastle, no. 49, 23 July 1862.
3   PRO 30/48/44, Evidence of Louis Q. Bowerbank.
4   *Papers* 1866b, Part 1, Cardwell to Eyre, 16 Dec. 1865, encl. Edenborough to Cardwell, Dec. 1865, 253.
5   Reprinted in the *Colonial Standard*, 26 Oct. 1865.
6   CO 137/395, Eyre to Cardwell, 23 Nov. 1865, encl. Statement of Bacchus Williams.
7   CO 137/394, Eyre to Cardwell, 7 Nov. 1865, encl. Report of John Parry.
8   *Jamaica Papers*, no. 3, Statement of the Committee, 27 July 1866.
9   CO 137/394, Eyre to Cardwell, 7 Nov. 1865, encl. Jackson to Eyre [n.d.].
10 *The Colonial Standard*, 9 Aug. 1865.
11 PRO 30/48/44, Evidence of Louis Q. Bowerbank.
12 *Jamaica Watchman and People's Free Press,* 21 Aug. 1865.
13 *Papers* 1866b, Part 1, Eyre to Cardwell, 23 Nov. 1866, encl. 10.
14 *Papers* 1866b, Part 1, Eyre to Cardwell, 23 Nov. 1866, encl. 11.
15 CO 137/394, Eyre to Cardwell, 8 Nov. 1865.
16 PRO 30/48/44, Evidence of Louis Q. Bowerbank.
17 CO 137/394, Eyre to Cardwell, 8 Nov. 1865.
18 *Papers* 1866b, Part 1, Eyre to Cardwell, 20 Oct. 1865, encl. 38, Westmoreland to Eyre, 19 Oct. 1865.
19 *Jamaica Watchman and People's Free Press*, 7 Aug. 1865.
20. *Jamaica Watchman and People's Free Press*, 21 Aug. 1865.
21 *Papers,* 1866b, Part 1, Eyre to Cardwell, no. 22, 7 Nov. 1865, encl. 18, Governor's Secretary to the Editor of the *Tribune*, 30 Oct. 1865, 113.
22 *Queen's Newsman*, Vol. 1, no. 1, 2 July 1870.
23 *Jamaica Watchman and People's Free Press*, [28] Aug. 1865, Resolutions from the Public Meeting at Saint Ann's Bay, 29 July 1865 (G. W. Gordon, Chair).

Bibliography

Manuscript sources

Jamaica

National Library of Jamaica, Kingston.

MS 74. Morant Bay Rebellion: Contemporary Newspaper Cuttings.
MS 106. Rev. E. B. Underhill's Letter to Governor Eyre, 5 Jan. 1865.
MS 841. Rev. G. Rouse, six letters to Baptist Missionary Society, 1844–58.
MS 865. Letter from Mrs. E. Holt to Rev. E. B. Underhill, 26 Oct. 1853.
'Thirty-six letters and reports of Baptist Missionaries re condition of Church and Church Schools in Falmouth, Montego Bay'. [1850–1862].
'Thirty Five Letters to the Baptist Missionary Society'. [1841–1863].

England

Baptist Missionary Society Archives, Angus Library, Regents College, Oxford.

WI/5. Jamaica correspondence.
E. B. Underhill: 'Extracts from Correspondence with Missionaries in Jamaica on the Disturbances, 1864–66.'
'Extracts from letters written by B.M.S. missionaries', Bound Vol., 1840–46.

Public Record Office, London.

CO 137. Original Correspondence of Jamaican Governors.
FO 35/1 — 35/29, Foreign Office, General Correspondence, Haiti, 1825–1844.
PRO 30/48/42, 30/48/43, 30/48/44. Edward Cardwell Papers.
Report of the Jamaica Royal Commission, 1866. Parts 1 and 2. London: G. E. Eyre & Wm. Spottiswoode, 1866. [JRC].

School of Oriental and African Studies, University of London.

Wesleyan Methodist Missionary Society Archives [WMMS].
West Indies Correspondence, Haiti, 1834–1857.
West Indies Correspondence, Jamaica, 1838–1865. Boxes 195–199.
Special Series, Biographical, West Indies.
Box 581: Journal of William Towler, 1838–1853.
Box 588: Autobiography of James Hartwell, 1817–1902.
Box 590: Journal of John Brown, 1816–1819.
London Missionary Society Archives (Council for World Mission) [LMS].
Boxes 2–9, 1837–1869.

France

Archives du Ministère des Affaires Étrangères, Paris [AMAE].

Corréspondence Consulaire et Commerçial.
CCC, Le Cap Haitien, 1825–1856. 2 vols.
CCC, Les Cayes, 1825–1831. 1 vol.
CCC, Port-au-Prince, 1825–1901. 13 vols.
Corréspondence Politique [CP], Haïti. 1838–1844. Vols. 8–12.

Archives Nationales, Paris [AN].

Colonies, Archives Ministerielles Anciennes.
Séries C9a–b. Saint Domingue, 1664–1792.
Séries CC9a–c. Saint Domingue (sous-séries).
Marine, Archives du Ministère des Marines.
Séries GGII.1 Papiers du Amiral Charles Baudin.

United States

New York Public Library [NYPL]

Haitian papers, 1811–1846 [microform]: comprising proclamations, decrees, occasional numbers of official gazettes, e.g. Le Telegraphe, and other official and nonofficial papers, both printed and ms. [Port-au-Prince: s.n., 1811–1846].
Haitian papers, 1842–1846 [microform]: comprising proclamations, decrees, constitutions and other official and nonofficial publications. [Port-au-Prince: s.n., 1842–1846].
James Redpath, Scrapbook of Clippings of articles mostly relating to Haiti and John Brown,1859–1861.

Other government papers

Jamaica

Papers Relating to the Affairs of Jamaica. London: Eyre & Spottiswoode, Feb. [*Papers* 1866a].
Papers Relating to the Case of Lewis Celeste Lecesne and John Escoffery. [Bound pamphlets, 1823–26].
Papers Relating to the Disturbances in Jamaica and *Further Papers Relative to the Disturbances in Jamaica.* Parts I, II and III. London: Harrison & Sons, 1866. [*Papers* 1866b].
'The Queen's Advice'. The Right Hon. E. Cardwell to Gov. Eyre, Downing St., 14 June 1865. (Copy — Jamaica — no. 222) Spanish Town: Jordon & Osborn.
'Report of the Central Board of Health of Jamaica'. Printed by Order of the House of Assembly, Spanish Town: F. M. Wilson Printer, 1852.

England

'Pièces officielles rélatives aux négotiations du gouvernement français avec le gouvernement haïtien, pour traiter de la formalité de la réconnaissance de

l'indépendence d'Haïti.' Port-au-Prince: Impr. du gouvernement, 1824.
'Pièces rélatives aux communications faites au nom du gouvernement français, au Président d'Hayti, par Mr. le Général Dauxion Lavaysse, Deputé de S. M. Louis XVIII, Roi de France et de Navarre.' New York: Impr. Joseph Desnoves, 1816.
'Royaume d'Hayti. Procés verbal des Séances du Consul général de la nation.' Cap-Henry, 1814.

United States

United States Consular Despatches [microfilm]: Cap Haitien, 1827–1849 [M9].

Newspapers

Haitian

L'Abeille Haytienne, journal politique et littéraire, 1818–20 (Port-au-Prince)
L'Eclaireur Haytien ou le parfait patriote, 1818–1819 (Port-au-Prince)
La Feuille du Commerce, 1833–1860 (Port-au-Prince)
Le Manifeste, journal commerçial, politique et littéraire, 1841–44 (Port-au-Prince)
Le Patriote, 1842–1844 (Port-au-Prince)
Le Propagateur haïtien, 1824 (Port-au-Prince)
Le Républicain, récueil scientifique et littéraire, 1837 (Port-au-Prince)
L'Union (Port-au-Prince)

Jamaican

The Baptist Herald and Friend of Africa (Kingston)
The Colonial Standard and Jamaica Despatch (Kingston)
The County Union, 1864–65 (Montego Bay)
The Falmouth Post [and Jamaica General Advertiser] (Falmouth)
The Jamaica Watchman and People's Free Press, 1859, 1865 (Kingston)
The Morning Journal, 1838– (Kingston)
The Queen's Newsman, 1870 (Kingston)
The Sentinel, 1865 (Kingston)
The Watchman and Jamaica Free Press, 1829–1830 (Kingston)

Printed primary sources

d'Alaux, Gustave [Maxime Reybaud, French Consul General]. *La République dominicaine et l'empereur Soulouque*. Detached from *Révue des deux mondes*. 10 (15 Apr. and 1 May, 1851), pp. 193–210.
——. *L'Empereur Soulouque et Son Empire*. 2d ed. (Paris: Michel Levy Frères, 1860).
Anon., *Addresses to His Excellency Edward John Eyre, Esq., 1865, 1866* (Kingston: DeCordova & Co., 1866).
Anon., *Jamaica: It's State and Prospects* (London, 1867).

Ardouin, Beaubrun. *Réponse du Sénateur B. Ardouin à un écrit anonyme* (Port-au-Prince: Imprimérie Pinard,1840).

——. *Réponse du Sénateur B. Ardouin à une lettre de M. Isambert* (Port-au-Prince: Imprimérie Pinard, 1842).

——. *Études sur l'histoire d'Haïti*. 11 vols. (Paris: Dezobry, Magdeleine et Ce, 1860).

Banbury, Rev. T. *Jamaica Superstitions; Or, the Obeah Book: A Complete Treatise on the Absurdities Believed in By the People of the Island* (Kingston: Mortimer De Souza, 1895).

Bigelow, John. *Jamaica in 1850. Or, The effects of Sixteen Years of Freedom on a Slave Colony.* Reprint. Including Appendix A: 'A Visit to the Emperor of Haiti'. (Westport, CT: Negro Universities Press, [1851] 1970).

Bird, Mark B. 'Has Freedom Proved a Failure in Hayti'. *Methodist Quarterly Review*, 46 (1862), 561–579.

——. *The Black Man; Or, Haytian Independence* (New York: n.p., 1869).

Bonneau, Alexandre. *Haïti: ses progrès — son avenir* (Paris: E. Dentu, 1862).

Brown, Jonathan. *The History and present Condition of St. Domingue*. 2 vols. Reprint. (London: Frank Cass, 1972). [Philadelphia: William Marshall, 1837].

Dewey, Loring D. *Correspondence Relative to the Emigration to Hayti of the Free People of Colour in the United States* (New York: Day, 1824).

Fletcher, Rev. Duncan. *Personal Recollections of the Hon. George W. Gordon, late of Jamaica* (London: Elliot Stock, 1867).

Franklin, James. *The Present State of Hayti (Saint Domingo), with remarks on its agriculture, commerce, laws, religion, finances, and population, etc.* (London: J. Murray, 1828).

Griggs, Earl and Clifford Prator, eds. *Henry Christophe and Thomas Clarkson, A Correspondence* (New York: Greenwood Press, 1968).

Harvey, Thomas and William Brewin. *Jamaica in 1866: A Narrative of a Tour Through the Island, with Remarks on its Social, Educational, and Industrial Condition* (London: A. W. Bennett, 1867).

Holly, James Theodore. 'A Vindication of the capacity of the Negro race for self-government and civilized progress' in Howard Bell, ed., *Black Separatism and the Caribbean, 1860* (Ann Arbor: University of Michigan Press, [1857] 1970).

Inginac, Joseph B. *Mémoires de Joseph Balthazar Inginac, Général de Division, Ex-Sécrétaire-Général, près S. E. l'Ex-Président d'Haïti, 1797–1843* (Kingston, Jamaica: J. R. DeCordova, 1843).

Jamaica Baptist Union. 'Distress in Jamaica: letter of the Ministers of the Jamaica Baptist Union, to His Ex. Edward John Eyre… . In Reference to the Letter Addressed by Dr. Underhill to the Rt. Hon'ble Mr. Cardwell, Secretary of State for the Colonies'. (Montego Bay: *County Union* Office, 5 June 1865).

Jamaica Committee, *Facts and documents re alleged rebellion in Jamaica and the Measure of Repression; including Notes of the trial of Mr. Gordon*, Jamaica Papers, no. 1. (London: The Jamaica Committee, 1866).

Janvier, Louis Joseph. *Du gouvernement civil en Haïti*. (Lille: Le Bigot Freres, 1905).

——. *Les Constitutions d'Haïti (1801–1885)*. Reprint (Paris: Fardin [1886] 1977).

Lake, A.W.H. *The Riot in St. Thomas in the East: Trial of Mr. George William Gordon* (Spanish Town: Robert Osborn, 1866).

Linstant, Baron S. *Essai sur les Moyens d'extirper les préjugés des Blancs contre la couleur des Africains et des sang-mêlés* [Ouvrage couronné par la société française pour l'abolition de l'esclavage, 1840]. (Paris: Pagnerre Ed., 1841).

——. *Récueil général des Lois et Actes du Gouvernement d'Haïti, depuis la proclamation de son indépendence jusqu'à nos jours*. 5 vols. (Paris: Auguste Durand, 1851–1860).

Mackenzie, Charles [British Consul General]. *Notes on Haiti, Made During a Residence in that Republic*. 2 vols. Reprint. (London: Frank Cass [1830] 1970).

Madiou, Thomas. *Histoire d'Haïti*. 8 vols. Reprint. Ed. Michèle Oriol. (Port-au-Prince: Editions Henri Deschamps, 1985–1991 [originally published: Port-au-Prince: Impr. J. Courtois, 1847–1848]).

Price, George. *Jamaica and the Colonial Office: Who Caused the Crisis?* (London: Sampson Low, Son and Marston, 1866).

Redpath, James, ed. *A Guide to Hayti*. Reprint. (Westport, CT: Negro Universities Press [1861] 1970).

Saint-Rémy, Joseph (Lepelletier de). 'La République d'Haïti; ses dernières révolutions et sa situation actuelle'. Detached from *Révue des Deux Mondes*. (15 Nov. 1845), pp. 662–685.

Schoelcher, Victor. *Colonies Étrangères et Haïti: Résultats de l'Émancipation Anglaise* (Paris: Pagnerre, 1843).

Sewell, William G. *The Ordeal of Free Labor in the British West Indies* (London: Frank Cass, [1861] 1968).

St. John, Spenser Buckingham. *Hayti: or, The Black Republic*. Reprint, 2d ed. (London: Frank Cass, [1889] 1971).

Stewart, John. *A View of the Past and Present State of the Island of Jamaica* (Edinburgh: n.p., 1823).

Sturge, Joseph and Thomas Harvey. *The West Indies in 1837* (London: Hamilton, Adams & Co, 1838).

Underhill, Edward Bean. *The Tragedy at Morant Bay: A Narrative of the Disturbance in the Island of Jamaica in 1865* (London: Alexander & Shepheard, 1895).

Waddell, Rev. Hope Masterton. *Twenty-Nine Years in the West Indies and Central Africa: A Review of Missionary Work and Adventure, 1829–1858*. Reprint. (London: Frank Cass, [1863] 1970).

Ward, Samuel [Ringold]. *Reflections Upon the Gordon Rebellion* [Pamphlet, 1866].

Williams, James. *A Narrative of Events since the First of August, 1834, by James Williams, An Apprenticed Labourer in Jamaica*. Bound with Lord Brougham's Speech on the Slave Trade in the House of Lords, Monday, Jan. 29, 1838 (London: J. Rider, 1838).

Secondary sources

Alleyne, Mervyn C. 1985. 'A Linguistic Perspective on the Caribbean'. In *Caribbean Contours*, ed. Sidney Mintz and Sally Price, pp. 155–180. Baltimore and London: Johns Hopkins University Press.

Anderson, Benedict. [1983] 1991. *Imagined Communities: Reflections on the Origin and Spread of Nationalism*. London and New York: Verso.

Andrews, George R. and Herrick Chapman, eds. 1995. *The Social Construction of Democracy, 1870–1990*. New York: New York University Press.

Anglade, Georges. 1982. *Éspace et Liberté en Haïti*. Montréal: ERCE & CRC, Université de Quebec.

d'Anjou, Leo. 1996. *Social Movements and Cultural Change: The First Abolition Campaign Revisited.* Hawthorne, NY: Aldine de Gruyter.

Anstey, Roger. 1975. *The Atlantic Slave Trade and British Abolition, 1760–1810.* London: Macmillan.

Antoine, Régis. 1978. *Les Écrivains français et les antilles: des premiers pères blancs aux surréalistes noirs.* Paris: G. P. Maisonneuve et Larose.

Aptheker, Herbert. [1943] 1993. *American Negro Slave Revolts.* 50th Anniversary Edition. New York: Monthly Review Press.

Auguste, Yves L. 1979. *Haïti et les États-Unis: 1804–1862.* Sherbrooke, Quebec: Editions Naaman.

Austin, Diane J. 1984. *Urban Life in Kingston, Jamaica: The Culture and Class Ideology of Two Neighborhoods.* New York: Gordon and Breach.

Austin-Broos, Diane J. 1997. *Jamaica Genesis: Religion and the Politics of Moral Orders.* Chicago and London: University of Chicago Press.

Bakan, Abigail B. 1990. *Ideology and Class Conflict in Jamaica: The Politics of Rebellion.* Montreal and Kingston: McGill-Queen's University Press.

Barthélémy, Gerard. 1989. *Le Pays en Déhors.* Port-au-Prince: H. Deschamps.

Bastide, Roger. 1978. *The African Religions of Brazil: Toward a Sociology of the Interpretation of Civilizations.* Trans. Helen Sebba. Baltimore, MD: Johns Hopkins University Press.

Beckford, George. 1972. *Persistent Poverty: Underdevelopment in Plantation Economies in the Third World.* New York: Oxford University Press.

Beckles, Hilary McD. 1988. 'Caribbean Anti-Slavery: the Self-Liberation Ethos of Enslaved Blacks'. *Journal of Caribbean History*, 22: nos. 1/2: 1–19.

——. 1989. *Natural Rebels: A Social History of Enslaved Black Women in Barbados.* London: Zed Books.

——. 1998. 'Historicizing Slavery in West Indian Feminisms'. *Feminist Review* 59 (Summer): 34–56.

Beckles, Hilary and Verene Shepherd, eds. 1993. *Caribbean Freedom: Economy and Society from Emancipation to the Present.* Kingston, Jamaica: Ian Randle.

Beckwith, Martha. 1969. *Black Roadways: A Study of Jamaican Folk Life.* Reprint. New York: Negro Universities Press [University of North Carolina, 1929].

Bell, Howard H., ed. 1970. *Black Separatism and the Caribbean, 1860.* Ann Arbor: University of Michigan.

Bellegarde-Smith, Patrick. 1980. 'Haitian Social Thought in the Nineteenth Century: Class Formation and Westernization'. *Caribbean Studies*, 20: 1: 5–33.

——. 1990. *Haiti: The Breached Citadel.* Boulder and London: Westview.

Besson, Jean. 1979. 'Symbolic Aspects of Land Tenure in the Caribbean'. In *Peasants, Plantations and Rural Communities in the Caribbean*, ed. Malcolm Cross and A. Marks, 86–116. Guildford, England: University of Surrey.

——. 1993. 'Reputation and respectability reconsidered: a new perspective on Afro-Caribbean peasant women'. In *Women and Change in the Caribbean: a Pan-Caribbean Perspective*, ed. Janet Momsen, 15–37. London: James Currey.

——. 1995. 'Land, Kinship and Community in the Post-Emancipation Caribbean: A Regional View of the Leewards'. In *Small Islands, Large Questions: Society, Culture and Resistance in the Post-Emancipation Caribbean*, ed. Karen F. Olwig, 73–99. London: Frank Cass.

Blackburn, Robyn. 1988. *The Overthrow of Colonial Slavery, 1776–1848.* London: Verso.

Blackett, R. J. M. 1983. *Building an Antislavery Wall: Black Americans in the Atlantic Abolitionist Movement, 1830–1860.* Baton Rouge and London: Louisiana State University Press.

Bohstedt, John. 1983. *Riots and Community Politics in England and Wales, 1790–1810.* Cambridge, MA: Harvard University Press.

Bolster, Jeffrey W. 1997. *Black Jacks: African American Seamen in the Age of Sail.* Cambridge, MA: Harvard University Press.

Bradley, James E. 1986. *Popular Politics and the American Revolution in England: Petitions, the Crown and Public Opinion.* Macon: Mercer University Press.

Brown, Elsa B. 1995. 'Negotiating and Transforming the Public Sphere: African American Political Life in the Transition from Slavery to Freedom'. In *The Black Public Sphere: A Public Culture Book,* ed. Black Public Sphere Collective, 111–151. Chicago and London: University of Chicago Press.

Brown, Karen McCarthy. 1997. 'The Power to Heal: Haitian Women in Vodou'. In *Daughters of Caliban,* ed. Consuelo Lopez Springfield, 123–42. Bloomington and Indianapolis: Indiana University Press.

Bryan, Patrick. 1984. *The Haitian Revolution and its Effects.* Kingston and Exeter, NH: Heinemann.

Burton, Richard D. E. 1997. *Afro-Creole: Power, Opposition and Play in the Caribbean.* Ithaca and London: Cornell University Press.

Bush, Barbara. 1990. *Slave Women in Caribbean Society 1650–1838.* London: James Currey; Kingston: Heinnemann; Bloomington: Indiana University Press.

Calhoun, Craig, ed. 1992. *Habermas and the Public Sphere.* Cambridge, MA: MIT Press.

Campbell, Mavis.1976. *The Dynamics of Change in A Slave Society: A Sociopolitical History of the Free Colored of Jamaica, 1800–1865.* Ph.D. Dissertation, University of the West Indies, Kingston, Jamaica.

——. 1988. *The Maroons of Jamaica 1655–1796: A History of Resistance, Collaboration and Betrayal.* Granby, MA: Bergin & Garvey.

Cassidy, Frederic G. 1982. *Jamaica Talk: Three-hundred Years of the English Language in Jamaica.* London: Macmillan Educational.

Castera, Justin. 1986. *Brèf coup d'oeil sur les origines de la presse haïtienne, 1764–1850.* Port-au-Prince, Haiti: Impr. H. Deschamps.

Catherall, Rev. Gordon A. 1990. *Baptist War and Peace: A Study of British Baptist Involvement in Jamaica, 1783–1865.* Typescript (Liverpool), BMS.

Césaire, Aimé. 1981. *Toussaint L'Ouverture: la Révolution Française et le Problème Coloniale.* Paris: Présence Africaine.

Chevannes, Barry. 1994. *Rastafari: Roots and Ideology.* Syracuse, NY: Syracuse University Press.

Clarke, John H. with Amy J. Garvey. 1974. *Marcus Garvey and the Vision of Africa.* New York: Vintage Books.

Comaroff, Jean and John Comaroff. 1991. *Of Revelation and Revolution: Christianity, Colonialism and Consciousness in South Africa.* Chicago and London: University of Chicago Press.

Cooper, Carolyn. 1995. *Noises in the Blood: Orality, Gender, and the 'Vulgar' Body of Jamaican Popular Culture.* Durham: Duke University Press.

Cooper, Frederick, Allen Isaacman, Florencia Mallon, William Roseberry, and Steve Stern. 1993. *Confronting Historical Paradigms: Peasants, Labor, and the Capitalist World System in Africa and Latin America.* Madison: University of Wisconsin Press.

Courlander, Harold. 1960. *The Drum and the Hoe: Life and Lore of the Haitian People*. Berkeley and Los Angeles: University of California Press.

Craton, Michael. 1974. *Sinews of Empire: A Short History of British Slavery*. London: Doubleday.

——. 1982. *Testing the Chains: Resistance to Slavery in the British West Indies*. Ithaca: Cornell University Press.

——. 1997. *Empire, Enslavement and Freedom in the Caribbean*. Kingston: Ian Randle; Oxford: James Currey; Princeton: Markus Weiner.

Cross, Malcolm and Gad Heuman, eds. 1988. *Labour in the Caribbean: From Emancipation to Independence*. London: Macmillan.

Curtin, Philip. [1955] 1975. *Two Jamaicas: The Role of Ideas in a Tropical Colony, 1830–1865*. Cambridge, MA: Harvard University Press.

——. 1990. *The Rise and Fall of the Plantation Complex: Essays in Atlantic History*. Cambridge: Cambridge University Press.

Dann, Martin E. 1971. *The Black Press, 1827–1890: The Quest for National Identity*. New York: Capricorn Books.

Dash, J. Michael. 1997. *Haiti and the United States: National Stereotypes in the Literary Imagination*, 2nd ed. New York: St Martin's Press.

Davis, David Brion. 1975. *The Problem of Slavery in the Age of Revolution, 1770–1823*. Ithaca: Cornell University Press.

——. 1984. *Slavery and Human Progress*. New York: Oxford University Press.

Dayan, Joan. 1995. *Haiti, History and the Gods*. Berkeley, Los Angeles and London: University of California Press.

Desquiron, Jean. 1993. *Haïti à la Une: Une anthologie de la presse haïtienne de 1724 à 1934*. 2 vols. Port-au-Prince, 1993.

Drescher, Seymour. 1977. *Econocide: British Slavery in the Era of Abolition*. Pittsburgh: Pittsburgh University Press.

——. 1982. 'Public Opinion and the Destruction of British Colonial Slavery'. In *Slavery and British Society, 1776–1846*, ed. James Walvin, 22–48. Baton Rouge: Louisiana State University Press.

——. 1987. *Capitalism and Anti-Slavery: British Mobilization in Comparative Perspective*. New York: Oxford University Press.

——. 1994. 'The Long Goodbye: Dutch Capitalism and Antislavery in Comparative Perspective'. *American Historical Review* 99 (1): 44–69.

Du Bois, W. E. B. [1935] 1992. *Black Reconstruction in America, 1860–1880*. Reprint. New York: Atheneum.

Duncker, Sheila. 1960. 'The Free Coloured and Their Fight for Civil Rights in Jamaica, 1800–1830'. Unpublished M.A. thesis, University of London.

Dupuy, Alex. 1989. *Haiti in the World Economy: class, race and underdevelopment since 1700*. Boulder, CO: Westview Press.

Egerton, Douglas. 1990. 'Gabriel's Conspiracy and the Election of 1800'. *Journal of Southern History*, 56: 191–214.

Eltis, David. 1987. *Economic Growth and the Ending of the Transatlantic Slave Trade*. New York: Oxford University Press.

Emirbayer, Mustafa and Mimi Sheller. 1999. 'Publics in History'. *Theory and Society,* 28: 145–97.

Evans, Sara and Harry Boyte. 1986. *Free Spaces*. New York: Harper and Row.

Fanon, Frantz. 1967. *Black Skin, White Masks*. Trans. Charles Markmann. New York: Grove Weidenfeld

Farmer, Paul. 1994. *The Uses of Haiti*. Monroe, ME: Common Courage Press.

Fick, Carolyn E. 1990. *The Making of Haiti: The Saint Domingue Revolution from Below*. Knoxville: University of Tennessee Press.

——. 1988. 'Black Peasants and Soldiers in the Saint-Domingue Revolution: Initial Reactions to Freedom in the South Province (1793–94)'. In *History From Below*, ed. Frederick Krantz. Oxford and New York: Basil Blackwell.

Fogel, Robert W. and Stanley L. Engerman. [1974] 1989. *Time on the Cross: The Economics of American Negro Slavery*. New York: W. W. Norton.

Foner, Eric. 1983. *Nothing But Freedom: Emancipation and Its Legacy*. Baton Rouge: Louisiana State University Press.

——. 1988. *Reconstruction: America's Unfinished Revolution, 1863–1877*. New York: Harper & Row.

Franzosi, Roberto. 1994. 'From Words to Numbers: A Set Theory Framework for the Collection, Organization, and Analysis of Narrative Data'. In *Sociological Methodology*. 24: 105–137 (Ed. Peter Marsden) Oxford: Blackwell.

Fryer, Peter. 1984. *Staying Power: Black People in Britain Since 1504*. Atlantic Highlands, NJ: Humanities Press.

Gaspar, David B. and David P. Geggus. 1997. *A Turbulent Time: The French Revolution and the Greater Caribbean*. Bloomington and Indianapolis: Indiana University Press.

Gates, Henry Louis, Jr., ed. 1987. *The Classic Slave Narratives*. New York and London: Mentor.

Gayle, Clement. 1982. *George Liele: Pioneer Missionary to Jamaica*. Kingston: Jamaica Baptist Union.

Geggus, David P. 1982a. *Slavery, War and Revolution: The British Occupation of Saint Domingue, 1793–1798*. Oxford: Clarendon Press.

——. 1982b. 'British Opinion and the Emergence of Haiti, 1791–1805'. In *Slavery and British Society, 1776–1846*, ed. James Walvin. Baton Rouge: Louisiana State University Press.

——. 1985. 'Haiti and the Abolitionists: Opinion, Propaganda and International Politics in Britain and France, 1804–1835'. In *Abolition and its Aftermath*, ed. David Richardson. London: Frank Cass.

——. 1997. 'Slavery, War and revolution in the Greater Caribbean, 1789–1815'. In *A Turbulent Time*, ed. Gaspar and Geggus, *op. cit.*, pp. 1–50.

Genovese, Eugene. [1979] 1981. *From Rebellion to Revolution: Afro-American Slave Revolts in the Making of the New World*. New York: Vintage.

Gerzina, Gretchen. 1995. *Black London: Life Before Emancipation*. New Brunswick: Rutgers University Press.

Gilroy, Paul. 1991. *'There Ain't No Black in the Union Jack': the Cultural Politics of Race and Nation*. Chicago: University of Chicago Press.

——. [1993] 1995. *The Black Atlantic: Modernity and Double Consciousness*. Cambrdige: Harvard University Press.

Green, William A. [1976] 1991. *British Slave Emancipation*. Oxford: Clarendon.

Griffiths, Leslie. 1991. *A History of Methodism in Haiti*. Port-au-Prince: Imprimerie Methodiste-D. E. L.

Habermas, Jurgen. [1989] 1992. *The Structural Transformation of the Public Sphere*. Cambridge, MA: MIT Press.

Hall, Catherine. 1992. *White, Male and Middle Class: Explorations in Feminism and History*. Cambridge: Polity Press.

——. 1995. 'Gender Politics and Imperial Politics: Rethinking the Histories of Empire'. In *Engendering History*, ed. V. Shepherd et al., *op. cit.*, pp. 48–59.

Hall, Douglas. 1959. *Free Jamaica, 1838–1865: An Economic History*. New Haven: Yale University Press.

_____. 1978. 'The Flight from the Estates Reconsidered: The British West Indies, 1838–1842'. *The Journal of Caribbean History*. No. 10/11: 7–24. Reproduced in Beckles and Shepherd, *Caribbean Freedom*, 1993, pp. 55–63.

Harding, Vincent. 1981. *There is A River: The Black Struggle for Freedom in America* (New York: Vintage Books, 1981).

Helg, Aline. 1995. *Our Rightful Share: The Afro-Cuban Struggle for Equality, 1886–1912*. Chapel Hill and London: University of North Carolina Press.

Herskovitz, Melville J. [1937] 1971. *Life in a Haitian Valley*. New York: Anchor Books.

Heuman, Gad J. 1981. *Between Black and White: Race, Politics and the Free Coloreds in Jamaica, 1792–1865*. Westport, CT: Greenwood.

_____. 1994. *'The Killing Time': The Morant Bay Rebellion in Jamaica*. London: Macmillan.

_____. 1995. 'Post-Emancipation Protest in Jamaica: The Morant Bay Rebellion, 1865'. In *From Chattel Slaves to Wage Slaves: The Dynamics of Labour Bargaining in the Americas*, ed. Mary Turner, 258–274. London: James Currey; Kingston: Ian Randle; Bloomington: Indiana University Press.

Heuman, Gad J., ed. 1986. *Out of the House of Bondage: runaways, resistance and marronage in Africa and the New World*. London: Frank Cass.

Higginbotham, Evelyn Brooks. 1993. *Righteous Discontent: The Women's Movement in the Black Baptist Church, 1880–1920*. Cambridge, MA and London: Harvard University Press.

_____. 1997. 'The Black Church: A Gender Perspective'. In *African-American Religion: Interpretive Essays in History and Culture*, ed. Timothy E. Fulop and Albert J. Raboteau, 201–26. New York and London: Routledge.

Higman, Barry. 1988. *Jamaica Surveyed: Plantation Maps and Plans of the eighteenth and nineteenth Centuries*. Kingston: Institute of Jamaica.

_____. 1995. 'Post-Emancipation Historiography of the Leeward Islands'. In *Small Islands, Large Questions*, ed. K.F. Olwig, *op. cit.*, pp. 8–28.

Higman, Barry, ed. 1980. *The Jamaican Censuses of 1844 and 1861*. Kingston, Jamaica: University of the West Indies.

Hoetink, H. 1982. *The Dominican People 1850–1900: Notes for a Historical Sociology*. Trans. Stephen Ault. Baltimore: Johns Hopkins University Press.

_____. 1985. ' "Race" and Color in the Caribbean'. In *Caribbean Contours*, ed. S. Mintz and S. Price, *op. cit.*, pp. 55–84.

Holm, John. 1988. *Pidgins and Creoles*. NY: Cambridge University Press.

Holt, Thomas C. 1992. *The Problem of Freedom: Race, Labor and Politics in Jamaica and Britain, 1832–1939*. Baltimore: Johns Hopkins University Press.

Huber, Evelyne. 1993. 'The Future of Democracy in the Caribbean'. In *Democracy in the Caribbean: Political, Economic and Social Perspectives*. ed. Jorge Dominguez, Robert Pastor and R. Delisle Worrell, 74–95. Baltimore & London: Johns Hopkins University Press.

Hunt, Alfred. 1988. *Haiti's Influence on Antebellum America: slumbering volcano in the Caribbean*. Baton Rouge: Louisiana State University Press.

Hurbon, Laënnec. 1995. *Voodoo: Truth and Fantasy*. Trans. Lory Frankel. London: Thames and Hudson [Paris: Gallimard, 1993].

Hurston, Zora Neale. [1938] 1990. *Tell my Horse: Voodoo and Life in Haiti and Jamaica*. Reprint. New York: Harper & Row.

Isaacman, Allen F. 1993. 'Peasants and Rural Social Protest in Africa' in *Confronting Historical Paradigms* Cooper, et al., *op. cit.*, pp. 205–317. University of Wisconsin Press.

Jackson, James O. 1976. 'The Origins of Pan-African Nationalism: Afro-American and Haytian Relations, 1800–1863'. Ph.D. dissertation, Northwestern University.

Jacob, Margaret C. 1991. *Living the Enlightenment: Freemasonry and Politics in Eighteenth-Century Europe*. New York and Oxford: Oxford University Press.

James, C. L. R. [1938] 1989. *The Black Jacobins: Toussaint l'Ouverture and the San Domingo Revolution*. New York: Vintage Books.

James, Winston. 1998. *Holding Aloft the Banner of Ethiopia: Caribbean Radicalism in Early Twentieth-Century America*. London and New York: Verso.

Jordan, Winthrop D. 1968. *White Over Black: American Attitudes Toward the Negro, 1550–1812*. Chapel Hill: University of North Carolina Press.

Keane, John. 1984. *Public Life and Late Capitalism: Toward a Socialist Theory of Democracy*. Cambridge: Cambridge University Press.

Kelley, Robin D. G. 1996. *Race Rebels: Culture, Politics and the Black Working Class*. New York: The Free Press.

Knight, Franklin. 1990. *The Caribbean: The Genesis of a Fragmented Nationalism*. 2d ed. New York and London: Oxford University Press.

LaCerte, Robert K. 1993. 'The Evolution of Land and Labour in the Haitian Revolution 1791–1820'. In *Caribbean Freedom*, ed. H. Beckles and V. Shepherd, *op. cit.*, 42–47.

——. 1975. 'The First Land Reform in Latin America: The Reforms of Alexander Pétion, 1809–1814'. *Inter-American Economic Affairs*. 28: 4: 77–85.

——. 1981. 'Xenophobia and Economic Decline: The Haitian Case, 1820–1843'. *The Americas*. 37: 4: 499–459.

Laguerre, Michel. 1993. *The Military and Society in Haiti*. Knoxville: University of Tennessee Press.

——. 1989. *Voodoo and Politics in Haiti*. New York: St. Martin's Press.

Landes, Joan. 1988. *Women and the Public Sphere in the Age of the French Revolution*. Ithaca: Cornell University Press.

Larose, Serge. 1975. 'The Haitian Lakou: land, family and ritual'. In *Family and Kinship in Middle America and The Caribbean*, ed. Arnaud Marks and Rene Romer, 482–512. Curacao: University Netherlands Antilles.

Lawless, Robert K. 1992. *Haiti's Bad Press*. Rochester, VT: Schenkman Books.

Léger, Abel-Nicolas. 1930. *Histoire Diplomatique d'Haïti: Tome Prémier, 1804–1859*. Port-au-Prince: Impr. Aug. Heraux.

Lewis, Gordon K. 1968. *The Growth of the Modern West Indies*. New York: Monthly Review Press.

——. 1983. *Main Currents in Caribbean Thought: The Historical Evolution of Caribbean Society in Its Ideological Aspects, 1492–1900*. Baltimore: Johns Hopkins University Press.

Logan, Rayford. 1941. *The Diplomatic Relations of the United States with Haiti, 1776–1891*. Chapel Hill: University of North Carolina Press.

Lorimer, Douglas A. 1992. 'Black Resistance to Slavery and racism in Eighteenth-Century England'. In *Essays on the History of Blacks in Britain*, ed., Jagdish S. Gundara and Ian Duffield, 58–80. Aldershot: Avebury.

Lowenthal, David. 1995. 'The Wayward Leewards' in *Small Islands, Large Questions,* ed., K. F. Olwig, *op. cit.*, 179–87.

MacLeod, Murdo J. 1970. 'The Soulouque Regime in Haiti, 1847–1859: A Reevaluation.' *Caribbean Studies*. 10: 3: 35–48.

Maingot, Anthony. 1996. 'Haiti and the Terrified Consciousness of the Caribbean'. In *Ethnicity in the Caribbean*, ed. Gert Oostindie, 53–80. (London and Basingstoke: Macmillan Caribbean).

Mallon, Florencia. 1983. *The Defense of Community in Peru's Central Highlands: Peasant Struggle and Capitalist Transition, 1860–1940*. Princeton: Princeton University Press.

———. 1995. *Peasant and Nation: The Making of Postcolonial Mexico and Peru*. Berkeley and Los Angeles: University of California Press.

Mannheim, Karl. [1928] 1952. 'The Problem of Generations'. In *Essays on the Sociology of Knowledge*. Trans. P. Keckemet. New York: Oxford Univ. Press.

Martin, Tony. 1976. *Race First: The Ideological and Organizational Struggles of Marcus Garvey and the Universal Negro Improvement Association* (Westport, CT and London: Greenwood Press).

Martinez-Alier, Verena. [1974] 1989. *Marriage, Class and Colour in Nineteenth Century Cuba*. 2d ed. Ann Arbor: University of Michigan.

Martinez-Fernandez, Luis. 1994. *Torn Between Empires: Economy, Society, and Patterns of Political Thought in the Hispanic Caribbean, 1840–1870*. Athens, GA and London: University of Georgia Press.

Marx, Karl. [1913] 1926. *The Eighteenth Brumaire of Louis Bonaparte*. Trans. Eden and Cedar Paul. New York: Allen and Unwin.

Marx, Anthony. 1998. *Making Race and Nation: A Comparison of the United States, South Africa, and Brazil*. Cambridge and New York: Cambridge University Press.

Matos-Rodriguez, Felix V. 1995. 'Street Vendors, Peddlars, Shop-Owners and Domestics: Some Aspects of Women's Economic Roles in Nineteenth Century San Juan, Puerto Rico, 1820–1870'. In *Engendering History*, ed. V. Shepherd et al., *op. cit.*, pp.176–96. Kingston: Ian Randle; London: James Currey.

McAdam, Doug. 1982. *Political Process and the Development of Black Insurgency, 1930–1970*. Chicago: University of Chicago Press.

McAdam, Doug, John D. McCarthy, & Mayer Zald. 1996. 'Introduction: Opportunities, mobilizing structures, and framing processes: toward a synthetic, comparative perspective on social movements'. In *Comparative Perspectives on Social Movements: Political Opportunities, Mobilizing Structures and Cultural Framings*, ed. D. McAdam, J. D. McCarthy and M. Zald. Cambridge: Cambridge University Press.

McClellan, James. 1992. *Colonialism and Science: Saint Domingue in the Old Regime*. Baltimore, MD: Johns Hopkins University Press.

McGlynn, Frank and Seymour Drescher, eds. 1992. *The Meaning of Freedom: Economics, Politics and Culture after Slavery*. Pittsburgh & London: University of Pittsburgh Press.

Métraux, Alfred. 1960. *Black Peasants and Their Religion*. Trans. Peter Lengyel. London: George Harrap & Co.

———. 1972. *Voodoo in Haiti*. Trans. Hugo Chartiris. New York: Schocken Books.

Mintz, Sidney. 1958. 'Historical Sociology of the Jamaican Church-Founded Free Village System'. *De West-Indische Gids* 1–2 (Sept.): 46–70.

———. 1964. 'The Employment of Capital by Market Women in Haiti'. In *Capital, Savings and Credit in Peasant Societies*, ed. Raymond Firth and B. S. Yamey, 256–296. Chicago: Aldine.

———. 1973. 'The Rural Proletariat and the Problem of Rural Proletarian Class Consciousness'. *Journal of Peasant Studies*. 1: 1: 291–325.

———. 1979. 'Slavery and the Rise of Peasantries'. *Historical Reflections*. 6: 1: 213–42.

———. 1985. *Sweetness and Power: The Place of Sugar in Modern History*. New York: Penguin.

——. [1974] 1989. *Caribbean Transformations*. New York: Columbia University Press.

Mintz, Sidney and Douglas Hall. 1960. *The Origins of the Jamaican Internal Marketing System*. New Haven: Yale University Publications in Anthropology, no. 57, pp. 3–26.

Mintz, Sidney and Sally Price, eds. 1985. *Caribbean Contours*. Baltimore: Johns Hopkins University Press.

Mohanty, Chandra Talpade 1991. 'Cartographies of Struggle'. In *Third World Women and the Politics of Feminism*, ed. C. Mohanty, A. Russo and L. Torres 1–50. Bloomington and Indianapolis: Indiana University Press.

Moïse, Claude. 1988. *Constitutions et Luttes de Pouvoir en Haïti (1804–1987)*. Vol. 1: 'La Faillite des Classes Dirigéantes (1804–1915)'. Quebec: CIDIHCA.

Momsen, Janet.1988. 'Gender Roles in Caribbean Agricultural Labour'. In *Labour in the Caribbean*, ed. M. Cross and G. Heuman 141–58. London: Macmillan.

Momsen, Janet H., ed. 1993. *Women and Change in the Caribbean: a Pan-Caribbean Perspective*. London: James Currey.

Monroe, Fordham. 1975. 'Nineteenth Century Black Thought in the United States: Some Influences of the Santo Domingo Revolution'. *Journal of Black Studies*, 6: 2: 15–26.

Moore, Barrington Jr.. 1966. *Social Origins of Dictatorship and Democracy: Lord and Peasant in the Making of the Modern World*. Boston: Beacon.

Moreno Fraginals, Manuel. 1976. *The Sugarmill: The Socioeconomic Complex of Sugar in Cuba, 1760–1860*. Trans. Cedric Belfrage. New York and London: Monthly Review Books.

Morris, Aldon D. 1984. *The Origins of the Civil Rights Movement*. New York: Free Press.

Morrissey, Marietta. 1989. *Slave Women in the New World: Gender Stratification in the Caribbean*. Lawrence, K. S.: University of Kansas Press.

Moya Pons, Frank. 1985. 'The Land Question in Haiti & Santo Domingo: The Socio-political Context of the Transition from Slavery to Free Labor, 1801–1843'. In *Between Slavery and Free Labor: The Spanish-Speaking Caribbean in the 19ᵗʰ Century*, ed. M. Moreno Fraginals, F. Moya Pons and S. Engerman. Baltimore: Johns Hopkins University Press.

Negt, Oskar and Alexander Kluge. 1993. *Public Sphere and Experience: Toward an Analysis of the Bourgeois and Proletarian Public Sphere*. Foreword Miriam Hansen. Trans., Peter Labanyi, Jamie Daniel, and Assenka Oksiloff. Minneapolis and London: University of Minneapolis Press.

Nicholls, David. 1974. 'A Work of Combat: Mulatto Historians and the Haitian Past, 1847–1867'. *Journal of Interamerican Studies and World Affairs*. 16: 1: 15–38.

——. 1985. *Haiti in Caribbean Context: ethnicity, economy and revolt*. New York: Saint Martin's.

——. 1996. *From Dessalines to Duvalier: Race, Colour and National Independence in Haiti*. 3d ed. London: Macmillan Caribbean.

Northrup, David. 1995. *Indentured Labor in the Age of Imperialism, 1834–1922*. Cambridge: Cambridge University Press.

Okihiro, Gary. 1986. *In Resistance: Studies in African, Caribbean & Afro-American History*. Amherst: University of Massachusetts Press.

Olwell, Robert. 1996. '"Loose, Idle and Disorderly": Slave Women in the Eighteenth-Century Charleston Marketplace.' In *More than Chattel: Black Women and Slavery in the Americas*, ed. David B. Gaspar and Darlene C. Hine, 97–110. Bloomington and Indianapolis: Indiana University Press.

Olwig, Karen Fog, ed. 1995. *Small Islands, Large Questions: Society, Culture and Resistance in the Post-Emancipation Caribbean*. London. Frank Cass.

Omi, Michael and Howard Winant. 1994. *Racial Formation in the United States: from the 1960s to the 1990s*. New York: Routledge.

Ott, Thomas. 1972. *The Haitian Revolution, 1789–1804*. Knoxville: University of Tennessee Press.

Paige, Jeffery M. *Coffee and Power: Revolution and the Rise of Democracy in Central America*. Cambridge, MA and London: Harvard University Press.

Paquette, Robert. 1988. *Sugar is Made With Blood: The Conspiracy of La Escalera and Conflict Between Empires over Slavery in Cuba*. Middletown, CT: Wesleyan University Press.

———. 1997. 'Revolutionary Saint Domingue in the Making of Territorial Louisiana'. In *A Turbulent Time*, ed. Gaspar and Geggus, *op. cit.*, pp. 204–25.

Patterson, Orlando. 1987. 'The Unholy Trinity: Freedom, Slavery and the American Constitution'. *Social Research*. 54: 3: 543–578.

———. 1991. *Freedom in the Making of Western Culture*. Vol 1. Cambridge, MA: Harvard University Press.

Payne, Anthony. 1993. 'Westminster Adapted: The Political Order of the Commonwealth Caribbean'. In *Democracy in the Caribbean: Political, Economic and Social Perspectives*, ed. Jorge Dominguez, Robert A. Pastor and R. Delisle Worrell, 57–73. Baltimore and London: Johns Hopkins University Press.

Petras, Elizabeth M. 1988. *Jamaican Labor Migration: White Capital and Black Labor, 1850–1930*. Boulder & London: Westview Press.

Plummer, Brenda G. 1992. *Haiti and the United States: The Psychological Moment*. Athens, GA: University of Georgia Press.

———. 1988. *Haiti and the Great Powers, 1902–1915*. Baton Rouge: Louisiana State University Press.

Polletta, Francesca. 1999. '"Free Spaces" in Collective Action'. *Theory and Society,* 28: 1–38.

Price, Richard, ed. 1973. *Maroon Societies*. New York: Anchor.

Raboteau, Albert J. 1980. *Slave Religion: The 'Invisible Institution' in the Antebellum South*. Oxford: Oxford University Press.

Reddock, Rhoda. 1985. 'Women and Slavery in the Caribbean: A Feminist Perspective.' *Latin American Perspectives*. Issue 44, 12: 1 (Winter): 63–80.

———. 1994. *Women, Labour & Politics in Trinidad & Tobago, A History*. London: Zed Books.

Robotham, Don. 1981. '"The Notorious Riot": The Socio-Economic and Political Bases of Paul Bogle's Revolt'. Working Paper 28, Institute of Social and Economic Research, University of the West Indies, Kingston.

Rodney, Walter. 1981. *A History of the Guyanese Working People, 1881–1905*. Baltimore: Johns Hopkins University Press.

———. 1982. *How Europe Underdeveloped Africa*. Howard University Press.

Romain, Jacques. 1974. *Quelques Moeurs et Coutumes des Paysans Haitiens*. Révue de la Faculté d'Ethnologie, no. 2, Folcroft Library ed. [originall published in Port-au-Prince: Impr. De l'Etat, 1958].

Roseberry, William. 1989. *Anthropologies and Histories: Essays in Culture, History and Political Economy*. New Brunswick and London: Rutgers University Press.

Roseberry, William, Lowell Gudmundson and Mario S. Kutschback, eds. 1995. *Coffee, Society, and Power in Latin America*. Baltimore and London: Johns Hopkins University Press.

Rueschemeyer, Dietrich, Evelyne Huber Stephens and John Stephens. 1992. *Capitalist Development and Democracy*. Chicago: University of Chicago Press.

Ryan, Mary. 1990. *Women in Public: Between Banners and Ballots, 1825–1880*. Baltimore: Johns Hopkins University Press.

———. 1997. *Civic Wars: Democracy and Public Life in the American City during the Nineteenth Century*. Berkeley and Los Angeles: University of California Press.

Saville, Julie. 1994. *The Work of Reconstruction: From Slave to Wage Laborer in South Carolina, 1860–1970*. Cambridge: Cambridge University Press.

Schuler, Monica. 1980. *'Alas, Alas, Kongo': A Social History of Indentured African Immigration into Jamaica, 1841–1865*. Baltimore: Johns Hopkins Univ. Press.

———. 1991. 'Myalism and the African Religious Tradition in Jamaica'. In *Caribbean Slave Society and Economy*, ed. H. Beckles and V. Shepherd, 295– 303. New York: New Press [original article, 1979].

Scott, James. 1976. *The Moral Economy of the Peasant*. New Haven: Yale Univerity Press.

———. 1985. *Weapons of the Weak: Everyday Forms of Peasant Resistance*. New Haven: Yale University Press.

———. 1990. *Domination and the Arts of Resistance: Hidden Transcripts*. New Haven and London: Yale University Press.

Scott, Julius Sherard, III. *The Common Wind: Currents of Afro-Caribbean Political Communication in the Era of the Haitian Revolution*. (Ph.D. Dissertation, Duke University).

Scott, Rebecca. 1985. *Slave Emancipation in Cuba: The Transition to Free Labor, 1860–1899*. Princeton: Princeton University Press.

———. 1988. 'Exploring the Meaning of Freedom: Postemancipation Societies in Comparative Perspective'. *Hispanic American Historical Review*, 68: 407–28.

Semmel, Bernard. 1968. *The Governor Eyre Controversy*. London: Macgibbon & Kee.

Sewell, William H., Jr. 1980. *Work and Revolution in France: The Language of Labor from the Old Regime to 1848*. Cambridge: Cambridge University Press.

———. 1992. 'Introduction: Narratives and Social Identities'. *Social Science History* 16: 3: 479–488.

Sheller, Mimi. 1997. 'Sword-Bearing Citizens: Militarism and Manhood in Nineteenth Century Haiti'. *Plantation Society in the Americas*, 4: 2/3: 233–78.

———. 1998. 'Quasheba, Mother, Queen: Black Women's Public Leadership and Political Protest in Postemancipation Jamaica, 1834–65'. *Slavery and Abolition*, 19: 3: 90–117.

———. 1999. 'The "Haytian Fear": Racial Projects and Competing Reaction to the First Black Republic', in Research in Politics and Society, Vol. 6, The Global Perspective, ed. Pinar Batur-Vanderlippe and Joe Feagan (Greenwich, CT: JAI Press), pp. 285–303.

Shepherd, Verene. 1994. *Transients to Settlers: The experience of Indians in Jamaica, 1845–1950*. Leeds, England: Peepal Tree.

Shepherd, Verene, Bridget Brereton and Barbara Bailey. 1995. *Engendering History: Caribbean Women in Historical Perspective*. Kingston: Ian Randle; London: James Currey.

Smith, Dorothy. 1987. *The Everyday World as Problematic*. Boston: Northeastern University Press.

Smucker, Glenn R. 1984. 'The Social Character of Religion in Rural Haiti'. In *Haiti: Today and Tomorrow*, ed. Charles Foster and Albert Valdman, 35–56. Lanham, MD: University Press of America.

Solow, Barbara and Stanley Engerman, eds. 1987. *British Capitalism and Caribbean Slavery*. Cambridge: Cambridge University Press.

Somers, Margaret R. 1992. 'Narrative, Narrative Identity, and Social Action: Rethinking English Working-Class Formation'. *Social Science History*. 16: 4: 591–630.

——. 1993. 'Citizenship and the Place of the Public Sphere: Law, Community, and Political Culture in the Transition to Democracy'. *American Sociological Review*, 58: 587–620.

Stanley, Brian. 1992. *The History of the Baptist Missionary Society, 1792–1992*. Edinburgh: T. & T. Clark.

Steinberg, Marc W. 1994. 'The Dialogue of Struggle: The Contest Over Ideological Boundaries in the Case of the London Silk Weavers in the Nineteenth Century'. *Social Science History*, 18: 505–542.

Steinmetz, George. 1992. 'Reflections on the Role of Social Narratives in Working Class Formation: Narrative Theory in the Social Sciences'. *Social Science History,* 16: 3: 489–516.

Stepan, Alfred. 1985. 'State Power and the Strength of Civil Society in the Southern Cone of Latin America.' In *Bringing the State Back In*, ed. P. Evans, D. Rueschemeyer, and T. Skocpol 317–43. Cambridge: Cambridge University Press.

Stephens, Evelyne Huber and John D. Stephens. 1986. *Democratic Socialism in Jamaica: The Political Movement and Social Transformation in Dependent Capitalism*. Princeton, NJ: Princton University Press.

Stern, Steve. [1988] 1993. 'Feudalism, Capitalism and the World-System in the Perspective of Latin America and the Caribbean'. In *Confronting Historical Paradigms,* Cooper, *op. cit*, pp. 23–83.

Stern, Steve, ed. 1987. *Resistance, Rebellion and Consciousness in the Andean Peasant World: Eighteenth to Twentieth Centuries*. Madison: University of Wisconsin Press.

Stewart, Robert J. 1992. *Religion and Society in Post-Emancipation Jamaica*. Knoxville, TN: University of Tennessee Press.

Stinchcombe, Arthur L. 1994a. 'Class Conflict and Diplomacy: Haitian Isolation in The 19th-century World System.' *Sociological Perspectives*. 37: 1: 1–23.

——. 1994b. 'Freedom and Oppression of Slaves in the Eighteenth-Century Caribbean'. *American Sociological Review*. 59 (Dec.): 911–929.

——. 1996. *The Political Economy of the Caribbean, 1775–1900: The Sociology of Slavery and Freedom*. Princeton, NJ: Princeton University Press.

Stuckey, Sterling. 1987. *Slave Culture: Nationalist Theory and the Foundations of Black America*. New York: Oxford University Press.

Swidler, Ann. 1986. 'Culture in Action: Symbols and Strategies'. *American Sociological Review*. 51: 273–286.

Tilly, Charles. 1993. 'Contentious Repertoires in Great Britain, 1758–1834.' *Social Science History*. 17: 2: 253–280.

——. 1995a. *Popular Contention in Great Britain, 1758–1834*. Cambridge, MA: The Belknap Press of Harvard University Press.

——. 1995b. 'Democracy is a Lake'. In *The Social Construction of Democracy, 1870–1990*, ed. George Andrews and Herrick Chapman, 365–38. New York: New York University Press.

Tinker, Hugh. 1993. *A New System of Slavery: The Export of Indian Labour Overseas, 1830–1920*. 2d ed. London: Hansib Publishing.

Trouillot, Michel-Rolph. 1990. *Haiti: State Against Nation: The Origins and Legacy of Duvalierism*. New York: Monthly Review Press.

——. 1992. 'The Inconvenience of Freedom: Free People of Color and the Political Aftermath of Slavery in Dominica and Saint-Domingue/Haiti'. In *The Meaning of Freedom*, ed. F. McGlynn and S. Drescher, *op. cit.*, pp. 147–82.

——. 1993. 'Coffee Planters and Coffee Slaves in the Antilles: The Impact of a Secondary Crop'. In *Cultivation and Culture: Labor and the Shaping of Slave Life in the Americas*, ed. Ira Berlin and Philip D. Morgan, 124–137, 331–335. Charlottesville and London: University of Virginia.

——. 1995. 'The Three Faces of Sans Souci: Glory and Silences in the Haitian Revolution'. In *The Production of History: Silences and Commemorations*, ed. Gerald Sider and Gavin Smith.

Turner, Mary S. 1982. *Slaves and Missionaries: The Disintegration of Jamaican Slave Society, 1787–1834*. Urbana: University of Illinois Press.

——. 1988. 'Chattel Slaves into wage slaves: A Jamaican case study'. In *Labour in the Caribbean*, ed. Cross and Heuman, *op. cit*, pp. 14–31.

Turner, Mary, ed. 1995. *From Chattel Slaves to Wage Slaves: The Dynamics of Labour Bargaining in the Americas*. London: James Currey; Kingston: Ian Randle; Bloomington: Indiana University Press.

Vlach, John M. 1993. *Back of the Bighouse: The Architecture of Plantation Slavery*. Chapel Hill and London: University of North Carolina Press.

Wallerstein, Immanuel. 1980. *The Modern World System II: Mercantilism and the Consolidation of the European World Economy, 1600–1750*. New York: Academic Press.

Watts, David. [1987] 1990. *The West Indies: Patterns of Development, Culture and Environmental Change Since 1492*. Cambridge and New York: Cambridge University Press.

Weinstein, Brian and Aaron Segal. 1992. *Haiti: The Failure of Politics*. New York: Praeger.

White, Harrison. 1995. 'Where do Languages Come From?', Prt I and II. Center for the Social Sciences at Columbia University, Pre-print Series.

Williams, Eric. 1944. *Capitalism and Slavery*. Chapel Hill: University of North Carolina Press.

Wilmot, Swithin. [1977] 1984. 'Political Development in Jamaica in the Post-Emancipation Period, 1838–1854'. D. Phil thesis, Oxford University.

——. 1986. 'Emancipation in Action: Workers and Wage Conflict in Jamaica, 1838–1840'. *Jamaica Journal*, 19: 55–62.

——. 1994. 'The Growth of Political Activity in Post-Emancipation Jamaica. In *Garvey: His Work and Impact*, ed. Rupert Lewis and Patrick Bryan, 39–36. (Trenton, NJ: Africa World Press).

——. 1995. '"Females of Abandoned Character"? Women and Protest in Jamaica, 1838–65.' In *Engendering History: Caribbean Women in Historical Perspective*, ed. Shepherd et al., *op. cit.*, pp. 279–295.

Wilson, Peter J. 1973. *Crab Antics: The Social Anthropology of English-Speaking Negro Societies in the Caribbean*. New Haven: Yale University Press.

Womack, John. 1969. *Zapata and the Mexican Revolution*. New York: Knopf.

Index

Numbers in **bold** indicate Tables; those in *italics* indicate Figures.